3000 800068 60147
St. Louis Community College

W9-DGN-211

Florissant Valley Library
St. Louis Community College
3400 Pershall Road
Ferguson, MO 63135-1499
314-513-4514

For Reference

Not to be taken from this room

Ethnic Dress in the United States

Ethnic Dress in the United States

A Cultural Encyclopedia

EDITED BY
ANNETTE LYNCH
AND
MITCHELL D. STRAUSS

ROWMAN & LITTLEFIELD
Lanham • Boulder • New York • London

Published by Rowman & Littlefield
A wholly owned subsidary of The Rowman & Littlefield Publishing Group, Inc.
4501 Forbes Boulevard, Suite 200, Lanham, Maryland 20706
www.rowman.com

Unit A, Whitacre Mews, 26-34 Stannery Street, London SE11 4AB, United Kingdom

Copyright © 2015 by Rowman & Littlefield
Illustrations © 2015 J. Susan Cole Stone

All rights reserved. No part of this book may be reproduced in any form or by any electronic
or mechanical means, including information storage and retrieval systems, without written
permission from the publisher, except by a reviewer who may quote passages in a review.

British Library Cataloguing in Publication Information Available

Library of Congress Cataloging-in-Publication Data
Ethnic dress in the United States : a cultural encyclopedia / edited by Annette Lynch and
Mitchell D. Strauss.
       pages cm
       Includes bibliographical references and index.
       ISBN 978-0-7591-2148-5 (cloth : alk. paper) — ISBN 978-0-7591-2150-8 (electronic)
    1. Ethnic costume—United States—History—Encyclopedias. 2. Clothing and dress—United
States—History—Encyclopedias. 3. Minorities—Clothing—United States—Encyclopedias. 4.
United States—Social life and customs. I. Lynch, Annette (Annette Ferne) II. Strauss, Mitchell D.
       GT605.E35 2015
       391.0089—dc23
                                                                                    2014025511

∞™ The paper used in this publication meets the minimum requirements of American
National Standard for Information Sciences—Permanence of Paper for Printed Library
Materials, ANSI/NISO Z39.48-1992.

Printed in the United States of America

CONTENTS

FOREWORD

JOANNE B. EICHER

The kaleidoscope of items of dress worn in the United States comes from the wide variety of ethnicities that immigrants represent. The A-to-Z list captures commonly known terms such as "muʻumuʻu" and "Aloha shirt" from Hawaiʻi as well as ones unfamiliar to me such as "busserull" or "rubaha." If you don't recognize these either, you have the opportunity to look them up! In the United States, many ethnic groups comprise our population, and dress may visibly symbolize heritage as a way to connect individuals with their ethnic background, in contrast to Japan and Korea, for example, where the population is largely homogeneous. Of special interest, however, is the fact that although some items like lederhosen or sari are identified easily with a specific background or country, other items filter into the population at large, like the cloche, fedora, and turban, or huaraches, espadrilles, and Birkenstocks, and become fashion items whose wearers do not recognize that the item has an ethnic heritage. I am particularly fascinated that in this list of over 150 items, roughly thirty are headwear and fifteen footwear, accounting together for almost one-third of the total. Perhaps something about adopting apparel for head and feet happens relatively quickly, thrusting some examples into what may become known as world fashion (Eicher and Sumberg, 1995).

I have been involved in the conception and execution of two encyclopedia projects (Steele, 2005; Eicher, 2010), but Lynch and Strauss have gone beyond either contribution by focusing on and collecting a list of primarily apparel items worn in the United States at various times. Some choices we select as members of an ethnic group to highlight heritage during holiday celebrations. Other choices sneak into a fashion cycle, worn because the footwear or hat is comfortable or attractive, and "everyone is wearing it." I was surprised to see textiles included, such as Battenberg lace, batik, and calico, but realized that these also link to our pasts. Some readers may find an example from their own background missing from the A–Z list, which should not be a surprise in a nation like ours, but hold the promise of another volume or perhaps a revised edition. The economist John Kenneth Galbraith once wrote of "pockets of poverty." The United States has many "pockets of ethnicity," like my Twin Cities community of Minneapolis and St. Paul, Minnesota, with two fairly recent examples of Hmong peoples coming from Laos and Thailand and Somalis from East Africa. With a country as large as the United States, not only in population but in geographic size and regional differences, awareness of new words that represent our backgrounds is inevitable.

REFERENCES

Eicher, J. B., ed. *Encyclopedia of World Dress and Fashion*. New York: Oxford University Press, 2010 (also *Berg Encyclopedia of World Dress and Fashion*, Berg Publishers, Oxford, UK).

Eicher, J. B., and B. Sumberg. "World Fashion, Ethnic, and National Dress." In *Dress and Ethnicity*, edited by J. B. Eicher, 295–306. Oxford/Washington, DC: Berg Publishers, 1995.

Steele, V., ed. *Encyclopedia of Clothing and Fashion*. New York: Scribner, 2005.

INTRODUCTION

The clothes we wear tell stories about us and are often imbued with cultural meanings specific to our ethnic heritage. This concise A-to-Z encyclopedia uses a material culture approach to explore over 150 different and distinct items of ethnic dress, their history, and their cultural significance in the United States. The clothing artifacts we have chosen to document have been or are now regularly worn by Americans as everyday clothing, fashion, ethnic or religious identifiers, or style statements. As identity-linked material culture artifacts, the selected clothing items embody the cultural history of the United States and its peoples, from Native Americans, white Anglo colonists, and forcibly relocated black slaves to the millennium influx of immigrants from around the world. Entries consider how dress items may serve as symbolic linkages to home country and family or provide insight into the ethnic-based core ideologies, myths, and cultural codes that have played a role in the formation and continued story of the United States.

In many ways the ethnic and cultural diversity characterizing millennium America can be attributed to the myths surrounding immigration to America and the tenacious will of individual people to land on our shore and make a home here, rather than a seamless history of open immigration policies. Dating back to the colonial period, Americans have expressed ambivalence about welcoming new immigrants to our shores, with early colonial leaders complaining about the boorish German population influx into Pennsylvania, decrying the newcomer's unwillingness to learn English (Archdeacon, 1983). Significant periods of the United States, including several decades of the first half of the twentieth century, have included the passage of immigration restrictions formalizing popular culture attitudes toward what was deemed undesirable immigration patterns by white-dominant culture.

Despite these both formal and informal barriers, immigrants made it to America. The growth of the U.S. population from less than 4 million in 1790 to 315 million in 2013 was largely fueled by immigration. The American population analysis done in the 1990s by Edmonston and Passell (1994, p. 61) estimated that almost two-thirds of the citizenry in the last decade of the twentieth century was composed of immigrants and their descendants arriving after 1800. The clothing artifacts documented in this encyclopedia tell the story of the diversity that existed prior to the large waves of immigration and the forcible relocation of Native Americans and black slaves, and provides a visual record of the influx of immigrants to the United States in the nineteenth, twentieth, and twenty-first centuries.

The first period of mass migration from 1880 to 1924 was primarily made up of European immigrants, followed forty years later by a post-1965 pattern of immigration from Latin America and Asia. The late nineteenth and early twentieth centuries brought a multitude of Italians, Slavs, Greeks, Poles, and Eastern European Jews into the country, resulting in approximately half the white population being first- and second-generation white at the turn of the century. The post-1964 migration, composed of a mix of Mexicans, Puerto Ricans, Cubans, Asians, and Africans, resulted in the overall share of the nonwhite national population in the United States increasing from around 13 percent in 1970 to over 30 percent in 2000, with the white majority now slated to be gone by 2043. Added into our cultural diverse mix is a small percentage of American Indian/Native Americans, in 2000 approximately 1 percent of the total population. This encyclopedia covers entries from all of these populations and cultures, in addition to the original white Anglo colonists.

One of the most revealing facts about the cultural meaning of ethnic dress in America is that we have no official national costume. Nationalism, as expressed by dress in America, is an expression of cultural diversity and immigration history. When asked for an answer about American national dress, Google searches over and over again reiterate, "America is a nation of immigrants." This is in dramatic contrast with much of Europe, whose countries have a formal uniform of national identity despite the now complex diversity within national borders throughout the eurozone. The popular-culture depiction of America as a land of immigrants is thematically explored by sociologist Charles Hirschman who puts forward the argument that "American identity is not rooted in nationhood but rather in the welcoming of strangers" (2005, p. 595). Siting the iconic symbolic weight of the Statue of Liberty as a beacon of welcome, Hirschman persuasively posits that a core ideology driving America as a nation is that of an open door to immigrants, a country where you can come to make your way in the world.

The second major cultural myth surrounding immigration in the United States analyzed by Hirschman (1983) is the concept of America as a melting pot, a land of opportunity, an even playing field for all nationalities, races, and ethnicities, free of barriers to social mobility. This myth has rung true for many ethnic groups, with the notable exception of populations originating from black Africa and Puerto Rico. Traditional clothing styles and accessories linked to a homeland are portable ethnic markers often hand carried out of countries of origin, imported, or handcrafted within the United States. For ethnic groups who are for the most part already largely assimilated into American culture, the dress items often serve as symbolic linkages to the home country and family, perhaps worn during a rite of passage or for a special occasion. For cultural groups still experiencing discrimination, the dress items may be worn as a visible form of opposition to the more powerful and dominant cultural norms.

The mixing together of the core ideology of a nation of immigrants and the myth of the American melting pot results in ethnic dress artifacts maintaining cultural meaning and value, even after immigration and assimilation. America as a nation of immigrants does not have a national costume or a national identity that all assume when landing on her shore. Diversity is America, and the wearing of apparel marking ethnic origins becomes a meaningful exploration of what it means to be an American. Material culture is pliable and fluid in terms of how it is used to construct and transform identity. Well-established demographic trends toward intermarriage among ethnic populations, coupled with the contemporary acceptance of constructed identities apart from heritage and history, point to the wide relevance of the items included in this encyclopedia not only to the members of the specific ethnic group but to the wider population.

Artifacts were chosen to be included in the encyclopedia to represent the ethnic diversity and the settlement and resettlement patterns of cultural groups in the United States. Priority was given to clothing items that have retained cultural significance and meaning, and in some cases have been mainstreamed into American culture. Each entry opens with a description of the artifact, followed by sections outlining its history and its entrance into the United States. The closing portion of each entry focuses on the influence and impact of the clothing artifact, often with an eye to cultural meaning and significance.

REFERENCES

Archdeacon, T. J. *Becoming American: An Ethnic History*. New York: Free Press, 1983.

Edmonston, B., and J. Passel. *Immigration and Ethnicity: The Integration of America's Newest Arrivals*. Washington, DC: Urban Institute Press, 1994.

Hirschman, Charles. "America's Melting Pot Reconsidered." *Annual Review of Sociology* 9 (1983): 397–423.

———. "Immigration and the American Century." *Demography* 42, no. 4 (November 2005): 595–620.

A

AFRICAN HEAD WRAP

African head wraps are also known as a turban, a rag, a head tie, or a head handkerchief. The African head wrap has a long history both in Africa and in the United States. They are believed to have originated in West Africa and are still worn today to commemorate rites of passage and to indicate social status or religion, or they are simply worn for adornment. Unlike the head wraps worn by eastern Europeans (babushkas), the African head wrap is a rectangular piece of fabric that is wrapped from the back of the head and tied or tucked on top of the head, exposing and enhancing the face.

History

Considerable historical evidence indicates that the head wraps worn by African-Americans originated in Africa where the head has always held special significance as the root of intelligence and personality. Headdress of Africa has not only served utilitarian purposes to protect the wearer from environmental elements; they have also been historically used as ethnic markers. Some evidence points to an African origin derived from the male Muslim turban like that worn by the Tuaregs of North Africa, which is symbolic of his gender and adult status. Tuareg women also adopted a head wrap, but as a stylish adornment to attract suitors. Further evidence points to the Muslims on the west coast of Africa who also wore the turban, but as a sign of high status and prestige, regardless of their ethnic affiliation.

The most accepted argument is the West African origin of the African head wrap because of the slave trade off the West Africa coast during the eighteenth century. Hair ornaments, such as beads and shells, were originally more popular than head wraps because of the scarcity of woven cloth until European expansion into Africa in the eighteenth century that made inexpensive cloth more readily available for personal aesthetic use in West Africa. For many African women, especially in West Africa, head wraps were not directly affiliated with Islamic practices and identity, but rather they marked their status as wives and mothers, or simply as an expression of style.

African Head Wrap

African Head Wraps in the United States

West Africans traded fellow human beings destined for slavery in the United States in exchange for goods from the Europeans, including the much-sought-after cloth. Pictorial evidence shows both enslaved African men and women in the United States wearing head wraps, but it ultimately became associated with just women. In the United States, the African head wrap became a sign of servitude. Whites imposed dress codes upon enslaved women, which required them to cover their heads, thereby outwardly differentiating them from the white women—the women of status and power. Slave owners and plantation owners often gave the slave women scraps of cloth or handkerchiefs as part of their servant uniforms to reinforce the necessity of binding their hair in the head wrap. The head wrap was also functional for the laboring slave, as it helped to absorb perspiration and keep her hair pulled away from her face as she worked. At a time when personal hygiene was unfeasible, the head wrap was a quick and easy solution to maintain unruly hair and make oneself look presentable and to even help prevent the spread of lice during infestations.

Influence and Impact

Well into the twentieth century the head wrap as a symbol of servility is perpetuated with images of the turbaned "Black Mammy" servant in Hollywood films and even advertising logos, such as Aunt Jemima by the Quaker Oats Company.

It was not until much later that wearing the head wrap reflected continuity with African tradition and a conscious bond with the women of their past. African-American women adopted the head wrap as a way to set themselves apart from the customs of the white woman. The use of the head wrap reemerged in the 1960s and 1970s in conjunction with the civil rights movement, redefining the head wrap as a symbol of black empowerment.

Even today, generations are left with little knowledge of their ancestral origin, except for possibly a symbolic ethnicity in the form of a constructed collective ethnic identity associated with a country that they probably have never seen. African-Americans have sought symbolic ties to their continent of origin ever since people were forced into slavery in the Americas. One of the most common types of symbolic association has been through the preservation of ethnic clothing, such as the African head wrap through which African-American women reclaim their "Africanism" and ties to West Africa. Pop-culture icons such as Beyoncé, Brandy, and Erykah Badu are widely known for showing their Afrocentricity through the use of head wraps. However, it has become en vogue for those with no African ties to adopt the deeply symbolic garment. Jennifer Lopez wore an African head wrap in her music video "I'm Into You" featuring Lil' Wayne in 2011. The white models for Stella Jean's fall/winter 2013 line were not only dressed in ethnic wax-resist print dresses and skirts but had their outfits completed with complementary head wraps.

The African "return to your roots" craze is no longer reserved only for African-Americans. It has bridged the racial divide thanks to the fashion industry.

See also CHURCH HAT; DO-RAG; GELE; HAWLI; TURBAN
Compare to BANDANA; BLANGKON; KUFI; RASTA HAT

Further Reading

Arnoldi, Mary Jo, and Christine Mullen Kreamer. *Crowning Achievements: African Arts of Dressing the Head.* Los Angeles: Fowler Museum of Cultural History, 1995.

Griebel, Helen Bradley. "The African American Woman's Head Wrap: Unwinding the Symbols." In *Dress and Identity*, edited by Mary Ellen Roach-Higgins, Joanne B. Eicher, and Kim K. P. Johnson, 445–60. New York: Fairchild, 1995.

———. "The West African Origin of the African-American Head Wrap." In *Dress and Ethnicity: Change across Space and Time*, edited by Joanne B. Eicher, 207–26. Oxford and Washington, DC: Berg, 1995.

■ JESSICA STRÜBEL

ALBORNOZ

See BURNOUS

ALOHA SHIRT (HAWAI'IAN SHIRT)

The aloha shirt has become an iconic representation of Hawai'i. Known throughout the rest of the world as the "Hawai'ian Shirt," the brightly colored shirt made of woven fabric in tropical prints with a collar and buttons down the front has come to represent the casual, laid-back lifestyle of resort living.

History

The history of the aloha shirt is as complex as the history of the Hawai'ian Islands. These Polynesian islands developed without western intervention until the late eighteenth century when they were discovered by Captain Cook. Hawai'i was a monarchy. Once missionaries arrived in 1820, rapid changes occurred throughout the nineteenth century. The Hawai'ian Islands continued as a kingdom until American business interests overthrew the monarchy and the Hawai'ian queen was imprisoned in her palace. In 1898 Hawai'i became an American territory, and in 1959 it became the fiftieth American state. This political history is quite relevant to the development of material culture in Hawai'i, as the textile history reflects the sociocultural changes as they occurred.

The Aloha Shirt in the United States

The origins of the aloha shirt are in the 1930s when Hawai'i was an American territory. The development of the shirt coincided with the multiethnic Hawai'ian Islands Westernizing into an American state, and it symbolizes the constant interplay between ethnic expression and Westernization in Hawai'i. In the nineteenth century, the need for plantation laborers led to importing workers from China, Japan, Korea, the Philippines, and other nations, who then lived and worked together on the plantations.

Due to the harshness of sugarcane, work clothing needed to be sturdy to protect the workers. Fabrics were imported from Europe and the United States to provide denim for trousers, and a heavy cotton plaid for long-sleeved jackets. The plaid was called *palaka* in Hawai'ian. The jackets had collars and buttons down the front and were worn into the early twentieth century. At this time *palaka* was also available in lighter weights that were used for short-sleeved *palaka* shirts. The vast majority of men worked on plantations and there was little leisure time, but what was worn after work was often their traditional ethnic dress, or the lightweight *palaka* shirts. The design lines of the *palaka* shirt would become the basic style of the aloha shirt—only the fabric would change.

In 1930s Hawai'i, apparel was produced by Chinese or Japanese tailors, using fabric primarily imported from Japan. The majority of fabric was intended for use in kimonos and Hawai'ian dresses (mu'umu'us and *holoku*). In the early 1930s a group of boys from a private school in Honolulu asked a Chinese tailor to make matching shirts for them from Japanese *kabe* crepe. These fabrics were very brightly printed designs intended for use in little girls' kimonos. The brightly printed shirts were a fad that spawned a fashion. Until World War II, these proto-Hawai'ian shirts would be produced with Japanese fabrics and designs.

The proto-Hawai'ian shirts became aloha shirts once the textiles drew their inspiration from Hawai'i. In the mid-1930s, textile design in Hawai'i was in the developmental stage. There were a few people creating Hawai'ian designs for cotton prints. Ethyl Lum produced designs using small linoleum blocks. Her designs were usually limited to two or three colors for the small motifs that were stamped onto cotton broadcloth to make shirts for tourists. Her brother, Elery Chun, trademarked the term "aloha shirt" in 1936, and the aloha attire industry began in earnest.

Tropical flowers have consistently been a favored theme for aloha shirts, although it may have started with drapery fabric. By the 1940s, fabrics with large tropical motifs on heavy cotton fabrics were imported for drapery and slipcovers. Wong's drapery company began using the remnants for aloha shirts. These were so popular (but heavy) that artists scaled down the designs for lightweight fabrics more suitable for apparel. Floral prints were imported from Polynesia, particularly Tahiti, and used in aloha attire.

While the earliest aloha shirts were made in small tailoring shops (often Chinese or Japanese), the scale of production increased in the late 1930s as the Hawai'ian garment industry began with its initial focus on the production of aloha shirts for tourists and servicemen. They ordered fabric with tropical print designs from Asia until shipping was curtailed by World War II. At that time the apparel companies found that they needed to create their own textile designs in order to stay in business, and this led to the development of unique textiles for aloha shirts. The larger aloha shirt companies began to design and silk-screen their own designs. One of the benefits of Hawai'ians creating the designs themselves is that they were able to create large and very bold designs for the shirts. When ordering fabric from mills, the companies were limited to no more than three colors in a print, and the scale of the designs was small. When they began producing their own silk screens, they went to a twenty-four-inch repeat with as many as five different colors screened onto the fabric. After World War II they began using heavy rayons that would take a great deal of dye. The end result was the production of aloha shirts that were essentially art pieces. The heyday of the aloha shirt was the late 1940s through the late 1950s when the bright, bold rayon aloha shirts were in style. Because of the feel of the rayon, these shirts were called "silkies" and today are highly collectible. The highest auction price thus far for a silkie is $15,000.

Hawai'i is well known as a multicultural state that has no ethnic majority. It is no surprise that textile designers in Hawai'i drew on inspiration from the cultural diversity all around them. Aloha shirts use Hawai'ian prints, but those prints do not focus only on Hawai'ian themes; indeed, the cultural diversity in the islands is seen visually in the aloha shirts. The prints feature Hawai'ian flora and fauna, sea life, and Hawai'ian cultural themes, but they also feature design elements from Polynesia, Indonesia, China, Japan, and Korea. The art of the aloha shirt is a visible manifestation of ethnicity in Hawai'i. This theme was well established even before Hawai'i became a state.

After World War II the territory of Hawai'i began a concerted effort to become an American state. During this time Hawai'i's garment industry developed quickly to meet the demand for aloha attire (*holoku*, mu'umu'us, and aloha shirts) by both tourists and locals. The golden age of the aloha shirt was the decade following World War II, when rayon silkies with realistic depictions of flora, fauna, and cultural elements dominated. As with any other fashion, tastes changed, and so did the styles. Realistic textile art on the aloha shirts went out of style as modernism came into vogue. Abstract design came into textile design for aloha shirts.

How Worn, by Whom, and Cultural Meaning in Hawai'i Following Statehood

There are two different forms of aloha shirts—the style discussed thus far was the form developed for tourists. An entirely different type of shirt was developed for local residents who, until recently, had more subtle tastes. In 1965, Honolulu passed an ordinance allowing aloha shirts to be worn to work on Fridays only if they were very simple and understated. From the 1960s to the 1980s, locals in Hawai'i continued to favor simple, subtle aloha shirts with smaller design motifs in more subtle colorations. The aloha shirt has usually been worn outside the pants (or shorts), but by the end of the twentieth century, shirts were tucked into trousers when worn to the office. Today, the aloha shirt is the basic garment for men in Hawai'i who wear either type of aloha shirt to work, church, or social events.

Servicemen brought aloha shirts home to the U.S. mainland, and they were eagerly embraced. Notable celebrities wore aloha shirts. By the time Hawai'i became the fiftieth state in 1959, the aloha shirt had become a fashion in California and Florida. Many apparel companies in California began producing their own versions of aloha shirts, which they called Hawai'ian shirts. By the end of the century, Hawai'ian shirts were being produced all over the United States and offshore as well. By the end of the twentieth century, the aloha shirt had been embraced by men of all ages and lifestyles throughout the mainland United States.

Influence and Impact

As surfers from California began traveling to and from Hawai'i in the 1960s, they brought the aloha shirt back to California along with the laid-back lifestyle of surfers. The aloha shirt became a badge of this carefree attitude toward life, and aloha shirts became the rage throughout California's high schools and colleges. Aloha shirts were adopted as a badge of a casual lifestyle and became an important part of surfers' wardrobes as they evolved. Many of the 1960s surfers became tech entrepreneurs in the Silicon Valley in Northern California, and they brought the idea of Aloha Friday to the workplace in California. Today it is called Casual Friday.

See also KOSOVOROTKA; MUʻUMUʻU
Compare to BARONG TAGALOG; DASHIKI; KIMONO; OXFORD SHIRT

Further Reading

Arthur, Linda. *Aloha Attire: Hawaiian Dress in the Twentieth Century.* Atglen, PA: Schiffer Publications, 2000.
Brown, David, and Linda Arthur. *Art of the Aloha Shirt.* Honolulu, HI: Island Heritage, 2002.
Hope, Dale, and Greg Tozian. *The Aloha Shirt.* Portland, OR: Beyond Words Publishing, 2002.

■ LINDA ARTHUR BRADLEY

ALPACA SWEATER

Alpaca sweaters are knit or woven from 100 percent alpaca fiber or alpaca combined with other fibers such as silk, nylon, acrylic, and wool. Alpaca is considered a specialty fiber that is highly prized for its thermal properties and because it is light, soft, and strong. Sweaters come in a plethora of natural shades of crème, brown, gray, and black, brightly dyed colors, and patterns influenced by Andean architecture, iconography, and natural wonders.

History

Alpacas are members of the camel family along with the wild vicuña and guanaco and the domesticated llama. Alpacas are native to the high plateau region of the Andean Mountains of South America known as the Altiplano that spreads across Peru, Bolivia, Chile, Argentina, and Ecuador. The height of the Altiplano averages over twelve thousand feet, and the climate is harsh, with temperatures that can fluctuate dramatically between day and night. Alpacas have been domesticated for centuries, bred for their fiber and docility. Incan royalty treasured their fleeces, and the introduction of camelid fibers into South American textiles resulted in a textile revolution. Hundreds of burials in the Paracas Peninsula from the end of the first millennium BCE incorporate over 120 different colors from dyed camelid wool. A multitude of textiles in the Neutrogena Collection gifted to the Museum of International Folk Art in Santa Fe, New Mexico, identify a common use of cotton in the warp and alpaca fiber in the weft. The Spanish conquest brought the alpaca to the brink of extinction because of the introduction of Spanish sheep. The alpacas survived because of their adaptability to harsh climates and their importance to the indigenous populations.

Englishman Sir Titus Salt is credited with developing the modern alpaca market in the mid-1830s. Already a successful mill owner, in 1834 he discovered alpaca fiber bales at a Liverpool warehouse. After some experimentation, he produced a beautiful cloth perfect for expensive dresses for the wealthy. Salt's mills made him a very rich man, and alpaca came to represent the height of fashion for over a century. While produced in South

America, alpaca fiber was processed primarily in England and Europe until the end of World War II when efforts were made to modernize and vertically integrate the Peruvian alpaca industry. The first company to do this successfully was founded by Englishman Frank Michell. Today, the Michell Company and Grupo Inca, both based in Arequipa, Peru, furnish most of the world's finished alpaca products.

The Alpaca Sweater in the United States

Around the world, products such as alpaca sweaters made from alpaca fiber index many things including the Peruvian Andes, the ancient Inca city at Machu Picchu, exotic came-lids, and artisanal hand production. While there had been a market for finished alpaca products in the United States since the nineteenth century, the U.S. alpaca industry began in the 1980s when small numbers of alpacas were imported from Chile. The U.S. market for alpacas grew out of the well-established llama market and focused on the animal's rarity. Today, however, it is shifting to a focus on fleece quality and the development of a high-end product market that focuses on distinguishing alpaca from wool. Breeders and the public are enamored with alpacas and alpaca products because of the sacred quality or mystique that surrounds the breed and the association of alpaca fiber with success, money, and glamour.

Influence and Impact

Alpaca sweaters are marketed to individuals who are interested in artisan apparel—prod-ucts, often handmade from high-quality materials, associated with indigenous or ethnic communities and/or traditions. One hundred percent alpaca products are quite expen-sive and are considered luxury items. Customers who have purchased alpaca sweaters self-describe themselves as classic, stylish, high-end shoppers, comfort oriented, practical, trendy, and fashionable. They identify the product's softness, warmth, and light weight as important attributes. In addition, supporting indigenous community organizations is something "fun to explain to friends." Alpaca sweater product descriptions often reference Andean sites such as Puno, Cuzco, Lima, or Aymara and local architecture and natural wonders as direct inspiration for patterns and colors. In addition, pre-Columbian textiles, pictograms, and patterns are highlighted, as is the 3,500-year tradition of alpaca fiber use. Brighter colors are sometimes considered too ethnic, while natural-colored sweaters are classic and sophisticated.

Today, the alpaca market is small; however, it has a certain kind of cachet that indexes the past through the mystique of Peru and the modern through its association with high status and luxury. Any Internet search will bring up numerous sites where, through the consumption of images, history, and products associated with the doe-eyed and docile alpaca, the past and present are forged. Differences in fiber content, whether 100 percent alpaca or a blend; colors, whether bright or natural; and textile patterns, such as llamas or geometric shapes, attract either high-end shoppers or those looking for more "rustic" products. Ultimately, alpaca sweater producers and marketers argue that the purchase of alpaca products contributes to social and environmental sustainability.

See also ARAN SWEATER; CH'ULLU; NORWEGIAN SWEATER; SCOTTISH SWEATER
Compare to PASHMINA SHAWL AND SCARF; SERAPE

Further Reading

Flores-Ochoa, Jorge A. *Pastoralists of the Andes: The Alpaca Herders of Paratía*. Philadelphia: Institute for the Study of Human Issues, 1968.

Harris, Jennifer, ed. "Latin America." In *Textiles 5000 Years: An International History and Illustrated Survey*. New York: Harry N. Abrams, 1993.

Kahlenberg, Mary Hunt, ed. "Andes." In *The Extraordinary in the Ordinary: Works in Cloth, Ceramic, Wood, Metal, Straw, and Paper from Cultures throughout the World*. New York: Harry N. Abrams, 1998.

McMullen, Cathi. "Romancing the Alpaca: Passionate Consumption, Collection, and Companionship." *Journal of Business Research* 61 (2008): 502–8.

Safley, Michael. *Alpacas: Synthesis of a Miracle*. Hillsboro, OR: Northwest Alpacas, 2001.

■ BLAIRE O. GAGNON

ANORAK/PARKA

Simply defined, an anorak is a water-repellant, waist-length, hooded pullover jacket with elastic gathers on the hood and at the waist and wrists and does not have a zipper, button, or frogged opening. The parka, although similar in nature to the anorak, differs in that it is a hip-length jacket stuffed with down or synthetic insulting materials that has a fur-lined (real or faux) hood and a front closure. Both the anorak and the parka are worn in extreme weather conditions and serve to protect the wearer from frigid temperatures, water, and high winds.

History

Both the anorak and parka hail from arctic regions. The origin of the anorak dates back to the early 1920s from the Greenlandic Inuit Eskimo. The term "anorak" comes from the Kalaallisut word *anoraq* that refers to a beaded garment worn by Greenland women or brides. Originally made of animal skins such as caribou or seal by the Inuit (Eskimo) of the Canadian Arctic and Greenland, the anorak proved to be a necessity in the harsh Arctic environment. The heavy jacket was typically coated in oil (usually fish) to protect the wearer from wind and wetness while hunting and kayaking. To retain their water-resistant property, the jackets were regularly coated in train (fish) oil. The parka, or *kamleika*, translated as "animal skin" in the Nenets language, originated in the Aleutian Islands, Alaska. For women, the traditional parka was made out of seal or sea otter skins and possibly lined with fur or feathers. A parka worn by a man could be made out of bird skin and feathers. If participating in water activities, the male parka could be made out of large mammal guts and entrails.

The Anorak/Parka in the United States

The anorak was first adopted by American and British pilots in the late 1930s at the beginning of World War II and referred at the time to a jacket made of any weather-resistant material. The anorak reached its height of popularity in the 1950s, at which time it was commonly made of nylon. The poplin anorak first appeared as a fashion item in a 1959 issue of *Vogue* magazine. By 1984, the anorak had declined in popularity. During this time the term "anorak" took on a derogatory meaning in the British (slang) language to mean "a socially inept person." The thought was that only an inept individual would wear an anorak.

Eddie Bauer is often credited with mainstreaming the parka when he introduced/produced a quilted, waterproof jacket called the Skyliner in 1936. It is said that his inspiration came from the insulating garments his grandfather wore in 1904 during the Russian-Japanese War. The broader adoption of the parka was also linked to military use. The snorkel and fishtail parkas were developed in the early 1950s for military use during the Korean War. The snorkel parka was mainly used by airmen stationed in extremely cold areas, whereas the fishtail parka was designed for infantry and lacked the insulation the snorkel parka provided. The fishtail parka reached its height in pop culture during the 1960s in the United Kingdom. The cheapness and availability of the material made the fishtail parka the ideal outer garment for the mod culture that relied on the garment to protect their clothing while riding their scooters. The snorkel parka became widely accepted in the popular culture during the late 1970s through mid-1980s as a school jacket.

Influence and Impact

Even though the anorak and parka originated as two separate clothing items, today the anorak and parka have become synonymous, and the names are often interchangeable with each other. The term "parka," however, is the more universal name, being used in both the United States and Canada, with "anorak" being used more so in the United Kingdom. Other names associated with the anorak include "windbreaker" or "windcheater." Currently the anorak/parka is considered a form of sportswear worn for any outdoor sporting event/occasion, with the general term today meaning a puffy, insulated coat designed to be worn in cold winters. The anorak/parka of today is not defined by the original description alone. While the main properties may be similar, the modern anorak is no longer defined as a pullover jacket but can also have a full-length front opening and be made of modern and even lightweight materials.

In terms of fashion today, both the anorak and parka are considered to be a necessity in cold-weather climates, and fashionable. The anorak is a popular form of outerwear among sororities across college campuses during cold and inclement weather. Here the anorak is used as a symbol of membership, with the sorority's colors and Greek letters displayed on the jacket. Today, the parka is often worn for cold-weather sporting events and activities such as snowboarding and skiing. You can even find the parka on display during the Winter Olympics. Thanks to the Baby Phat brand, the parka has also become a popular form of outerwear in the hip-hop subculture. Both the anorak and parka are popular forms of outerwear and have been so for the past few years, with the parka being featured in a past issue of *Harper's Bazaar*. Brands from Alexander McQueen and Burberry to H & M and Zara offer many modern takes on the traditional form of these jackets. The anorak is no longer relegated to fall/winter wear only. A lighter-weight version has become a popular form of outerwear for the spring and summer months. Current styles of these jackets may have adaptations to the materials, hemlines, trims, and ornamentation that make them modern and current with today's style.

See also HIP-HOP FASHION
Compare to MEXICAN TOURIST/SOUVENIR JACKET; PELISSE; PONCHO; SERAPE

Further Reading

Calasibetta, C. *Essential Terms of Fashion*. New York: Fairchild, 1986.

King, J. C. H., Birgit Pauksztat, and Robert Storrie. *Arctic Clothing of North America: Alaska, Canada, Greenland*. London: British Museum Press, 2005.

Oakes, J., and R. Riewe. "Comparison of Historical and Contemporary Skin Clothing Used in North Greenland: An Ethnohistorical Approach." *Clothing & Textiles Research Journal* 10 (1992): 73.

■ MICHELLE M. JONES

APRON

Aprons are protective coverings for clothing that can also be used to decorate or ornament dress. They can be made of many materials: sturdy washable fabrics, leather, rubber, or plastic for dirty work, or lightweight fabrics decorated with colored trim or lace for a dressy look. They can cover a full outfit from neck to toe, with ties or loops to go around the neck and ties at the waist, or they can be a simple square of cloth gathered into a band that ties around the waist and covers the lower half of the body.

History

The most ancient aprons can be seen on figures in Minoan archaeology. By the Middle Ages, using some cloth to cover up clothing in work, preparing food, or when eating was prevalent for many classes of people. According to the *Oxford English Dictionary*, the word "apron" comes from the Old French *naperon*, meaning tray cloth or tablecloth, which implies a covering of sorts. Craftsmen in the Middle Ages wore aprons for protection and to hold work items. Women followed suit in the home, creating aprons that just covered the skirt, sometimes called a half apron. The idea of the apron spread across Europe and evolved over time. These European immigrant groups brought aprons with them when they settled the American continent. Aprons in the nineteenth century became ubiquitous for women to wear during their household chores. Some aprons became decorative items for dressy occasions, while others were to be put aside when entertaining visitors. In the early twentieth century, aprons often covered the entire front of a woman's dress. They evolved through the 1950s to smaller lap coverings that were often more decorative than functional.

The Apron in the United States

Both male and female European immigrants to the colonies in the seventeenth and eighteenth centuries brought the practical apron style with them. Men wore aprons as protective coverings in their occupations. Blacksmiths, wagon makers, carpenters, cobblers, machinists, and those handling chemicals understood the apron's purpose as a garment protector or, with large pockets, as a way to keep one's tools close at hand for work. Men also wore ceremonial aprons for secret societies. Freemasonry took its symbols from the tools and clothing of actual stonemasons, including the apron, and the degree of master mason is recognized with an apron.

Pinafore-style aprons, where a square of cloth attached to a waist tie above the waist was pinned to the upper body, became a useful apron for women starting in the eighteenth century. Aprons became more closely associated with the cult of domesticity throughout the nineteenth century. The idea of a decorated and fashionable half apron with minimal functional purpose began in the mid-1700s and continued into the 1950s. However, the symbolic link between aprons and domestic work remained the most salient meaning of the apron. This symbolic association was most strongly felt in the 1950s when women were encouraged to leave the World War II workplaces and return to domestic work in the home, and aprons were used in advertising and popular culture to capture the lifestyle of the 1950s housewife. As a result, during this postwar period, society closely tied the image of a woman in an apron, whether doing actual housework or serving cocktails or dinner in a fancier version, with the woman's perceived role as a homemaker. With rise of feminism in the 1960s, the formal apron with its symbolic link to a confining domestic role for women became outdated.

Influence and Impact

An apron's role as a practical covering for clothing from some kind of mess has changed little from medieval times. In the late twentieth century, as men's and women's work roles became less rigidly defined, gender-neutral aprons were developed and worn by both men and women, on the grilling deck, in the kitchen, and in the garage workshop. There has been a small revival for fashionable aprons for women, as well as a return to the designs of the 1950s at the turn of the twenty-first century with fabric stores, pattern makers, and retailers featuring decorative aprons as a part of their inventory.

See also PINAFORE
Compare to DIRNDL

Further Reading

The Adorned Apron. "History of Aprons." http://www.theadornedapron.com/?page_id=18 (accessed June 1, 2013).
Cheney, Joyce. *Aprons: Icons of the American Home*. Philadelphia: Running Press, 2000.

■ JENNIFER VAN HAAFTEN

ARAN SWEATER

Aran sweaters are named for the Aran Islands, which are located off of the west coast of Ireland. Intricate stitching on the sweaters almost forms a language of their own for those who know how to interpret the meaning behind the stitches. Traditionally, women would knit a potential husband a sweater to show that she would make a good wife. The type of stitch she used represented the Irish clan or family. The sweaters were handmade from 100 percent untreated sheep's wool, which has the ability to absorb water, offers breathability, and wicks moisture away from the skin. For the extreme elements workers faced, this sweater was ideal to protect and insulate the body. An Aran sweater can take an experienced knitter approximately sixty days to finish and a novice several months. Estimates indicate that each sweater consists of over one hundred thousand stitches. The first Aran sweater was sold around 1935 in Dublin.

History

Galway Bay experiences intense weather, and many of the workers have traditionally been fishermen or farmers. Records indicate that hand knitting of stockings in the Aran Islands can be traced back as early as the 1600s. The Aran sweater developed as a practical workingmen's sweater, comfortable to the climate of the island. Even in modern times, inhabitants of the island took care of their own needs. Electricity and running water were not available on the island until the 1960s; telephones were not available until the 1970s.

After church on Sundays, many of the women would sit around and share their skill to others in the family. It was a typical pastime activity. There were not any written records of the stitches, as everything was passed on verbally from generation to generation. Legend has it that some men who died at sea and washed up on the shores were able to be identified by their sweater since each was unique. Another use was for young males to wear Aran sweaters for their first holy communion, which heightened awareness for the family unit. This was not a tradition for all of Ireland, but mainly focused on areas close to the Aran Islands.

Aran Sweater in the United States

Vogue magazine featured an article on Aran sweaters in the 1950s after a knitting pattern was published in England during the 1940s and sold in a Galway shop. Once the *Vogue* magazine article hit, exports of the sweaters from Ireland to the United States began.

Influence and Impact

Aran sweaters have become a staple of native Ireland, but also a popular garment for tourists, gaining worldwide acceptance. With the advancement of machine knitting, hand-knit sweaters have become very hard to find due to the increase in their cost. Today most are created by machine. Today many other types of yarn are used besides the traditional wool, including mohair, alpaca, cashmere, and silk.

See also ALPACA SWEATER; NORWEGIAN SWEATER; SCOTTISH SWEATER
Compare to PASHMINA SHAWL AND SCARF; PONCHO; SERAPE

Further Reading

Antonio. "The Aran Sweater." http://www.realmenrealstyle.com/the-aran-sweater.
Misiaszek, E. "The Irish Aran Sweater." http://www.tenontours.com/irish-history/irish-aran-sweater.
Payne, Blanche, Geitel Winakor, and Jane Farrell-Beck. *The History of Costume.* 2nd ed. New York: Addison Wesley Longman, 1992.

■ LUANNE MAYORGA

BANDANA

A bandana is a twenty-two-inch brightly printed square scarf that serves a multitude of practical uses, including handkerchief, neckerchief, face mask, forehead band, and a means by which to wrap small possessions for transport, such as food or personal items. The most popular bandana design is the red cotton cloth square with a black-and-white paisley border. This paisley bandana is also available in a range of colors and varying paisley patterns and borders. Bandanas are produced in cotton fabric, for more practical and robust usage, or silk fabric for a more fashionable and delicate accessory. The popular red bandana enjoys a long history and has historically been associated with the American cowboy and the Wild West of the nineteenth century.

History

As a precursor to the modern-day paisley bandana, the printed commemorative scarf was popularized during the American Revolution, when eighteenth-century textile printmakers began documenting historical events on cloth. George Washington, founding father of the United States, was depicted on a cloth square, and the bandana became a venue for advertising military and political opinion. Printed bandanas were utilized during political campaigns and featured politicians or political causes that warranted promotion. During times of war, especially during World War I and World War II, bandanas were printed with motifs to encourage war support and to increase morale on the home front. By wearing a printed bandana, wearers felt as though they were invested in the conflict and physically demonstrated support by wearing the bandana.

Printed commemorative scarves were utilized in lighthearted marketing methods as well. Bandanas were printed to commemorate fun events, such as world fairs or other important social and cultural events. Printed bandanas promoted movies and famous sporting events, such as the World Series, the annual baseball championship played since 1903. Souvenir bandanas proved to be a profitable marketing venture for many organizations.

When Germans immigrated to the American West in the early nineteenth century, they most frequently settled in Texas hill country and Nuevo Leon, a northern Mexican state bordering on Texas. The dress styles of German settlers in Nuevo Leon influenced cowboy dress of the region, which included leather-fringed vests and coats, bandanas, and cowboy hats. The bandana was used as a functional accessory to protect the mouth and nose from dust, to protect the back of the neck and sometimes the face from the sun, and in cold weather worn under the hat to keep the ears warm.

In 1937, the French couturier Hermes began printing silk scarves in a range of creative designs and colors, which rapidly became a highly sought fashion accessory. In the 1950s, Hermes scarves were endorsed by British royalty, including Queen Elizabeth, as well as Hollywood royalty, including Grace Kelly, who wore the Hermes version of the bandana as a head scarf, a neckerchief, and as a sling for her injured arm. Hermes scarves, the fabric of which is characterized by strong twill silk fabric and which featured labor-intensive hand-sewn hems, were a high-end version of the humble cotton bandana with its simple, often machine-stitched hems.

Bandanas in the United States

Bandanas were made the most famous by cowboys wearing them in old Western movies. However, a wide range of blue-collar working-class men, including farmers, railroad workers, and coal miners, commonly wore the bandana. The main purpose of the bandana for these men working in environmentally demanding conditions was to wipe sweat from the face, protect the nose and throat from dust, and keep dust out of their collars. This working-class cultural code resulted in the inclusion of the bandana in the Rosie the Riveter poster created in 1943 during World War II, a promotional campaign focused on urging women to help out the war effort by working the assembly lines while their boyfriends, husbands, and fathers were overseas.

Because laborers and outdoorsmen used printed bandanas instead of white handkerchiefs, and banditos and raiders used them to conceal their identity, this clothing item came to be associated with the working classes and social revolution. In the early twentieth century in West Virginia and Kentucky, miners wore red bandanas to protect themselves from coal dust but also as a symbol of solidarity. Black and white miners alike identified with the bandana as a symbol of solid working-class masculinity, in contrast with upper-level management at the mines whose masculinity was often challenged by the rank-and-file miners. Red bandanas were handed out at strikes and demonstrations to clearly mark labor organization members during shootouts and other altercations with the coal-mining management. This was particularly useful to union organizers who were attempting to unite men working at different mine locations, and from differing ethnic and racial groups. Red bandanas were a central rallying symbol for the 1921 Battle of Blair Mountain in West Virginia, a labor uprising of between ten and fifteen thousand coal miners.

Influence and Impact

Labor organizers continue to use the red bandana as a means of rallying and flamboyantly identifying supporters. For example, the Red Bandana Brigade in Boston keeps the spirit of the labor movement alive by wearing red bandanas and marching in the annual Honk! Festival of Activist Street Bands parade. In a more general sense, the bandana has been adopted as a symbol of working-class masculinity, with Harley-Davidson motorcycle riders and country-and-western icons such as Willie Nelson sporting the look. The bandana was also widely adopted in the late 1960s and 1970s as a fundamental element of alternative dress styles of the counterculture movement of the period.

Beginning in the 1970s, traditional paisley bandanas were utilized in inner-city gang culture to identify members. Each gang member wears the colored bandana that corresponds to their gang's colors. For example, two long-standing rival gangs that originated in Los Angeles, California, wear bandanas to distinguish loyalty. The Crips gang is identified by the blue bandana while the Bloods gang is identified by the red bandana. Just as bandanas serve as a means of identification within gang culture, bandanas also served as a means of communication within the homosexual community, with the trend peaking in urban United States in the 1970s and 1980s. Different colored bandanas and differing placements on the body communicated within the urban gay community various preferences for different sexual acts. This communication system was referred to as the bandana code and was used by potential partners to convey sexual availability and preferences.

See also BRICOLAGE; CHOLO STYLE; SERAPE; WESTERN WEAR
Compare to DO-RAG; KEFFIYEH; POWWOW ACCESSORIES; PASHMINA SHAWL AND SCARF; TURBAN

Further Reading

Albrechtsen, Nicky, and Fola Solanke. *Scarves.* New York: Thames & Hudson, 2011.
Cisneros, Jose. *Riders across the Centuries: Horsemen of the Spanish Borderlands.* El Paso: Texas Western Press, 1984.
Coleno, Nadine. *The Hermes Scarf: History & Mystique.* New York: Thames & Hudson, 2010.
Harelson, Randy. *The Bandanna Book: 101 Uses for an American Classic.* New York: Perigee Books, 1984.
Huber, Patrick. "Red Necks and Red Bandanas: Appalachian Coal Miners and the Coloring of Union Identity, 1912–1936." *Western Folklore* 65, nos. 1–2 (2006): 195–210.
Slatta, Richard. *Cowboys of the Americas.* New Haven, CT: Yale University Press, 1990.
Weiss, Hillary. *The American Bandana.* New York: Random House Value Publishing, 1995.
Wilson, Laurel. "American Cowboy Dress: Function to Fashion." *Dress* 28 (2002): 40–52.

■ JENNIFER DALEY

BANDEAU

See BIKINI

BANNER GOWN

See CHEONGSAM

BARONG FILIPINO

See BARONG TAGALOG

BARONG TAGALOG

The barong tagalog, also known as the barong Filipino or simply the barong, is the national men's shirt of the Philippines. It is a long-sleeved, collared shirt, buttoning halfway down the front. Traditionally, the barong is made of white, transparent cloth with embroidery around the buttons. The shirt is usually woven out of piña fiber, which is harvested from the leaves of the pineapple plant.

History

The history of the barong tagalog can be traced to precolonial times. The name literally translates to "the dress of Tagalog." Tagalog is the language of the Philippines and the name of the people who lived on the island of Luzon before the Spaniards arrived. The original type of dress of the Tagalog people with its front opening, white color, and loose, tucked-out style resembles today's barong tagalog. Before being conquered by the Spanish in the sixteenth century, native Filipinos hand wove piña, cotton, *jusi*, banana, and abaca fibers. The combination of Filipino weaving skills and Spanish embroidery led the way to articles of clothing made from piña that eventually became staples of dress in the Philippines.

The shirt may be transparent and worn tucked out because of the hot climate or because the embroidery was meant to be shown, but it also had political motives. During the Spanish colonial era, 1565 to 1898, the Spanish rulers forced the Indios, native Filipino men, to wear their shirts tucked out to show inferiority. The material was transparent, so weapons could not be hidden under the shirt, and there were no pockets in order to prevent stealing. As a middle class started to form, businessmen still had to wear the barong tagalog, but they added embroidery to the front of the shirt for decoration. During the American colonial period, 1902 to 1946, Filipino dress still represented colonization. Westernized formal wear was the norm during the American colonization because it symbolized wealth and political power, as well as modernity. The upper class wore Westernized clothing to signify their equality to Americans.

After achieving independence, the barong symbolized the Filipino "man of the masses." Soon the shirt became a symbol of colonial resistance. In 1953, President Ramon Magsaysay wore a barong for his inauguration and other formal occasions to identify himself with the common people instead of the elite. Previous presidents embraced Westernized formal wear, but he wanted to project the image of simplicity and embody the "man of the masses." In 1975, President Ferdinand Marcos came to power and also popularized the barong by wearing it on all occasions. Finding a picture of him without it is very rare. He even declared an official Barong Tagalog Week from June 5 to 11 to promote the shirt even further to the nation and expand its export opportunities.

The rise in barong popularity may also be accounted for because of the Filipinos' new desire to have pride in their products, people, and nation as a whole. It was a staple in a man's wardrobe by the end of the 1900s. The polo barong is the short-sleeved, more casual version of the barong tagalog. It was even further transformed into a shirt made of cotton or polyester and with little embroidery. Soon it became the uniform of government employees, many private companies, and even President Fidel Ramos, the twelfth president of the Philippines from 1992 to 1998. It was not until the 1990s that it became the norm for grooms to wear barongs at their weddings.

Today, Filipino men wear the barong at special formal events, and grooms traditionally wear long-sleeved ones for their wedding. They wear it not tucked in as a formal dress shirt with black pants. Eventually the barong tagalog became the dress given to foreign dignitaries on official visits to the Philippines. It is also a tradition for leaders at Asia Pacific Economic Cooperation (APEC) meetings to wear the clothing of the host country for a leader's family photo.

The Barong Tagalog in the United States

The barong came over to the United States with Filipino immigrants. Mass immigration started in the twentieth century when the Philippines was ceded to the United States. It is mostly prevalent in large Filipino communities in California, Hawai'i, and Chicago. Pierre Cardin, who opened the front, made it a full button-up instead of a pullover, pointed the cuffs, thickened the collar, and minimalized the embroidery, redesigned the barong in 1971. This style only remained popular until the 1980s. The Pierre Cardin barong tagalog was revolutionary because the silhouette was tapered in instead of loose fitting. This alteration of the traditional barong was proof that Filipino dress was internationally stylish and a gateway to introducing the shirt into couture fashion.

Influence and Impact

In the United States, Filipino men wear it the same traditional way as an alternate to a suit or tuxedo. For example, Quentin Tarantino wore a barong tagalog to the Golden Globes nominations following his visit to the Philippines. Lesser-quality barongs can be made of *jusi*, which is a combination of silk and piña, and mechanically woven instead of handmade.

Because of the Filipinos' independence, the traditional dress became equal to other nations in the world. The barong tagalog originated as a sign of inferiority to the Spanish rulers, but with the promotion by several presidents, it turned into a symbol of overcoming colonialism and gaining independence.

See also ALOHA SHIRT (HAWAI'IAN SHIRT)
Compare to BUSSERULL (NORWEGIAN WORK SHIRT); DASHIKI; KIMONO; OXFORD SHIRT; POLO SHIRT

Further Reading

Roces, Mina. "Gender, Nation and the Politics of Dress in Twentieth-Century Philippines." *Gender & History* 17, no. 2 (August 2005): 354–77.

■ SABRINA SKERSTON AND ELLEN C. MCKINNEY

BATA CUBANA
See RUMBA DRESS

BATIK CLOTH APPAREL

An ancient resist technique commonly associated with the use of a melted, hot wax mixture being applied to fabric prior to being dyed to prohibit the dye from coloring the fabric in areas where the wax-resist medium has been applied. Other types of liquid resists that have been associated with batik include paste resists of flour, rice, mud, resin, or starch.

After the fabric is waxed, dyed, and dried, it is often rewaxed and dyed again to create multiple layers of colors and more intricate designs. This process can be repeated over and over until the desired effects are achieved. Each time the fabric is dyed, the current color being dyed is affected by the previously applied colors, typically progressing from light to dark. To complete the batik process, the dye must be set to ensure color/wash fastness, and then the wax must be removed from the fabric. Traditionally the wax is a combination of beeswax and paraffin (a petroleum product) and possibly a resin. The differing properties of beeswax (being a softer wax) and paraffin (being more brittle) allow artists to control the amount of crackle in their designs. Dye flowing into the wax cracks creates thin, variegated lines of color, which is a distinct quality of batik. The challenge of a well-crafted batik, in addition to being well designed, is to achieve a delicate balance of wax application, overlay of dyed colors, and successful removal of wax while maintaining the strength of the colors dyed. Batik fabrics are typically cotton or silk but may also be rayon or linen.

History

There is much speculation as to when and where the earliest resist-dyed fabrics came into existence since they have existed in many cultures before written records and possibly have developed cross-culturally. Some form of batik has been practiced at different times in the majority of countries in the world. Evidence of resist dying has been found on Egyptian burial cloth as early as 1000 BCE. But it has been suggested that the origin of that particular cloth is from India.

Java, Indonesia, the area most widely recognized for batik fabrics, was a cultural melting pot and sat on a major trade route that included India, Egypt, China, and Persia where goods and knowledge were traded. Much discussion has occurred over the centuries as to how Java became a recognized center for batik. Who influenced whom? Dutch traders brought batik to Holland in the late 1800s. As it passed into Europe in the early 1900s, batik rapidly became popular with artists and found its way into the fashion of the day, becoming a part of Art Nouveau.

In contemporary Malaysia, government officials are expected to wear batik (or batik printed) clothing on Fridays.

A traditional batik tool for applying wax is a canting, also known as *tjanting* tool, used to draw fine lines. A canting/*tjanting* tool is a teaspoon-sized copper bowl with one to seven copper tubes projecting out. This is attached to a stick/handle for ease of use. The copper (best metal for even heat retention) bowl holds hot liquid wax that flows through the tube(s) to enable fine lines to be drawn on the fabric. Finely drawn batiks (known as batik *tulis*) are labor intensive and may take months to complete.

In the 1880s, caps, also known as *tjaps*, started being manufactured. Caps/*tjaps* are copper blocks designed with copper bands to simulate the hand-drawn lines of the canting/*tjanting* tool. Caps/*tjaps* are dipped in a wax mixture and stamped on the fabric in repeat patterns, allowing for a much faster and more affordable production of intricate-looking batiks.

Contemporary, nontraditional artists employ a wide variety of application techniques to create multiple-surface designed batiks, including painting wax with assorted brushes, dipping found objects or cut sponges in wax for stamping repeated motifs on fabric, pouring wax on fabric, using tools for scratching or scraping away wax already applied to the fabric, rubbing hard wax onto the fabric, making wax crayons for drawing, applying wax to screens for use as a stencil to screen print on fabric, and more.

Batik in the United States

Javanese dance costumes made of batik fabrics were seen in the United States in 1893 at the Chicago World's Columbian Exposition. Interest in batik grew from 1907 to 1936. Numerous manuals and how-to articles were published in the United States during that time; the process and fabrics became popular in mainstream America. In the mid-1960s, 1970s, and early 1980s, there was another revival of interest from the world of art, fashion, and home furnishings, sparked in part by more people traveling to Asia. More books and articles were published during this time as artist interest in hand-dyed textiles grew. Batik fabrics and imitations of batik fabrics were seen in fashion and home furnishings.

Batik has seen a recent revival in popularity among artists since the emergence of soy wax. Soy wax, hydrogenated soy oil, was invented in 2001 for candle making by Iowan Michael Richards. In 2002, Dorothy Bunny Bowen started experimenting with soy wax and in June 2005 presented a paper, "Soy Wax: An Alternative Resist," at the World Batik Conference in Boston, Massachusetts, and again at the Kuala Lumpur International Batik Convention in Malaysia in December 2005. Since that time, interest in soy wax has been on the rise, with online forums popping up and many textile publications both online and in print emerging with the inclusion of soy wax, recognizing it as an eco-friendly alternative in the batik process.

With the invention of soy wax, artists have started experimenting with its properties. This is a recent trend, and much of its application is still in the experimental stages, but there appears to be a growing interest in the possibilities of soy wax. Soy wax offers some unique advantages, most notably the fact that it is environmentally friendly, it melts at a lower temperature, and it is significantly easier to remove from the fabric through steaming, ironing, or washing in a washing machine. Since soy wax is water soluble, low-immersion dye baths are required, and extra care is needed in the process of overdyeing, since multiple dye baths will break down the wax barrier. Another significant difference is its viscosity. Soy wax tends to be less viscous, making it more challenging to create a finely detailed design. As interest increases, more information is becoming available, and more artists are researching/experimenting with the possible uses of soy wax.

Influence and Impact

Batik, along with tie-dye, was incorporated into the fashion of the 1960s, being seen on brightly colored halter dresses, granny dresses, minidresses, and midi- and maxiskirts, which were mostly worn by young women. It was a time of protest and freedom of expression. Batik provided a way for people to express their individuality. Procion fiber reactive dyes came on the market. These dyes changed the home dyeing industry, being much easier to use, providing intense color that did not easily wash out, and working with hot or cold water. The fact that fiber reactive dyes could be used with cold water was critical to the batik process, since hot water would melt the wax applied to the fabric. Artists began using the fiber reactive dyes in batik wall hangings, and eventually the use of fiber reactive dyes spread to the general public, with people creating psychedelic T-shirts, fabrics for dresses, and bedspreads with these new, easier-to-use dyes on the market.

Since the 1980s there has been much interest in hand-dyed, batik fabrics among America quilt makers. Most quilt shops sell a variety of these types of fabrics. In 2005, the World Batik Conference was held in Boston, Massachusetts. At that event, the World Batik Council was formed.

See also BLANGKON; PAJ NTAUB (HMONG FLOWER CLOTH); SARONG
Compare to CHAMBRAY; MADRAS CLOTH; TIE-DYED APPAREL

Further Reading

Li, Y., C. Hu, and X. Yao. "Innovative Batik Design with an Interactive Evolutionary Art System." *Journal of Computer Science and Technology* 24, no. 6 (2009): 1035–47. doi:10.1007/s11390-009-9293-5.
Welters, L. "Batik from Courts and Palaces: The Rudolf Smend Collection and Batik Fashion/American Style." *Textile* 4, no. 3 (2006): 368–74.

■ JOAN WEBSTER-VORE

BATTENBERG LACE

Queen Victoria is credited for defining the term "Battenberg lace" in the late 1800s as a tribute to her son-in-law, the Duke of Battenberg. It was common practice in England for laces to be named for dukes. The lace gained enormous popularity during the Victorian and Edwardian time periods and was used for collars, cuffs, lace jackets, and dresses.

There are several different types of lace that involve various techniques. A tape lace is made with a base flat strip of stitches that can then be manipulated into designs. Bobbin lace is made on a firm pillow in which a design is laid on the pillow. Bobbins come in two primary types: spangled and continentals. The thread is wrapped around the bobbin and then intertwining the bobbins following the patterns makes the design of the lace.

The category of tape laces consists of those that have a base that is shaped to make a design. Some tape laces, such as Renaissance or Brussels, consist of shapes or scallops. Battenberg lace is a flat tape lace that normally does not have any ornamentation and is filled with special stitching that holds the design in place. Battenberg tape has small wires on each side that allow the tape to be shaped as the wires are pulled in one direction or another. The majority of lace tapes today are machine made, which gained in popularity during the nineteenth century, allowing for quicker Battenberg lace designs. From the sixteenth to the nineteenth century, lace tapes were made by hand, normally out of bobbin lace. Other Irish laces include Carrickmacross, Limerick, and Youghal.

History

In the nineteenth century, laces with a foundation of woven tapes became popular. Patterns were outlined with the tapes then stitched in the center to connect motifs and help hold their shapes. Manufacturers during this time were able to mass produce the tapes; then lace makers created the designs.

The seven-year potato famine in Ireland in 1845 was devastating to the country. Potatoes provided roughly 60 percent of food to the majority of Ireland. Approximately one million people died, and hundreds of thousands left Ireland for other countries including the United States, Canada, Wales, and England. No matter where they went, they were unwelcome, taken advantage of, and put into slums, and multitudes died from disease. For those remaining in Ireland, people were starving, work was scarce, families were destitute, and enormous populations were homeless as landlords evicted people for not being able to pay their rent.

Lady Harriet Kavanagh decided to set up a tape lace industry in 1846 in Ireland to help support women who were located on the Borris estate at the time of the potato famine. Lady Kavanagh had traveled throughout Europe and frequently viewed various types of laces. She took those ideas to begin her own variation. In other parts of Ireland, nuns taught others about lace making as a way to provide income to families during the famine. Cork became well known for its laces, and each area developed its own form or style of lace. Orders were received from royalty, and lace was also sold to people aboard ships in the coastal towns. For many families, selling lace helped keep them alive.

Battenberg Lace in the United States

Lace making has had a strong influence in America since the 1600s when it was first introduced by the East Midland countries. Early American settlers used lace on the edge of clothes, although its primary use was for special occasions. There were sumptuary laws in existence during that time that prohibited settlers from displaying excess. In addition, many were skilled in bobbin lace prior to leaving their homeland, so they were able to continue making lace and teaching others the skill. This lace-making technique thus became popular in the United States. Needle lace, on the other hand, was very tedious and challenging to make. It did not really catch on in America. Tape laces came to America during the Industrial Revolution. Up to that time, lace tapes were made by hand using bobbin lace techniques and were primarily floral designs. They were very popular in America, and their popularity increased with the invention of machine-made tapes. Battenberg and other tape laces had multiple uses, including household linens and handkerchiefs, because of their durability.

Sara Hadley was a lace maker in Brooklyn, New York, in the late 1800s. Even though she made different types of lace, Battenberg was one of her specialties. Her work was featured in numerous fashion magazines, which heightened the interest in Battenberg lace.

Influence and Impact

Battenberg lace has had an influence on more than just clothing. It can be found in home decor, including curtains, table linens, and bedsheets, as well as in hair ornaments and Irish dance dresses. Special occasion garments including wedding dresses, christening gowns, and first communion dresses are often seen with accents of this beautiful lace.

See also APRON; SNOOD
Compare to BARONG TAGALOG; CHAMBRAY; DASHIKI

Further Reading

Bullock, Alice-May. *Lace and Lace Making.* New York: Larousse, 1981.
Chase, Michelle C. "American Lace." Master's thesis, Winthrop University, Spring 2004.
Powys, Marian. "Lace in America." *Arts & Decoration* 12 (1919–1920).
Robinson, Mabel F. "Irish Lace." *Art Journal* 50 (1887).

■ LUANNE MAYORGA

BERET

A beret is a soft hat made of felt, usually black, gathered at the head so that it tapers outward or slumps, and tipped with a small single-shaft tassel at its center. Since the 1920s, it has been associated with the quintessential Frenchman; however it is also worn extensively in Spain and as part of military uniforms. Variants are also worn in Scottish traditional dress as well as by Rastafarians. The soft woolen hat has a long history and can be traced back to the Bronze Age in Crete and Italy where it was worn by the Greeks, Minoans, and Romans.

History

The word "beret" is a French variant of the English *biretta* and the Spanish *birette*, used to name a square clerical cap. Early etymologies link it to the vernacular Latin *birrum*, the Gaulish *birros*, and the Old Irish *birros*, all relating to "short." Given the beret's simplicity, its exact roots are difficult to trace, and it can be assumed that it was a generic form of head wear since ancient times. Although mainly worn by the common classes, in the Middle Ages and the Renaissance, variants were worn by the nobility. These were typi-

Beret

cally adorned with jewelry and feathers and were made from more opulent materials such as fur.

Its more modern incarnations have come to be associated with the Basque region associated with the Pyrenees Mountains on the border of France and Spain where it is traditionally worn with espadrilles. It was here that berets began to be produced in more than an informal way, with production beginning in the seventeenth century in Oloron-Sainte-Marie in France. By the early nineteenth century, industrial production began to displace local artisanal production, with the first beret factory opening in 1810 in Beatex-Laulhere. By the early twentieth century, there were around twenty factories in France as well as others in Italy and Spain.

The military beret began in an informal way with the militia of France and Spain who wore their own clothing, with the beret being a common denominator. The most famous of these were the Volontaires Cantabres that came from the Basque country and who were active between 1740 and 1760. At a similar period, Scottish troops wore the blue bonnet, a capacious version of the beret. More formally, it began to be worn in 1889 by the French Chasseurs Alpins (alpine cavalry). This prompted the World War I general Hugh Elles to recommend them for the uniform for the Royal Tank Regiment. Not only did the adoption of the hat mark the creation of the new regiment, but it was less likely to come off in various movement in and out of hatches. The military beret achieved lasting fame when it was worn by Field Marshall Montgomery in World War II. It is also worn by the French Foreign Legion as well as the Canadian military. In the Vietnam War, the beret was worn by the Special Forces Unit. Today it is used across the world as part of official uniform, and especially as part of noncombat military dress. The beret is also worn by various police forces.

In the military and police uniform, the beret is expected to be worn slumped, usually to feature the official insignia of the battalion or unit. But the beret has also been worn by dissident, revolutionary, and guerilla groups. Perhaps outmatching Montgomery as the most iconic example of the beret is Che Guevara, whose most famous portrait has him wearing a black beret with a red star. Already in the 1960s the black beret was used as the item of clothing registering belonging to other groups of resistance fighters such as the Black Panthers in the United States and the black power brigades of Bermuda. It has also been used by the Provisional Irish Republican Party and the ETA guerillas. Berets were also worn by the Latino revolutionary movement in the 1960s and 1970s, the Young Lords Party.

The Beret in the United States

The beret's entry into the United States initially occurred in the military in 1943 when a battalion of the 509th Parachute Infantry was given maroon berets by their British counterparts for their service in World War II. Subsequently, the U.S. army adopted the beret for their counterinsurgency forces fighting in Vietnam, the famous Green Berets. In recent times, outside of traditional usage, berets have been worn by beatniks, bohemians, and otherwise individuals who wish to show off a sense of creative daring. Along with the archetypal Frenchman, berets are de rigueur for the cliché of the artist. Larger versions that are knitted and often multicolored are used by Rastafarians when they wish to contain their dreadlocks. In cities throughout the Western world, berets are largely worn by women, in all colors and accented with complementary decoration.

Influence and Impact

Berets are worn most persistently in the Basque region, for which there are specialized names such as *béret basque* in French and *basco* in Italian. Historically the colors included red, white, and blue, with the latter being the most widely worn. In France and Spain, the beret is chiefly black. Although industrial beret production began in France, it is not so commonly worn except in rural areas. Nonetheless it remains strongly tied to national identity. The persistent caricature propagated in Anglo-Saxon culture accompanies the beret with a striped shirt, a baguette, and a bicycle. In many ways the beret is the unofficial national dress of France. As such, Americans often adopt the beret as a symbol of a linkage to France and as a mark of cosmopolitan character.

See also DASHIKI; SNOOD; TAM-O'-SHANTER
Compare to BOWLER HAT; FEZ; RASTA HAT

Further Reading

Amphlett, Hilda. *Hats: A History of Fashion in Headwear*. New York: Dover, 2003.
Denisoff, Serge. "Fighting Prophecy with Napalm: The Ballad of the Green Beret." *Journal of American Culture* 13, no. 1 (Spring 1990): 81–93.

■ ADAM GECZY

BERMUDA SHORTS

Bermuda shorts are knee-length, pleated-front shorts made from lightweight but durable materials such as cotton twill in a range of colors. They are still worn on Bermuda as part of a business suit, where they are made of summer-weight suiting fabrics in neutral colors and paired with long socks, a dress shirt, and a tie.

History

In the early twentieth century, shorts became an appropriate alternative to pants on business or formal occasions for men working in tropical colonies of the British Empire. Edward VIII, then Duke of Windsor (1894–1972), was an international style icon who made Bermuda shorts popular throughout the West when he wore them extensively while governor of the island during World War II. As women took on traditionally male roles in society, they also adopted many aspects of male dress, such as Bermuda shorts. Women attending college in the 1940s were inspired by the returning GIs, many of whose uniforms had included a pair of shorts for comfort in warmer climates.

Bermuda Shorts in the United States

Beginning in the early twentieth century, the American beauty ideal was based on youth and exercise, and young people led fashion trends. Young men at universities such as Princeton and Yale adopted a mode of dress called "Ivy style," which many continued to wear throughout their lives. The classic Ivy-style wardrobe included Oxford shirts, Bermuda shorts, sack suits, penny loafers, and repp ties. When these men took office jobs in the early 1950s, they continued to wear the clothing of their college days, including suits comprised of a matching jacket and Bermuda shorts for summer days before air conditioning; socks long enough to cover the lower legs were necessary for propriety's sake. It is also possible that men picked up the Bermuda suit from British colonial islands such as Bermuda, Jamaica, and the Bahamas, which were popular vacation spots in the 1950s.

As the Bermuda suit gained popularity, American retailers introduced a "two-and-a-half-piece suit," which included a jacket, pants, and shorts cut from the same fabric. When air conditioning was installed in office buildings, the Bermuda suit largely disappeared in favor of full-length pants. However, men still wore many different lengths of pant for vacation and leisure activities. Women and teenage girls also wore Bermuda shorts as leisurewear, especially on vacation. Lilly Pulitzer (b. 1931), whose bright, Palm Beach–inspired prints would become preppy classics, began making Bermuda shorts for both men and women in her graphic, brightly colored fabrics in the 1960s. As pants and shorts became appropriate alternatives to skirts and dresses, women began to wear Bermuda shorts for daily activities. This style was adopted widely by suburban housewives, whose lives often included casual sports and many hours of leisure. Former president John F. Kennedy (1917–1963), a style icon of the early 1960s, codified Bermuda shorts as part of the casual preppy wardrobe after pictures of him wearing an untucked Oxford shirt and Bermuda shorts in Hyannis Port, Massachusetts, were published in *Time* magazine. The style remained popular throughout the twentieth century, used with greater frequency as American fashion became more casual. The 1990s and early 2000s saw a resurgence of fashionable Bermuda shorts for women, and this casual day wear was even considered appropriate for business and fashionable evening wear, available in satins and worn with high heels. Throughout the second half of the twentieth century, Bermuda shorts have been known as an unflattering hallmark of American tourists in Europe.

Influence and Impact

Bermuda shorts now come in a variety of colors and fabrics, from seersucker, madras, and linen to heavy cottons and sometimes wool. In America, they are most often worn as separates (no longer as part of a suit) and are generally not appropriate for office wear. They continue to be identified most strongly with Ivy League dress, and certain styles, such as "Nantucket reds" (cotton dyed a specific red hue), are a staple of preppy summer wardrobes. The term "Bermuda shorts" is now applied to most shorts that hit above the knee, regardless of cut or material. Shorts for men in the 2010s are by default Bermuda length; women wear a wider range of lengths, and Bermuda shorts might be considered dowdy or conservative.

See also ALOHA SHIRT (HAWAI'IAN SHIRT); FLIP-FLOPS (GETA); MADRAS CLOTH; OXFORD SHIRT
Compare to CAPRI PANTS; LEDERHOSEN; SIRWAL

Further Reading

Banks, Jeffrey, and Doria de la Chappelle. *Preppy: Cultivating Ivy Style*. New York: Rizzoli, 2011.
Green, Nancy. *Ready-to-Wear, Ready-to-Work: A Century of Industry and Immigrants in Paris and New York*. Durham, NC: Duke University Press, 1997.
Hill, Daniel Delis. *American Menswear from the Civil War to the Twenty-First Century*. Lubbock: Texas Tech University Press, 2011.

■ ARIANNA E. FUNK

BIKINI

Also referred to as the bandeau, the bikini is a two-piece bathing suit where up to 85 to 90 percent of the body is bare. The top is usually made from two isosceles-shaped fabric triangles placed over the breasts, held in place by thin straps. Vertical placement is secured by straps attached in the front to the uppermost triangle points then attached around the neck, and horizontal stability is achieved by a strap that is attached to the lower edge of the triangles and ties in the back. The bottom sits well below the hipbone and has thin side straps that connect the front triangular fabric to a rounded triangle in the back.

History

The bikini's historical origin can be traced to ancient Greece when pictures of women barely covered by pieces of fabric were included in mosaics. As civilization evolved, bathing shifted from focusing on health and cleanliness to bathing for leisure and sport. Up to the mid-twentieth century, swimwear focused on modesty and protecting the woman's body from onlookers. The modern bikini emerged during the 1940s from zeitgeist forces, including the sumptuary laws of World War II in which fabric for women's beachwear was reduced by 10 percent to reserve fabric for the war effort. Women initially rejected the bikini, which revealed a majority of bare skin, because it symbolized lack of decency. French designer Jacques Heim launched his version of a bikini the summer after the end of World War II on the French Rivera, but no French model dared to wear it in public and the bikini was banned from beauty pageants and from many European beaches.

Public acceptance of the bikini improved when Michele Bernardini, a French show-girl turned model, wore a bikini at a fashion show in Paris in 1946. Swimsuits in the 1950s included two-piece styles with a bare midriff, but the majority of suit bottoms sold to the consumer-at-large had waists well above hip level and covered most of the upper leg. The true bikini was mostly seen on pinup girls or women in films such as Brigitte Bardot, Jayne Mansfield, and Diana Dors. Swimsuits also began to be showcased in beauty contests in Florida and California. In the 1960s, the bikini, embraced by the youth culture, gained widespread acceptance, and new textile innovations including the discovery of spandex inspired new styles. By the 1970s, the bikini had lost some of its shock value and became available to the common consumer. By 1974, the string bikini emerged and became popular on exotic beaches in Rio and Saint Tropez and in the United States. In Rio de Janeiro and Saint Tropez, women pushed the bikini miniaturization concept further by wearing the "tanga," also known as the thong.

Bikini in the United States

Americans didn't wear the bikini on beaches until the 1960s. The bikini infiltrated popular culture in the United States through music and film; its first appearance was in the song "Itsy Bitsy Teenie Weenie Yellow Polkadot Bikini" by Brian Hyland. In 1962, Ursula Andress wore a bikini in the film *Dr. No*, the first James Bond movie, and a series of surf/beach movies followed. Bikinis were epitomized in films such as *Beach Party* (1963), *Bikini Beach* (1964), *How to Stuff a Wild Bikini* (1965), and *Dr. Goldfoot and the Bikini Machine* (1965). The cultural shifts toward freedom of expression in the 1960s resulted in designer

Rudy Gernreich's monokini that was revealed in California in 1962; however its commercialization was short-lived.

Influence and Impact

The success of contemporary lingerie firms such as Victoria's Secret can be traced to the sociological shift that enabled widespread acceptance of swimsuits that bare much of a woman's body. Because women in Western society were freed from the moral barriers related to body covering when swimming, lingerie firms were able to build on that sense of freedom, applying it to the lingerie sector.

See also KIMONO; SARONG
Compare to CAFTAN

Further Reading

Cohen, M. "An Itsy-Bitsy History of the Teeny Weeny Bikini, 1946–2003." *Shape* 22 (2003): 232–33.
Lencek, Lena, and Gideon Bosker. *Making Waves: Swimsuits and the Undressing of America.* San Francisco: Chronicle Books, 1989.
Spencer, K. "Our Crash Course on the Bikini." *Cosmopolitan* 237 (2004): 178.
Webber-Hanchett, T. "Bikini." In *Fashion, Costume, and Culture: Clothing, Headwear, Body Decorations, and Footwear through the Ages*, edited by S. Pendergast and T. Pendergast, vol. 5, 853–55. Detroit, MI: UXL, 2005.

■ MARY RUPPERT-STROESCU AND REBECCA VANG

BIRKENSTOCKS

The word "Birkenstock" is a family name indicating any pair in a line of shoes manufactured or distributed by the Birkenstock family and company or its U.S. counterpart, Birkenstock USA. Birkenstocks are made with a contoured cork-latex sole designed specifically with features such as deep heel cups, arch support, and a toe gripper to more naturally fit the human foot. The eco-friendly cork is sandwiched by a suede liner on top for comfort, a jute liner to wick away moisture, and a shock absorbing, durable sole on bottom to resist wear and tear. The upper part of the shoe is often made with natural materials such as leather, suede, nuback, or boiled wool, though more recently synthetic alternatives have been used. Most commonly, the term "Birkenstocks" has come to refer to one of the company's two most popular styles: either a half clog (the Boston) or a two-strapped sandal style (the Arizona). Less accurately, the term has come to refer to any knockoff with similar styling.

History

In 1774, medieval church records in a small German town record Johann Adam Birkenstock as "subject and shoemaker." As was traditional for the era, it is likely that Johann's sons were apprenticed to his trade, as well as their sons to them, and so on. Johann's grandson, Konrad, hypothesized in 1897 that since the human foot was naturally contoured, a sole that was curved would be more comfortable for the wearer, and he developed an insole in 1902 intended to be inserted into other premanufactured German shoes. In the early twentieth century, Carl Birkenstock began exporting the insoles to other European countries and gave training seminars to European physicians extolling the virtues of a contoured sole. Carl's son, Karl, also joined the family business and in 1964 evolved the idea from mere insole to manufacturing the entire shoe in-house, which resulted in the first Birkenstock sandal. Though created in Germany, Birkenstocks were never identified as part of any specific German traditional or cultural dress.

Birkenstocks in the United States

The popularity of the brand might have remained primarily a European secret except that Californian Margot Fraser took a trip to Germany in 1966. The large walking demands of her trip left Margot with uncomfortable foot pain. While in a spa seeking relief, Fraser was recommended the Birkenstocks brand. Fraser felt immediate relief and was further impressed that after a few months using the sandals back in California, all her chronic foot pain disappeared. Fraser was so amazed that she began importing the shoe to the United States, giving birth to the company Birkenstock USA. The Arizona, the two-strap sandal most eponymous for the brand, was introduced in 1973. The brand continued to grow, and in 1997 they were inducted into the Footwear News Hall of Fame "in honor of extraordinary business practices, outstanding contributions to the Marin County community, and for dramatically influencing what Americans wear on their feet." In 2002, Fraser passed on her shares in the company to her employees, transitioning the business to an employee-owned model. Fraser herself retired from the company in 2005.

Influence and Impact

When Fraser initially tried to import Birkenstocks, she was rejected by shoe retailers on the basis that the shoe was too ugly to be salable in the United States. The first places to stock Birkenstocks were actually health food grocery stores in Berkeley, California. Rather than conforming, the homely appearance of the Birkenstock has been embraced by its wearers as a way to make a personal statement in their dress, that they are unwilling to be slaves to fashion. The hippie culture of the United States during the 1970s strongly identified with Birkenstock's core values of quality and comfort over fashion, high-quality craftsmanship, environmentally friendly materials, and long-lasting products. Birkenstocks also flourished in popularity during the late 1990s during the grunge culture. Even though Birkenstocks have become a common piece of American footwear, they are still stereotypically representative of a granola-crunchy, bohemian individual, if not optimistic naivete. Often they will be used as a device to help further characterizations of a role; in the popular sitcom *Friends*, Phoebe Buffay is shown to have purchased cowhide-colored Bostons off of eBay, mistakenly believing them to have belonged to the "late" Shania Twain.

Birkenstocks were also a conscious wardrobe choice in the 2005 mockumentary *Thank You for Smoking*. In the film they were worn by environmentalist senator Ortolan Finistirre; in one scene the camera pans distinctly to his footwear. In an interview by the *New York Times*, director Jason Reitman is quoted as saying, "Nothing says, 'I want to tell you how to live your life' more than Birkenstocks."

Though Birkenstock has partnered with several designers such as Stella McCartney, Giambattista Valli, and Céline's Phoebe Philo, presumably to bring more fashion appeal to the brand, they have been unable to shed their frumpy image. The popular *Manolo's Shoe Blog* (not representational of the brand Manolo Blanik) has consigned the Boston style to the "Gallery of Horrors," declaring it "the ugliest, most unstylish shoe ever manufactured. This shoe, it looks like it was put together by the blind medieval monks, for wear by the peasants of the mud." Despite this, Birkenstocks continue to be popular with many consumers. Birkenstocks have been photographed being worn in street settings by several celebrities such as Anne Hathaway, Heidi Klum, Amy Poehler, and Liev Schreiber. To date, Birkenstocks have not made a "red carpet" or other formalized appearance. While arguments for or against their fashionability abound, Birkenstocks are firmly established as acceptable casual footwear in American culture.

During the height of its popularity in the late 1990s, the Birkenstock style was knocked off by several retailers. To offer the style at a lower price point, most of these manufacturers would retain the clog or two-strap style upper body, if not the signature contoured soles that made the brand popular in the first place. With the decrease in popularity, the production and availability of knockoffs of the Boston style have waned. The two-strap style of the Arizona remains a popular sandal style for both men and women across many price points. Nevertheless, it can be argued that the popularity of Birkenstocks in general paved the way for other comfortable, albeit not traditionally stylish, footwear brands to debut on the market such as the Croc and UGG brands.

See also CLOGS
Compare to BLUNDSTONE BOOTS; BRITISH RIDING BOOTS; CHINESE FLATS; JELLIES; UGG FOOTWEAR

Further Reading

Birkenstock USA Official Site. "Birkenstock History." http://www.birkenstockusa.com/about/birken stock-history (accessed May 5, 2013).
Carr, Coeli. "Thank You for Insulting Our Sandals." *New York Times*, March 12, 2006, http://www .nytimes.com/2006/03/12/fashion/sundaystyles/12birkenstock.html# (accessed May 6, 2014).
Moon, Youngme. *Different: Escaping the Competitive Herd*. New York: Crown Business, 2011.
Official Birkenstock Website Germany. "Our Company." http://www.birkenstock.de/birkenstock/ index_e1280.html (accessed May 5, 2014).

■ LAURA VAN WAARDHUIZEN

BLANGKON

The blangkon is a traditional Javanese male headdress made from batik fabric and sewn into the shape of a human head. The term originated from the Javanese word *blangko*, meaning "a form to be filled in," referring to the human head. Blangkon are made with square batik fabric usually measuring 105 by 105 centimeters. The batik cloth is traditionally pleated (*wiru*) and glued onto the head pattern and then carefully stitched.

There are several different styles of blangkon, but among them, blangkon Yogya (Jogja or Yogyakarta) and Solo are the most popular. These styles were named after their cities of origin. Blangkon Jogja, also known as blangkon Mataraman, came from the Mataram kingdom tradition in Yogyakarta, whereas blangkon Solo came from the court of Sura-karta. The distinction between these two blangkon is evident through the shape of the *mondholan*—a bugle (bundle) attachment on the back of the blangkon. The Yogyakartan blangkon has a full-volumed shape of the *mondholan* bugle on the back, while in the blangkon Solo, the *mondholan* shape is relatively flat and is therefore also known as blang-kon *trepes* (Javanese for "flat"). The original function of the *mondholan* bugle in the blang-kon is to keep the male's topknot hairstyle, giving him a more neat and tidy appearance.

History

The shape of the blangkon is believed to be a form of Islamic customization from earlier Javanese male head cloths known as *udheng* or *iket*—a head cloth worn by men using batik cloth winding around their heads. Compared to *udheng* or *iket*, the function of the blangkon is to fully cover the head. The modification of the turban design into the blangkon correlates with the purpose of economic efficiency, as the blangkon only used half the amount of cloth that was required for a turban.

A Javanese legend communicating the value of the blangkon in society tells a narrative of a man named Aji Saka (Aji Soko) who saved Java from the monstrous Javanese ruler, King Dewata Cengkar. In this legend, Saka offers himself to become a sacrificial meal for the king. His dying request of the king is for the land of Java to be the same size as his turban. When Saka's request is granted, he spreads his turban over the land. The cloth magically grows wider, longer, and bigger, pushing King Dewata Cengkar into the sea, leaving Java in peace. This legend places the blangkon as a symbol of heroic manhood in Java.

The wearing of the Javanese blangkon in the early twentieth century was also used to distinguish the aristocrats. Since the mid-twentieth century, Javanese civilians have typically worn blangkon when attending special occasions such as cultural festivals, cere-monies, and formal parties. From 1890 to 1939 there were massive migrations of Javanese people to labor in Surinamese plantations; therefore the blangkon is also known as an ethnic male headdress worn by Javanese Surinamers in Suriname, South America.

The Blangkon in the United States

The migration of Javanese Indonesians to study in the United States has contributed to the introduction of the blangkon in this region. History suggests that the introduction of the blangkon to the United States was brought about by American and Indonesian academics who studied *wayang*, the Javanese traditional puppet show, and gamelan, the Javanese traditional orchestra, in the mid-twentieth century. Furthermore, the migration of Javanese Surinamers to the United States after the independence of Suriname in 1975 and after the military migration of Suriname in 1987 has most likely contributed to the existence of the blangkon headdress as one of the ethnic costumes of the United States.

Influence and Impact

Indonesian and American *wayang* puppeteers and gamelan musicians in United States practice the continued wearing of the blangkon. As the blangkon symbolizes Javanese culture and identity, the wearing of the blangkon by Americans, Indonesians, and Javanese Surinamers is often seen in cultural events held by the Indonesian diplomatic office in the United States.

The wearing of the blangkon as a performance costume of the *wayang* puppet show and gamelan orchestra in the United States has shifted the original function of the blangkon as a formal and traditional civil costume into a form of ethnic performance art. Broadly speaking, the wearing of the blangkon by puppeteers and musicians contributes to the richness of performance art costumes in the United States.

See also BATIK CLOTH APPAREL; HAWLI
Compare to AFRICAN HEAD WRAP; BANDANA; FEZ; KUFI; RASTA HAT; TAQIYA; TURBAN

Further Reading

Cohen, Matthew Isaac. "Contemporary *Wayang* in Global Context." *Asian Theatre Journal* 24, no. 2 (2007): 338–69.

D'Almeira, William Barrington. *Life in Java: With Sketches of the Javanese.* Vol. 1. London: Hurst and Blackett, 1864.

Dijk, Kees van. "Sarong, Jubbah, and Trousers: Appearance as a Means of Distinction and Discrimination." In *Outward Appearances: Dressing State and Society in Indonesia*, edited by Henk Schulte Nordholt, 39–83. Leiden: KITLV Press, 1997.

Muryanto, Bambang. "Blangkon Craftsmen: Yogyakarta, Central Java." *Blangkon Traditional Headdresses from Jogja*, 2008, http://blangkon-jogja.blogspot.com.au.

Nordholt, Henk Schulte. *Outward Appearances: Dressing State and Society in Indonesia.* Edited by Henk Schulte Nordholt. Leiden: KITLV Press, 1997.

■ APRINA MURWANTI

BLUNDSTONE BOOTS

Blundstone boots are elastic-sided boots produced by an Australian company. The best-known product is its steel-capped work boots known colloquially as "Blunnies." Blundstone also produces gumboots, lace-up safety footwear for men and women, heavy industrial footwear, school shoes, men's casual footwear, and a range of footwear for children.

History

Operating since 1870 in Hobart, Tasmania, Blundstone boots established a strong presence in Australia as reliable and long-lasting footwear for blue-collar and agricultural workers as well as for use in specialized industrial, mining, and safety occupations. Marketed as "Stylish, Serviceable and Durable," Blundstone boots became a national icon helped by their contract to supply boots to the Australian military in World Wars I and II. By the late 1960s, Australia's apparel and footwear industries were under threat from tariff reductions and cheap imports. Blundstone

Blundstone Boots

was one of the first companies to start exporting products and later manufacturing in offshore countries including New Zealand, Vietnam, China, Singapore, India, and Europe. Although it won an Australian Export Award in 1986, the offshore move and closure of its Australian factory proved controversial, and Blundstone subsequently committed to maintaining at least some local production. A new high-tech factory opened in Hobart in 2012 for the manufacture of its gumboots.

While its reputation had been forged as a hard-wearing practical boot, Blundstone acquired a whole new image as a fashion and art icon following a Design Award from the Industrial Design Council of Australia in 1979 and initiating a competition, "Do Something with a Blundstone," in 1992. Won by an Aboriginal artist with a boot decorated in dot-style painting, the subsequent exhibition toured nationally and internationally to great acclaim and publicity for Blundstone, especially in Europe and North America. Exports grew as Blunnies rivaled the popularity of the punk-resonant Doc Martens and soon were stocked in the most fashionable boutiques of London and outdoor-apparel stockists in North America. The other boost to its image came with the formation of the Tap Dogs musical stage show in 1995 which featured tap-dancing men dressed as construction workers in jeans, flannelette shirts, and Blundstone boots. Tap Dogs became a global hit, the basis of the 2000 film *Bootmen*, and is still touring today.

Blundstone Boots in the United States

Blundstone had entered a new phase and responded to its changing status as iconic if slightly edgy fashion by expanding its range of products to over eighty styles, establishing Internet sales in 1997, and initiating a stylish range for children in 1999. The development of waterproof footwear was an especially successful innovation. The company expanded rapidly from making annually five hundred thousand boots in the early 1990s to 1.5 million today. Dedicated online websites were created in the United States, Canada, New Zealand, Israel, Denmark, Spain, Poland, the Netherlands, and Germany. One of the biggest suppliers is Sugar River Outfitters in America, which stocks Blundstone alongside other iconic outdoor footwear and apparel.

Influence and Impact

The success of Blundstone boots in America stemmed from the American connection with the image of iconic Australian national identity as a rural-based tough people pitting their energies against a harsh and formidable terrain and climate. This image had been promoted in films like *Crocodile Dundee*, *Mad Max* (also known as *The Road Warrior*), *Australia*, and *The Man from Snowy River*. It was also reprised in the opening and closing ceremonies of the 2000 Sydney Olympic Games where Blundstone boots made a spectacular appearance in the Tap Dogs segment as reworked symbols of Australian identity. Like other iconic Australian rural apparel such as Akubra, R. M. Williams, Redback, and Drizabone, Blundstone has created a dual niche as both heavy-duty and fashionable footwear that appeals to multiple market segments. Deals have been struck also for the exclusive supply of Blundstones with impact-absorbing soles for extreme sports such as marathons and motorsports.

Unlikely as it seems, Blundstone boots have had a major cultural impact not only as icons of Australian identity but as symbols of contemporary lifestyle fashion and casual clothing. They have also become collectors' items featured in the Powerhouse Museum of Applied Arts and Science in Sydney, Australia, and the Bata Shoe Museum in Toronto, Canada. Blundstone Canada holds an annual Blundstone boot design competition called "Art to Boot" which tours nationally before entries are auctioned at a gala fund-raising event. Concern about lower manufacturing standards offshore led to controversy about the quality of its polyurethane soles, which were prone to "exploding." Due to hydrolysis damage, the company addressed this issue in 2013.

See also BRITISH RIDING BOOTS; DR. MARTENS; UGG FOOTWEAR
Compare to BIRKENSTOCKS; CHINESE FLATS; JELLIES

Further Reading

Attard, Kristy. "Best Foot Forward." *Business in Focus*, October 2011, 26–33.
Bata Shoe Museum. "'Art to Boot' at the Bata Shoe Museum." *A Step into the Bata Shoe Museum*, August 17, 2010.
Blundstone Australia. Company website, 2013, http://www.blundstone.com.
Business Outlook. "Blundstone Boots: How Ideas Triumphed over Isolation." *Business Outlook*, 2008, www.businessoutlook.com.au/08/archives/.../Blundstone%20boots.pdf.
Sutton, Candace. "The 'Exploding Soles' of Blundstone Boots." News.com.au, May 27, 2013.

■ JENNIFER CRAIK

BLUNNIES

See BLUNDSTONE BOOTS

BOHEMIAN DRESS

The term "bohemian," as it came to be used to refer to the unconventional lifestyles of artists, writers, and other nonconformists, originates from the name Europeans gave to various nomadic and refugee groups who moved throughout Western Europe also referred to as "gypsies." These groups were erroneously believed to have originated from Czechoslovakia, formerly known as Bohemia.

History

While the sartorial style of groups labeled as "gypsy" or "Bohemian" by Europeans and Americans varies widely depending on where these groups have settled, one group in particular, the Roma (who actually came from India and Persia to Europe around the fourteenth century), had a unique style of dressing that became associated with all of these groups in the popular imagination. Roma women wear separate skirts and shirts, which are also laundered separately, as a means of demarcating the upper part of the body as pure, and lower part as impure. In addition to long skirts, kerchiefs or scarves covering women's hair and elaborate jewelry are also associated with Roma or "gypsy" women's dress. Roma men have adopted the clothes of men in the various places they have settled but often exaggerate that style, for example, with large black hats, or coats sometimes adorned with coins that mimic buttons from military uniforms.

Images of Bohemians or "gypsies" in European and American popular culture have historically exoticized these groups as existing outside conventions of nationality, politics, and polite society. "Gypsies" have been depicted through primitivist tropes as connected to nature and exhibiting primal urges, particularly sexuality. The image of Bohemian groups living on the fringes of society, outside of social conventions, national identity, and traditional commerce has made them an appealing group for European and Americans seeking to resist the cultural norms of their societies. By the mid-nineteenth century in the face of the rising bourgeoisie, these groups styled themselves as Bohemians and adopted the name.

Bohemian Dress in the United States

The French writer Henry Murger in a series of literary sketches immortalized bohemians in the mid-1840s, and by 1850 an American version of Bohemia was developing in New York. Modes of dress became a key part of how these groups, often populated by artists, intellectuals, and writers, differentiated themselves. These modes of dressing were as varied as those of the peoples whose name was applied to them, and often have little to do with the ways in which actual Roma people or other groups historically labeled Bohemian dressed and continue to dress.

Influence and Impact

Of the styles that emerged from the imagined image of the Bohemian in the nineteenth and early twentieth centuries, long flowing skirts, worn without crinolines, petticoats, or corsets, were a key part of the female bohemian's wardrobe. Bright colors and patterns were used by both men and women as a means of setting themselves apart from the more somberly and respectably dressed middle and upper classes, as were more casual clothes.

In New York's Greenwich Village, a thriving community of bohemian artists, writers, and thinkers developed in the 1910s. Many of these bohemian women wore simple tunics or embroidered peasant-inspired blouses, like those that might have been sported by Roma women. Sandals, bare legs, and sometimes even bare feet were also modes of exhibiting an allegiance to bohemian culture and creating a look of poverty—which might have been real or affected—as well as a connection to nature.

Sandals continued to be a part of bohemian dressing into the 1950s, worn by both men and women who were part of the beat scene. Beat women also adopted ballet flats as a means of rejecting high-heeled styles popular at the time. Peasant shirts and bold jewelry were a means of expressing their nonconformist identity. These styles continued to be used by hippie women into the 1960s and 1970s, along with long skirts and kerchiefs. Bright colors were worn by both men and women, as was the bold jewelry. Many of these styles maintain their popularity to the present day in so-called boho style, referencing the 1960s and 1970s hippie bohemian rather than the original "gypsy" reference.

See also Birkenstocks; Bricolage; Broomstick Skirt; Caftan; Gypsy Skirt; Peasant Blouse
Compare to Cholo Style; Hip-Hop Fashion; Western Wear

Further Reading

Hasdeu, Iulia. "Imagining the Gypsy Woman: Representations of Roma in Romanian Museum." *Third Text* 22, no. 3 (May 2008): 347–57.
Levin, Joanna. *Bohemia in America, 1858–1920*. Stanford, CA: Stanford University Press, 2010.
Saville, Deborah. "Dress and Culture in Greenwich Village." In *Twentieth-Century American Fashion*, edited by Linda Welters and Patricia A. Cunningham, 33–56. New York: Berg, 2005.
Wilson, Elizabeth. "Bohemian Dress and the Heroism of Everyday Life." *Fashion Theory* 2, no. 3 (September 1998): 225–44.

■ VICTORIA PASS

BOHO STYLE
See Bohemian Dress

BOLA TIES
See Bolo Tie

BOLERO JACKET

The bolero jacket is conventionally a woman's outer garment characterized by its sleek transition from front to back. It is not meant to go below the waist and is usually worn open; in most cases the jacket is cut in such a way that it cannot join, or only with fasteners. The dramatic yet compact line of the bolero jacket has ensured its endurance since it began to be worn in the early nineteenth century. Its curvaceous, tapered cut is able to show off decorative brocading or other types of facing; or it can be plain, its curvature used as a foil to the vertical lines of an ensemble. Worn over a blouse or bodice, the cropped shape of the garment tends to emphasize the waist, thus helping to enhance or give the illusion of an hourglass silhouette. The jacket is occasionally accompanied with a small collar, which can be worn turned up for dramatic effect. Although mass-produced and popular versions have used all manner of basic fabrics, in the nineteenth century when it was most worn, it was made of velvet, silk, or satin. It was an important decorative centerpiece, its accented lines used to accompany the straight lines of a shawl. While the original versions of the jacket were devised for men, it is now most commonly worn by women, with the exception of Spanish traditional and ceremonial dress, such as that of the toreador.

History

The word "bolero" is the name of a traditional kind of Spanish dance, which also has strong connotations to the very popular orchestral work by Maurice Ravel, which itself draws heavily from Spanish music. Yet the name obscures the actual origins of the garment, which is traceable to the outfit of the Spanish vaquero and the French-Algerian Zouave. The vaquero that emerged from Spain in the late eighteenth and nineteenth centuries was the precursor to the American Wild West cowboy. They were typically free spirits, known for their horsemanship, dexterity, and courage, which were then mirrored in their flamboyant clothing. These traits are important to mention for the way in which they are sublimated in the jacket as it came to be worn by women, ensuring that the garment remotely suggested danger and adventure. The vaquero was known to wear a short jacket of wool, silk, or velvet, typically with braiding on the front and back in a color contrasting strongly with the core fabric, finished with one or two silver buttons. These jackets are said to have been derived from the short-waisted jackets worn by Andalusian cattle herders, cut short to assist in movement while on a horse. Given that the pants were coarser or simpler, usually of canvas or leather, the jacket was the centerpiece of the vaquero's dress, its style and color acting similarly to heraldic colors marking the individual.

The Bolero in the United States

The Zouaves were a regiment of the light infantry in French North Africa active between 1831 and 1962. The uniform included baggy trousers, a fez or slumped hat, and a characteristic short jacket that was worn open to feature a sash or belt. "Zouave" was a term used in other armies, notably the volunteer regiments of the American Civil War. They did not, however, adopt the kind of clothing of their French counterpart. By the end of the nineteenth century, "Zouave" was the more common name for what would only later be called the bolero jacket. The *Daily News* of November 14, 1893, commented that "the Zouave is as great a favourite as it has been for some seasons, and though it varies in form—being sometimes a bolero, sometimes a toreador, and sometimes a cross between an Eton jacket and a Zouave." On July 6, 1899, the *Westminster Gazette* commented, "Robbing the coat of its basque has created the bolero corsage, really an actual bodice, though appearing a bolero coat and skirt."

Influence and Impact

Women's fashions of the second half of the nineteenth century leading to the First World War, with their tapered, corseted waistline and flared skirt, lent themselves to the bolero jacket, particularly in adding width to the shoulders and chest. Since they could be worn over the undergarment, they could serve to add extra color, or to be a jacket for an afternoon stroll, or as evening wear in which it might be trimmed with fur. In keeping with European fashions, boleros were popular in women's fashions in the United States from the 1850s onward, especially braid-trimmed Zouave jackets. These carried the double connotation of the exotic East as well as the more proximate Wild West and Mexico. The simple armature of the bolero made it available to all manner of decorative fashioning that could be modified to suit the motifs, patterns, colors, and trimmings popular at any given time.

In modern times the bolero has been used not only to add color but as a modest counterpoise to more risqué clothing underneath, such as small, skimpy shirts or tube tops. Bolero jackets have also been sympathetic to hybrid styles and to East-West mixing such as with the *quipao*, the tight silk dress popular in Shanghai and Hong Kong in the 1920s and now being revived in China as an example of national woman's dress.

The contemporary offshoot of the bolero jacket is what in the United States is known as the shrug. As the name suggests, it is a garment that emphasizes the shoulders, not with shoulder pads, however, but by being cropped above the waist. Shrugs are more like cardigans than jackets, are characteristically knitted, and can have either short or long sleeves. In some respects, it is an amalgam of a jacket and a shawl. If they have a fastener, it is tied under the bustline. Like the bolero jacket, it is typically worn to tone down more suggestive clothing on the upper body and helps to accent the waist and hips.

See also WESTERN WEAR
Compare to MEXICAN TOURIST/SOUVENIR JACKET; PASHMINA SHAWL AND SCARF; PELISSE; WAISTCOAT

Further Reading

Mulholland, Mary-Lee. "Mariachi, Myths and Mestizaje: Popular Culture and Mexican National Identity." *National Identities* 9, no. 3 (2007).

■ ADAM GECZY

BOLO TIE

The bolo tie is a form of men's neckwear, sometimes worn by women, favored in the southwestern region of the United States. The tie consists of a single or multi-strand of braided cord or leather connected by a rigid front plate (also called a buckle, clasp, or slide), with metal tips or aglets on the ends of the strands. It is worn beneath the collar of a dress or western shirt, often with a suit, in place of a more formal, traditional necktie and includes an ornamental front plate designed to slide along strands to adjust fit. The original purpose of the aglets was to prevent the ends of the braided cord from unraveling.

The bolo tie is also referred to as a bola tie, a string or shoe-string tie, a gaucho tie, a mono loop tie, an emblem lariat, a neck rope, a lariat tie, a cowboy tie, a western tie, a thong tie, or a sport tie. The bolo tie name comes from having an appearance similar to a *boleadora*, a projectile weapon consisting of cords and weighted balls, used by South American cowboys to capture prey by entangling their legs or wings, similar to the way a lasso was utilized by North American cowboys.

Bolo Tie

History

Although the name of the bolo tie came from South America, it is thought by many to be a uniquely American accessory. The actual origin of the tie is uncertain. Historians describe the wearing of kerchiefs or modified ties around the neck by American pioneers during the mid- to late 1800s. Both men and women wore metal jewelry necklaces in the same general form in the late 1800s. The extent of the influence of these articles on the development of the bolo tie is not known.

The Bolo Tie in the United States

Manny Goodman, onetime owner of a New Mexican craft store called the Covered Wagon, recalled that in the 1930s, when Navajo, Hopi, and Zuni men began clasping together bandanas around their necks, a shell or a silver conch was used to hold the ends together and to adjust fit. Perhaps others used a string rather than a bandana in its development. Another story credits its origin to Victor Cedarstaff, an Arizona silversmith. Not wanting to lose his silver-trimmed hatband when his hat kept slipping off, Cedarstaff looped the band around his collar. After a friend remarked that it was a nice-looking tie, he created what may have been the first bolo tie. Cedarstaff filed a patent for his "slide for a necktie" in May 1954; the patent was issued in July 1959.

Some of the earliest printed documentation in advertising appeared in a 1953–1954 western-wear catalog that described a new "String-A-Long" tie. In December 1953, a Phoenix, Arizona, western store advertised a "Slide A Tie" in the *Arizona Republic*. William H. Meeker applied for a patent in 1953 on what he called "apparel for neckwear"; the patent was granted in 1958. *Arizona Highways* published its first feature article about bolo ties in October 1966.

Western wear and bolo ties were brought to the attention of a wider audience by television shows and movies of the 1950s. The bolo tie is associated with film characters and stars of the period including the Cisco Kid, Hopalong Cassidy, and Roy Rogers. From the mid-twentieth century forward, the bolo tie was a widely accepted western-wear accessory. Although most often associated with traditional western wear, the bolo tie has also become a modern style icon of pop culture. In the mid-1980s, Brian Setzer and his band the Stray Cats helped make bolo ties one of the official accessories of "rockabilly" musicians. The tie appeared in 1980s films *Urban Cowboy*, *Pretty in Pink*, and *Cocktail*. Celebrities Patrick Swayze, Robin Williams, David Carradine, Richard Pryor, Johnny Carson, and Bruce Springsteen wore bolo ties.

More recent examples of celebrities wearing bolo ties include American Idol contestant Paul McDonald, the Killers frontman Brandon Flowers, and Cord Overstreet from *Glee*. Bolo ties have appeared on ready-to-wear runways of U.S. designers Rag and Bone and the Italian fashion house of Bottega Veneta. Apart from western wear, bolo ties continue to be used primarily by individuals to be "cool," hip, stylish, and/or distinctive or unique, thus making a fashion statement or expressing artistic individuality.

Influence and Impact

The bolo tie is designated as official neckwear in three U.S. states—Arizona, New Mexico, and Texas. Numerous politicians from western states and presidents Dwight D. Eisenhower, Jimmy Carter, and Ronald Reagan wore bolo ties. Bolo ties produced in silver by Native American artists, featuring turquoise or other semiprecious stones available in the west, are respected as exquisite works of art and demonstrate craftsmanship characteristic of Navajo and Hopi Indian jewelry. Classic and traditional bolo ties were featured in a fall 2011 exhibit at the Heard Museum in Phoenix entitled *Native American Bolo Ties: Vintage and Contemporary*, underscoring their popular-culture recognition as a classic western-wear accessory and a mark of "hipster" celebrity status and creative individualism.

See also BOOTLACE TIE; ETHNIC JEWELRY; WESTERN WEAR
Compare to NORIGAE

Further Reading

Kramer, William J. *Bola Tie: New Symbol of the West*. Flagstaff, AZ: Northland Press, 1978.
Pardue, Diana F., and Norman L. Sandfield. *Native American Bolo Ties*. Santa Fe: Museum of New Mexico Press, 2011.
Ullmann, Eleanor E. "The Bola Tie." *Arizona Highways*, October 1966, 2–7.

■ REBECCA W. GREER

BOOTLACE TIE (UK TEDDY BOYS)

A thin strip of leather, the width of a bootlace, worn around the collar of a shirt, with decorative metal tips (aglets) and a metal slide, often chased or stamped with designs or inlaid with hard or semiprecious stones, which can be pushed up or down to loosen or tighten the tie. In North America this tie is more commonly known as a "bolo tie."

History

The origin of the tie is not certain: Navajo artists were making very similar ties in the 1940s, but the most common explanation of its invention is that it was created in the 1940s and patented in 1959 by goldsmith Victor E. Cedarstaff, who invented it after tying his cowboy hat chin strap around his neck with a silver buckle in order to stop it from blowing off repeatedly in the wind. It is named because of its resemblance to the "bolas" used by Argentinian gauchos to capture animals. The bola tie is now the state tie of Arizona, after legislation was passed in 1971 and in 2007, when the tie was also made the state tie of Texas.

During the 1960s, the bolo tie in North America was especially popular in Arizona and among men working in traditional ranch roles. However, in Britain the bootlace tie, as it was known, was adopted by members of the revivalist youth movement the Teddy Boys, or "Teds." The original Teds were one of the first teenage-led subcultural movements, beginning among young, urban, working-class men circa 1953. Combining the "New Edwardian" look, worn by officers purchasing clothes from Savile Row, which consisted of slim straight trousers and long drape jackets with velvet collars, and the flamboyant zoot suit style, which originated in North America and was imported to England by GIs and West Indian immigrants after World War II, the first Teds appreciated all things American, especially rock and roll, which provided a glamorous contrast to the gray austerity of postwar Britain. They invented a unique style, simultaneously copying and parodying both American gangsters and English Edwardian gentlemen. The original Ted uniform consisted of drainpipe trousers; long drape jackets with half-velvet collars; a long slim necktie or a leather bootlace tied in a bow; "broth-el-creeper" shoes (with crepe soles), also imported from the United States; and a large greased quiff, a look much more peacock and stylized than anything worn by men in England during the previous fifty years.

The movement saw a resurgence once more in the 1960s and 1970s, with a slightly adapted look. The prevalence of Western films made in Hollywood, as well as the continuing appreciation of American masculine styling, and the appropriateness of the trope of the "urban cowboy" or "lone ranger" to young, underprivileged men, ensured that this revivalist movement paid more homage to Western styling than the original Teds. The influence of new rockabilly and country music, as well as rock and roll, also had an effect on styling. Drape jackets began to resemble the frock coats worn in saloons in Western films, and slim neckties were replaced by bola ties, known as "bootlace ties" in England, which were often advertised as imported, for an authentic American look.

Bootlace Ties in the United States

This dissemination of trends across the Atlantic worked in both directions, and American teen movements, especially rockabillies, adopted the bolo tie, both as a youth trend and also in homage to the area of origin of rockabilly music and to previous generations of cowboys, who had worn the bola ties in the course of their working day.

Influence and Impact

Today, bootlace and bola ties are worn both as traditional, conservative leather-wear ac-cessories, but also as part of a rockabilly outfit. The ties have entered variously into main-stream fashion, noticeably in the fall of 1988 and in Bottega Veneta's fall 2010 collection, which was inspired by rockabilly icons such as Jerry Lee Lewis.

See also BOLO TIE
Compare to ETHNIC JEWELRY; WESTERN WEAR

Further Reading

Horn, Adrian. *Juke Box Britain, Americanisation and Youth Culture, 1945–60.* Manchester and New York: Manchester University Press, 2009.
Montana, Hunter, and Shelkie Montana. *Cowboy Ties.* Layton, UT: Gibb Smith, 1994.
Mosconi, Davide, and Riccardo Villarosa. *The Book of Ties.* London: Tie Rack, 1985.
Polhemus, Ted. *Street Style: From Sidewalk to Catwalk.* 2nd ed. London: Thames & Hudson, 1997.
Steele-Perkins, Chris, and Richard Smith. *The Teds.* 2nd ed. London: Travelling Light/Exit, 1987.

■ HELEN RITCHIE

BORSALINO
See FEDORA

BOUBOU

The boubou originates from the Wolof word *mbubb*, meaning a garment that can be slipped on over the head and used generically to describe long, flowing, ankle-length robes worn by both men and women across Muslim West Africa from Senegal to Nigeria. The traditional boubou is an ample tunic with open sleeves and a triangular or rectangle breast pocket. The boubou is both formal dress and everyday wear, and it is made in all materials for both genders and all ages, income levels, and contexts. Well suited to the hot arid climate of the Sahara Desert, the loose flowing robe and layered clothing ensemble provides thermal protection against daytime high temperatures and cold nights. The boubou is both comfortable and practical and provides a high degree of covering in keeping with Islamic beliefs. Requiring about ten meters (eleven yards) of cloth, the men's boubou is constructed in three parts. The central panel serves as the body of the garment with two panels sewn to each side. The sleeves extend to the hand and are draped up onto the shoulders when wearing. Classic boubous have a slashed neckline and a large triangular or rectangular pocket attached just below the neck opening.

The most elegant boubous are made from high-quality imported damask and are heavily embroidered with the same color or contrasting silk thread. Ornate embroidered patterns of circles and swirls adorn the pocket, neck opening, upper right side of the body, and upper back of the robe. White and light blue are the classic colors and are commonly worn in Mauritania, Western Sahara, Mali, and Niger. Bright colors such as green, pink, and rich purple with multicolor embroidery are worn in Senegal and Gambia. Less expensive boubous are made from lower-quality cotton damask and lighter-weight broadcloth and voile imported from China and India and have minimal or no embroidery.

History

The traditional men's boubou is known by various names depending on the ethnic group and the region in which it is being worn. In Senegal and Gambia, everyday wear is a caftan or boubou with pants. The formal ensemble for men is a three-piece outfit consisting of caftan, *tchaya* pants (Wolof word for loose trousers), grand boubou, and a white embroidered skullcap, pillbox cap, or red or brown fez. In Mauritania and Western Sahara a similar garment with gold embroidery is called *deraa* and is commonly worn with sirwal (Arabic word for loose trousers) in matching damask fabric and a Western-style men's dress shirt and hawli (Hassaniya dialect word for a long rectangular piece of cloth that is used as a head wrap or turban). The hawli is three and a half meters (nearly four yards) long and is made of lightweight cotton or rayon fabric, usually white, light blue, or black. As part of the formal and everyday ensemble, the hawli is draped around the neck with long tails ready to be wrapped about the head when needed to protect from the wind and blowing sand. Across Niger a similar style of boubou is worn, and Tuareg men (the seminomadic people who speak the local Berber language called Tamazight) commonly wear wrap turbans and face veils. In Mali, *tilbi* and *lomasa* are two styles of luxury boubous, both with extensive hand embroidery. The *tilbi* made of white damask with white silk thread is associated with the towns of Djenne and Timbuktu, and the *lomasa* is primarily associated with Soninke chiefs and notables and is an indigo-dyed boubou embroidered with multicolored silk threads. The voluminous robe flows and billows in the wind creating a sense of dignity and allure. The embroidered boubou is the attire of the traditional Muslim man in West and Northwest Africa, the pinnacle of prestige and a symbol of national pride and identity.

The Boubou in the United States

In the United States today the boubou is associated with Africa and African immigrants in a very general way. Traditional garments travel with immigrants, American Peace Corp volunteers, and tourists to the United States.

Influence and Impact

Many versions of the boubou are more commonly worn in immigrant communities within urban centers. The boubou is not worn in everyday working contexts but is more often worn on important social occasions and religious holidays and is a symbol of national pride and identity.

The idea of Africa has been an inspiration for European fashion designers for centuries. Europe's close proximity and colonial ties to the region has been a source of aesthetic inspiration in terms of form, design, and unique and often exotic raw materials. In the 1950s Madame Carven was one of the first designers to use African textiles to manufacture dresses, bathing suits, and wraps. Inspiration came from the unique draping systems, voluminous shapes, and bright color combinations observed during travel to Cameroon, Senegal, Ghana, and other African countries. In 1967 Yves Saint Laurent produced a landmark African collection. In 1984 Kenzo designed flowing boubou dresses. Boubou dresses created by Paco Rabanne in the 1996 spring/summer collections emphasize the recurring influence of shape, form, and color on European and Western fashion. As many midlevel brands take inspiration from high-fashion brands, elements of African-inspired styling find their way into American fashion.

See also CAFTAN; FEZ; HAWLI; SIRWAL
Compare to BURNOUS; DOLMAN; HANFU CHINESE ROBES; KIMONO; MELHFA; THAWB

Further Reading

Gardi, Bernhard. *Le Boubou c'est Chic. Les Boubous du Mali et d'Autres Pays l'Afrique de l'Ouest*. Basel, Switzerland: Christoph-Merian-Verlag, 2000.

Loughran, Kristyne. "The Idea of Africa in European High Fashion: Global Dialogues." *Fashion Theory* 13, no. 2 (2009): 243–72. doi:10.2752/175174109x414277.

Mendy-Ongoundou, Renee. *Elegances Africaines. Tissus Traditionnels et Mode Contemporaine*. Paris: Editions Alternatives, 2002.

Rabine, Leslie. *The Global Circulation of African Fashion*. Oxford: Berg, 2002.

Rovine, Victoria I. *Bogolan: Shaping Culture through Cloth in Contemporary Mali*. Washington, DC: Smithsonian Institution Press, 2001.

■ VIRGINIA M. NOON

BOURNOUS
See BURNOUS

BOWLER HAT

The bowler hat is a close-fitting hard felt hat with a domed crown and rolled narrow brim originally introduced by the British in the Victorian era as a workingman's hat, and later adopted by the middle and upper classes. The bowler was the first mass-produced hat, and it was one of the first clothing-related items that blurred the lines of social status. The bowler-style hat is also referred to as a derby hat, particularly in the United States.

History

William Coke, a soldier and politician in England, commissioned the London hatmakers Thomas and William Bowler to create a sturdy hat with a low crown for his gamekeepers. Top hats were in fashion at this time, and the hats were always being knocked off when riding horses under low branches. The harder hat would also provide protection for the rider. The Bowlers were part of the London business Lock & Company. Gamekeepers were people who maintained the land owned by others. These duties consisted of keeping poachers off the land as well as preparation work for hunting and shooting expeditions.

Bowler Hat

The hat was first introduced in the 1850s, gaining in popularity during the 1860s. It became popular as a key accessory worn by shooting parties, and later became a part of the wardrobe of a British businessman or barrister, as well as a part of the official uniform of the Queen's Guard. Linked to the name of its manufacturers, the Bowler brothers, the hat became a classic and remained standard wear through the 1890s, with women even adopting the style, wearing it as part of their horse-riding outfits. The end of the century saw a slight decline, but the hat regained popularity in the early part of the 1900s.

The Bowler Hat in the United States

Edward Stanley, the Twelfth Earl of Derby, was very involved in horse racing in England. He was responsible for starting the Derby Races that were held at Epsom Oaks. When he visited the United States he wore the bowler hat, which then was coined as the derby hat in America after the Earl of Derby. Therefore it was first introduced to America by the horse-racing community. Those attending horse races saw the hats being worn and began adopting their style.

As an inexpensive practical mass-produced hat that crossed class boundaries, the bowler became a central element of men's wardrobes in the latter half of the nineteenth century in Europe. As a result, American immigrants crossing over from Europe often brought along the bowler, thus moving it into wardrobes in the United States. In the American West, the bowler was a practical solution to the wind and weather and as a less expensive alternative to the Stetson was often worn by men settling the frontier.

Influence and Impact

Prior to the development of the bowler, hats typically marked rather than blurred class distinctions. For instance, if someone was seen wearing a top hat, they were of the upper class, whereas floppy hats were worn by working men. In the United States, working-class men either immigrated over with or adopted the bowler, which as in Britain was then adopted by the American upper class. Irish and other immigrant laborers were the backbone of the Industrial Revolution in America. Some of their common jobs included establishing the westward expansion of the railroad and working in steel factories and mines.

Many immigrants were clustered into neighborhoods restricted to their ethnicity, so it was important to fit in. During this time, one's appearance greatly influenced the family's status. The neighborhoods in larger cities tended to segregate people by ethnicity, which also contributed to social isolation. One of the ways to overcome discrimination based on ethnic background was to adopt more of an acceptable uniform or stereotypical look that blended with others and helped hide the ethnic identity of the wearer. For the Irish, this was particularly hard, as most did not want the Irish working for their companies, and some even had signs in their windows indicating that "No Irish Need Apply." Men were the breadwinners of the family, so they were the first to be outfitted and often appeared in the latest trends. The suit with a bowler-style hat became the standard and acceptable uniform for a workingman in the United States; it afforded all immigrant men a means of looking the part and breaking into American social life.

Bowler hats along with other menswear styles began to cross over into women's wear in the early years of the twentieth century. The fashion bowler has been included in women's wear collections throughout the twentieth and twenty-first centuries. As an example of the enduring style importance of the bowler in women's fashion in the United States, Diane Keaton first wore the bowler as a central identifying component of her look in the 1970s, and she continues to wear the bowler in the twenty-first century.

See also CH'ULLU
Compare to BERET; FEZ; RASTA HAT

Further Reading

Winakor, Geitel, and Jane Farrell-Beck. *The History of Costume.* 2nd ed. New York: Addison Wesley
    Longman, 1992.

■ LUANNE MAYORGA

BRICOLAGE

Bricolage is not a name for an item of ethnic dress or any specific object. Instead, bricolage names the act, or the product of the act, of combining unrelated elements into a new whole. Elements may be meanings as in literature, or materials as in architecture, or both as in dress styles. The term emerged in the mid-twentieth century in the United States with the development of postmodern theory. Art criticism harnessed bricolage to describe artworks formed of multiple found objects, as opposed to artworks created using a single highly developed medium. This usage continues; however "bricolage" is also employed to characterize dress ensembles or looks created from simultaneous combination of materials, garments, accessories, and bodily grooming practices originating from multiple cultures or ethnicities and social strata, rather than from one source. Following the meaning used in art criticism, bricolage in dress implies an improvised creativity and a do-it-yourself ethos that eschews couture craftsmanship.

History

The root word *bricoler* was in use in early nineteenth-century France, meaning to fix things with cleverness. A *bricoleur* is a person who improvises solutions, an alternative to a trained craftsperson. A *bricoleur* makes do with what is at hand, using found materials, non-task-specific tools, and unrefined skills to solve a problem.

From this everyday usage, "bricolage" then entered philosophical discourse in the 1960s when French anthropologist Claude Lévi-Strauss (1908–2009) suggested that "bricolage" describes the reuse of mental constructs in mythical thought creation in new ways. French philosopher Jacques Derrida (1930–2004) furthered the meaning by describing bricolage as cultural and antihistorical "borrowing" that is implicit in postmodern contexts. Although his attention was on words, he has been interpreted to suggest that bricolage permeates contemporary social exchange. The core concepts of bricolage are observable in worn ensembles, from looks crafted by individuals to mass-market designs, that borrow elements from outside the native identity and context but which are "at hand" either by chance or because the market has provided them.

Bricolage in the United States

The first use of the term "bricolage" in relation to dress was used to describe punk fashions. Punk style emerged in 1970s London and New York, spreading to other cities and eventually appearing in American suburbia on teens. Punk style used hardware, trash bags, torn clothes, and most notoriously safety pins. The rule-breaking looks broadcast the movement's antiestablishment stance toward society and dominant stylistic taste. Punks appropriated the Native American Mohawk hairstyle and other native dress practices including facial piercings, adding antimodernity as a meaning layer to their rebellion. One punk style, made by tying the long sleeves of a shirt around the waist and placing the shirt body in the front, resembled a Native American loincloth while also subverting the normal mode. Although punk style brought "bricolage" to dress as a descriptor, punk did not place actual ethnic garments or accessories out of context.

Influence and Impact

The 1960s hippie movement also broke with past conformist modes, including dress. Although the term "bricolage" was not used in the 1960s to refer to hippie styles, clearly hippies engaged in bricolage to create their looks. They embraced ethnic dress, drawing items from many cultural sources. American preferences included Native American moccasins and moccasin lace-up boots, Southwest Asian curly lamb garments decorated with embroidery, and European clog-style shoes and women's embroidered peasant blouses. Hippies also adopted many Indian elements, from scents to shirts. Their exuberant engagement of bricolage in dress has not been replicated.

In the early twenty-first century, engaging in bricolage seldom sends widely cast messages. Instead, meaning is with the individual. For example, young people in the United States enjoy tattoos with personal meaning. Although tattooing is modeled on indigenous practices of Pacific and South American natives, most people in the United States remain unaware of the motifs' cultural meaning as rites-of-passage symbols. The New Zealand Maori feel offense when nonnatives borrow their motifs because the meaning is ignored.

Fashions created for the mass market employ bricolage, but the meaning is simply to be stylish. Anna Sui (b. 1964), a prominent American fashion designer and retailer, often designs with bricolage. Her spring 2007 collection combined European ethnicities including Viennese and English elements. Target Corporation's *Go International* collection series included a season by Patrick Robinson. Greek folk-dress motifs, originally embroidered symbols of female fertility and other local meanings, were enlarged and printed on the collection's textiles. Consumers wore the garments oblivious to the original meaning.

See also CORSET; DR. MARTENS; MOCCASINS; PEASANT BLOUSE
Compare to CHOLO STYLE; HIP-HOP FASHION; WESTERN WEAR

Further Reading

Derrida, Jacques. "Structure, Sign, and Play in the Discourse of the Human Sciences." In *Writing and Difference*, trans. Alan Bass, 278–94. London: Routledge, 2001 (1967).
Polhemus, Ted. *Streetstyle: From Sidewalk to Catwalk.* New York: Thames & Hudson, 1994.

■ ABBY LILLETHUN

BRITISH RIDING BOOTS

There are two main types of British riding boots, long and short. Essentially simple in form, leather, originally handcrafted, and with little embellishment, they are more usually colored black, though they can be brown or tan. The "long" boot is commonly smooth and shiny surfaced, tight fitting, and sits slightly below the knee. Referred to as "dress" boots and with a slightly higher outer top than inner, the rounded edge is known as the "Spanish" top. The high boot is soled so as to prevent slippage through the stirrup, with a moderate heel of an inch or less. The handmade leather tall boots are favored, but for economy and service use, stable staff often prefer the same style in a tall rubber boot. The ankle-length "jodhpur" boot has a rounded or squared toe, commonly with a slim, smooth leather or reinforced rubber sole, with an elasticized or leather-strapped outer side cuff. Similarly, "paddock" boots lace up the front, tend to have a more substantial sole, and often come with a toecap.

History

There are several adaptations of the British riding boot linked to different usage patterns and riding styles, whether show jumping, eventing, dressage, or riding for leisure. Most "tall" boots encompass variations on the "field" boot, noted for its lace frontage at the ankle. These include "Newmarket," "dress," "hunt," and "polo" boots. The "field" boot entered the United States in around 1917 during World War I, having originated in England via the armed forces and so-called since it was worn by higher-rank officers in the field. Officers preferred leather gaiters (now known as "chaps"), field boots, or pull-on "polo" boots, and many men spent years wearing riding boots and spurs as air force pilots (thus primarily as a fashion garment) simply to impress.

Jodhpur boots developed from the sport of polo in India (post jodhpur "breeches") in 1920 and are presently used for "saddle seat" riding in the United States. Significantly, polo entered the United States around 1888, bringing with it English-style saddles and riding, then gradually adopted by elements of the widespread American equine community. Competitive sports and notably the Olympics equestrian section (only introduced in 1912) was in part responsible for team uniforms influenced by British riding boots as reflected in Vogel's of Manhattan, established in 1879 and the current suppliers to the U.S. team.

British Riding Boots

British Riding Boots in the United States

In 1925 the Texas University Corps of Cadets officially adopted the knee-high British riding boot when they changed from West Point–style uniforms to seniors. High-end retail stores such as Saks and Macy's supplied a "ready-to-wear" collection of clothing influenced by Hollywood film and glamour in the 1920s and 1930s. Footwear formerly primarily "couture" became more accessible. Romanticized and stylized, the dress boot especially appealed to both sexes with its regal look and connotations. Equally, magazines such as *Vogue* and *Harper's Bazaar* were setting trends with equine attire and sportswear spreads, spawning a classic style still current. Advertising and branding helped develop the regal and elite associations of the riding boot. Church's store on Madison Avenue since 1929, when purchased by Prada in 1999, was given a higher-fashion focus with chic adapted riding-boot styles favored by the fashion fraternity. Lobb of London in 1863 became official boot maker to the Prince of Wales, and their "ready-to-wear" collection was purchased in 1976 by Hermes Paris (whose horse-associated branding arose as a result of founder Thierry Hermes working as a saddler), bringing this handcrafted tradition to a wider audience interested in heritage and fashion, and in 2000 the first shop in the United States opened.

Post–World War II, the clean lines of the "tall" boot and related adaptations were primarily used in areas of service, industry, and sports, occupying a ceremonial, formal, and functional role, which meant the boot translated well to uniform, especially motorcycle/mounted police. Developing from a basic "pull-on" boot, the incorporation of zips enabled greater practicality as well as fashionability. During the 1960s, British style inspired the United States and particularly the Beatles, whose Chelsea boots were influenced by the jodhpur boot. Contemporary musicians and global "style setters" Madonna and Lady Gaga further utilized the "riding-boot look" in a costume context of performance, acknowledging its sexual connotations, as does burlesque star Dita Von Teese with her high-heeled "riding" boots.

Influence and Impact

Footwear styles of the riding tradition are a regular "uniform" at contemporary fashion events and "Fashion Week." With such reverence in the United States given to British aristocracy, inevitably its influence is manifest in art and fashion. Suppliers of paddock boots to the United States and cherished for their handcrafted art, Schnieders, bootmaker to the queen and her "Household Cavalry," personify horse heritage and its cultural influence as further pioneered by contemporary British designers. In particular, the collections of Alexander McQueen and Vivienne Westwood incorporate its debonair style with anarchist subversion, whereas American designers, especially Donna Karan and Ralph Lauren, romanticize, popularize, and "Americanize" the look while adding signature accessories that translate cross-culturally and stylistically.

See also BLUNDSTONE BOOTS; JODHPURS; UGG FOOTWEAR
Compare to BIRKENSTOCKS; CHINESE FLATS; JELLIES

Further Reading

Barney, Sydney. *Clothes and the Horse*. London: Vinton & Comp, 1953.
Cicolini, Alice. *The New English Dandy*. London: Thames & Hudson, 2005.

■ WENDY ROSIE SCOTT

BROOMSTICK SKIRT

The broomstick skirt, traditionally made of a lightweight, 100 percent cotton plain weave, generally has a wide, sweeping hem, has three equal tiers, and falls to ankle length. Obtaining its name from a method of wrapping the wrinkled or folded wet cotton tightly around a long thin, rounded piece of wood, most likely at the origin a broomstick, the defining characteristic of this skirt is a permanent wrinkle or pleat that may be regular or irregular throughout the entire fabric.

History

The origin of the broomstick skirt is not definitively clear, as qualities of the broomstick skirt can be found in Native American, particularly Navajo, traditional clothing, as well as in Southeast Asian dress. The Native American version was typically more structured and made from a plain-weave, medium-weight cotton with regular pleats. The Southeast Asian version, brought to the West primarily through the migration of the Romani people, also known as gypsies, was made from a very lightweight plain weave and had irregular pleats. Examining the evolution of pleating techniques, an integral part of the broomstick skirt, reveals origins of *arashi shibori* in eighth-century Japan. In the early twentieth century, Mario Fortuny, an Italian luxury fashion designer, influenced the fashion industry by developing a technique for pleating silk that could be reproduced and commercialized.

Broomstick Skirt

The Broomstick Skirt in the United States

The broomstick skirt was a staple in the Native American woman's traditional wardrobe; however, it was not until the 1940s that the broomstick skirt became popular with non–Native Americans. Initially distributed as a two-piece dress labeled the "squaw dress," the market absorbed the skirt alone, and it was seen worn in a Southwest tradition with various blouses, concho belts, and cowboy boots. Through the 1950s, fashion-conscious women wore the broomstick skirt as part of the structured habits of the time, wearing binding undergarments and conforming to the formal rules that dictated proper accessories for appropriate occasions. The Southeast Asian version of the broomstick skirt, with its elastic waist, soft touch, light weight, and irregular pleating, did not enter the wider American culture until the late 1960s when the youth, guided by cultural icons such as the Beatles, began to embrace ethnic dress from the country of India.

Influence and Impact

Initially adopted by the hippie culture, the Southeast Indian broomstick skirt was comfortable, easy to wear, and symbolized freedom from convention. Martha Reed, a designer whose collaboration with the Taos Pueblo Indians resulted in a broomstick skirt style that was adopted by upper-class women as well, commercialized the Native American version of the broomstick skirt. Wealthy society women such as Millicent Rogers included the Martha of Taos broomstick skirt in their wardrobes and wore it to events as prestigious as dinner at the White House. The Native American broomstick skirt became a symbol of respect and appreciation for the Navajo and Pueblo Indians' craftsmanship and techniques and continues to be worn regularly in the Southwest United States, where women in the area around Santa Fe still consider it a wardrobe staple.

When the American fashion designer Ralph Lauren adopted the broomstick skirt as part of his Southwest United States brand image in the 1970s, the style became mainstream and took on various names, such as the gypsy skirt and the tiered skirt. The broomstick skirt has experienced several revivals in the cyclical tradition of fashion trend adoption, coming back into popularity in the late 1990s and then in the late 2000s, when Isabel Toledo designed a broomstick dress with irregular pleats for Anne Klein's 2008 spring collection. The simple, lightweight, irregularly pleated broomstick skirt continues to sell both nationally and internationally, typically considered to be a low-cost, fast-fashion item. In addition to the aesthetic and functional characteristics the broomstick skirt embodies, it continues to project a "boho/hippie" impression. Fashion designers in India such as Priyadarshini Rao from Mumbai have included the broomstick skirt in contemporary clothing collections. This continued interest in the aesthetic and symbolic value of the broomstick skirt secures its place in the repertoire of both southwestern American and southeastern Asian fashion.

See also BOHEMIAN DRESS; GYPSY SKIRT
Compare to POWWOW ACCESSORIES; WESTERN WEAR

Further Reading

Metcalfe, J. R. "Native Designers of High Fashion: Expressing Identity, Creativity, and Tradition in Contemporary Customary Clothing Design." PhD dissertation, University of Arizona, 2010. ProQuest Dissertations and Theses, 409, http://search.proquest.com/docview/577639724?accountid=4117 (577639724).
Parezo, N. J., and A. R. Jones. "What's in a Name? The 1940s–1950s 'Squaw Dress'" *American Indian Quarterly* 33, no. 3 (2009).

■ MARY RUPPERT-STROESCU

BUCKSKIN

Buckskin is the leather of a deer or elk (though today it is most often created from sheep) which is prepared in the same manner or in a way that resembles the traditional Native American style. Originally, the animal's brain matter was applied to the skin, which was beaten with stones and smoked in a kiln-like setting for an extended period of time. The brain tanning process softens the deerskin to emphasize a suede-like finish for which buckskin is known.

History

Buckskin has been found in primitive societies around the globe and is generally regarded as one of the most utilized prehistoric materials. However, contemporary thought attributes buckskin to Native Americans, who fabricated the abundant resource into items such as hunting, ceremonial, and everyday garments. Though specifics varied from tribe to tribe and by region, in general buckskin was worn in similar fashions and might include moccasins, leggings, coats, vests, aprons, dresses, and shirts. In cold climates, the hair was left on the skin and could be turned inward for warmth, or reversed to shed snow and water. In some regions, shirts and dresses were made from adjoining two full body skins. Left in their natural shape, the front legs were sewn together to form sleeves while the rear legs hung down, creating a fringe. In addition to serving as a decorative component, buckskin fringe functioned as a way for water to drip off of the garment. Though many examples exist, scholars have long debated the extent to which European interaction influenced the Native Americans' desire or necessity to clothe the body.

Buckskin in the United States

Interestingly, European settlers had long worn buckskin garments. The nobility wore breeches made of tanned leather for hunting. Due to overhunting, the dwindling resource had become a luxury item in parts of Europe. The New World, however, seemed to have an unlimited supply, and its export soon became an integral part of the economy. By the middle of the eighteenth century, colonists were exporting thousands of pounds per year, some of which the Native Americans had already tanned. During the Revolutionary War (1775–1783) American militia wore buckskin hunting shirts and later buckskin breeches and vests as part of their official uniforms. The material could be supplied from native sources, thus not relying on British trade. "Buckskins" became the nickname of the Continental troops. The material continued to be the patriots' preferred choice during frontier warring, worn most famously by General Armstrong Custer (1839–1876). It was there, on the frontier, that our modern-day connotations of buckskin developed.

Influence and Impact

Nineteenth-century hunters, fur trappers, and explorers were the first to develop relationships with the native peoples who had for centuries developed extensive trade routes crisscrossing the continent. As they began trading goods, they also adopted each other's clothing styles, making the borrowed clothing entirely their own. Buckskin vests that had been cut from a European pattern and adorned with beadwork were found among the Plains and Woodland Indians. Frontier people, too, adapted clothing worn by the Native Americans. Buckskin was found to be durable and better suited for the rugged and extreme environment of the Wild West. Furthermore, manufactured fabrics were often not available on the frontier. Buckskin, however, was abundantly available and could be cut into pants and suits that met the frontiersmen's sartorial styles as well as their environmental needs. Miners and migrants adopted the combined styles, and this soon developed into traditional western wear. For those who did not go west, there was the buckskin-suit-clad celebrity frontiersman, "Buffalo Bill," born William Frederick Cody (1846–1917). Buffalo Bill's popular Wild West Show toured for twenty years and presented a fantastical version of the frontier to North American and European audiences.

By the end of the nineteenth century, the self-fringed buckskin suit became the most recognizable identifier of the American West. Railway expansion brought vacationing tourists to western dude ranches during the early twentieth century. Participation on the ranch demanded the donning of appropriate attire, but the buckskin rarely left the ranch. It was not until the 1960s that buckskin reached the urban streets. The folk-inspired hippie movement popularized styles such as the iconic fringed vest. An interest in buckskin garments continued through the 1970s. Far more memorable was the popularity of buckskin during the 1980s. Both the urban cowboy and the rebellious rocker found commonality in fringed buckskin, the styling of which could be found on nearly every type of garment. Buckskin exemplifies strength, independence, and patriotism. Whether worn by the Native American, the revolutionary, or the frontiersman, buckskin is the embodiment of the American West and its traditional folk attire.

See also COONSKIN CAP; MOCCASINS; WESTERN WEAR
Compare to POWWOW ACCESSORIES

Further Reading

Cordwell, Justine M., and Ronald A. Schwarz. *The Fabrics of Culture: The Anthropology of Clothing and Adornment.* The Hague: Mouton, 1979.

Cunningham, Patricia A., and Susan Voso Lab. *Dress in American Culture.* Bowling Green, OH: Bowling Green State University Popular Press, 1993.

■ ERICA SUZANNE SCOTT

BURNOUS

The burnous, also *burnouse* or *bournous*, is a floor-length mantle or cloak with a hood. Originating from the Arabic word *burnus*, it is an upper garment worn extensively today and for centuries past, dating back to the Roman era, by Berbers and Arabs of North Africa. Worn as an outer garment, the burnous is part of a traditional wardrobe of Berber populations before the Arab conquest. Usually made from coarse fabric of wool, camel hair, or a mixture of both, the circular cape-style cloak, with its large pointed hood, served as an item of clothing by day and a blanket by night. The burnous was most often brown, black, blue, beige, or white.

History

The Algerian East was famous for producing fine white woolen burnouses that were imported throughout North Africa and the Arab world. In the seventeenth century the Arabic word was incorporated into Spanish as *albornoz*, a hooded traveling cloak. In Southern Morocco and Mauritania, the same garment is referred to as a *silham*. The styling of the burnous worn in Libya varies from other North African countries and is a rectangle of cloth five to six feet (about one and a half to two meters) in width and eighteen to twenty feet (about five and a half to six meters) in length. The Libyan burnous may or may not have a hood, and the edges and body are sometimes decorated with embroidery using a technique known in Libya and Tunisia as *kobbita*.

In Libya today, the most typical item of dress identifying its wearer as a Libyan man is the Berber burnous. The garment is said to be symbolic for many Libyan men, being associated with bravery and courage. North African men wear the burnous in several ways, but typically Libyan men place the burnous under the right arm and over the left shoulder, without the hood covering their heads, allowing freedom of movement. The burnous was introduced to Western fashion through the Spahi, the French cavalry troops from Algeria, Tunisia, and Morocco in the 1830s.

Today the burnous remains part of the official uniform of the one remaining Spahi regiment of the French army. During the French colonial period in Algeria, the French were fascinated with Algerian fashion and adopted the burnous as a way of demonstrating and maintaining hierarchical structure. From the first years of colonial rule onward (French Algeria, 1830–1962), French Algerian soldiers were elaborately dressed in wide trousers, short waistcoats, and brightly colored hats. The official burnous, always in bright colors, represented rank within the colonial administration. During the fight for independence from France (1954–1962), Algerian nationalists returned to the coarse peasant burnous as a symbol of opposition to colonial rule.

The Burnous in the United States

In the 1850s the burnous was introduced to Western fashion by photographs of Spahi troops wearing it, which popularized the style of wearing cloaks. A burnous was very suitable to be worn over mid-nineteenth-century women's fashions, with the very loose shape easily draping over the large hoopskirts of the day, and the large hoods could be easily drawn over bonnets. Throughout history in Western fashion, the burnous for women was made of exotic Eastern fabrics, with plain and broad stripes, plaid trim, and often in solid velvet with passementerie, Indian embroidery, and tassels. The shape of the burnous evolved with Western fashion and became shorter and less voluminous as the hoop skirt went out of fashion and the bustle came in in the 1870s.

Influence and Impact

The burnous was mainly a Victorian and early twentieth-century garment, but it sometimes makes a sporadic return to the fashion scene in the West. In the United States today, similar-style cloaks are sometimes worn by brides over wedding gowns for weddings held in cooler temperatures. The voluminous cloak with hood and sometimes fur trim provides warmth and adds glamour to winter-wonderland-themed weddings. In Algeria today, the burnous is an important component of the wedding ensemble. A symbol of Berber identity, the elaborately embroidered and embellished bridal gown and matching burnous is just one of many wedding ensembles worn by the bride as part of a wedding celebration. In addition, styling similar to the burnous worn by the Spahi regiment is sometimes a component of marching-band uniforms worn by high school and university students.

See also CHADOR; HIJAB; JILBAB
Compare to PELISSE; TALLIT

Further Reading

Loughran, Kristyne. "The Idea of Africa in European High Fashion: Global Dialogues." *Fashion Theory* 13, no. 2 (2009): 243–72. doi:10.2752/175174109x414277.
Payne, Blanche. *History of Costume: From the Ancient Egyptians to the Twentieth Century.* New York: Harper & Row, 1965, 517.
Spring, Christopher, and Julie Hudson. *North African Textiles.* London: British Museum Press, 1995.

■ VIRGINIA M. NOON

BURNOUSE
See BURNOUS

BURQA
See HIJAB

BUSSERULL (NORWEGIAN WORK SHIRT)

The busserull, or Norwegian work shirt, was historically worn as a loose-fitting overshirt, constructed with squares and rectangles cut to allow a full range of movement for physical labor. There are a number of variations in the cut, but most include a band collar, a shoulder yoke that extends over the upper arm, and a body with a button-front closure either ending with a placket to mid-chest or open to the waist. Loose sleeves are attached from the midpoint of the yoke at the shoulder, and greater movement and ease around the body is allowed by inserting square gussets at the underarm. The waist is usually half belted with an adjustable belt at the back. When used for work, the most common fabric was striped cotton or linen, and the most typical color was blue with white stripes. Plain or twill woven cotton was used for warm-weather work wear; wool shirts were used for colder seasons.

History

Throughout the late nineteenth century in Norway, the shirts were used by railroad workers, lumberjacks, builders, agricultural workers, harbor workers, and fishermen as one layer of protection against the weather. Photographs show the shirt worn as a single garment or with a woolen vest, and in the coldest weather under a woolen jacket. Shirts in Norwegian museum collections are well worn and are often patched, or there are new sections sewn in to replace collars, cuffs, or shirttails. A variety of sturdy wool and half-wool shirts are available for study at the Norwegian Forestry Museum in Elverum, Norway. Records at the National Council of Folk Costumes in Fagernes, Norway, reflect that historically, a new work shirt might have been used for occasions other than work, but this garment was not considered suitable for church on Sunday. As sentiment grew for independence from Sweden near the turn of the nineteenth century, some forms of rural dress took on a nationalistic meaning, and the busserull, especially in the colors of the Norwegian flag (red or blue with white stripes) became more symbolic than functional. They were used for leisure activities outdoors, or for occasions such as folk dance or rural folk festivals. Rural forms of clothing were revived in the 1960s and 1970s in international fashion, and this was true also of the busserull in Norway.

Busserull in the United States

When Norwegian immigrants settled in agricultural areas throughout America, they continued sewing work shirts for use within the family. Photographs from the 1870s in rural Wisconsin by the Norwegian-American photographer Andreas Dahl show men in variations of the busserull. The loose-fitting busserull eventually went out of favor for agricultural work as farm operations became mechanized and overalls became ubiquitous. In America, the busserull evolved into an outdoor leisure garment, or it was worn, as in Norway, primarily for festival occasions. Shirts were imported or brought from Norway by tourists as souvenirs, often embellished with decorative pewter buttons.

Influence and Impact

Today these shirts in blue or red striped fabrics are worn in both informal and formal settings among Norwegian-Americans. A bridegroom might wear a busserull for a heritage-style wedding. Classes in sewing the shirts are popular where traditional folk crafts are taught, such as at the Vesterheim Norwegian-American Museum in Decorah, Iowa, and North House Folk School in Grand Marais, Minnesota. Whether or not of Norwegian-American heritage, students enjoy customizing their shirts to suit their work or leisure activities, with adaptations appropriate for festivals, folk dance, hiking, fishing, sailing, gardening, woodworking, or building.

Currently, busserull traditional fabrics as well as ready-to-wear work shirts are manufactured by the Norwegian company Grinakervev at their small factory in Brandbu, located in the central agricultural region of Hadeland, Norway. Now sized for men, women, and children, they are sold online to an international market. In addition to the traditional styles, unique models available include Pilgrimsskjorte (pilgrim shirt) in dark brown fabric and Statsrådsbusserull (cabinet meeting shirt), appropriate for formal wear, in blue fabric with red damask woven bands at the front closure, collar, cuffs, and pocket. In America, the current revival of hands-on sustainable skills has created an interest in sewing and wearing these comfortable, adaptable, and natural-fiber shirts. Individuals who choose their own fabric and create their own work shirts understand the satisfaction of a custom-made garment for leisure or work.

See also Kosovorotka; Norwegian Sweater
Compare to Aloha Shirt (Hawai'ian Shirt); Barong Tagalog; Chambray; Dashiki; Oxford Shirt

Further Reading

The National Council of Folk Costumes in Norway. www.bunadogfolkedrakt.no.
Vesterheim Norwegian-American Museum Decorah, Iowa. http://vesterheim.org.

■ CAROL ANN COLBURN

BUSTIER
See Corset

C

CABBIE HAT
See FLAT CAP

CAFTAN
"Caftan," or *kaftan*, is a Persian word that traditionally describes a full-length robe with full sleeves that is open at the front and sometimes buttoned. It can be made from almost any fabric, though caftans are primarily made of silk, wool, or cotton and are often bound with a sash. Both men and women in variations wear caftans across the Iranian plateau, through North Africa, and into West Africa. Primarily worn in hot climates, the loose silhouette of the caftan aids in proper ventilation, therefore lowering the body temperature. In Morocco, only women wear caftans, while in West Africa, "caftan" describes a woman's pullover robe (the male version is called a boubou). In the West, "caftan" has become the catchall term for any kind of loose-fitting robe or tunic of vaguely Middle Eastern or North African style.

History
This style of garment is believed to have originated in Ancient Mesopotamia. The Ottoman sultans from the fourteenth to the eighteenth centuries wore lavishly decorated caftans; they were also given as rewards to important dignitaries and generals. In Europe and North America, traditional caftans were rarely worn other than by a small number of travelers and eccentrics, who brought them back from exotic expeditions and usually wore them around the house—this was in keeping with the fad for Orientalism and Turkish-style interiors during the nineteenth century.

The Caftan Dress in the United States
The caftan was adapted by French couturiers, including Christian Dior and Balenciaga, in the 1950s and early 1960s as a new form of loose-fitting evening gown or a robe over matching trousers. Usually sashless, the Westernized caftan dress was sold by American designers and manufacturers in the 1960s as a style of hostess gown, usually made of embellished silks or patterned synthetics.

Influence and Impact

By 1966, *Vogue* was describing the caftan as an essential garment for every member of the jet set and photographed "the beautiful people" in an array of imported traditional styles and Western adaptations. Trickling down, the caftan dress became worn by women entertaining at home, while at the same time more traditional forms of the caftan were being brought into the United States by young people who had traveled the nascent "Hippie Trail" from North Africa to Afghanistan. The loose fit and long history of the caftan contributed to it becoming a staple of the hippie and flower-child wardrobe of the late 1960s, as its more primitive silhouette and manufacture appealed to a generation displeased with Western consumer culture. In keeping with their rejection of the "establishment," the counterculture returned to nature—an interest in rural living, health foods, and bodies unconstrained by heavily structured clothes. Often worn without undergarments, the shapeless silhouette of the caftan—often in earthy colors and less refined textiles—aligned with the back-to-the-land ethos of commune culture and also became associated with the rising number of cults in the early 1970s. First bought cheaply from small import stores, as the hippie counterculture gained notice, caftans began to be produced in the Middle East, India, and North Africa strictly for the American market and were imported in large numbers, while these more traditional styles were also replicated by American mass merchandisers.

The caftan dress, therefore, became associated with both the high end and with youth culture. Celebrities such as Elizabeth Taylor continued to popularize the luxurious caftan dress into the 1970s; Taylor collected ornate patchwork caftans by the London-based designer Thea Porter—seven of which were sold at an auction of her clothes at Christie's in 2011, each for over $20,000. The American designer Halston produced expensive caftan evening dresses in a sleek and minimal style. In addition to being used for evening gowns, caftan dresses were also reworked into loungewear and nightdresses.

Since the 1980s the caftan dress has moved from evening wear to primarily being worn as a beach cover-up. Off the beach, it is most closely associated with bohemian lifestyles and still to a certain degree with fringe religions and cults.

See also BOHEMIAN DRESS; BOUBOU; DASHIKI
Compare to CHIMA; MUʻUMUʻU; THAWB

Further Reading

"The Beautiful People in Caftans." *Vogue*, July 1, 1966, 66–72.
Welters, Linda. "The Natural Look: American Style in the 1970s." *Fashion Theory* 12, no. 4 (2008): 489–510.
Yablonsky, Lewis. *The Hippie Trip*. New York: Penguin, 1973.

■ LAURA MCLAWS HELMS

CALICO AND CHINTZ

"Calico" comes from Kozhikode or Calicut, a port in India, where these fabrics were originally produced. In the United States and Canada, "calico" refers to medium-weight unglazed plain-weave fabric printed with small all-over floral repeats or abstract motifs, often with pale white or beige background. However, in the United Kingdom, Australia, and New Zealand, "calico" refers to simple, cheap white, off-white, or unbleached plain-weave cotton fabric (muslin). Calicoes can be classified into two categories—abstract (dots, squiggles, and other geometric shapes) or figurative.

"Chintz" is derived from the Hindi word *chint* meaning variegated and from the Sanskrit word *chitrak* meaning shiny, gaily colored, and speckled. Chintz is calico only if it is block printed on cotton. Chintzes are characterized by large, bright floral patterns and representational motifs, which may be painted or printed on glazed cotton or silk that is usually dense. One of the most exquisite and expensive chintzes in India is known as *kalamkari*, derived from the Persian terms *kalam* (pen) and *kari* (craftsmanship).

History

Calico fabrics originated in India during the eleventh century. In the Mughal period, the chief centers of calico printing were Gujarat, Rajasthan, and Madhya Pradesh. These were initially traded for pepper, spices, gold, ivory, and horses with the Middle East and Africa. An early fragment of calico that dates back to the fifteenth century has been found near Cairo. During the seventeenth and eighteenth centuries, these were traded between India and Europe. The Dutch and English began to dictate the styles and designs of these fabrics, which resulted in the development of block printing in Holland, England, and France. By 1680, the Europeans had patented their own "Callicoe"-making process. The simplest, cheapest, and most prevalent calicoes were composed of orange-red, black, and cream colors from an alizarin dye bath, with iron and alum used for imparting black and red colors, respectively. These came to be known as Indienne Ordinaire. Some of the traditional calicoes in India had darker backgrounds such as orange-red and black, while some others were composed of black and red on cream backgrounds and multicolored floral prints on cotton, which were inspired by Chinese silk. Gold tinseling was used to impart richness to the material. European calicoes had cream-colored backgrounds predominantly. In England, printed calicoes were generally used for hangings, bedcovers, and clothes. These transitioned from modest home furnishings to dominating fashion that signified the elite. In India, it is primarily printed on the sari—an Indian attire. In the 1770s, silk and wool manufacturers and weavers of England protested against the import of cotton.

Calicoes and Chintzes in the United States

In 1770 John Hewson of Philadelphia printed calico for the first time in the United States, the process and designs of which were imported from Europe. By the end of the eighteenth century, most of the patterns became smaller, regular, and closer. Also, pale colors were reserved for evening wear, and some were embroidered instead of being printed. Day wear had darker colors and was usually patterned. With the advent of the American Revolution, American culture separated from its British roots. Calico in the United States was associated with fabrics with small floral repeats, whereas in England, calico referred to muslin, an inexpensive cotton fabric used for making test or fitting garments, and for lining quilts.

Influence and Impact

By the late 1850s, the Americans were the biggest consumers of calico in the world. From 1810 to 1815 was a notable era in American textile and quilt-making artistry, with pieced and whole-cloth quilts made from calicoes and chintzes, which were imported from France and England. Polychromatic chintzes with large floral motifs and calicoes were used to create kaleidoscopic quilts, some of which were commemorative, honoring political figures or memorializing events.

Bolts of calico were bought to make matching garments for family members. Traditional North American Indian long shirts and skirts were often made from calicoes and chintzes in the 1890s. Calico sunbonnets and everyday gowns were commonly worn by American women.

Today, these novelty fabrics have made a comeback. Calico and chintz designs are incorporated in spring and summer fashion clothing, home interiors, and even crockery, to provide a refreshing, ethnic, and vintage touch.

See also MELHFA; MUʻUMUʻU
Compare to BATIK CLOTH APPAREL; BATTENBERG LACE; CHAMBRAY; TIE-DYED APPAREL

Further Reading

Brackman, Barbara. *Clues in the Calico: A Guide to Identifying and Dating Antique Quilts.* Concord, CA: C&T Publishing, 2009.
Oakes, Leimomi. "Calico, Muslin and Gauze: A History of Fabric Terminology." *The Dreamstress,* June 4, 2010. http://thedreamstress.com/2010/06/calico-muslin-gauze-a-history-of-fabric-terminology -part-i.

■ HARINI RAMASWAMY

CAPRI PANTS

The original capri pants, created by Italian designer Emilio Pucci (1914–1992), featured a slim silhouette with a length ending just below the knee and had a small inverted V at the hem on each side, which enabled ease of movement, encouraging wearers to participate in an active lifestyle. The cropped pant had a flat front, a figure-hugging cut, and was made of the finest cotton poplin or silk shantung, which was dyed in shades reminiscent of the Mediterranean seascape. The addition of Pucci's long-sleeved, tailored, square-cut shirts and a cashmere sweater draped casually over the wearer's shoulders created a fashion uniform for women of the mid-twentieth century.

The name and style of capri pants can often be confused with "pedal pushers" and "clam diggers," but there are subtle differences between the styles. Capri pants have a very slim silhouette and end right below the knee, whereas pedal pushers provide a looser fit and are generally longer in length as they end at the calf. While clam diggers also extend to the calf, they are considerably looser in fit than capri pants and pedal pushers.

History

Originally created by Pucci in 1949, the capri pant came to symbolize the sporty casual way of life for American women in the 1950s. The capri pant, named for the island of

Capri Pants

Capri off the coast of Naples in Italy, is a calf-length trouser that was first sold in Emilio of Capri, the boutique Pucci opened on the popular summer destination of Capri. By 1949 Pucci felt the time had come for casual, colorful resort fashions that accommodated travelers to the island of Capri who were seeking pleasure and relaxation. Pucci was astute in his business plan, for international clientele, such as American-born Italian countess Consuelo Crespi (1928–2010), American socialite and fashion icon Mona Harrison von Bismarck (1897–1983), and French actress Maxime de la Falaise (1922–2009), were frequent customers of Emilio of Capri and helped popularize the casual clothing Pucci was designing. Tourists to the island, and customers of Pucci's, approved of the sportswear style that was the epitome of casual chic. Within a short period of time the capri pant, paired with Pucci's brightly colored silk shirts, became a popular style and altered the way women dressed when they were not required to dress up.

Capri Pants in the United States

The slim style of the capri pant was in direct opposition to the highly feminine and luxurious New Look created by French couture designer Christian Dior (1905–1957) in 1947. Despite the stylistic opposition to the New Look, the capri pant was a popular piece of clothing during the 1950s, especially within the California beach lifestyle. In the United States, the capri pant could be worn six months out of the year, either during the day or at night, when women would dress up the style with the addition of accessories such as gold jewelry and jeweled sandals. Mid-twentieth-century designers of American sportswear such as Claire McCardell (1905–1958) created pant styles reminiscent of the capri pant for American women across the country.

Influence and Impact

Much like today, Hollywood stars of the 1950s were trendsetters for American women. During the 1950s, Audrey Hepburn (1929–1993) was the height of popularity and was often looked to for stylish wardrobe choices because of her on-screen and off-screen fashion decisions. The 1954 film *Sabrina* featured Hepburn wearing capri pants throughout the movie, as did the popular films *Roman Holiday* (1953) and *Funny Face* (1957). Along with movie stars, television stars had a strong influence on the wardrobe choices of the modern American woman. Mary Tyler Moore (1936–), who is well known for her roles on the *Dick Van Dyke Show*, which ran during the 1960s, and *The Mary Tyler Moore Show* of the 1970s, wore capri pants throughout her time on the *Dick Van Dyke Show*. The proliferation of Hollywood and television stars wearing capri pants catapulted the style into the realm of classic day wear for women of all ages. Pucci's clientele also included wealthy and sophisticated women such as American actresses Lauren Bacall (1924–2014) and Marilyn Monroe (1926–1962) and First Lady Jacqueline Kennedy Onassis (1929–1994). During the 1970s,

Jacqueline Kennedy Onassis often vacationed on the island of Capri with her children and was commonly seen wearing capri pants with a short-sleeved shirt, evoking the casually elegant style that became essential in women's wardrobes.

While Pucci's success can partly be attributed to his international clientele, the general interest in Italian culture and way of life that swept through the United States and Europe during the middle of the twentieth century had a dramatic effect on the success of all things Italian. This included fashion designers, Vespas, movie stars such as Sophia Loren (1934–) and Gina Lollobrigida (1927–), chart-topping songs like "Arrivederci, Roma" (1955) from the popular movie of the same name, and novels like *Woman of Rome* (1949) by Alberto Moravia (1907–1990). At the time, Italians were looked to for stylistic advice and guidance, leading to the increased popularity of design houses like Emilio Pucci and Missoni, among others. The capri pant remains a classic item in women's wardrobes throughout the twentieth century and is continually cycled in and out of fashion. Pucci's chic capri pant contributed to the increasingly casual nature of women's dress, while retaining class and grace for women across the globe. The capri pant remains a popular choice for women of the twenty-first century, when the style became a mainstream choice for women across the globe, especially in the United States. Women of all ages in the United States began wearing the capri pant as an alternative to both long, more formal pants and more casual shorts. Commonly worn during warmer months, capri pants became available in a wide range of fabrics, including denim, chino, and a combination of man-made fibers for a figure-conscious fit. As the business of fitness clothing grew, companies such as Lululemon began offering fitness pants in styles reminiscent of capri pants. In the twenty-first century, a number of men also adopted the capri style into their daily wardrobe, although this has not become a widespread occurrence in men's fashion. Today, it is common to see women wearing capri-style pants in the workplace as well as within their daily lives outside of the office.

See also CHINESE FLATS
Compare to BERMUDA SHORTS; JODHPURS

Further Reading

Arbuckle, Joanne, and Francesca Sterlacci. *The A to Z of the Fashion Industry*. Lanham, MD: Scarecrow Press, 2008.

Kennedy, Shirley. *Pucci: A Renaissance in Fashion*. New York: Abbeville Press, 1991.

Stalder, Erika. *Fashion 101: A Crash Course in Clothing*. San Francisco: Orange Avenue Publishing, 2008.

■ JESSICA SCHWARTZ

CHADAH
See CHADOR

CHADAR
See CHADOR

CHADDAR
See CHADOR

CHADER
See CHADOR

CHADOR

The chador (also *chadah, chad(d)ar, chader, chud(d)ah,* or *chadur*) is the open cloak worn by women and young women of Islam in public spaces. It is the shape of a semicircle and tossed over the head. While it has an opening at the front, it is worn closed. It has no hand openings. It is typically worn with a head scarf (*rousan*), a blouse (*pirahan*), and a long skirt (*damaan*), or a skirt over pants (*shalvar*). The chador is part of the conformity to the Qu'ranic standard that a woman dress modestly. This modesty of dress is known under the umbrella term of "hijab." What is important to note is that hijab, which also includes the burqa, is not dress as such but continuous with belief and the proper sense of self as it applies to Islam.

History

The chador probably originated in ancient Mesopotamia. Persian custom differentiated respectable women from prostitutes and servants by the wearing of veils. Thus veils carried the sign of class and were a component of strict sumptuary laws. Covering women was practiced by the Achaemenid rulers of Persia to hide both concubines and wives from public view. While this continued in the Seleucid, Pathian, and Sassanid periods, it is also known that upper-class Greek and Byzantine women were also shielded from the public gaze. It is, however, uncertain at what point the chador took the form that is used today.

As part of the modernizations that occurred in the Muslim world, particularly in Turkey, in 1936 the Pahlavi ruler Reza Shah placed a ban on all hijab, which included the chador. This caused public upheaval since many women refused to abide by this law, causing them to be housebound or otherwise risk assault by the police. Feeling in violation of their religious beliefs, during this period many women committed suicide. The extremity of his measures eventuated in Reza Shah's abdication in 1941.

From 1980 onward, after the Islamic Revolution in Iran, the wearing of hijab began to be reinforced. But in recent years disenchantment with the Iranian regime has caused such conventions to be relaxed. Women can be seen wearing the scarf pushed back on their heads and even wearing makeup. Traditionally the chador was worn with a veil that was usually white (*ruband*), but more recently, the veil has been dispensed with. Equally, in urban households the chador is removed indoors in favor of lighter garments. But in rural areas they continue to be worn at all levels of life. Black chadors were conventionally worn only for funeral occasions and for mourning. But after the Islamic Revolution of 1979, they are worn on a day-to-day basis, with lighter colors and patterned fabrics reserved for domestic life and for prayer.

The Chador in the United States

The chador is largely an Iranian fashion. When seen in the United States, it is primarily worn by Iranian women who wish to reflect the practices, both religious and culturally, of their home country.

See also HIJAB; JILBAB; MELHFA
Compare to BURNOUS; PELISSE; TALLIT

Further Reading

El-Guindi, Fadwa. *Veil: Modesty, Privacy, and Resistance.* Oxford and New York: Berg, 1999.
Geczy, Adam. *Fashion and Orientalism: Dress, Textiles and Culture from the 17th to the 21st Century.* London and New York: Bloomsbury, 2013.
Özdalga, Elisabeth. *The Veiling Issue: Official Secularism and Popular Islam in Modern Turkey.* Richmond, Surrey: Curzon, 1998.

■ ADAM GECZY

CHADUR

See CHADOR

CHAMBRAY

Named after the French town of Cambrai, chambray is a lightweight woven fabric, with colored warp and white filling. Though the textile was originally made of linen, cotton became chambray's weave of choice with the rise of the textile industry in the United States. Commonly found in button-front shirts today, chambray is a staple of quintessential American style.

History

Chambray was first used in the town of Cambrai, in northern France, in which the weaving industry prospered during the Middle Ages. The fabric's invention is frequently attributed to Jean-Baptiste Cambrai or Cambray, though the era in which he lived is unknown—suggested dates range from the early fourteenth to the late sixteenth century. Cambric or batiste, as chambray was then called, was made of linen and used for a number of purposes such as lace and needlework, fine shirts, sunbonnets, and handkerchiefs. Stiff cambric ruffs were especially fashionable in Elizabethan England and remained the prevalent choice in neckwear and cuffs throughout the centuries for clerical, legal, and academic dress.

Advances in textile technology in the eighteenth century allowed the industry to flourish around the world. Samuel Slater, celebrated as the "father of American manufacturers" for his role in extending the British Industrial Revolution to the United States, opened the country's first cotton mill in Pawtucket, Rhode Island, in 1790. His firm soon began producing cambric, and both company and fabric gained recognition as textile manufacturing increased throughout New England in the nineteenth century. The term "chambray" appeared in the United States between 1805 and 1815, thus replacing "cambric," and the fabric subsequently became known for its cotton composition as opposed to linen.

Chambray quickly became accepted as an ideal fabric for utility shirts. In 1901, the U.S. Navy began issuing shirts in chambray—paired with denim trousers, this uniform carried on through World War II. Along with the similar-looking denim, chambray remains a key element within American fashion, which has long added military and "workingman" references to timeless pieces.

Chambray in the United States

Though used over the centuries in Europe for formal dress, chambray is often synonymous in the United States with work wear. Its lightweight and durable qualities render it practical for manual labor, especially in hot or outdoor environments. Clothing manufacturers generally use chambray for shirts, dresses, and linens, as well as various fashion accessories. The fabric can also be dyed in a range of colors, though the traditional blue and gray remain the most popular hues. With its naturally faded appearance, chambray gives the wearer a casual appearance, similar to denim or khaki, two other popular textiles in American sportswear.

In the United States, chambray is associated with a culture of heroic, hardworking people, thus reflecting enduring American values. The fabric's widespread use in and after World War II helped establish its connection to strong, working-class symbols. J. Howard Miller's iconic "We Can Do It!" poster, produced in 1943, features Rosie the Riveter in a chambray work shirt with rolled-up sleeves—this illustration has since endured in the American psyche. The textile's previous use in the navy, commonly worn with denim jeans and a white cap, also lends itself to recurring military influences in fashion trends. In the 1950s and 1960s, male American movie stars such as Marlon Brando, Steve McQueen, and James Dean wore chambray shirts, solidifying the garment as essential in order to achieve a rugged, adventurous look. Paul Newman even donned such a shirt in 1967's *Cool Hand Luke*.

Influence and Impact

Chambray has impacted not only worldwide textile and fashion industries but also the English language. The term "blue-collar worker," coined in the United States in the early twentieth century, stems from the image of manual workers wearing blue denim and chambray shirts as part of their uniforms. The expression spread during World War II and is used to this day, in addition to having been translated in a number of languages.

Today, the button-front chambray shirt plays a major role in classic American style, alongside other ubiquitous pieces such as jeans, polo shirts, leather jackets, and boat shoes. For decades, established U.S. designers Ralph Lauren and Tommy Hilfiger have been praised for their adoption of the classic American look, creating chambray garments for men, women, and children. Fashionable crowds from Paris to Tokyo have since appropriated the aesthetic; as a result, the chambray shirt has gained international appeal.

See also OXFORD SHIRT

Compare to BATIK CLOTH APPAREL; BUSSERULL (NORWEGIAN WORK SHIRT); CALICO AND CHINTZ; KENTE CLOTH; TIE-DYED APPAREL

Further Reading

Brackman, Barbara. *Making History: Quilts & Fabric from 1890–1970*. Lafayette, CA: C&T Publishing, 2008.

Little, Frances. *Early American Textiles*. New York: The Century Co., 1931.

Thompson, Eliza Bailey, Lee Galloway, and Beulah Elfreth Kennard. *The Cotton and Linen Departments*. New York: Ronald Press, 1917.

■ MARIE-CLAIRE EYLOTT

CHEMISE

The chemise is described in two different but related ways. Generally, the chemise is a loose-fitting shirt-like undergarment, usually of cotton or linen. It is also a specific style of women's dress designed to hang straight from the shoulders in a semifitted tube.

History

The word "chemise" originates with a combination of the Anglo-Norman *chemés* and the Latin *camisia*. The chemise was originally a tunic-like garment with rectangular front, back, and sleeves sewn together using widths of uncut linen or wool right off the loom. (The South Asian *kameez* carries on this efficient use of cloth.) Because it was worn as an undergarment, next to the skin and not visible, it was usually not dyed. Both men and women wore the tunic/chemise under a second tunic or toga in Roman times (500 BCE–400 CE). This "unders and overs" combination was standard dress throughout the early Middles Ages (300–1300 CE). The chemise protected skin from harsh outerwear, protected luxury fabrics from body oils and perspiration, added a layer of warmth, and was easily washed.

In thirteenth-century Europe, men wore knee-length breeches and a chemise under a *cote* (tunic) and *surcote* (over tunic). Women wore a distinctive *surcote* with large cutaway armholes called a sideless surcote. In warm weather, some women wore the sideless *surcote* directly over the chemise, but this was considered immodest. In the Late Middle Ages (1300–1500), the chemise was equivalent to an undershirt for men—linen, short-sleeved, knee length, and invisible. Women also wore the chemise, but it was full length. Some *cotes* and *surcotes* were exceptionally long, requiring the woman to hold her dress up, revealing the chemise, perhaps an early example of underwear used as outerwear. By the Renaissance (1400–1600), the English called the chemise a smock or shift and the Italians a *camicia*, with typical style features including tubular sleeves, a rounded or gathered neckline, and blackwork embroidery for the well-to-do. The chemise was again visible, now at the necklines of dresses and jackets, at the armscyes where sleeves were laced to the body of the garment, and below wide-flowing oversleeves. Linen cloth was produced with such fineness that sometimes the chemise is hardly visible in sixteenth-century portraits. A small ruffle was added to the gathered neckline, which grew into the ruff characteristic of the late sixteenth century. Ruffles also appeared at sleeve cuffs pointing to the ongoing transformation of the men's chemise into the modern dress shirt. With the formation of the European East India companies, cotton was introduced, and fine cotton muslin became a choice for undergarments because it was lighter weight than linen, softer on the skin, and less bulky. As cotton became more accessible in the eighteenth century, the *chemise a la reine* style of gown was fashionable. It was white cotton muslin and resembled a chemise, but with a fitted waist and full gathered skirt.

The Chemise in the United States

The chemise arrived in the United States with the Pilgrim women in 1620. In spite of their Puritan emphasis on simplicity, the colonists followed fashion, which included a boned bodice that was a forerunner of the corset, worn over the chemise. In the early 1800s, poor white women and African slave women are pictured wearing chemises and petticoats as street wear, indicative of their social position. In reaction to female Hawai'ian dress covering only the genitals, American Congregational missionaries in the 1820s developed the *holoku*, a loose-fitting floor-length gown with a yoke, long sleeves, and high neck. Missionary women also gave the Hawai'ian women chemises to wear under their *holoku*. The Hawai'ians called chemises mu'umu'us, meaning "cut off," and wore them as outerwear for sleeping and swimming. Over time, the mu'umu'u was culturally authenticated into the Hawai'ian ethnic dress of the same name favored by both locals and tourists.

By the mid-nineteenth century the chemise settled into the style features we picture today: fine linen or cotton, short set-in sleeves, low round or square neck, falling straight from shoulders to knees, wide but not voluminous, and often with embellishment. The corset fell out of use in the early twentieth century as the fashionable shape of women's bodies changed from hourglass to flapper after World War I (1914–1917). The style of the flapper dress, a body-skimming tube falling from the shoulders, was called a chemise, perhaps to provoke awareness that times had changed. Meanwhile, the need for a layer between skin and clothing remained, and the chemise gradually transformed into the slip, worn with brassiere and panty.

Influence and Impact

A societal shift similar to the 1920s occurred in the United States with the countercul-ture movement in the 1960s. Youth turned their backs on corporate gray flannel suits in favor of work wear, ethnic dress, and articles from grandma's attic. The historical chemise returned to favor as dresses and tops. At the same time, the post–World War II full figure was replaced by the gamine, and the chemise dress style replaced the full skirts and nipped waists characteristic of the 1950s. Panty hose, go-go boots, and double-knit polyester in psychedelic colors facilitated the adoption of this short, carefree garment. The chemise dress, sometimes called a shift or sack, made a comeback in 2012. After decades of clinging spandex, the ponte knit chemise offered women freedom of movement, easy care, and a return to elegance.

The chemise has staying power. The idea of underwear developed early in human history. The chemise is one point of origin and lives on in the slip. A layer of cloth between skin and garment serves multiple practical uses, and the chemise evolved into many sartorial eco-niches. As underwear, meant to remain unseen, the chemise was the first example of using underwear as outerwear. In the United States, changing times are marked by the classic chemise dress.

See also MUʻUMUʻU
Compare to CORSET; PEASANT BLOUSE

Further Reading

Tortore, Phyllis, and Keith Eubank. *Survey of Historic Costume.* New York: Fairchild, 2010.

■ SANDRA LEE EVENSON

CHEONGSAM

"Cheongsam," a name adopted from Cantonese, literally means long gown. It is mostly known as a one-piece dress that generally features a mandarin collar, an asymmetric closure extending from the neckline to the underarm on the right side, frog buttons, slits on one or both sides, piping effect on the edges, and a fitted silhouette. It was a popular dress form for urban Chinese women in Mainland China from the 1920s to the 1950s and continued to be worn until the late 1960s in Hong Kong and Taiwan.

History

In Mandarin, the cheongsam is called the *qipao*, literally meaning "banner gown," which alludes to one of its commonly believed origins: the dress of the female Manchu members of the Eight Banners. The Eight Banners were the administrative and military divisions of the Qing dynasty (1644–1911), of which the Manchu were the ruling ethnic minority. During the Qing dynasty, both Manchu men and women wore the banner gown. The women's banner gown was paired with loose trousers underneath. In the late Qing period, the round neckline of the banner gown was replaced with a mandarin collar. Although the banner gown shared attributes such as the mandarin collar and the asymmetric closure with the cheongsam, the two differed in many respects. For example, the cheongsam was not paired with trousers and was instead worn with high or low stockings. Neither did it feature heavy, meticulous surface designs in silk. The cheongsam used various materials, including synthetic fibers, cotton, and artificial silk, with their designs influenced by Western trends. The shape of the cheongsam was also narrower than the bell-shaped banner gown. The decorated wide borders of the banner gown were also replaced with narrow, delicate piping.

While Manchu women wore the one-piece banner gown during the Qing dynasty, the daily dress of the women of the Han majority was a combination of jacket and a long, pleated skirt or loose wide pants. This two-piece ensemble followed the long sartorial tradition of Han Chinese women, which distinguished them not only from Manchu women, but also from Han men, who wore a one-piece long gown, or cheongsam. The long gown worn by Han men during the Qing dynasty was usually neutral in color with subdued patterns or plain, and paired with long pants underneath. Chinese novelist Zhang Ailing (1920–1995) made the earliest reference to the cheongsam being worn by female students in Shanghai circa 1921. The early form of the cheongsam resembled nearly exactly the Han men's long gown: an ankle-length, spacious cut with no hint of the body lines and a plain surface in neutral colors. Scholars interpreted this adoption of the male dress form as a sign of female emancipation, modernity, and gender equality. But under Western influence, the cheongsam evolved to differ from the men's long gown in its shape, structure, and accessories.

At the peak of its popularity among fashionable women in the 1930s, the cheongsam became more body fitting and thus more feminine. And its hemline, sleeves, fabrics, and trim followed closely what was in fashion in the West. For example, the hemline was calf length in the 1920s, ankle or floor length in the 1930s, and middle calf or knee length in the 1940s and 1950s. From the 1930s on, Western construction techniques, such as darts, set-in sleeves, snap fasteners, and shoulder pads were incorporated to give the cheongsam a more fitted and structured three-dimensional form. Meanwhile, nylon stockings or panties were worn underneath the cheongsam, accessorized with heeled leather shoes.

The Cheongsam in the United States

Immigrants brought the cheongsam to the United States, first from Hong Kong and Taiwan and later from the mainland. The influence of Hollywood movies also reinforced the image of the cheongsam as embodying a Chinese ethnic identity in the United States. Anna May Wong, an American actress with Chinese heritage, showcased the cheongsam as early as the silent movie era. A hit drama of 1961, *The World of Suzie Wong*, further associated the cheongsam with a sensual image of Chinese women. *Life* magazine featured Nancy Kwan, the actress who starred as Suzie Wong in the movie, in a golden cheongsam on its October 1960 cover.

Influence and Impact

Although the cheongsam was a popular daily dress for decades in China, it is now only worn on special occasions both in the United States and in China. It is also a common uniform of the service industry in China. In the United States, new Chinese immigrants and Americans with Chinese heritage often wear the cheongsam for wedding ceremonies and traditional Chinese festivals or holidays, such as the Chinese New Year and Full Moon Festival. Due to its symbolic Chinese appeal, regardless of one's nationality and ethnicity, donning the cheongsam gives a sense of participation and celebration of Chinese culture. Thus, Americans can also be seen in the cheongsam on special Chinese occasions or festivals. Modified forms of the cheongsam exist both in daily life and on the catwalk. High-fashion designers or couturiers, including Yves Saint Laurent, Karl Lagerfeld, Christian Lacroix, Valentino, John Galliano, Donna Karan, and Jean Paul Gautier, have used the cheongsam as an inspirational source for their exotic designs.

Both the meaning and the form of the cheongsam have undergone gradual changes over time. Its dual origin and Western influence have made the cheongsam a hybrid design with complex meanings vested in its changing form. At the time of its inception, the cheongsam signified gender equality, female emancipation, and modernity. As the cheongsam metamorphosed into a sensual, body-hugging silhouette in the 1930s, it came to represent Chinese femininity, female sexuality, and fashionability. The high slits, high stockings, and high heels all contributed to the popular image of a hypersensual Chinese female. But in the 1940s, as it became the daily dress of urban women from all walks of life, it was seen as practical, economical, and socially appropriate. During the Mao era (1949–1977), the cheongsam was disfavored and abandoned by the masses due to its association with bourgeois taste and a capitalist lifestyle. Later on, the cheongsam came to serve as a representative form of Chinese identity, especially to outsiders. Chinese women from various backgrounds, such as movie stars and wives of political leaders from both the Republic era (1912–1949) and the People's Republic of China (1949–present), chose to wear the cheongsam on diplomatic occasions and visits. As now the cheongsam is worn mainly as a ceremonial dress, it has also come to represent Chinese culture and tradition more generally.

See also CHINESE FLATS
Compare to CAFTAN; CHIMA; JILBAB; KIMONO; MUʻUMUʻU; RUMBA DRESS; THAWB

Further Reading

Bao, Mingxin, Wu Juanjuan, Ma Li, Yang Shu, and Wu Di. *Zhongguo qipao* [Chinese *qipao*]. Shanghai: Shanghai Wenhua Chubanshe, 1998.
Clark, Hazel. *The Cheongsam.* New York: Oxford University Press, 2000.
Finnane, Antonia. *Changing Clothes in China: Fashion, History, Nation.* New York: Columbia University Press, 2008.
Garrett, Valery M. *Chinese Dress: From the Qing Dynasty to the Present.* Rutland, VT: Tuttle, 2007.
Steele, Valerie, and John Major. *China Chic: East Meets West.* New Haven, CT: Yale University Press, 1999.
Wu, Juanjuan. *Chinese Fashion from Mao to Now.* Oxford: Berg, 2009.

■ JUANJUAN WU

CHIMA

The word "chima" became a Korean noun indicating a woman's skirt in general; however, from an ethnic aspect, a "chima" is a wrap skirt that women wear as part of the hanbok, which is traditional Korean attire. A chima consists of the body of the skirt, a belt, and straps. The outline of the skirt maintains the beauty of volume and natural curves. A chima is wrapped, crossed, and tied around the torso to stabilize the skirt.

History

In the period of the Three Kingdoms of Korea (57 BCE–330 CE), there were two different kinds of skirts: *gun* and *sang*. *Gun* is a wider skirt, and many were gathered, as can be seen in the Goguryeo Tombs complex. In the unified Shilla (676–935), women wore

Chima

a skirt in which the vertical gathers appeared only at the top of the skirt. Loyal women layered two *sang* decorated with gold prints and embroideries. After that, in the period of Goryeo (918–1392), women also wore similar skirts to those in the unified Shilla period. During the Chosun dynasty (1392–1910), the period after Goryeo, women wore chima (skirts) and layered jeogori (top). Women wore different decorations and colors of skirts according to their class or the events. Noble ladies wore many garments under the chima such as *sokgot* or *sokbaji*, which are undertrousers to give the chima volume. Royalty and noble families wore chima decorated with gilt printed patterns or embroideries with colorful threads. For formal events such as a wedding, people wore *daeran* chima and *suran* chima, which are about twelve inches longer and also wider than ordinary chima. In winter, women wore a skirt padded with cotton batting under silk or cotton fabrics. In this period, the jeogori top became shorter, so the skirt's waistline became higher, worn at the high waistline or even under the breasts. In the early and mid-1900s, newly educated women started to wear knee-length skirts with wide flares. After the 1950s, many started to wear Western-style skirts but continued to wear Korean-style chima for special events and holidays.

The Chima in the United States

In the early and mid-1900s, Korean women wore traditional Korean-style skirts and Western skirts in daily life. When they came to the United States, they brought hanbok chima, and as time went on, hanbok chima was worn at special events and on holidays. After the 1980s, many designers presented modernized hanbok and hanbok-inspired designs in the United States. Now people can easily purchase hanbok chima online and in stores in varying ranges of prices and designs in the United States.

Influence and Impact

Hanbok chima was worn as a skirt bottom, with the chima matched to a jeogori (top), which are the main items of women's traditional hanbok attire. In the early and mid-1900s, immigrants and their descendants, workers or students, wore Western skirts in daily life. From that time to the present, their descendants and women who have interest in Korean culture wear hanbok chima for special events such as a wedding day, engagement ceremony, baby's first birthday, sixty-plus birthdays, and on holidays such as New Year's Day and Korean Thanksgiving Day. Women in Korea wear white or black chima at funeral ceremonies. Hanbok chima represents the Korean culture and historical identity of Koreans and their descendants in the United States. Now hanbok chima is modernized and combined with Western and updated designs to create unique ethnic aesthetics.

Many fashion designers are inspired by hanbok chima for its silhouette, fabrics, and colors. For example, hanbok chima was always paired with jeogori, but currently, hanbok chima–inspired dresses are worn by celebrities as unique strapless evening dresses. The beauty of the curvy silhouette, wrapped and tied with a belt, in various natural colors and fabrics, is combined with Western-style modern designs.

See also HANBOK; JEOGORI; NORIGAE
Compare to JILBAB; KANGA; KEBAYA AND SKIRT; KILT; PINAFORE; POLLERA; RUBAHA; SARI

Further Reading

The History of Korean Dictionary. *The Korean Literature Dictionary*. South Korea: The History of Korean Dictionary Publisher, 1998.
Korea Tourism Organization. "The Story of *Hanbok*." http://english.visitkorea.or.kr/enu/CU/CU _EN_8_1_2_1.jsp (accessed November 21, 2012).
Republic of Korea's Ministry of Culture, Sports and Tourism. 2008. "The Beauty of Korean Tradi-tion-*Hanbok*." http://www.mcst.go.kr/english/issue/issueView.jsp?pSeq=960.
Yang, S. *Hanbok: The Art of Korean Clothing*. Korea: Hollym, 1997.
Yoo, H., and M. Kim. *The History of Korean Costume*. Seoul, South Korea: Kyo Mun Sa, 2004.

■ HELEN KOO

CHINESE FLATS

"Chinese flats" is an American-created style term to describe flat, slipper-type shoes that are made out of cloth with a thin sole. Often they have one cloth strap that extends across the instep of the foot. Other synonyms for the same style are "Chinese slippers" and "Chinese Mary Janes." They are very similar in styling to ballerina flats.

History

Out of all ancient civilizations, the Chinese stood out for the wide variety of footwear they developed. A study of Qin Shi Huang's Terra Cotta Army reveals neat stitching on the soles of the clay warriors' feet. This reveals that the Chinese were stitching cloth shoes over two thousand years ago, while most civilizations either eschewed formal foot coverings or only utilized animal skins.

Although the foot binding of the Tang dynasty (618–907 CE) is probably the most well-known example of the practice, it is unlikely that the Chinese flats style is derived from this. Foot binding is a practice where young girls' feet would be bound tightly with bandages. The idea for this body modification was the lotus foot, a foot that was three inches in length. Because of the disfigurement, women who had bound feet would always wear white bandages over their feet, even in intimate moments with their husbands. Lotus shoes were special footwear designed to cover the whole foot, including the whole of the instep.

Given the radical difference in silhouette, it is unlikely that the lotus shoe was the driving inspiration behind the Chinese flat. What did perhaps translate is the exquisite embellishment and embroidery that often adorned lotus shoes. More likely, Chinese flats were derived from Manchu shoes that were developed during the Qing dynasty (1644–1911 CE). It was actually during the Qing dynasty that a royal edict was enacted forbidding the practice of foot binding. Noblewomen of the time displayed their wealth and status by wearing elaborative embroidered *qipao* gowns. These gowns were full and long, extending past a wearer's toes. To keep the hem of their gowns off the ground and clean, Manchu women wore silk slippers that were attached to a tall wooden platform. The strange silhouette of this shoe earned them the nickname of "horse-hoof" shoes. Though these slippers do not have a cross strap, if you remove the slipper portion from the wooden platform, they are closer in styling to Chinese flats. Women in China continued to wear this distinctive style well into the twentieth century, considering them a distinct "Chinese" alternative to the Western-style high heel.

Chinese Flats in the United States

Another possibility for the inspiration for Chinese flats may be found with the attire of Chinese immigrants who came to the United States in the mid-nineteenth and twentieth centuries. Typically, Chinese men would come over first and then work in manual labor, such as building railroads, to save up enough money to bring their families to America. Immigrant families would face economic hardships in the new country. To clothe their families, Chinese women would fashion slipper-type shoes by quilting several layers of cotton for soles and then sewing cloth uppers to the tops of them. This shoe could be easily created with the scraps of other old garments, making them an economical choice for the immigrant family.

Influence and Impact

Since Chinese flats are not actually part of authentic Chinese historical dress, there is no great cultural significance to this style of footwear. Since there are no strong cultural ties, Chinese flats are not worn exclusively by any particular ethnic group. Ironically (considering that the style was primarily an American invention), most Chinese flats are, in fact, made in China. Some people choose them to accessorize traditional Asian and Asian-inspired attire such as the cheongsam and Mandarin collared shirts, but the pairing is aesthetic and not prescribed by any strong cultural traditions.

Depending on style and ornamentation, Chinese flats can range from casual to formal. Plain cotton canvas styles can easily be worn with capris, while silk ones with intricate embroidery are appropriate accessories for formal wear. Although their classic style is acceptable in a wide range of settings, Chinese flats have never truly been considered "high fashion" on the American fashion scene.

See also BOHEMIAN DRESS; CAPRI PANTS
Compare to BIRKENSTOCKS; FLIP-FLOPS (GETA); HUARACHES; JELLIES

Further Reading

Chou, Shengfang. "Manchu Horse-Hoof Shoes: Footwear and Cultural Identity." http://www.vam .ac.uk/content/journals/research-journal/issue-02/manchu-horse-hoof-shoes-footwear-and -cultural-identity (accessed May 28, 2013).

Ministry of Culture. "History of Shoes in China." http://www.chinaculture.org/gb/en_chinaway/2003-09/24/content_29304.htm (accessed May 20, 2013).

Pendergast, Sara, and Tom Pendergast. *Fashion, Costume, and Culture: Clothing, Headwear, Body Decorations, and Footwear through the Ages.* Vol. 2, *Early Cultures across the Globe.* Edited by Sarah Hermse. Detroit, MI: UXL, 2004.

■ LAURA VAN WAARDHUIZEN

CHINESE SILK PAJAMAS

Chinese silk pajamas are a two-piece silk ensemble consisting of a boxy jacket and loose trousers. The jacket can range from high hip to low hip length, when side slits are employed to facilitate movement. The jacket is distinguished by a stand-up mandarin collar, patch pockets, and frog closures down the center front. Frog closures are made by forming fabric or braid into elaborately coiled knot buttons and loops. Sleeves are kimono style and rectangular. The trousers are fitted with a drawstring waistband or elastic. The jacket and trousers are usually the same color and woven in crepe-backed satin or a jacquard pattern of medallions or flowers.

History

Ancient Chinese dress was based on wrapped and draped robes with long flowing sleeves and asymmetrical closures of belts, ties, and knots. After Manchu warriors from northeast China crossed the Great Wall and settled in central China, founding the Qing dynasty (1644 CE–1911 CE), new forms of dress were introduced. Manchu society was based on the horse, and dress was designed for riding, utilizing bifurcated garments and short jackets buttoning down the center front. Wide-legged trousers became a part of both men's and women's dress, worn under their robes, as did short jackets worn over their robes. Trousers and jackets in cotton or hemp were particularly useful for peasant laborers because of their loose fit and range of movement.

Chinese dress in the Qing dynasty was characteristic of imperial societies. Nobility and commoners wore the same styles, but with different fiber content, embellishment, and number of layers. In addition, the production of cloth was not mechanized. All fabrics were created by hand, from cultivation of the fiber to weaving, representing an enormous amount of time, labor, and skill. Because cloth was precious, clothing was styled to use all the fabric. The traditional Chinese jacket and trousers exemplify this economy of dress, creating a boxy silhouette.

Eighteenth- and nineteenth-century European traders found Chinese dress more comfortable than their woolen suits and uniforms and so often adopted indigenous dress for leisure. Traders were equally practical about terminology; many had become familiar with loose cotton trousers worn by men in India, called *pajamas*, which in turn became the term for loose-fitting top and pants in general. With the development of photography in the late nineteenth century, people in the West became familiar with Chinese dress, from the plain cotton jackets and trousers of commoners to the ornate silk brocades of the court. In both cases, the style elements were exotic to Euro-American eyes and crystallized into what the West thought of as "Chinese."

Chinese Silk Pajamas in the United States

Chinese dress arrived in the United States with Chinese immigrants in the nineteenth century. Laborers preferred their familiar loose jackets and pants for work on the pineapple and sugarcane plantations of Hawai'i, in the gold fields of the American West (1848–1855 CE), and on the transcontinental railroad (1863–1869 CE). A hundred years later, Western-themed films and television programs stereotyped the Chinese jacket and trouser (and long braid and conical bamboo hat) into a familiar "coolie" costume.

China experienced much political upheaval in the twentieth century. In 1911, the Qing dynasty was overthrown and a republic was formed, which in turn was replaced in 1949 by the People's Republic of China. Hong Kong remained a British colony until 1997, offering a window into Chinese culture even when the People's Republic was inaccessible. Chinese dress was a regular inspiration to European designers, from French couturier Paul Poiret who introduced frog closures in 1903 to Yves Saint Laurent's *China of My Dreams* collection that received rave reviews in 1994. American designers synthesized what they saw as the most interesting elements of Chinese dress into luxurious versions of the peasant costume in rich shades of flowing silk with exotic motifs, Mandarin collars, and frog closures. The traditional Chinese jacket and trousers were transformed into Chinese silk pajamas.

Meanwhile, books like *The Good Earth* (1931) by Pearl S. Buck, movies like *The Inn of the Sixth Happiness* (1958) starring Ingrid Bergman, and musicals like Rogers and Hammerstein's *Flower Drum Song* (1961) popularized the complexity of Chinese peasant life, bringing the Chinese jacket and trouser aesthetic to a wider audience. Simultaneously, actresses such as Marlene Dietrich and Katherine Hepburn popularized pants as day wear for women, and ethnic styles were initially more acceptable. Foreign aid workers, diplomats, and Christian missionaries, like the traders before them, rediscovered the advantages of indigenous dress and brought ensembles home at the end of their service. During the 1960s counterculture in the United States, hippies donned the dress of peasants worldwide as a statement on antifashion and solidarity with the working class. When relations normalized between China and the United States in the 1970s, Chinese silk pajamas made a comeback and continue as a fashion classic.

In the United States, both men and women wear Chinese silk pajamas as casual evening wear, loungewear, or sleepwear. Because the fabric is a silk satin or a fine jacquard weave, the tactile quality of the ensemble lends itself to romance. Among Chinese-Americans, men wear the suit as ethnic dress for martial arts exhibitions or with family.

Influence and Impact

The term "Chinese silk pajamas" is something of a misnomer because the Chinese themselves do not wear this outfit; the original versions were worn by peasants and made of cotton, and they were work clothes, not sleepwear. Chinese silk pajamas are an example of a process called cultural authentication, in which the people of one culture choose an object from another culture, give it a new name, incorporate the object into everyday life, and transform it into something completely different, often barely recognizable from the donating culture. Cultural authentication describes what happens when humans interact with and get new ideas from each other. Dress is culturally authenticated because it meets a need or satisfies an aesthetic, documenting social change. To Americans, Chinese silk pajamas are quintessentially Chinese. Some Chinese view Chinese-American ethnic dress as cultural appropriation. In any case, it is likely that many Chinese silk pajamas are produced in the mills and factories of the People's Republic of China.

See also CHEONGSAM; CHINESE FLATS
Compare to KIMONO; MAO SUIT; SIRWAL

Further Reading

Garrett, Valery. *Chinese Dress from the Qing Dynasty to the Present.* Tokyo: Tuttle, 2007.

■ SANDRA LEE EVENSON

CHITENGE
See KANGA

CHOGURI
See JEOGORI

CHOLI

A choli is a midriff-baring bodice with short sleeves and open neckline and back, worn with a length of fabric called a sari. The word originates from the Indian word *chola*, meaning "the body." Cholis and saris are the traditional dress of India and have been worn since the tenth century. Cholis in their original form had an open back tied with laces. The choli provided coverage across the front while still keeping the wearer cool in the warm climate of India, Bangladesh, Nepal, Sri Lanka, and Pakistan.

History

In parts of Southern India, bodices were not worn before the nineteenth century even though they can be seen rendered in early Indian paintings. They are generally made from colorful and elaborate fabric embellished with embroidery and beading, including mirrors, patchwork patterns, and rows of small metal beads or shells. In nomadic, tribal communities, wealth was displayed through adornment worn as jewelry or as embellishment on textiles. This practice made cholis a valued example of tribal needlework.

The fabric was cut in simple shapes so that the entire surface could be embellished. The specific design of a choli and the type of embellishment used varied from region to region. The simple design preserved the embellishment, and as the garment wore out, sections were added or removed and repurposed into other garments. This ensured the preservation of skills throughout the community and enabled stitching techniques to be handed down from generation to generation.

In India, a length of sari fabric includes a heavily decorated section of fabric woven into one end specifically made for making up a choli. Cholis made from saris in this way are a sign of a more formal occasion such as weddings. Cholis were made for young girls on the occasion of their marriage. Girls were married as young as thirteen; as a result, cholis that are imported into the United States can be too small for American adult women and must be altered to fit. In daily life, cholis and saris are made of cotton fabrics and are worn in a less formal, mix-and-match way.

The Choli in the United States

Cholis were first seen in the United States in 1893 at the Great Columbian Exposition in Chicago, worn by Baladi/Ghawahzee dancers. In the twentieth century, travel between the United States and India became more common with the development of aviation and extended train travel. As visitors to India and immigrants brought back traditional clothing and textiles to the United States, fashion designers such as Donna Karan, Halston, and Oscar de la Renta began to incorporate decorative elements from the choli into their collections. Beginning in the year 2000, the United States was exposed to the choli through the costumes of the main female characters in popular Bollywood films that focus on Indian culture, dress, and dance.

Influence and Impact

In the twentieth and twenty-first centuries, first-generation Indian immigrants living in the United States still wear the choli as a method of preserving Indian culture. Second- and third-generation Indians living in the United States adopt predominantly Western clothing and wear cholis only for formal, traditional events such as marriages and funerals. Indian brides wear white or brightly colored cholis and saris, elaborately beaded and embroidered in gold for traditional wedding ceremonies.

With the increasing popularity of tribal belly dance in modern culture, the choli was reinvented with three-quarter sleeves, a low, V-shaped neckline, and construction from brightly colored cottons and luxurious stretch velvets. The choli is the first item of costuming that differentiates tribal-style belly dance from the traditional forms of Oriental and Egyptian style belly dance. Oriental/Egyptian dancers perform in an elaborately decorated bra, drawing attention to the body and the sensuality of the dance. By covering more of the torso and arms, tribal dancers are focusing attention on the movement and feminine power of the dance.

The influence of Western culture on India and the recent popularity of Indian dance culture in the United States transformed the choli in both countries. In India, cholis now resemble garments such as tank tops and sports bras worn in the United States. Made in nontraditional fabrics such as lycra and suede, designers are reinterpreting the choli as a more casual, functional garment. In the United States, the opposite is happening: tank tops and bathing-suit tops have adopted the decorative aspects of the choli with embroidery and beading, allowing for a more formal presentation of what was once seen as athletic wear.

See also SARI
Compare to DIRNDL; JEOGORI; PEASANT BLOUSE

Further Reading

Djoumahna, Kajira. *The Tribal Bible*. Santa Rosa, CA: Kajira Djoumahna/Black Sheep Bellydance, 2003.
Fabri, Charles. *Indian Dress*. New Delhi: Disha Books, 1994.
Kumar, Ritu. *Costumes and Textiles of Royal India*. Ritu Kumar, 2006.
Shukla, Pravina. *The Grace of Four Moons: Dress, Adornment, and the Art of the Body in Modern India*. Bloomington: Indiana University Press, 2008.

■ JENNIFER ROTHROCK

CHOLO STYLE

Cholo style is a tough street-culture trend among millennium East Los Angeles Mexican-Americans that features low-slung chinos, bandanas layered low on the head, over-sized layered shirts, and extravagant and colorful religious tattoos. The female version of the trend is similar but often includes flat black shoes, heavy makeup, and long hair. Instead of white T-shirts, females often opt for tank tops that are worn under plaid shirts.

History

The dissemination of the Los Angeles–based cholo style trend was fueled by millennium shifts in demographics leading to Hispanics being the largest minority group in the United States in the first two decades of the twenty-first century. Further solidifying the influence of this trend is the fact that eighteen- to twenty-four-year-olds are the fastest-growing segment within this ethnic group. Radio broadcasts and music videos provide the direct tracks for spread of the trend across the United States. For example a 2003 music video by the heavy-metal band Metallica, "St. Anger," was set in a Los Angeles jail, with focused display of chino pant styles and tattoos.

Cholo Style in the United States

Originating in the Los Angeles area, the cholo trend has spread to other concentrated pockets of Hispanic culture in the United States, including New York City, which has played a large role in disseminating the trend throughout the country.

Influence and Impact

Cholo street style, similar to African-American hip-hop style, was picked up by popular-culture celebrities such as Missy Elliott, Christina Aguilera, and Cher. Bolstered by these celebrity endorsements, retailers like the Gap developed a line of jeans embroidered with Latino-style gothic monogrammed motifs, modeled by Madonna. Social media has added to the influence of the trend with inside trend experts like Reynaldo Berrios, who wrote a book on cholo style, operating a Facebook site. Rodrigo Salazar, the editor in chief of *Urban Latino*, a magazine for young Hispanics, also helps to spread the trend.

See also BANDANA
Compare to JAPANESE STREET FASHION; WESTERN WEAR; ZOOT SUIT

Further Reading

Berrios, R. *Cholo Style: Homies, Homegirls and La Raza*. Port Townsend, WA: Feral House, 2008.

Ferla, R. L. "First Hip-Hop, Now Cholo Style." *New York Times*, November 30, 2003.

■ LUANNE MAYORGA

CHUDDAH

See CHADOR

CHULLU

See CH'ULLU

CH'ULLU (QUECHUA) OR CHULLO (HISPANICIZED)

A chullo is a men's knitted hat or cap with earflaps traditional to indigenous populations of Peru and Bolivia. The term comes from the Quechua language. Chullos are made from natural fibers such as vicuña, alpaca, llama, sheep's wool, and synthetics. Traditionally, chullos are knitted in the round with five straight, double-pointed knitting needles. Stitches include stockinette, garter, and rib stitches, while edges can be crocheted. Colors, patterns, and decorations link chullos to ethnic, village, and community identities. Some more elaborate varieties incorporate buttons, beads, and colorful tassels.

History

The origin of the hat's style is unclear, with some sources suggesting that it is pre-Hispanic and another noting similarity to Basque men's head wear of the fifteenth and sixteenth centuries, specifically the *papahigo* or *mantera*. The *mantera*, in particular, has a similar look to the way Andean men sometimes wear their chullos under a brimmed hat or sombrero. The knitting technique is attributed to the colonial period.

Generally, in Bolivia, men knit chullos, and in Peru, women. Traditionally, fathers knit their child's first chullo. Ideally, the chullo should vary in color and design according to the wearer's age and social status. In the late twentieth and early twenty-first centuries, unmarried Taquilean men were wearing a finely knit hat (ch'ullu *soltero*) with a colored base, white top, and no earflaps. Married Taquilean men, particularly those who had served their communities, wore a red and navy blue striped knit hat with designs along its entire length (*pintay* ch'ullu). Other men wore a style of chullo, known as a ch'ullu *oreja* or *ninri* ch'ullu, that had earflaps and many multicolored rows like a rainbow. Potential in-laws might evaluate a bachelor's chullo for clues to his character because it could give hints as to his patience, planning skills, and creativity. A chullo in the collection of the Haffenreffer Museum of Anthropology, Brown University, Bristol, Rhode Island, attributed to the village of Acora in the state of Puno, Peru, is described as a "virgin cap" that is worn until marriage, when it is replaced by a bowler derby.

Within the Andean context, ethnicity is central to social status and issues of discrimination. The chullo is a form of dress that marks an individual as an Indian or indigenous person, a relational status in the Andes associated with being of a lower class or someone who is crude. A decision not to wear a chullo by an indigenous person can be read as a visible and embodied form of identity transformation. However, it is also adopted as a purposeful political statement of affinity. The chullo, along with other pieces of ethnic or indigenous dress, was worn by the former Peruvian president Alberto Fujimori when visiting Taquile during his reelection bid. The political party Frenatraca (Frente Nacional de Trabajadores y Campesinos) adopted the chullo to symbolize the party's Andean roots and to attract the support of migrants who would have worn these types of caps. The October 2012 cover of *Vogue Brazil* sported a cover model wearing a chullo, much to the delight of Peruvian fashion followers.

The Chullo in the United States

Tourists from the United States are the most common visitors to Peru, and chullos are popular souvenir items that tourists bring home to memorialize their journey because of their ability to index cultural tourism and Andean indigenous dress in a functional souvenir form. Chullos often incorporate iconic Andean images such as llamas, the names of cities like Cuzco, dates, and geometric and human figures.

Influence and Impact

Contemporary chullos are handmade and mass produced, sold on the Internet, in street markets, and in brick-and-mortar stores. The chullo's affordability, light weight, durability, and warmth make it a popular form of casual winter attire; they became associated with snowboarders in the late 2000s. A chullo-style hat, known as the Jayne hat, worn in the TV show *Firefly* by the character Jayne Cobb, has become the unofficial symbol of the show's fandom. *Firefly* ran for only four months in 2002. Since its cancellation, the show's avid fan base began making and selling versions of the Jayne hat on sites such as Etsy. Central to the hat's popularity was its hand production and the symbol of their being "hand knit with love from a fan to a fan." In December 2012, a licensed version of the hat began to be sold online, and the Fox Group started going after unlicensed sellers for copyright infringement. By April 2013, it had become known as the Jayne hat controversy.

A January 21, 2009, *New York Times* editorial noted the visibility of the hat on the streets of New York. The author wondered if the hat's popularity signaled indigenous inclusiveness or globalization similar to seeing baseball caps on the streets of Lima. The chullo has become ubiquitous in the United States because of its reproducibility, innovative colors and designs, practicality, and ability to signify cultural capital and group membership, whether of a fan, an international tourist, or a winter sport enthusiast. While some may denigrate its commonality and describe it as unstylish, others draw upon hand production and group status to elevate the chullo to a visible marker of identity.

See also ALPACA SWEATER; TOQUE
Compare to BERET; BOWLER HAT; FEZ; FLAT CAP; KUFI; RASTA HAT; SIBENIK CAP; TAM-O'-SHANTER

Further Reading

Femenías, Blenda. *Gender and the Boundaries of Dress in Contemporary Peru.* Austin: University of Texas Press, 2005.

Heckman, Andrea M. *Woven Stories: Andean Textiles and Rituals.* Albuquerque: University of New Mexico Press, 2003.

Lecount, Cynthia Gravelle. *Andean Folk Knitting: Traditions and Techniques from Peru and Bolivia.* St. Paul, MN: Dos Tejedoras Fiber Art Publications, 1990.

Shevill, Margot Blum. *Costume as Communication: Ethnographic Costumes and Textiles from Middle America and the Central Andes of South America.* Seattle: University of Washington Press, 1986.

■ BLAIRE O. GAGNON

CHURCH HAT

A church hat is a structured, decorative head covering, worn by women and girls for church and other formal occasions. It is most commonly made of stiff materials like felt, wool, and straw. Church hats tend to be oversized and heavily decorated with netting, feathers, flowers, ribbons, and other brightly colored materials. This hat is much more lavishly decorated than the everyday hat and ranges in style, material, color, and composition.

History

The idea of the church hat originates in the African-American culture from the African tradition of head decoration. A majority of the African slaves being brought to the United States in the seventeenth century were from West Africa. African culture places importance on both the cut and the decorative motif of garments designed for special occasions, including head wear. The practice of adorning the head with elaborate hairstyles or headdresses was an important part of African dress, especially for spiritual ceremonies. Decorating the head for all sexes in the African culture served to show propriety, self-esteem, economic position, social status, and marriage eligibility. This aspect of African culture carried over into the emerging culture of African slaves brought to America.

The Church Hat in the United States

Church Hats

Africans coming to the United States in bondage had to assimilate into the dominant culture, which meant practicing that culture's religion. Covering one's head has its roots in Scripture. According to religious doctrine, the Apostle Paul decreed that "women must cover their heads when they come to worship." Heeding this decree, African-American female house servants would spruce up used, worn hats given to them by plantation owners with feathers, buttons, flowers, and ribbons for church. Field hands often wore hats made of palmetto or straw in order to keep the sun from beating down on them in the fields. These hats could be quickly decorated for church by placing a flower in the brim. Dressing up and looking respectable for church were important qualities for African-American slaves and their owners. Church was the one time they could remove their aprons and drab work attire, neaten up, and show their reverence. By the nineteenth and twentieth centuries, African-American women began making their own money, which allowed them to be independent and invest in hats, clothing, and accessories in order to look their best for church and other special occasions.

Influence and Impact

Church hats are a status symbol among women within the African-American community. Each new hat and a substantial collection of hats symbolized and exhibited material success and triumph over hardships. It is traditional to put on one's newest finery for church. Wearing fancy hats to church carries both a spiritual and cultural significance. While such hats used to be worn for everyday wear, shopping, luncheons, and other occasions, today they are most commonly worn only for Sunday church service. In some communities, church hats are worn by nearly every woman, whereas in others they are quite uncommon.

The head is the crowning glory. A church hat can also be called a crown. Church hats usually match the dress or suit of the wearer. A church hat should never be wider than the shoulders or darker than the wearer's shoes. Never put a hat on the bed; it is bad luck. Church hats for summer should be made of colorful, lightweight straw, reinforced fabric, or sisal. Feathers, ribbons, and chapel-length veils are used to add character and individuality to church hats. Church hats really became visible in the early 1980s during Lady Diana Spencer's wedding to Prince Charles of Wales where guests wore rich, ornamental hats. Philip Treacy and Stephen Jones are milliners who specialize in designing women's high-fashion hats.

See also AFRICAN HEAD WRAP; GELE
Compare to BERET; BOWLER HAT; CHADOR; CLOCHE HAT; TURBAN

Further Reading

Cunningham, Michael, and Craig Marberry. *Crowns*. New York: Doubleday, 2000.

Davies, Kevin. *Philip Treacy by Kevin Davies*. London: Phaidon Press, 2013.

Eicher Bulboz, Joanne, Kim K. P. Johnson, and Mary Ellen Roach-Higgins. *Dress and Identity*. New York: Fairchild, 1995.

Foster, Helen. *"New Raiments of Self": African American Clothing in the Antebellum South*. London: Berg, 1997.

Wares, Lydia. "Dress of the African American Woman in Slavery and in Freedom: 1500–1935." PhD dissertation, Purdue University, 1981.

White, Shane, and Graham White. *African American Expressive Culture: From Its Beginning to the Zoot Suit*. Ithaca, NY: Cornell University Press, 1998.

Williams, Lena. "In Defense of the Church Hat." *New York Times*, May 12, 1996.

■ KAREN J. GILMER

CLOCHE HAT

The cloche hat first appeared in the United States in 1923, at which time it was imported from Paris. During the 1920s, small hats were the height of fashion among stylish women. The close-fitting, bell-shaped cloche hat was commonly pulled down over the forehead and eyes and worn over bobbed haircuts, such as the short Eton crop, or featuring a Marcel wave, which was fashionable in the 1920s. While the materials, colors, and decorations of the cloche varied, the angled placement of the hat served as a unifying feature for the style during the Roaring Twenties in the United States.

History

While there is some debate concerning who originally designed the cloche hat, with its close-fitting and bell-shape design ("cloche" means bell in French), it is widely accepted that French couturiere Gabrielle "Coco" Chanel (1883–1971) is the originator. Widely known for her work in women's wear, Gabrielle Chanel was a milliner before she began her career in couture. In 1910 Chanel opened her first salon at 21 rue Cambon in Paris with the financial backing of her lover, polo player Arthur Capel (1881–1919). Early in her career, Chanel worked predominantly as a fashion leader and created simple shapes that were decorated sparingly in order to complement her aesthetic vision of dress for the modern woman. Chanel achieved financial independence by 1912, when her hats were worn by leading French actresses of the time such as Gabrielle Dorziat (1880–1979).

The Cloche Hat in the United States

The millinery business first began in the United States in the late eighteenth century with Betsy Metcalf (1786–date unknown) of Providence, Rhode Island. Metcalf is widely regarded as one of the first milliners in the United States and began making hats around the age of twelve. Later in life Metcalf set the trend for new straw-weaving techniques, and as a result of her innovative work, she is credited with founding the American millinery industry.

 While milliners flourished on each side of the Atlantic, Parisian milliners who set the style for high-fashion hats led the industry. With Paris leading the way in millinery, designers in the United States worked to establish their personal reputation through innovative design and by dressing notable clientele. Hollywood designer Gilbert Adrian (1903–1959) adopted the original cloche hat design for screen siren Greta Garbo (1905–1990). For the 1929 film *A Woman of Affairs*, Adrian designed the "slouch hat," which was created as a larger-than-normal cloche hat. The slouch hat was worn at an angle and was pulled down well over the forehead. Adrian's alteration of the cloche hat proved influential on hat design for the next decade. Other Hollywood stars, including American actress Clara Bow (1905–1965), adopted the cloche hat in the 1920s. The exposure the cloche hat gained within Hollywood led to an increase in popularity among American women.

Influence and Impact

Due to the boom in popularity of recreational dancing and sports, the 1920s required clothing and accessories that ensured greater freedom of movement. The cloche hat, which has become a classic design in fashion, was developed in the early 1920s and was well suited to the new short hairstyles associated with the modern woman of the time. Cloche hats were made of nearly any material, including straw, felt, satin, velvet, rayon, and cotton. The versatility in fabric enabled women of the 1920s and later decades to wear a cloche hat at any time of the year. Cloches were commonly decorated with a wide variety of materials including appliqué, ribbons, rhinestones, buckles, beads, and decorative clips. These decorative accessories were usually pinned over the ear rather than on the front of the hat. Flapper girls of the 1920s, including the quintessential flapper girl Zelda Fitzgerald, wore the cloche hat for nearly every occasion, whether during the day or for socializing well into the night.

Filtering in and out of fashion since its introduction in the 1910s, the cloche hat has remained a staple in the female wardrobe of the twentieth and twenty-first centuries. Cloche hats can be purchased from today's leading retailers, making the style accessible to a wide range of customers across all income levels. In the twenty-first century, cloche hats commonly feature embellishment along the brim, as was popular during the 1920s and 1930s. Along with the diversity of embellishment that is available, the cloche of the twenty-first century is available in a wide range of colors to suit the quickly changing nature of fashion. Originally introduced by Chanel in the 1910s and later popularized by the flapper girl of the 1920s and Hollywood actresses, the cloche hat has become a wardrobe staple in the twenty-first century.

See also SNOOD; TOQUE
Compare to BERET; BOWLER HAT; CONICAL ASIAN HAT; FEDORA; SLOUCH HAT (AUSTRALIAN)

Further Reading

Blum, Dilys E. "Ahead of Fashion: Hats of the 20th Century." *Philadelphia Museum of Art Bulletin* 89 (1993): 1–48.
Costantino, Maria. *Fashions of a Decade: The 1930s*. New York: Chelsea House, 2007.
Ginsburg, Madeleine. *The Hat: Trends and Traditions*. New York: Barron's Educational Series.
Lillethun, Abbey, and Linda Welters. *The Fashion Reader*. 2nd ed. New York: Berg, 2011.

■ JESSICA SCHWARTZ

CLOGS

Clogs are a standard type of footwear comprised of a thick, hard wooden or composite sole and either a wooden, leather, or cloth upper. They are used as a hardy, protective layer between the wearer's feet or daintier shoes and rough, flooded roads or bad weather. Wooden shoes carved as one are traditionally associated with peasant classes and prostitutes, some of whom were required by law to wear them. Nobility in the Middle Ages wore a more refined style with decorative cloth uppers or leather straps to protect nicer shoes. Clogs have been worn for centuries, with roots in Africa and Asia, but those used in America today evolved from the French *sabot*, Italian *zoccolo*, and Scandinavian *träsko*.

History

Wooden clogs carved as one solid shoe became popular in Scandinavia from either the late seventeenth or early eighteenth century, although Swedish farmers were wearing an all-leather version from the early seventeenth century. Farmers in the south of Sweden and Finland wore wooden clogs that were adapted from those worn in continental European countries, such as the Netherlands (which is commonly associated with solid wooden clogs today). The region of Skåne, in southern Sweden, is closest to the continent (now sharing a bridge with Copenhagen, Denmark, which shares a border with the Netherlands), which might be why the use of wooden clogs was most prevalent there. Some Swedish women's clogs became finely shaped and painted with traditional designs, and men's were adapted with wire or metal at the instep for reinforcement. In Scandinavia and England in the early nineteenth century, innovators developed basic overshoe-style clogs that used springs and hinges across the tread to make walking easier, and an ankle strap to secure it to the foot. This advancement caught on quickly and was popular until more substantial everyday footwear became popular in the 1850s, obviating the need for overshoes. Clogs were also a part of traditional regional dress in Scandinavia in the nineteenth and early twentieth centuries, often worn with a work outfit (as opposed to high holiday dress).

The use of wooden or wooden-soled clogs in Europe increased throughout the nineteenth century, probably because wood was cheaper than leather, and making these simple shoes did not require a shoemaker's skills. The growing population, especially in the countryside, was encouraged by civic leaders to adopt the wooden clog. Norwegian fishermen wore clog boots with leather legs nailed on, and many Norwegian examples from the late nineteenth century have a high toe spring. One extant Finnish clog from the early twentieth century even features buttons painted on the upper, in imitation of the button-up boots and shoes that were popular in Europe at the time.

Clogs in the United States

Clogs made their way to America through waves of immigration in the late nineteenth century. Scandinavian immigrants had been arriving in America since the 1820s, and many settled in midwestern states with a climate much like that of their native lands. Although identifiably ethnic and rural—the antithesis of American style—wooden clogs were well adapted to life in the cold, snowy northern midwestern states of America.

Perhaps for comfort or due to increased circumstances, clogs of leather uppers nailed or stapled to wooden soles became more common than solid wooden versions in twentieth-century Sweden. In the 1960s and 1970s, interest in Scandinavian design made Swedish-built clogs extremely popular in America, most commonly in a mule style open at the heel with a thin rubber sole reinforcement to dampen the noise. Along with Earth shoes and Frye boots, wearing clogs imported from Sweden implied a relaxed attitude, a desire for comfort, and an interest in natural materials; some were even made with cork bottoms and wool or leather uppers, such as German label Birkenstock.

Influence and Impact

At the turn of the twenty-first century, Scandinavian clogs made a comeback, with modern, fashionable takes on the traditional wood bottom and leather upper; the brand Swedish Hasbeens produced a range of styles, sometimes in outlandish colors such as neons and silver. Dansko makes composite-soled clogs with leather uppers in a range of modern styles, popular with cooks, hospital employees, and others who work on their feet.

Crocs are an even lighter version, made of extremely light foam; these are also popular with restaurant employees, and chef Mario Batali (b. 1960) is famous for his orange pairs.

See also BIRKENSTOCKS
Compare to CHINESE FLATS; HUARACHES; JELLIES; MOCCASINS

Further Reading

Riello, Giorgio, and Peter McNeil, eds. *Shoes: A History from Sandals to Sneakers*. Oxford: Berg, 2006.
Swann, June. *History of Footwear in Norway, Sweden and Finland*. Stockholm: Kungl. Vitterhets Historie och Antikvitets Akademien, 2001.
Vigeon, Evelyn. "Clogs or Wooden-Soled Shoes." *Costume* 11 (1977): 1–27.

■ ARIANNA E. FUNK

CLOTH HAT
See FLAT CAP

CONCHO BELT

A concho is a circular or oval decorative object most often made of silver and uniform in design. Conchos are recognizable by their iconographic scalloped edges, stamped detail, and turquoise inlays. Navajo Indians began making conchos during the last quarter of the nineteenth century and affixed them to belts in groupings. Prided for their adornment as well as their monetary value, conchos have become nearly synonymous with the south-western region of the United States.

History

The concho is a blend of Native American and Spanish Mexican cultures and crafts-manship. For hundreds of years, Native American Indians exchanged exotic commodities along elaborate trading routes that reached far across the continent. European settlers continued trading along these routes, bringing with them even more sophisticated objects from foreign places. European-made silver brooches found their way to Plains Indians who fashioned them into elaborate hairpins. These disc-like buttons were strung, several at a time, together and onto cloth, horsehair, or leather cords. The lengthy hair plates were attached to the nape of the neck, often reaching the floor or draped over the shoulder when seated. One theory about the concho's origin is that through trade or warring raids, the Navajo Indians acquired the hair plates; inspired, they began to create their own.

The Concho in the United States

Believed to be the first Navajo silversmith, Chief Atsidi Sani (c. 1830–c. 1870) shared this skill with his sons and later, while imprisoned at Bosque Redondo (1863–1868), with other Navajo tribesmen. Scholars debate whether to credit Sani's teachings to Mexican blacksmiths, silversmiths, or leatherworkers. Nevertheless, it is undeniable that silversmith-ing quickly became an integral part of the Navajo lifestyle.

Influence and Impact

By the 1870s, the Navajo smiths were melting Mexican and U.S. silver dollar coins to create silver discs. Using primitive tools, the early smiths patiently created detailed filings and scalloped edges on the conchos. They incorporated leather-stamping tools to adorn the center of the concho, employing symbols that were reminiscent of the ornate ironwork created by Mexican blacksmiths. In the center of each concho the craftsman cut two triangles. These cutouts or "diamond slots" allowed the conchos to be strung with fabric or leather bands, thus creating the concho belt. Though no two craftsmen shared the same technique, by the end of the nineteenth century Navajo smiths were refining their skills. New soldering practices allowed copper loops to be attached to the back side of the concho, freeing space for even more intricate embellishment.

The jewelry, which could be quite valuable, was not just for adornment. Early button-like conchos could be removed from the belt and traded for goods and services or to secure credit. Silversmithing and the creation of conchos as well as other jewelry significantly contributed to the evolution of a new economy in the Navajo tribes region. After the U.S. conquest, these young men, who might have otherwise become warring raiders, instead became sheepherders and practiced the prestigiously regarded silversmithing in their spare time. The turn of the twentieth century brought with it a westerly expanded railroad and subsequently led to an increase in tourism. A lighter-weight version of the concho and silver jewelry was produced for tourist consumption. Receiving popular acclaim, the Navajo silversmiths began to experiment with even greater variations in the design of the concho, eventually incorporating turquoise stones, buckles, and decorative spacers such as the butterfly spacer. Though they are most famously associated with the concho, Navajo Indians are not the only southwestern tribe to engage in the craft of silversmithing. The Hopi and the Zuni tribes also create concho belts, and do so each with their own distinct style.

During the late 1940s, Millicent Rogers (1902–1953), Standard Oil heiress and mid-century style icon, brought attention to southwestern style when she moved to Taos, New Mexico. Rogers purportedly traded her high-fashion couture garments, donating them to the Brooklyn Museum, for the native dress and jewelry of the region. Upon her death, she asked that she be buried in her beloved Navajo concho belt. The remainder of her extensive jewelry, garments, and artifacts would go on to become part of the founding collection for the Millicent Rogers Museum. When the hippie culture of the 1960s and 1970s embraced Native American clothing, the concho belt again came into vogue. Two notable celebrities, often seen depicted in their concho belts, Jim Morrison (1943–1971) and Cher (1946–), are credited with popularizing Navajo jewelry and helping to solidify the association of concho belts with free-spirited outsiders and rock-and-rollers. On the cusp of the 1980s the concho belt made a reappearance, this time as a highly fashionable "it" accessory sent down the runway by influential and decidedly American designers such as Ralph Lauren (1939–) and Calvin Klein (1942–). These successful fashion collections, ultimately to become known as Santa Fe style, focused on western and southwestern styles and embodied the pioneer spirit of the American culture. Appealing to a wide though often affluent audience, the concho belt—an intrinsic part of the Santa Fe style—made a lasting impression on fashion history as an iconic part of the traditional American style.

The concho belt, which may not have begun as an indigenous art form, has developed into an essential element of the Navajo peoples of the Southwest, vital not only to their local economy but also to the development and pride of their artisans. Similarly, the concho belt has been appropriated into traditional American fashion. The concho belt continues to be associated with the free, bohemian, and pioneering lifestyle associated with the American Southwest that has come to symbolize the classic and iconic American tradition.

See also BOLO TIE; ETHNIC JEWELRY; MOCCASINS; WESTERN WEAR
Compare to BOHEMIAN DRESS; BRICOLAGE; PORCUPINE ROACH; POWWOW ACCESSORIES

Further Reading

Frank, Larry, and Millard J. Holbrook. *Indian Silver Jewelry of the Southwest, 1868–1930.* Boston: New York Graphic Society, 1978.
Matthews, Washington. "Navajo Silversmiths." *Annual Report of the Bureau of Ethnology*, 1883.

■ ERICA SUZANNE SCOTT

CONICAL ASIAN HAT

The conical Asian hat is a wide cone with the point at the top of the wearer's head and the sides of the cone spreading out from the head, creating shade for the face and neck. The hat has a ribbon, string, or piece of silk fabric to tie under the chin to keep it on the head. If for fieldwork or everyday wear, it is made of natural materials such as palm leaves, rattan, bamboo, or other plant material. They can also be colored, stitched with poetic verses, bound with colored threads, or decorated with beading. Hats made for the Western market are also made in silk or imitation silk fabrics.

History

The conical hat can be found for work and everyday wear throughout the histories of eastern and southern Asian countries including Vietnam, China, Taiwan, Korea, Cambodia, Indonesia, Japan, and the Philippines. Most often it is found on farmers or women, its shape useful for keeping the heat of the sun or rainfall off the wearer's head. The hat style came to the United States with Chinese immigrants who came to work on the transcontinental railroad in the mid-nineteenth century. Until the twentieth century, these hats remained with first-generation Southeast Asian immigrants. In the late 1930s and early 1940s, couture designer Valentina Schlee began and frequently used the hat shape for ensembles she created.

Conical Asian Hat

Over the next several years into the twenty-first century, the hat occasionally made an appearance in high-fashion shows.

The Conical Asian Hat in the United States

The original hats that came with Chinese immigrants in the mid-nineteenth century remained within Chinese and other Southeast Asian cultural groups, separate from the mainstream American culture well into the twentieth century. Valentina, an émigré Russian actress turned fashion designer, in the 1930s appropriated the hat design and wore it with her daytime creations for herself and her clients through the early 1950s. Her conical hats were made of fabrics that complemented her suit ensembles. In 2011, clothing company American Apparel offered the hats as casual wear for its customer base.

Influence and Impact

During depressed economic times in the later nineteenth century in the United States, Chinese immigrants were more often used as cheaper labor than the American-born Europeans. The name "coolie," a corruption of a Hindu or Chinese word referring to hired laborers or slave workers, was used as a derogatory term in political cartoons to express frustration with the use of cheap Chinese labor. Though the cartoon coolie was shown without his hat to display his bald head and a single braid, the actual Chinese immigrants wore the conical hats for their work outside. Besides calling the hats coolie hats, those who live in Western culture also describe the hats as "paddy hats" or "rice hats," due to the fact that images of Asians wearing them usually depict farmers in rice fields. In Western culture, the visual image of a person wearing this hat is a cultural shorthand to indicate an Asian. Asian-Americans consider the term "coolie hat" and the use of the hat in Asian depictions offensive. It is a reminder of impoverished farm laborers in the countries they left to immigrate to the United States. After the American Apparel company offered it for sale, much online debate ensued about the fact that wearing it as a fashion statement rather than as a protective piece of clothing could be construed as offensive and racist.

Asian influences on the haute couture of Western culture have been cycling in and out since the nineteenth century. Valentina brought the hat shape itself to her fashion lines in the late 1930s and early 1940s. Christian Dior used the same hat shape with his New Look in the late 1940s. The hats were rendered in the fashion fabrics of the ensembles with which they were paired. The conical hat in natural materials has continued to be sold as a practical covering in gardening catalogs in the late twentieth and early twenty-first centuries. With the American Apparel offering, the company attempted to make it part of mainstream American fashion, but its sale was derided as offensive by Asian-American people.

See also CHEONGSAM; CHINESE FLATS; CHINESE SILK PAJAMAS; HANFU CHINESE ROBES; MAO SUIT
Compare to FEZ; FLAT CAP; RASTA HAT; TAQIYA; TOQUE; TURBAN

Further Reading

"American Apparel's 'Conical Asian Hat'—Nothing New." *Forbes*. http://www.forbes.com/sites/raquellaneri/2011/08/01/american-apparels-conical-asian-hat-nothing-new (accessed April 25, 2013).

Yêu anh vn. "Non La—Conical Hat." http://www.yeuanhvan.com/culture/1374-non-la-conical-hat (accessed May 28, 2013).

Yohannan, Kohle. *Valentina: American Couture and the Cult of Celebrity*. New York: Rizzoli, 2009.

■ JENNIFER VAN HAAFTEN

COOLIE HAT

See CONICAL ASIAN HAT

COONSKIN CAP

The coonskin cap is a fur or fur-like item of head wear. As the name suggests, the cap, which is designed to fit snugly on the head from the ears upward, is generally made from the skin and fur taken from a raccoon, a creature inhabiting North America in substantial numbers. The cap is sewn together from the body pelt of the animal in such a way as to envelop the head of the wearer. The fur of the pelt faces externally. Often, but not always, the deboned animal's tail is attached to the rear of the hat for the purpose of embellishment. Another option includes the deboned animal's face on the front portion of the cap. Similar caps can be made from the pelts of other creatures, such as the fox or rabbit, but as the name suggests, the raccoon provides the traditional fur of choice. Manufactured fibers have also been used to create a synthetic pelt for less expensive, more politically correct versions of the cap.

History

The indigenous people of North America used animal pelts and skins for a variety of purposes, including apparel. Buckskin breaches and tunics, for example, were closely associated with indigenous apparel. The initial use of the coonskin cap was also believed to originate among native inhabitants of the land. Raccoons were quite plentiful, and the pelt adapted quite nicely to the size of a human's head.

The Coonskin Cap in the United States

The coonskin cap preexisted the arrival of Europeans to North America. As a result of interaction, apparel of the indigenous inhabitants was adapted by those pioneering and exploring the continent for practical reasons, as the skins and fur of animals was an available resource in the frontier areas of the continent.

Influence and Impact

There is documentation from histories of locations including Pennsylvania, Virginia, Kentucky, Tennessee, and Florida indicating that early European inhabitants of those regions

Coonskin Cap

adopted the coonskin cap as head wear. In fact, the coonskin cap became a symbol of frontier exploration in North America, most likely as a result of Meriwether Lewis wearing one during his famous expedition of discovery with William Clark. Though popular culture associates the cap with Daniel Boone, historical records suggest he eschewed that form of head wear. When serving as ambassador to France, Benjamin Franklin arrived wearing a coonskin cap, which served as a national symbol for the newly emerged frontier nation. Without a doubt, the individual with whom the coonskin cap is most associated in the United States was Davy Crocket, frontiersman, legendary folk hero, and three-time congressman who perished at the Alamo, one of the most symbolically laden conflicts in the history of Texas and the nation. Though the coonskin cap was not worn by Crockett as part of his standard attire, he adapted it to augment his legendary status following James Kirke Paulding's *The Lion of the West*, a play in which the "Crockett" character wore the furry cap. Ironically the play was a satire lampooning Crockett's frontier mythology.

The intersection of frontier culture, the legendary "lost cause" battle for the Alamo, and folk hero Davy Crockett is significant and in many ways embodies several important mythologies underpinning the founding of the United States. Symbolically, the coonskin cap is embedded in that intersection simultaneously as symbolic frontier attire and head wear worn by Davy Crockett at the Alamo. From a cultural and historical standpoint, it is very important to note that the three-hour serial adventures of the life of Davy Crockett, starring Fess Parker as Crockett on the Disney television show in 1954 and 1955, exploded the Crockett/coonskin cap mythology into the national consciousness of the American public, particularly young male baby boomers of the time. The TV show, entitled *Davy Crockett, King of the Wild Frontier*, created a huge wave of interest in the Crockett/Alamo mythology. Sales of Davy Crockett T-shirts, toy muskets, lunch boxes, and most notably coonskin caps reached fad levels. At its peak, the coonskin cap, licensed by Disney, sold five thousand units per day. As with all fads, sales of coonskin caps to young Crockett admirers diminished fairly rapidly; however, the cap remains today as an enduring symbol of freedom and frontier, two highly held values in the U.S. national consciousness. Both authentic and synthetic versions of the coonskin cap are still available from a variety of vendors in the United States.

See also BUCKSKIN; WESTERN WEAR
Compare to BOWLER HAT; SLOUCH HAT (AUSTRALIAN)

Further Reading

Anderson, Paul. *The Davy Crockett Craze: A Look at the 1950's Phenomenon and Davy Crockett Collectibles*. Darien, CT: R & G Productions, 1996.
George-Warren, Holly. *How the West Was Worn*. New York: Harry N. Abrams, 2001.
Thompson, Frank. *The Alamo: A Cultural History*. New York: Taylor Trade, 2001.

■ MITCHELL D. STRAUSS

CORSET

A corset is a garment or accessory worn around the midsection that constricts the body in some way.

History

The earliest traces of the corset can be found in Minoan statues from 1550 BCE, and it was not until over three thousand years later that corsets began to be worn in Europe. In the early fifteenth century, paintings and sculptures from France, Germany, and Flanders depict women in gowns with fitted, small waists and abdomens, reflecting a restrictive undergarment to ensure the shape. At the birth of the Renaissance in sixteenth-century Italy, binding the midsection was a requirement for both men's and women's dress, as evidenced in the man's doublet and the woman's corset. Catherine de Medici introduced the corset to the French court from Italy when she wed Henry II, and corsets remained a mainstay of the upper-class woman's wardrobe until the twentieth century.

The early corsets were made from a stiff canvas material and reinforced vertically by stays made from iron and whalebone. The upper edge of the corset ranged from covering the bust to cupping under the breasts, and the lower edge might have stopped at the waist, extended to below the hip, or remained waist height in the back and plunged into a deep V in the front. Regardless of the style, the purpose of the corset was to restrain the body as much as possible. Over the centuries, women have endured binding their midsection in the pursuit of the ideal twenty-, eighteen-, or even sixteen-inch waist. Wearing tightly laced corsets reflected the woman's socioeconomic status, as it was impossible to perform manual labor while wearing this restrictive device. The resulting social/psychological environment created a troubling paradox. Although doctors warned women of the dangers associated with corseting and tight lacing, women continued to wear corsets despite the resulting health problems.

It was not until the 1900s, when French designer Paul Poiret shifted the focus from the waist to the ankle that the corset began to lose favor. The ensuing fashion change of the 1920s where desire for the curvaceous female body was replaced by a boxy, boyish "*garçonne*" silhouette signified the end of tightly laced steel-ribbed or whalebone corsets as a staple in the upper-class woman's wardrobe. Even when styles again focused on a tiny waist in the 1930s and 1950s, the corsets had become softer, lighter, and more flexible, incorporating textile innovations such as elastic, plastic boning, and knit fabrics. In the mid-twentieth century, designers in the French haute couture, such as Mme. Grès, began integrating the support structure directly into evening gowns, eliminating the need for a restrictive undergarment. From the punk subculture in 1970s London, designer Vivienne Westwood's interest in vintage clothing brought the Victorian corset back into the fashion limelight, and by the early 1980s the corset was transformed from an undergarment to an outer garment, sometimes called a camisole or a bustier.

The Corset in the United States

Because fashion trends up to the mid-twentieth century came to the United States primarily from France, women in the United States wore the corset as an undergarment in the same manner as described above.

Influence and Impact

American pop culture contributed significantly to global acceptance of wearing the corset as an outer garment when French designer Jean Paul Gaultier created a cone-busted corset for singer/celebrity Madonna during her 1993 Blonde Ambition tour. Widespread acceptance of wearing a corset as an outer garment paved the way for companies like Victoria's Secret and Frederick's of Hollywood to market lingerie as outerwear, blurring the lines between product categories.

As can be seen in department stores today, the tradition of compressing the body with corsets has evolved to include corsets worn either as under- or overgarments, as well as undergarments that are said to be "body slimmers" that are softer than the traditional corset but serve as restrictive shaping garments. While socioeconomic status in the early twenty-first century is not as directly reflected by wearing a corset as at the dawn of the twentieth century, women's self-image and confidence can certainly be subtly boosted by purchasing modern body shapers.

See also FAJA
Compare to BOHEMIAN DRESS; CHEMISE; GYPSY SKIRT

Further Reading

Fontanel, B. *Support and Seduction: The History of Corsets and Bras.* New York: Abradale Press, 2001.
Larson, C. "Of Corset Matters." *Washington Monthly* 34 (2002): 49–50.
Ouellette, L. "Cracking the Dress Code." *Women's Review of Books* 11, no. 8 (1994): 21–22.
Steele, V. *The Corset: A Cultural History.* New Haven, CT: Yale University Press, 2001.

■ MARY RUPPERT-STROESCU

CUBAN RUMBA DRESS
See RUMBA DRESS

D

DASHIKI

A dashiki is a loose-fitting, pullover, T-shaped shirt traditionally worn by men in East and West Africa. The dashiki is hip length, collarless, and often made with geometric embroidery along the neck. The word "dashiki" is derived from the Yoruba word for a similar style of garment called a *dansiki*, which means a short-sleeved work shirt for men. A dashiki is generally made of African print brocade, silk, lace, suiting, or cotton fabrics. The dashiki is usually worn with simple drawstring pants, or more currently it can be paired with jeans or linen pants. The ankle-length version, worn by both men and women, is referred to as a caftan.

History

The dashiki originated in West and East Africa as a loose-fitting shirt that was light enough to provide protection from the African sun and heat. Versions of dashikis have been found in burial mounds in Mali and date back to the twelfth and thirteenth centuries. The original garment was worn by both men and women and resembled the thawb or *qamis* worn by the Arab traders who brought Islam to West Africa. This is probable evidence of the Islamic origin of the dashiki.

Like all African textiles, the colors and symbols of the traditional dashiki are also culturally significant. Colors such as gold and yellow represent wealth and royalty, while colors such as white are reserved for weddings and religious events because of the symbolic association with purification.

The Dashiki in the United States

The dashiki shirt was brought to the United States by returning Peace Corps volunteers who served in West Africa during the 1960s, and there were also many African diplomats and dignitaries photographed in the 1960s wearing the colorful garment. During the civil rights movement of the 1960s, Afrocentric fashion, such as the dashiki, became an expression of black identity, cultural struggles, and nationalism. The dashiki became a central form of visual symbolism of the racial suppression against which black students were fighting in the 1960s.

Dashikis first started selling in 1967 from a two-room store in Harlem and quickly became a fashion item for men and women of all races in brightly colored cotton fabrics with modern patterns framing the neckline. While more militant individuals adopted the iconic black uniform of the Black Panthers, those members of the nonviolent black power movements adopted the traditional African clothing to promote racial pride and ethnic cohesion. However, some Black Panther men, such as Stokely Carmichael, were known to wear the dashiki as an expression of Afrocentricity in addition to the iconic black berets, black turtlenecks, and black leather jackets.

The dashiki in the United States has historically served as a significant symbol of black pride. Throughout the 1960s, the dashiki was part of the black power uniform. Political activists and celebrities alike adopted the symbolic garment to fashion a distinct ethnic look. Sammy Davis Jr., Stevie Wonder, and Putney Swope of *Soul Train* are just a few influential African-Americans who used the dashiki as a marker of their black identity.

About the same time as the black movement was starting, the "hippie" movement was becoming popular. Hippies and other white Americans soon began wearing the dashiki because they were drawn to the vibrant colors and embroidery, the loose fit, and the casual swapping of the top between both sexes.

In the 1960s, designers were looking everywhere for inspiration, including traditional ethnic clothing such as Afrocentric dress. In 1969, Simplicity Pattern 8177 was released (a man's tunic or woman's minidress) resembling a dashiki, but the drawings were of a white man and woman.

Influence and Impact

Today, wearing Afrocentric fashion such as the dashiki reflects African identity and black identity. Unlike the 1960s countercultural movement of the hippies, the dashiki is reserved more for ceremonial purposes. The dashiki is most visible during Black History Month in February or in celebrations of Kwanzaa. However, there are some individuals who choose to wear the dashiki as nonceremonial attire, but they have been known to be ridiculed and even discriminated against for looking "too ethnic" in the workplace.

Unfortunately, the dashiki has also become a cliché element of "African costumes" in costume shops and online costumer retailers for Halloween paired with exaggerated afros and beaded jewelry.

See also BERET; BOUBOU; CAFTAN; KUFI; THAWB
Compare to ALOHA SHIRT (HAWAI'IAN SHIRT); BARONG TAGALOG; OXFORD SHIRT; PONCHO

Further Reading

Joseph, Peniel E. "Dashikis and Democracy: Black Studies, Student Activism, and the Black Power Movement." *Journal of African American History* 88, no. 2 (2003): 182–203.
Lewis, VanDyk. "Afrocentric Fashion." In *The Berg Companion to Fashion*, edited by Valerie Steele, 14–17. Oxford: Berg, 2010.

■ JESSICA STRÜBEL

DENIM
See WESTERN WEAR

DERAA
See BOUBOU

DERBY HAT
See BOWLER HAT

DIRNDL

The word "dirndl" is the description for a peasant or bourgeois girl in South Germany or Austria. In fashion it is used as a description for a woman's folk dress that consists of a blouse, a full skirt, a laced-up bodice, and a separate apron.

The dirndl blouse comes in hundreds of different cuts; has short, puffed, or long sleeves; features different necklines; and ends above the waist. The skirt starts usually at the waist or lower and has various lengths depending on the dirndl type or current fashion trends. The bodice has a low or high, square or round neckline and is often decorated with buttons, hucks, or ribbons. The apron is nowadays a decorative item, formerly worn to protect the dress. It comes in simple fabrics for everyday use or for festive occasions with elegant fabrics. When tying the knot of the apron, the loop on the right side symbolizes that the wearer is engaged or married, the left side that she is available, the front side that she is a virgin, and the back side that she is a widow.

Different combinations of the dirndl components make up the traditional dirndl style, and the combination of elements reflects regional affiliation and the social class of the wearer. The fashion or fantasy dirndl comes in different styles, colors, materials, or patterns, reflecting trends of the locale and time period.

History

Dirndl style originally developed as a part of valley, regional, and local folk dresses developed in South Germany and Austria between the mid-eighteenth and nineteenth centuries. With the support of Emperor Franz Joseph, a new fashion trend was born: the aristocracy in Europe wore dirndls and lederhosen as country clothing during their summer vacation. The dirndl became fashionable in urban settings and separated itself from being exclusively considered a peasant-style dress. The international popularity of the dirndl was supported by the wearing of the costume during performances and society events at the Salzburg Festival in the 1920s, the Olympic Winter Games in Garmisch

Dirndl

in 1936, and the World Exhibition in Paris in 1937. Its international reputation was also enhanced by the worldwide success of the operetta *Weisses Roessl* in the early 1930s.

The Dirndl in the United States

Based on international recognition of the dirndl and the American popularity of the Johanna Spyri novel *Heidi*, the first branch office of the Austrian dirndl designer and manufacturer Lanz Trachtenmode opened in Los Angeles in 1935. Three years later the dirndl was one of the main features of Paris fashion collections. On the Paris runways the dirndl served as an inspirational design for U.S.-based fashion designers, including perhaps most significantly Claire McCardell. The dirndl fashion collections also attracted attention in the theater world. Austrian styles were the focus of Hollywood musicals in 1939. During World War II, immigrants from Europe brought their dirndls to America as a reminder of their home. The dirndl gained further popularity in the 1950s with the support of foreign travels of Austrian folk groups to the United States and the help of fashion catalogs featuring dirndl collections.

Around twenty years later, the dirndl again was spotlighted and gained international publicity with the Broadway musical and Hollywood movie *The Sound of Music*, including the rich history of the Trapp family who dressed in traditional Austrian dirndls. Also, Billy Wilder's movie *A Foreign Affair* and Carol Reed's *The Third Man* spread the worldwide popularity of the dirndl dress. Folklore-inspired fashion became a fashion trend in the 1970s, especially following the Diana Vreeland *Habsburger* exhibition in 1979 at the New York Metropolitan Museum, which inspired fashion designers around the world.

Influence and Impact

American immigrants and their descendants from Austria and Germany wear the dirndl in the traditional way with the traditional styling, color, pattern, and fabrics. It is worn at important points in life-cycle rituals: birth, puberty, marriage, and death. The traditional dirndl style has also been adapted for use by theme-based resorts, taverns, and restaurants. Bavarian theme towns (e.g., Little Bavaria in Frankenmuth, Michigan), Bavarian lodges in ski resorts, Oktoberfest, and beer gardens are places where the modern dirndl is worn by employees and visitors. The cultural meaning is based on this traditional dress style's ability to function symbolically to strengthen individual and group identity, emphasize togetherness, provide community education, and espouse belief and ideology.

More broadly the dirndl silhouette evolved from being a peasant dress in South Germany and Austria to a modern-day fashion dress, a fashion evergreen. It signals naturalness, simplicity, and authenticity and is even a genuine big-city advertising and marketing tool. The versatility guarantees the longevity of the dirndl. Folklore and country styles regularly cycle in and out of prêt-à-porter fashion. Furthermore, the influence and availability of international media in the form of movies, musicals, operettas, and print support the continued dissemination of the dirndl as a style classic.

See also APRON; PEASANT BLOUSE; PINAFORE
Compare to BROOMSTICK SKIRT; CH'ULLU; LEDERHOSEN; POLLERA

Further Reading

Frenkel, Stephen, and Judy Walton. "Bavarian Leavenworth and the Symbolic Economy of a Theme Town." *Geographical Review* 90, no. 4 (October 2000): 559–84.

Graml, Gundolf. "The Hills Are Alive . . . : Sound of Music Tourism and the Performative Construction of Places." *Women in German Yearbook* 21 (2005): 192–214.

Hollmer, Heide, and Kathrin Hollmer. *Dirndl: Trends, Traditionen, Philosophie, Pop, Stil, Styling.* Berlin: Edition ebersback, 2011.

Peine, Sheila. *Embroidered Textiles: A World Guide to Traditional Patterns.* London: Thames & Hudson, 2010.

Rieff Anawalt, Patricia. *The Worldwide History of Dress.* London: Thames & Hudson, 2007.

Tostmann, Gexi. *The Dirndl: Austrian National Fashion.* Vienna: Panorama, 1990.

■ SILKE HAGAN-JURKOWITSCH

DJELLABA

The traditional djellaba is a tubular-shaped tunic that falls loosely from the shoulder to the ankle, with long sleeves and a large hood.

History

The specific time frame of the origin of the djellaba has not been precisely documented; however, descriptions of the garment date back to ancient times. In the seventh-century writings of the Qu'ran, the djellaba is specifically mentioned in reference to recommended clothing for women. Considered by some to be the precursor to the Turkish caftan, the djellaba is commonly associated with countries in North Africa and is worn by both men and women; however the djellaba can be seen worn by Arab-Islamic people around the world. The traditional man's djellaba is a long and homespun woolen cloak that includes a hood. There can be variation in the woven pattern, but a vertical stripe is a dominating characteristic. The djellaba has various symbolic functions and yields complex meaning in both secular and religious settings. During World War II, Moroccan tribesmen, known as the Goumiers, wore cloth turbans and djellabas. The djellaba was the main distinct clothing piece that distinguished a man as a Goumier. In the late twentieth century, Moroccan djellabas for women have reflected diverse aesthetic influences through the addition of embellishments such as embroidery, traditional Moroccan braided trim, and variations in sleeve depth, shape, and length. Initially these adaptations from the simple, traditional djellaba may have been prompted by a sense of national pride to demonstrate the talent of Moroccan craftsmen and women; however, djellaba production today clearly shows the influence of the Western concept of fashion, where specific styles are popular for short periods of time.

The Djellaba in the United States

The djellaba made its way into the United States during the mid-twentieth century, introduced first through film. Peter O'Toole was seen wearing the white djellaba in the film *Lawrence of Arabia* during the 1960s, which told the story of T. E. Lawrence and his involvement with the Arabs during World War I. In addition, film star Elizabeth Taylor wore a djellaba in the film *Boom* in 1968. The youth culture in the 1960s was influenced by celebrity musicians such as the Beatles to express individuality through ethnic dress. A sure sign that the djellaba was embraced by the mainstream consumer is the fact that McCall's pattern company included a djellaba pattern in their selection in 1967, providing the home sewer with access to this traditional garment.

The popularity, in the 1970s, of simple maxi-length tunic shapes embellished around the neckline clearly reflected the influence of the djellaba as well. Characters in the 1977 box office hit *Star Wars* wore the djellaba and familiarized an entire generation with the concept of wearing a long rough-hewn tunic with a hood in a desert-like environment. The effect of the djellaba on popular fashion continued, and in the latter part of the twentieth century a clear revival of the djellaba's influence can be seen on the global fashion stage. In 1995, Rifat Ozbek offered djellaba-inspired looks on the runway shows for Christian Lacroix. Long sleeveless versions floated over mini hipster skirts and body-conscious pants. A mini-djellaba was veiled in a transparent nylon slip, and a hooded mini-djellaba in a white jersey. Tom Ford, then designer for Gucci, also introduced the mod mini-djellaba in his spring 1996 collection. In 1997, even John Galliano showcased a djellaba tucked under a Chinese-style blazer for Dior. Early twenty-first-century celebrities photographed in djellabas range from U.S. Secretary of State Hillary Clinton while on an official visit with King Mohammed VI of Morocco to Jessica Simpson wearing a Moroccan caftan for Halloween.

Influence and Impact

Continued interest in the djellaba, both the traditional and modern versions, may be evidenced in fashion designers' quest for inspiration and in the consumer's quest for comfort and style. Countries rich in the Arab-Islamic tradition have developed variations on the original design that resemble fashion change, and Western countries have adopted essential elements of the djellaba into commercialized products desired by the non-Arab-Islamic consumer as well.

See also BOUBOU; BURNOUS; CAFTAN; CHADOR; THAWB
Compare to DASHIKI; JILBAB; KOSOVOROTKA

Further Reading

Bimberg, L. *Moroccan Goums: Tribal Warriors in a Modern War.* Westport, CT: Greenwood Press, 1999.
White, C. C. R. "At Lacroix Show, Excess Is a Minus." *New York Times*, October 16, 1995, B10.

■ MARY RUPPERT-STROESCU

DOC MARTENS
See DR. MARTENS

DOLMAN

The term "dolman" is used to describe several distinct items of dress as well as a sleeve style. "Dolman" originally referred to a long loose garment with narrow sleeves and a front opening. Originating from the Turkish word for robe, *dolaman* or *dolamah*, the dolman robe was similar in shape to a cassock, the ankle-length, close-fitting robe traditionally worn by Christian clergymen. The dolman coat or *dolmany* is an Oriental garment of Turkish origin derived from the caftan that was worn by men in Hungary for many centuries in the form of a coat. The uniform jacket with several rows of buttons and a horizontal braid across the front originally worn by the Hussars was also called a dolman. The dolman mantle, a popular women's fashion in Western Europe and the United States during the 1870s and 1880s, was characterized by loose sling-like sleeves cut with the body of the garment resembling a half jacket, half cape. The dolman or batwing sleeve is cut all in one with the bodice, giving a very deep armhole and narrowing at the wrist. The dolman sleeve style was worn in the early Middle Ages and has reappeared at intervals throughout history and remains a popular sleeve style today.

History

From the sixteenth until the early nineteenth century, Hungary was dominated by Ottoman fashion. Basic dress for men included the wearing of two coats, dolman and *mente*, hose or trousers, and boots. The outer coat, or *mente*, was generally worn slung over one shoulder. The dolman was worn over a finely embroidered white shirt and was a fitted garment to the waist, where it flared out in a so-called *csakora*-cut style with a diagonally cut piece of fabric overlapping the front of the garment at an angle. The flared skirt went nearly to the knee and was worn shorter as time passed. Originating from a Turkish military doublet with a Western-styled stand-up collar, the dolman was most often made from rich ornamental velvet or brocade fabrics.

The body of the garment was usually decorated and trimmed with rich and intricate braid-work passementerie, often embroidered all over in gold or silver. The dolman closed with loops and buttons that were sometimes coated in enamel and set in semiprecious stones. The opulent features were both decorative and functional, historically intended to protect the wearer from sword attacks to the chest. The dolman was worn with a silver or gold sash wrapped around the waist with a decorative sword hung from it. By the eighteenth century, this style of dress became a symbol of the noble lifestyle and began to be referred to as *diszmagyar*, meaning "magyaros gala dress," and has been worn throughout history as a symbol of patriotism.

The dolman mantle became popular for outdoor women's wear in the 1870s. It was cut to fit over the bustle style of gown, and the semifitted style revealed the shapely contours of the fashionable silhouette. The semifitted coat/cape-like styling was less restricting and cumbersome than a coat, and dolmans were cut in a variety of lengths, from rich velvet brocade and paisley fabrics, and were lavishly trimmed. Ornate trimmings often positioned on the back of the dolman accentuated the bustled silhouette. Rich passementerie with tassels, rosettes, braids, cords, tufts, and fringe frequently embellished women's fashionable dress, creating luxurious effects resembling the trimmings found on curtains and upholstery.

The dolman sleeve style was first seen during the early Middle Ages. The sleeve cut in one with the garment was more common during earlier centuries due to its simple construction compared with the set-in sleeve that required a higher skill level or standard of tailoring. The term "dolman" was used to describe the style in the nineteenth century, while "batwing" is the modern term for the same sleeve style. Both terms continue to be used today. Paul Poiret popularized the dolman-sleeve-style cut in one with the long, slim kimono-style coats in his first collection following World War I in 1919. The dominant silhouette in the first part of the 1920s was tubular and fairly long, and most coats were full cut with kimono or dolman sleeves.

The Dolman in the United States

The dolman military jacket came to the United States with European soldiers during America's War of Independence from England and in future American/European territorial conflicts in the formation of the continental United States as known today. The Hungarian dolman was not worn in the United States as originally styled, but its influence in fabrication and ornamentation style was seen in the dolman mantle worn by women for several decades in the late nineteenth century.

Influence and Impact

The term "dolman" has a rich history, and many distinct elements from each style of dress continue to be seen today in Western and American fashion. The term "dolman" is widely known today as a loose unstructured sleeve style, and the dolman or batwing sleeve cut all in one with the body remains a commonly seen sleeve style today. The original military dolman jacket worn by the Hussars has had a major impact on styling of military uniforms throughout history until today.

Today in the United States the dolman sleeve remains an important sleeve style and can be seen in every category of women's tops including blouses, sweaters, jackets, coats, and robes in a wide variety of fabrications. No special cultural meaning is attached to the sleeve styling.

See also INVERNESS COAT
Compare to BOLERO JACKET; CAFTAN; DUSTER; HANFU CHINESE ROBES; HAORI; HAPPI

Further Reading

Abler, Thomas. *European Empires and Exotic Uniforms: Hinterland Warriors and Military Dress*. Oxford: Berg, 1999.

Mathias, Paul. "A View of Hungary." In *The Imperial Style: Fashions of the Hapsburg Era*, 89–99. Metropolitan Museum Exhibition. New York: Rizzoli, 1980.

Poiret, Paul. *King of Fashion: The Autobiography of Paul Poiret*. Philadelphia and London: J. B. Lippincott, 1931.

Yarwood, Doreen. *Encyclopedia of World Costume*, 94–96. New York: Scribner, 1978.

■ VIRGINIA M. NOON

DOO RAG
See DO-RAG

DO-RAG

The do-rag, also spelled "doo rag" or "du-rag," is a nylon or polyester stretch-mesh head covering with a long panel draping the neck and a tie on each side of the head for securing. An authentic modern-day do-rag should not be mistaken for a bandana worn by motorcyclists to keep their hair from tangling while riding. A bandana is a single piece of cloth, folded in half to make a head covering, whereas a do-rag consists of several fabric panels sewn together to form a shape that fits the head snugly. There may be as few as two panels or up to five or more panels in the construction of a do-rag. Do-rags have also been referred to as pressing caps from the 1930s through the 1960s. Today do-rags are referred to as wave caps because they are used to create a wave pattern in hair or to keep cornrows and other hairstyles in place.

History

The earliest do-rag styling came in the form of a kerchief traced back to Ancient Egyptian times during the First Dynasty. These kerchiefs were usually made of a simple semicircle piece of linen rolled along the bottom hem and whipstitched. Much like the do-rag, the kerchief had a tie that was sewn to the top edge, allowing the kerchief to be tied tightly on the head. The kerchiefs were worn as a means of covering the head and hair while working in dirty or dusty environments.

The Do-Rag in the United States

More recently, do-rag-like head wraps made of cotton rags were worn by African slaves in the United States in the eighteenth century. The rags were tied tight to the head, and the tails were oftentimes tucked in the wrap. Slave men and women both wore a head wrap to help protect their hair and scalp from lice and ringworms. Biracial (usually African and white) slaves were instructed to wear a head wrap by their masters. Mulatto slaves, as they were called then, oftentimes could pass for white, and wearing the head wrap distinguished the slave from the white population as head wraps were signifiers of poverty and subordination. In the 1930s, do-rags were advertised with the use of pomades as a means of making African-American men's normally kinky-curly hair flat and slick. The pomade would be combed or brushed through the hair, and then the do-rag would be placed tightly on the head and worn to bed. Once chemical hair-straightening products were invented in 1948 by Jose Calva, some African-American men donned a straight hairstyle called a conk. The do-rag was worn in order to train newly conked hair to lie flat. Prior to changing his name from Malcolm Little and joining the Nation of Islam, Malcolm X wore a conk and oftentimes wore a do-rag to help maintain the sleek straight look. The conk was said to be worn by men who were low class, pimps, or hoodlums; thus there was an equally demeaning association with men who wore the do-rag.

Do-Rag

Influence and Impact

The do-rag can be tied tight around the head with the back panel/tails knotted tightly and tucked in. Some men wear the do-rag loosely with the ties undone, and many wear the do-rag under a hat. Do-rag manufacturing companies have designed a style with a sun visor built in, giving the do-rag versatility and functionality. In the present day, the do-rag is still associated with a particular population of people deemed as societal rebels or low caste. Consequently, the National Football League banned the use of do-rags from being worn under helmets in 2001. They ruled that do-rags violated the uniform code. Famous do-rag wearers today are rap artists L. L. Cool J, Snoop Dogg, and Nelly. The do-rag serves as a cultural symbol for a number of African-American males and has become an important part of the hip-hop culture and way of dress.

Since the 1990s the do-rag has become a popular urban/street-wear accessory and is not just worn indoors to bed but every day as part of some urban African-American men's wardrobes. The do-rag has evolved from being made of linen in Egyptian times, cotton during U.S. slavery times, and recently stretch nylon or polyester in today's era. However, do-rags' main purpose is very similar to ancient times: to keep hair in place and to protect the hair.

See also AFRICAN HEAD WRAP; HIP-HOP FASHION
Compare to BANDANA; BERET; CH'ULLU; KEFFIYEH; KUFI

Further Reading

Branch, Shelly. "If You Don't Have a 'Do,' Why Wear a Doo-Rag? White Suburbia's New Import Is the Inner City's Hair Tamer." *Wall Street Journal*, September 12, 2003. http://online.wsj.com/article/0,,SB106331677785644700,00.html.

Chandler, Robin M., and Nuri Chandler-Smith. "Flava in Ya Gear: Transgressive Politics and the Influence of Hip-Hop on Contemporary Fashion." In *Twentieth-Century American Fashion*, edited by Linda Welters and Patricia A. Cunningham. Oxford: Berg, 2005.

Claire. "Black History Fashion Trend: Do-Rags." *Fashion Bomb Daily*, February 19, 2010, http://fashionbombdaily.com/2010/02/19/black-history-fashion-trend-do-rags-or-du-rags.

Craig, Maxine. "The Decline and Fall of the Conk; or, How to Read a Process." *Fashion Theory: The Journal of Dress, Body and Culture* 1, no. 4 (1997): 399–419.

Griebel, Helen B. "The African American Headwrap." In *Dress and Ethnicity: Change across Space and Time*, edited by Joanne B. Eicher, 206–23. Oxford: Berg, 1995.

———. "The African American Woman's Headwrap: Unwinding the Symbols." In *Dress and Identity*, edited by M. E. Roach-Higgins, J. B. Eicher, and K. K. P. Johnson, 448–49. New York: Fairchild, 1995.

Volgelsang-Eastwood, Gillian. *Pharaonic Egyptian Clothing*. Leiden: Brill, 1993.

■ TAMEKA N. ELLINGTON

DRIVING CAP

See FLAT CAP

DR. MARTENS

A British footwear brand, Dr. Martens has a history that spans over fifty years. The brand's most notable and famous product is the classic "1460" eight-eyelet black leather boot, with its distinctive thick "Airwair" sole with yellow stitching that attaches the leather upper to the sole. The 1460 was so named after the date of its birth, April 1, 1960, and has been championed by bands, musicians, and popular-culture style tribes through the later decades of the twentieth century and well into the twenty-first. Dr. Martens, also known as Doc Martens, Docs, or DMs, have transcended their original function as the British workingman's footwear to become iconic symbols of antifashion, youth culture, and resistance, as well as being embraced by mainstream fashion across the globe. Frequently described as the boot that parents always disapproved of, the Dr. Martens boot maintains a unique position in contemporary culture, being desired and consumed by new generations. The 1460 is today sold alongside 250 other styles, including shoes, sandals, and Wellington boots.

History

The Dr. Martens boot was the original invention of a World War II German army physician, Dr. Klaus Märtens, after whom they were officially named. While on leave in 1945 on a skiing trip in the Bavarian Alps, Märtens injured his ankle, and while recuperating in the hospital he thought about how the design of boots could be improved to be more comfortable than the heavy army boots he was used to wearing. His idea was for a boot to be made out of soft leather with air-filled soles. Once the war had ended, Märtens purportedly bought a cobbler's last, some leather and needles, and made a pair of these boots. A chance meeting with an old colleague from the University of Munich, Dr. Herbert Funck, was to give Märtens the technical know-how, and thus started a new business partnership that was to see the Dr. Märtens boot come to fruition. Funck and Märtens bought up volumes of discarded aviation rubber from the Luftwaffe airfields, melted it down, and used it to create the air-filled cushion soles.

The first pairs, constructed from bits of old army uniforms, went on sale in 1947 and proved very popular among German housewives and older women who consumed them as a comfort shoe to help correct feet that had suffered from wearing ill-fitting shoes during the war. By 1952, Märtens and Funck had opened a factory in Munich and started advertising their invention in overseas trade magazines. One such advert caught the eye of the Griggs family, well-established shoe manufacturers from Northampton (then the heart of the British shoe and boot industry), and in 1960 the family bought the UK manufacturing rights for Märtens's boot. Before its UK launch, the design was reworked, the heel was reshaped, a yellow welt stitching was added, and the original sole was replaced with a two-toned, grooved sole-edge style. The cushioned sole was trademarked as "Airwair," and a black and yellow heel loop was added to the boot with the words "Airwair . . . with Bouncing Soles." Finally the name was anglicized to Dr. Martens. The first pairs of the classic 1460 boot were made in cherry-red leather. This new boot reflected German technology and functionality combined with British craftsmanship.

Initially the purpose of the Dr. Martens boot was a functional work-wear item to be worn by factory workers, Royal Mail postal service workers, and eventually policemen. However, 1966 saw a dramatic change in the meaning of the boot when it was worn by Pete Townsend from the British rock band the Who, and so began its story as an item of cultural and social significance. From the 1970s onward, the Dr. Martens boot was appropriated by British youth subcultures and worn as the uniform boot of the aggressively macho male. Most notable were the skinheads who wore the boots with button-fly red-tag Levi's and braces of different widths and colors. In some cases, the boots would be steel capped and categorized as offensive weapons. The colors of the laces were also meaningful, with red representing allegiance to the far left. The Dr. Martens has been reappropriated by many British subcultures, from mods, punks, to goths, as a symbol of resistance and antifashion. Feminists and lesbians as emblems of power have also worn the boots, and gay men have used it as a mark of masculinity. In the late 1980s and 1990s, the boot transcended its working-class, masculine roots and became worn by young women who teamed them with baby-doll dresses. It was from then that the Dr. Martens boot became consumed and marketed as a fashion accessory.

Dr. Martens in the United States

Dr. Martens' entry into the United States came from its association with youth subcultures and music, with the boot being the favored style of U.S. hardcore punk bands in the early 1980s. The boot was hard to come by then, and it did not go on sale in the United States until 1984. Dr. Martens' popularity in the United States was to soar in the 1990s with Seattle grunge and Kurt Cobain who famously wore the boots. Today two-thirds of Dr. Martens' global sales are to the United States, and men, women, and children wear the brand.

Influence and Impact

Grunge bands like Nirvana and the Smashing Pumpkins popularized the blue-collar chic uniforms of flannel lumberjack shirts teamed with Dr. Martens. The postfeminist subculture of the Riot Grrrls wore the Dr. Martens boot with frilly dresses and fueled its popularity among American women. It continues to be the favored boot of U.S. bands and musicians, from Madonna to the Strokes.

The boot has moved from being a symbol of working-class youth culture and rebellion to become an iconic fashion item worn by fashion followers, music fans, and celebrities alike. Pope John Paul II supposedly had a customized pair of 1460s in white leather. Through its long and subversive history, the Dr. Martens boot reveals the evolving relationship between youth and popular culture.

See also BLUNDSTONE BOOTS; UGG FOOTWEAR
Compare to BRITISH RIDING BOOTS; MEXICAN POINTY BOOTS; MOCCASINS

Further Reading

Brydon, Ann. "Sensible Shoes." In *Consuming Fashion*, edited by Ann Brydon and Sandra Niessen, 1–22. Oxford: Berg, 1998.

McDowell, Colin. *Shoes: Fashion and Fantasy*. London: Thames & Hudson, 1994.
Roach, Martin. *Dr. Martens: The Story of an Icon*. London: Chrysalis Impact, 2003.

■ NAOMI BRAITHWAITE

DU-RAG
See DO-RAG

DUSTER

The duster coat is a single-breasted, mid-calf-length, loose-fitting garment with a short shoulder cape and back slits. The coat is held together with buttons and often features leg straps to keep the coat flaps in place. The duster coat has long sleeves, and the bottom of the coat is flared to create ease for horseback riding. The fabric is usually light-colored canvas or linen-type cloth.

History

Sailors invented oilcloth in Abroath, Scotland, in 1795. For centuries they waterproofed their sails by soaking them in fish oil. Eventually the sailors discovered that linseed oil (from flaxseed) not only created waterproofed fabrics that were pliable and lightweight but also that were less odorous.

In the late 1800s, Scotsman Andrew LeRoy recycled boat sails soaked in linseed oil to create waterproof capes, which were then adopted by sailors for protection on the seas. The linen fabric used to make ship sails was heavy, and linseed oil turned yellow over time. Eventually linen sails were replaced by cotton because it was lighter and could be woven into stronger fabric. The earliest duster coats were called monsoon capes and were designed to repel wind and sea spray.

Australia's first pioneers settled in New South Wales, Victoria, and Tasmania and took their waterproof capes with them to these cold locations. The capes were redesigned to fit more closely for warmth but retained their original traits. Other than linseed oil, lanolin oil from sheep was mixed with beeswax to ensure longer wear. The new mixture serves as the basis for waterproofing the coats today.

After the introduction of the steamship, which required less manpower, Australian ports were abandoned, and sailors began work on the Australian outback, moving herds across the vast land. These men were called "drovers." Like sailors, drovers were exposed to harsh conditions, including wet, rainy conditions on the trail. Drovers used their waterproof capes not only for protection from wind and rain, but also for a shield against the brush. Other uses for the cape included a bedroll for sleep at night.

The capes evolved in style to become longer and bigger, with a voluminous waist to allow the drover to mount a horse with more ease. In addition, the new style of the cape allowed the coat to drape over the horse more fluidly, trapping the animal's body heat for additional warmth for the drover. The name of the coat began to evolve as its styling and function evolved; eventually the name of the garment changed from the "monsoon cape" to the "drover coat."

Dusters in the United States

It is commonly believed that the duster coat found its acceptance in the United States during the Civil War. Caden McCoy provided the Confederate cavalry with the coats, which became the staple for the soldiers. Caden McCoy left for Texas after the Civil War and took the coat with him. Cowboys at the time noticed that the "slickers" made excellent covers to keep trail dust out of their clothing. From this point, the name "duster coat" was born. The duster coats were the recommended uniform of the Texas Rangers and began being constructed of leather, hides, or other fabric.

The first "horseless carriages," or motorcars, were introduced in the early twentieth century, helping to establish the importance of duster coats for their function. These prototypical vehicles were "open" and so consequently collected dust and other irritants that soiled and became embedded in passengers' clothing. In addition, inclement weather was a threat to passengers. Well-dressed men and women of the time needed protection for their fine apparel. Duster coats became synonymous with the Industrial Revolution in the United States, as their acceptance was due to the emergence of the vehicle and the utilitarian need for protection. During the Industrial Revolution the "travel" fashions of the time included dusters, goggles, caps with visors, and veiled hats.

Influence and Impact

Dusters evolved into unlined coats with soft collars and large patch pockets for the motorists of America. The duster coat, with its many names, is worn as an overcoat by men and women. In the early days, however, people used an overcoat while working. Overcoats, including the duster coat and trench coats, have been worn as protective garments or as part of a prescribed uniform, particularly identifiable with war, with each period of time and war having its unique form of coat.

Articles of clothing have the capacity to state personal or cultural identity and to establish or defy social norms. The duster coat is linked to the deadly shootings that occurred at Columbine High School. The teenage shooters, often referred to as the "Trench Coat Mafia," were said to have been wearing long, black dusters at the time of the shooting. Dusters are also commonly associated with the "gothic subculture," a group of people who wear all-black clothing including long coats and combat boots. Dusters can be worn to not only make a statement or pose a threat but also as an ideal cover for weapons, tools, supplies, or other objects the wearer intends to remain unseen.

The duster is synonymous with the Australian outback, American cowboys, and the Wild West. The duster coat lost its popularity for a period of time but experienced resurgence with the appearance of the automobile. Western horsemen's dusters gained renewed popularity in the late twentieth century and are now a standard item of western wear and outer wear. In the late 1960s, Sergio Leone reintroduced the duster coat in his movies *The Good, the Bad, and the Ugly* and *Once Upon a Time in the West*. The coat quickly made its way into various films and books, including *The Man from Snowy River*, a 1982 classic. Other contemporary films in which the duster is a clothing symbol that personifies the main characters include *The Matrix* and *True Grit*.

Today, the duster coat has found its way to the fashion runway, being featured in the collections of Christian Dior, Missoni, Michael Kors, and countless others all the way from Paris to New York City and available at the world's largest and most renowned retailers, including Nordstrom, Neiman Marcus, and Saks Fifth Avenue. The popularity of the duster coat today may be due to changes in fashion silhouettes, including maxidresses and skirts, which make the long coat a more appropriate outerwear item. When worn as a fashion statement, the duster is popularized more for its form rather than its function.

Traditionally the duster coat was flammable due to the linseed oil coating. However, manufacturer Driza-Bone has improved its fabrication to produce duster coats with a nonflammable proofing compound. Cotton and linen have been replaced by fur, faux fur, and leather, while the fit has remained billowy to give the duster its signature, flowing look.

See also TRENCH COAT; WESTERN WEAR
Compare to ANORAK/PARKA

Further Reading

Andrus, D. "Cowboy Classics." *Wearable Business* 10, no. 11 (2006): 10–12.
Riley, R. E. "Of Dusters and Drovers: A Peek into the History of Outback Outerwear!" *Horse & Rider* 30, no. 8 (2012): 62–63.
Wilson, L. E. "The Cowboy: Real and Imagined." *Dress* 23, no. 1 (1996): 3–15.

■ JAIME R. CUPIT

E

ESPADRILLES

Espadrilles are cotton shoes with thin soles typically worn without socks, associated with the Basque region. Modern incarnations have the sole typically from rubber, faced with jute. Some still emulate the earlier versions in which the sole was made entirely from thick woven jute. It is this material that lends the shoes their name: *esparto* is the Catalan word for the thick grass fiber used to make rope and matting. In Aragonese dialect, they are known as *esparteñas*; elsewhere they can be called *alpargatas. Espadrille* is the French variant.

History

The history of espadrilles can be dated back to the fourteenth century in Catalonia between Spain and France where both men and women continue to wear them to the present day. They are particularly worn in the summer months, being too light and porous for colder, wetter weather.

While still produced in Catalonia where there are entire shops devoted to them, they are also produced throughout Asia, including India and Bangladesh. Bangladesh is one of the world's largest producers of jute products. More recently the emphasis on jute has added to the popularity of espadrilles, since jute carries strong associations of eco-friendliness. In their manufacture, the jute is first machine braided, then formed naturally into a sole which is hydraulically pressed into the correct shape, then stitched. To this is added the rubber sole or wooden heel. The cotton uppers are then sewn to the base.

The espadrille is related in style to moccasins and to the simple variety of cotton shoes commonly worn throughout Asia. But as opposed to the jute base, the upper cotton shell is built onto a vinyl sole.

Espadrilles in the United States

Since the 1960s, espadrilles have spawned hybrid varieties such as high-heeled versions, notable for the jute facing around what is usually a solid platform heel. They were made famous in the United States in the late 1940s, especially with the example of Lauren Bacall's espadrilles, which were laced at the ankle, that she wore in the move *Key Largo*

(1948). In the 1980s they were worn by Don John-son's character Sonny Crockett in *Miami Vice*. His character was suave and wore suits. This removed the shoes from their peasant origins and gave them a classic and stylish edge. Recently there have also been designer varieties in which the jute is replaced by other materials resembling rope, and the cotton upper replaced by synthetics and even leather.

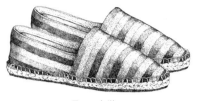

Espadrilles

Influence and Impact

Espadrilles as a style were revitalized in 2010 with the founding of the New York City–based Soludos brand. Using a mix of partnerships such as a line of print and pattern novelty shoes with Mara Hoffman and a custom line for J. Crew, the Soludos brand started trendsetting in the Soho district of New York City and has now captured a significant American market segment. The espadrille symbolizes the dressed down, easygoing appearance so many Americans favor. Design and manufacturing of espa-drilles for Americans with a variety of designs continues, reflecting the ongoing fashion appeal of this item.

See also CHINESE FLATS; FLIP-FLOPS (GETA); JELLIES
Compare to HUARACHES; MOCCASINS; WINGTIPS (BROGUE SHOE)

Further Reading

Cartner-Morley, J. "Espadrilles Look to Be Summer's Sole Success after Beyoncé Endorsement." *Guard-ian*, June 7, 2013, http://www.theguardian.com/fashion/2013/jun/07/espadrilles-summer-success-beyonce-tabitha-simmons.

■ ADAM GECZY

ETHNIC JEWELRY

The influence of non–Western cultures on jewelry in Europe and the United States has a long history. The twentieth century saw perhaps the most widespread adoption of ethnic styles in jewelry. The discovery of Tutankhamen's tomb in 1922, as well as various world expositions in the 1920s and 1930s, helped to bring global styles and materials to wide audiences that were adopted by designers of all kinds. Ethnic jewelry has historically been connected to the exoticization of the ethnic other. Africans, Native Americans, and other ethnic groups have been imagined to be more primitive, more closely aligned to nature, and more in touch with their sexuality. These imagined qualities have made ethnic jewelry appealing to American consumers. Women have worn ethnic jewelry as a way of expressing an exotic sex appeal, and both men and women have worn this jewelry as a way of resisting the homogenization of American mass culture by embracing the suppos-edly natural, authentic, or handmade.

Ethnic Jewelry in the United States

African Style Jewelry

In the 1920s, with the rising popularity of jazz music, African influences in jewelry became particularly popular. Jazz music's roots in African-American communities linked it in the popular imagination to Africa. Jazz clubs were often decked out as jungles in darkest Africa. Bangle bracelets, hoop earrings, and simple metal collar necklaces were all associated with African style, and by extension jazz music. These styles had little direct relationship to African jewelry and often borrowed freely from many different cultures at once. Geometric patterns of contrasting colors, tooth-shaped beads, and simple metal or wood bangles were all used to reference African style. Simple metal ring necklaces, sometimes worn in large numbers, as well as simple metal bangles may have been inspired by a photograph of a Masai woman wearing brass jewelry taken on "La Croisière Noire" (the Black Crossing), an expedition across the Sahara sponsored by the car manufacturer Citroën. A documentary film of the journey from Algeria to Madagascar between October 1924 and June 1925, released in 1926, as well as photographs published in several formats were some of the most widely distributed images of Africans and their modes of dress and adornments. These photographs continue to be used in texts on Africa and have been one of the primary means through which African jewelry has influenced designers and consumers.

Other African styles of jewelry were worn by Africans brought to America as slaves beginning in the seventeenth century. Archeological evidence of cowries, seashells, and glass beads has been found in slave sites around the United States. Both men and women of African descent in the lower coastal South as well as in Haiti and elsewhere in the Caribbean wore hoop-style earrings singly, most likely as protective amulets. Hoop earrings also appeared in the ears of caricatured images of female slaves.

African-inspired jewelry, some of which referenced these slave styles, became an important component of Afrocentric dressing in the 1960s and 1970s. Jewelry inspired by Ghana and Egypt, as well as large hoop earrings, wooden beads, and cowrie-shell jewelry were worn by African-Americans as a way of displaying their allegiance to the politics of civil rights as well as black cultural nationalism. African-style jewelry was also popular with hippies in the 1960s and 1970s who used ethnic-inspired jewelry of all kinds to create a "natural" look. They embraced natural materials and so-called primitive styles as a way of resisting the synthetic materials popular in the early 1960s as well as systems of mass production.

In 1997, Ralph Lauren showed a collection inspired by Africa that included simple metal collars, armlets, and large hoop earrings similar to styles popular in the 1920s. Despite the fact that the hoop earrings have been worn by a wide variety of cultures historically, they are often associated popularly with African culture, deployed by both those interested in the political message of Afrocentric dressing or in referring to an exotic image of Africa.

Native American Jewelry

Unlike the African-style jewelry marketed in the United States that by and large was not manufactured by Africans, Native Americans themselves have played an important role in the manufacture and sale of jewelry in the United States. The jewelry styles of tribes in the

Southwest were the most popular with Americans, made by various Pueblo peoples living in New Mexico and Arizona. The jewelry made by these groups historically represented an amalgamation of styles rather than an "authentically" Native American tradition. Two styles popular with Americans, concho belts and squash-blossom necklaces, are excellent examples of this fusion of styles, as both derive parts of their designs from Spanish motifs. Both were developed in the mid-nineteenth century when Mexican silversmiths introduced their techniques to Native artists; turquoise mined in the Southwest was integrated into silver work around the turn of the century.

The concho-style belt, adorned with shell-like disks of silver based on Spanish bridle ornaments, became incredibly popular throughout the latter half of the twentieth century, adopted as a reference not only to Native American style but also to western or cowboy style. Rock musicians in the 1960s and 1970s such as Jim Morrison embraced the belt as a symbol of rugged masculinity and the perfect adornment for their flamboyant performance ensembles. These belts continue to be popular with musicians such as guitarist Slash who adorns his signature top hat with one. The squash-blossom necklace combines a crescent-shaped *naja* pendant—influenced by Spanish designs which in turn were influenced by Moorish ones—with smaller pendants often shaped like pomegranate flower forms derived from Spanish designs but called squash blossoms.

At the turn of the century, when the Atchison, Topeka and Santa Fe Railway brought tourists to the Southwest, trading posts sprung up to sell them Native American handcrafts, in particular, jewelry. Fred Harvey, who operated Harvey House restaurants and hotels along the tourist route, added trading posts to his hotels, and Harvey House restaurants such as Hopi House opened in 1905 at the Grand Canyon. Collaborating with Native artists, the Harvey Company played a key role in marketing Native American jewelry to tourists. The pieces from 1890 to 1930 have been dubbed Fred Harvey style and were made lighter and less expensive with flashy designs that appealed to the tourist market: arrowheads, crossed arrows, thunderbirds, kachina spirits, and sun signs.

Ethnic jewelry purchased and collected by tourists became both a souvenir of a vacation as well as the evidence of a supposedly vanishing people, a metaphor for the changing face of America in the wake of rapid industrialization. The popularity of this jewelry expanded in the 1930s and 1940s with the explosion of costume jewelry in mainstream fashion. Dude ranches in the West became popular destinations for wealthier travelers and helped to popularize "western" or cowboy dress with often-included squash-blossom necklaces and concho belts.

Hippies embraced Native American jewelry in the late 1960s and 1970s as a way of aligning themselves with what they saw as the heroic resistance of the Native Americans to modern American homogenization. Singer Cher's adoption of Native American jewelry and fashion and her claim that she was part Cherokee tapped into the romantic image of the Native American, popular in the early 1970s. American designer Ralph Lauren helped to popularize concho belts with women in the early 1980s, along with turquoise and silver jewelry, and continues to show these styles as part of his classic relaxed American style.

See also BOHEMIAN DRESS; BOLO TIE; BRICOLAGE; CONCHO BELT
Compare to JAPANESE STREET FASHION; POWWOW ACCESSORIES; WESTERN WEAR

Further Reading

Baxter, Paula. "Cross-Cultural Controversies in the Design History of Southwestern American Indian Jewellery." *Journal of Design History* 7, no. 4 (1994): 233–45.

Foster, Helen Bradley. "African American Jewellery before the Civil War." In *Beads and Bead Makers: Gender, Material Culture, and Meaning*, edited by L. D. Sciama and J. B. Eicher. London: Berg, 1998.

Hannel, Susan L. "The Influence of American Jazz on Fashion." In *Twentieth-Century American Fashion*, edited by Linda Welters and Patricia A. Cunningham, 56–77. New York: Berg, 2005.

Howard, Kathleen L., and Diana F. Pardue. *Inventing the Southwest: The Fred Harvey Company and Native American Art*. Flagstaff, AZ: Northland Publishing, 1996.

Starke, Barbara M., Lillian O. Holloman, and Barbara K. Nordquist, eds. *African American Dress and Adornment: A Cultural Perspective*. Dubuque, IA: Kendall/Hunt, 1990.

Weigle, Marta, and Barbara A. Babcock, eds. *The Great Southwest of the Fred Harvey Company and the Santa Fe Railway*. Phoenix, AZ: Heard Museum, 1996.

■ VICTORIA PASS

F

FAJA

The faja is a compression undergarment, similar to a girdle. The faja is worn very tight on the body to create an extremely curvy hourglass figure. The undergarment shifts organs and flesh and has been said to reduce one's appetite. The degree of figure shaping and body compression depends on the fabric composition. Versions can be found in mixtures of spandex, cotton, nylon, or latex; the less forgiving the material, the more flattering the effect. The undergarment may be closed with hooks, a zipper, or both.

The faja typically extends from under the bust to below hip level. This type is often made of a material called Powernet, a very firm net-like fabric construction of spandex, nylon, and cotton. However, a variety of shapes and sizes can be found. One version is full-body jumpsuits, which may include covering of the upper arms, legs, and bust area. However, these jumpsuits are typically seen with the bust area open to show the bra. These full-body versions are also marketed as postsurgery garments. They appear to be engineered for function rather than aesthetic appeal. Another version is the tight bellyband, similar to a corset, closed with a center front row of hooks and eyes. These versions can be found in an array of colors and are often accented with lace to add sex appeal.

History

Faja is the Spanish word for wrap. The faja originated in Colombia as a postsurgery medical garment for liposuction patients. Its postoperative function is to reduce swelling to make sure that the skin tightens as desired. People then adopted it for everyday wear to mold their figures to a more idealized, curvy version as seen on celebrities. Colombian manufacturers designed and fabricated the fajas for nonmedical wear, as did manufacturers in Brazil, Chile, and other parts of the region. The Colombians' designs evolved most successfully, eventually earning them the veneration of the entire region. Colombian fajas are known for their ability to not roll up or bunch and are very compressive. This tight compression is known to help women instantly hide up to four dress sizes.

The Faja in the United States

The faja came to the United States as a result of immigration. Colombian women who moved to the United States continued to use the faja as a body-contouring device, with

Faja

a large population centered in Queens, New York. In the beginning, only Latinos and black women were interested in wearing the faja; however, it eventually spread to wider use, as U.S. consumers realized the effectiveness of the faja for figure control. Use began to spread throughout New York State, even to areas where Latino populations are small. Several companies import fajas from Colombia to sell in the United States.

Influence and Impact

While the faja continues to be marketed for postoperative wear as well as postpartum wear to reduce the size of the abdomen, its use has expanded as a tool to achieve a current fashion silhouette. This is similar to the roles that girdles have played over the years. Today, there are two major fashion trends that drive the popularity of the faja. The garment is especially popular among younger Latina women trying to achieve the idealized "Coke bottle" or "guitar-shaped" figure. Young women who are part of the counterculture that mimics 1950s pinup girls have also adopted the faja. Even slender young women use the faja to create the hourglass figure that allows them to fit into waist-emphasizing fashions such as capri pants, swing skirts, and halter tops. They see this sexy self-presentation as a type of female empowerment.

More well-known support undergarments, such as Spanx, introduced women to the concept of extra help for figure problems and made the idea of shaping the body with compressive undergarments more acceptable. The faja has taken this to the extreme, with the act of donning one often compared to a battle of woman versus fabric. This is in stark contrast to feminist women of the 1970s who cast off such constrictive undergarments as symbols of repression. It appears that young women of today are willing to endure some discomfort to create their desired appearance.

See also CORSET
Compare to CHEMISE

Further Reading

La Ferla, R. "A Sly Wink to Pinups of the Past." *New York Times*, May 17, 2012, http://www.nytimes .com/2012/05/17/fashion/a-sly-wink-to-pinups-of-the-past.html?pagewanted=all&_r=0.

Nir, S. M. "Rediscovering a Shortcut to an Hourglass Figure." *New York Times*, May 16, 2012, http:// www.nytimes.com/2012/05/16/nyregion/with-fajas-tight-as-corsets-shortcut-to-hourglass -figure-is-rediscovered.html.

■ ELLEN C. MCKINNEY

FEDORA

The fedora is a soft felt hat with a medium-width (approximately 2.5-inch), slightly curled brim. The brim is often worn with the front snapped down and curled up at the back, or completely flat. It features a crown (approximately 4.5 inches high) with a deep crease known as a gutter that runs from front to back and a pinched appearance at the front that creates a teardrop shape; however, the crown can be pushed in at several different places to create shallow depressions known as indentations for slight variations in style. Traditional colors include black, gray, and fawn. Classic styles also feature a black or brown ribbon band usually tied with a flat bow at the point on the hat where the crown meets the brim. Some styles include a feather tucked into the band. The fedora was usually worn as outerwear.

History

In the twenty-first century, the fedora saw a resurgence in popularity in the United States in both men's and women's fashion and became available in a variety of colors, patterns, and materials, such as canvas and straw. However, the classic fedora was first seen widely in French dramatist Victorien Sardou's 1882 play *Fédora*, for which the hat was created specially and worn by the American actress Sarah Bernhardt who played the lead role of Princess Fédora. At the time of the play's debut and for a decade thereafter, the hat was fashionable among middle- and upper-class women in Europe and the United States, but it became an almost exclusively male fashion item by the end of the nineteenth century. It was during this period that the hat soared in popularity, eclipsing the then-popular homburg-style hat for daily wear.

In the early twentieth century, the fedora was adopted by Orthodox yeshiva students and Chabad-Lubavitch Jews in Israel and the United States who began wearing the hats in black to distinguish themselves within the Orthodox community and to reify their culture so as not to assimilate into the mainstream. Within this community, the hat is commonly referred to as a Borsalino after one of the most well-known manufacturers of felt fedoras.

In South America, the fedora was popular in the Ecuadorian Highlands where it became ubiquitous among Quichua-speaking Otavalo men. The technology of felting sheep wool was brought to South America in the sixteenth century and was assimilated into local head-wear styles, but by the 1940s, the fedora had become a crucial marker of ethnic identity and a staple of everyday dress for Otavalo men who commonly paired the hat with white pants, a white shirt, and a poncho.

The Fedora in the United States

The fedora's popularity reached its apex in the United States in the first decade of the twentieth century when it signaled the end of the equestrian age and the rise of the automobile, as well as a loosening of rigid Victorian etiquette. In contrast to tall and stiff top hats, which were designed to protect the rider's head from low-hanging branches, the modern and malleable fedora could be molded to suit the wearer's individual tastes and did not need to be removed upon entering an automobile cabin with limited headroom. By the 1920s, handmade top hats had almost entirely fallen out of favor as felted styles could be easily and cheaply machine manufactured. It was during this period that soft felted hats of all kinds became a staple in every man's wardrobe, ushering in an era in which it was uncommon to see a man without a hat while outdoors.

Influence and Impact

In the 1920s and 1930s, the fedora became synonymous with Prohibition-era crime culture and was highly visible in the pulp films and literature of the 1940s that fetishized gangsters and the detectives who chased them. Infamous gangsters like Al Capone and Frank Costello, who rose to fame during Prohibition, customized the fedora in unique colors with bold ribbons and feather accents to fashion a signature look. When styled with a pinstripe suit and gum-soled shoes, the fedora became inextricably linked with tough-guy style. For Hollywood, the fedora was a great cinematic prop in the detective films of the 1940s, which when paired with a classic trench coat became synonymous with detectives and private investigators.

In the late 1930s and early 1940s, young African-American, Chicano, and Italian-American men popularized the zoot suit, a suiting style that features high-waist pants with tapered, pegged legs and a long jacket with extra wide lapels and padded shoulders that is usually topped off with a porkpie or fedora hat. In its styling, materiality, and proportions, the zoot suit was an exaggerated form of conservative business dress down to the manipulation of the fedora. Fashioned in loud colors with an exaggerated brim and finished with conspicuous flourishes like ostrich feathers, the fedora complemented the style's other exaggerated accompaniments, such as two-tone brogues and gold wallet chains.

By the late 1950s, hat wearing had fallen out of favor for everyday dress as men's fashions became increasingly casual for both work and leisure. Historians and culturists also point to the fact that President John F. Kennedy could often be seen in public hatless at a key period during which the fashion for wearing hats waned.

In the 1990s, the fedora saw a brief surge in popularity when Michael Jackson donned the hat in his "Billie Jean" music video and when Harrison Ford wore one in the *Indiana Jones* movie franchise. The fedora was rediscovered as a fashion item in the twenty-first century when celebrities could be seen donning the hat in a new array of colors and materials on Hollywood's red carpets. In the second decade of the twenty-first century, the fedora became closely associated with the hipster subculture. Worn by both men and women, the fedora can be found cheaply at most high street-fashion retailers and is most frequently worn in casual contexts paired with everyday dress. While the fedora is far removed from its associations to gangster and crime culture in the present moment, it maintains its status as a stylish accessory for a discerning arbiter of fashion in a climate in which the baseball cap is ubiquitous.

See also TRENCH COAT; ZOOT SUIT
Compare to BOWLER HAT; PANAMA HAT; SLOUCH HAT (AUSTRALIAN); SOMBRERO

Further Reading

Cotton, Elizabeth. *Hats*. New York: Stewart, Tabori & Chang, 1999.
Henderson, Debbie. *Hat Talk: Conversations with 20th Century Hatters*. Santa Cruz, CA: Wild Goose Press, 2011.
Steinberg, Neil. *Hatless Jack: The President, the Fedora, and the History of American Style*. New York: Plume, 2004.

■ LAUREN DOWNING PETERS

FEZ

A fez is a brimless hat of felt or cloth in the shape of a straight cylinder or slightly tapered cone. It is usually red with a black or dark blue tassel. The fez varies from tall and stiff to shorter, soft, and rounded. Often worn over a cotton skullcap, the fez serves as the outermost item of head wear or as the basis for a turban, through which its top may be visible. The fez is also called a tarbush/tarboosh, from the Arabic.

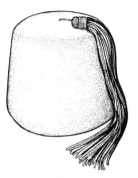

Fez

History

The fez serves roles ranging from the quotidian to the religious and/or ceremonial. It is an everyday item of dress worn by Muslims throughout the Eastern Mediterranean, and by some non-Muslims in North Africa. Islam requires its adherents to cover their heads in public and to touch their foreheads to the ground in prayer, hence the fez's lack of a brim. This also allows a clear, unblocked view of heaven. The tassel may be related to the custom of Muslim men shaving their heads except for a single lock of hair, by which Allah could lift them to Paradise.

The fez probably originated in ancient Greece, where a short, soft version was worn by the *euzonoi* (infantrymen). The tassel was thought to protect the wearer against evil. Fezzes are still worn by the Presidential Guard of Athens on ceremonial occasions and are also a component of traditional Cypriot dress. In Africa, the fez is ceremonial head wear for the Moba of northern Togo, worn by male initiates, priests, and chiefs. The Igbo of southeastern Nigeria add feathers and don the fez as a symbol of high office. In the Middle East, boys do not wear a turban over their fezzes until puberty, and for special occasions such as circumcision ceremonies, they may be elaborately embellished. The fez is most often associated with Turkey and the Ottoman Empire, where in 1796 Sultan Selim III introduced it into regimental uniforms as part of an early attempt at military modernization. The fez was made official army issue in 1827, at which time it was already in use by the army of the governor of Egypt and by the Zouaves, French soldiers serving in North Africa.

Early fezzes were imported to Turkey from North Africa. Despite the hat's name, its original center of production appears to have been Tunis, not Fez. Manufacture was later moved to Istanbul and staffed by Tunis workers, where the factory made 1,500 fezzes a month, selling surplus hats to the public. In 1829, the Ottoman Empire extended its Westernizing clothing reforms to include all but the highest-ranking religious leaders. Men were required by law to wear a frock coat, collared shirt, cape, European-style shoes, and a fez. After the 1850s, several fashionable shapes of fez became available, each model requiring a different block. But by the early twentieth century, reformers sought to abolish the fez as an outmoded symbol of Islamic orthodoxy, conservatism, and the Ottoman Sultanate. In 1925, the wearing of the fez was made a criminal offense by the government of the Turkish Republic; in approximately one hundred years it had shifted from a symbol of progress to one of antiquity.

The Fez in the United States

The fez's appeal in the United States and Europe was part of the vogue for Orientalism around the turn of the twentieth century. At-home wear for wealthy men emulating exotic—usually Eastern—cultures included robes and soft caps such as fezzes, often worn in similarly adorned smoking rooms. In the twentieth century the fez, like other regional head wear, was a source of inspiration for fashion designers. The fashion press of the 1930s and 1940s made numerous references to fezzes by contemporary designers and milliners, including Mainbocher and John-Frederics.

Fezzes are sometimes worn in the United States by immigrants who associate the style with commonplace work wear as worn in their home countries. Many fezzes arrive via tourism, as their connotation of romance and exoticism continues. But the most common use of the fez in the United States today is ceremonial: it is often custom made or adorned for private clubs and groups. The Shriners, an order of the Freemasons, are well known for wearing red fezzes for functions and parades. These hats are personalized with appliquéd or embroidered insignia to denote rank and membership in specific clubs and activities; a Shriner may own multiple customized fezzes.

Influence and Impact

The fez continues to be a reference point for contemporary fashion designers. One of Stephen Jones's earliest hats was a sequined fez worn for a cameo in Culture Club's "Do You Really Want to Hurt Me?" music video in 1982. Jean Paul Gaultier later asked Jones to design hats for him, including a riff on the traditional fez in which the tassels represent falling tears. John Galliano featured a bejeweled white fez with a veil for his fall/winter 2010/2011 show. Several recent men's runway looks have also incorporated fezzes. The fez has lately earned its place in popular culture via numerous appearances on the remake of the *Doctor Who* television series. It has been donned by several incarnations of the Doctor, serving as a crucial plot element each time it appears.

See also BOUBOU; KUFI

Compare to BERET; BLANGKON; FLAT CAP; RASTA HAT; SIBENIK CAP; TAM-O'-SHANTER; TAQIYA

Further Reading

Anawalt, Patricia Rieff. *The Worldwide History of Dress*. New York: Thames & Hudson, 2007.

Arnoldi, Mary Jo, and Christine Mullen Kreamer. *Crowning Achievements: African Arts of Dressing the Head*. Los Angeles: Fowler Museum of Cultural History, University of California, 1995.

Baker, Patricia L. "The Fez in Turkey: A Symbol of Modernization?" *Costume* 20 (1986): 72–85.

Chico, Beverly. "Gender Headwear Traditions in Judaism and Islam." *Dress* 27 (2000): 18–36.

Jirousek, Charlotte. "More than Oriental Splendor: European and Ottoman Headgear, 1380–1580." *Dress* 22 (1995): 22–33.

Kramer, Fritz. *The Red Fez: Art and Spirit Possession in Africa*. Translated by Malcolm Green. New York: Verso, 1993.

■ TRACY JENKINS

FIELD BOOTS

See BRITISH RIDING BOOTS

FLAT CAP

The flat cap is a round, wedge-shaped, soft men's cap with a short peak at the front and a stiff back and is traditionally made from wool or tweed. The flat cap has also been termed a "golf cap," "cloth cap," "driving cap," or "Windsor cap."

History

The cap's history can be traced back to fifteenth-century Northern England, during the reign of the Tudors, and is an accessory through which the social history of Britain's class system can be documented. Although the cap has been primarily recorded as a British creation, it could also be found in fifteenth-century Southern Italy. In 1571 an Act of Parliament passed in England held that all males over the age of six, except those of noble birth, were to wear wool caps or be fined three farthings (pre-decimal currency) a day. The objective of the act was to stimulate the important woolen trade that was the foundation of the British economy at that time. Although the act was repealed in 1597, the cap had become firmly entrenched as the mark of the rural working-class male.

Well into the twentieth century the flat cap was ubiquitous among English and Irish working-class males. However, in stark contrast it was also popular attire for the English gentry who wore it to go hunting, shooting, and fishing. In this class and social context, the cap would be worn with the Barbour jacket and Wellington boots, with the flat cap constructed from finer cloth, often a tweed. As the cap crossed over into the upper class, it became increasingly popular at golfing parties and shooting events. During the 1920s the cap took on a more stylish role, being worn by fashionable young men. In 1954, British hat manufacturer Kangol created their famous seamless flat "Carricap" made from stiffened materials in both men's and women's styles. The Beatles wore the flat cap during the 1960s, fueling popularity for the style, which led to the eventual distribution of the Kangol cap into the United States.

The Flat Cap in the United States

Immigrants first brought the traditional flat cap into the United States from Ireland and England during the nineteenth century. In contrast to how it was worn in England, the flat cap in the United States was a classless item. The style became extremely popular in the United States during the latter part of the nineteenth century and well into the twentieth century, with American men wearing the cap for both formal and casual wear. The flat cap was to become the distinguishing mark of the street-corner newspaper seller and was frequently worn by the New York cabbie, hence why it has been termed a cab driver or cabbie hat.

During the 1930s and 1940s, African-Americans in the South would don the flat cap to mimic jazz musicians. Hollywood also popularized the flat cap, bringing it further into the domain of popular culture. Robert Redford wore a white flat cap in *The Great Gatsby*

(1974). Warren Beatty and Faye Dunaway wore them in *Bonnie and Clyde* (1967). This association with Hollywood stars saw the cap move into the realms of urban fashion. As the Kangol brand with their flat-cap designs grew in popularity in the United States, so did their appropriation by different style groupings. The flat cap was taken up by American hip-hop culture during the 1990s when it was worn back to front by artists like Run DMC, Grandmaster Flash, and L. L. Cool J. Today it is a favored accessory of celebrities, worn by Madonna, David Beckham, Brad Pitt, and Samuel L. Jackson, who wore a Kangol cap back to front in the Quentin Tarantino movie *Jackie Brown*.

Influence and Impact

Through its British roots, the flat cap has at one end of the spectrum represented working-class solidarity, and at the other it has been a mark of upper-class status and their engagement in sporting and rural pursuits. The flat cap today has a wide array of different functions that include the wearing for country pursuits, golf, or just purely as an urban fashion accessory. Although the flat cap has been recorded as stereotypically working class and gendered, its history and transition into the U.S. market shows how it has transcended class and gender to become an item of popular culture.

See also BOWLER HAT; HARRIS TWEED; HIP-HOP FASHION
Compare to BERET; BLANGKON; RASTA HAT; SIBENIK CAP; TAM-O'-SHANTER; TAQIYA

Further Reading

Akbareian, E. "Kangol: You Can Leave Your Hat On." *Independent*, April 7, 2013, http://www.independent.co.uk/life-style/fashion/features/kangol-you-can-leave-your-hat-on-8563455.html (accessed May 12, 2013).
The Design Museum. *Fifty Hats That Changed the World*. London: Conran Octopus, 2011.
Porter, C. "If You Want to Get Ahead, Get a Flap Cap." *Telegraph*, November 4, 2010, http://fashion.telegraph.co.uk/news-features/TMG8108321/If-you-want-to-get-ahead-get-a-flat-cap.html (accessed May 12, 2013).
Romero, E. *Free Stylin': How Hip Hop Changed the Fashion Industry*. Santa Barbara, CA: Praeger, 2012.

■ NAOMI BRAITHWAITE

FLIP-FLOPS (GETA)

The name of these casual backless sandals comes from the sound they make when walking. The sandals have two straps configured in a Y shape, connected to a thin rubber or plastic sole by a thong. These inexpensive sandals have their origin in Japanese footwear where a direct line of descent can be traced from Japan, to Hawai'i, and then on to the U.S. mainland.

History

When Japanese immigrated into Hawai'i to work on the plantations in the 1880s, they came to the Islands wearing geta and *zōris*. The thong is in the middle of both types of

Japanese shoes, so there is no difference between left and right. Geta are thick wooden clogs held on the foot by a Y-shaped strap. *Zōris* are similarly styled, but the soles are thin and are made of a variety of materials. While straw, rice stalks, and bulrushes were common in the past, in the twentieth century, *zōris* were made from plastic, vinyl, or leather. Geta are now only seen worn with the traditional kimono, but *zōris* were adopted as everyday footwear in Hawai'i where they are commonly referred to as "slippers," "rubber slippers," or more correctly (and in Hawai'ian pidgin), "rubbah slippahs," which is iconic for Hawai'i's laid-back dress and lifestyle.

Flip-Flops in the United States

In 1932 Elmer Scott, a cobbler from Massachusetts, migrated to Hawai'i where he began making steel-toed rubber boots for plantation workers. During World War II he started producing sandals for the military. American soldiers stationed in Hawai'i bought *zōris* in Japan and "slippers" in Hawai'i and brought them home to be used in the shower or at the beach.

Influence and Impact

After the war, Clark reshaped the *zōris* for the local Hawai'ian market, and he produced the slippers with a left and a right. Consequently, it may well be Scott who put a Western spin on an Asian shoe style. In the 1950s many Honolulu shoe companies produced slippers. Soon thereafter, Japan began exporting inexpensive *zōris* and slippers to Hawai'i and to the western states. In 1959 Hawai'i officially became the fiftieth American state, and tourism exploded. As the sport of surfing was embraced by enthusiasts in California, surfers traveled to Hawai'i to learn how to ride the waves. In the process they adopted the Hawai'ian style of dress. The aloha shirt, board shorts, and slippers were the uniform of surfers who brought this style back to California. Surfers became important in the movement of slippers to the U.S. mainland, where they became known as "flip-flops." During the 1960s, California surfers traveled back and forth to Hawai'i and brought back slippers and aloha shirts to the U.S. mainland, thereby introducing ethnic forms of casual dress to California. Surfers and beatniks adopted slippers. They were renamed "flip-flops" as they became ubiquitous in the United States. By 1972, the term "flip-flop" was in use in dictionaries.

Flip-flops are still referred to as slippers in Hawai'i. They epitomize Hawai'i's multicultural ethos, in which humility, practicality, and casual living are key values. As an icon, slippers are seen in many images of Hawai'i and are often the focus of jewelry. Wearing slippers in Hawai'i is extremely common for most functions. They are not restricted to beach wear but are worn to restaurants, to many jobs, and even to weddings in Hawai'i. However, flip-flops are restricted to casual use on the U.S. mainland.

Influence and Impact

Throughout the United States, flip-flops have been embraced by all ages as acceptable beach dress, or as a utilitarian form of shoes for people who engage in water sports. Nonetheless, a bit of controversy arose in 2005 when the champion women's lacrosse team from Northwestern University visited the White House dressed in flip-flops. Whether this or President Obama's use of flip-flops while on vacation in Hawai'i signals a symbolic shift is debatable. What is not debatable is that these cheap shoes are big business. The Atlanta-based company Flip Flop Shops reported that this category of shoes was a $20 billion industry in 2009.

Podiatrists caution that flip-flops should not be worn for long, as the shoes do not protect the foot, nor do they provide adequate support to the foot. Problems from tendonitis to overpronation are reported.

See also BIRKENSTOCKS; HUARACHES; JELLIES; TABI
Compare to BOHEMIAN DRESS; ESPADRILLES

Further Reading

"Appropriate? Obama Becomes First Flip-Flop President." Fox News, January 5, 2011, http://www.nation.foxnews.com/culture/2011/01/05/appropriate-obama-becomes-first-flip-flop-president Fox News.
Kawakami, Barbara. *Japanese Immigrant Clothing in Hawaii.* Honolulu: University of Hawaii Press, 1993.
"Rubbah Soul." *Hana Hou!* 14, no. 3 (2012).

■ LINDA ARTHUR BRADLEY

FRONTIER WEAR
See BUCKSKIN; CALICO AND CHINTZ; COONSKIN CAP

FUSTANELLA

The fustanella is a men's pleated knee-length skirt made from folded layers of linen. It is worn by men for ceremonial and military purposes in Eastern Europe and the Mediterranean, including the countries of Greece, Albania, and Macedonia. Albanian fustanellas are less full than Greek fustanellas, and styles vary with time period and region. Today's fustanellas are associated with bright white color, but at times the fustanella was coated with a layer of fat to protect soldiers from rain. It may be worn with wool trousers and black jackets, and it is a familiar sight in the traditional folk dress of these regions.

History

The fustanella has a long history, but there is contention over who introduced the fustanella to whom and when. In Athens, a statue dating from the third century BCE wears a fustanella-like garment. The fustanella may have been introduced to Western Europe during the Roman conquest, influencing Celtic kilts and other fashion trends. The Albanians also introduced the fustanella to the Greeks during the fourteenth century. The fustanella was prominent military dress during the reign of the Ottoman Empire and continued to have prominence in Eastern European military dress for centuries.

The fustanella is often associated with traditional folk dress, rather than with fashionable clothing trends. Some young people in these regions do not feel that fustanellas reflect their own identity and style. In the last decade, Greek designers have worked to reinvent the fustanella for contemporary fashion. A museum exhibition during the Athens Olympics entitled "Ptychoseis = Folds + Pleats: Drapery from Ancient Greek Dress to 21st Century Fashion" featured new possibilities for the fustanella. This exhibition challenged visitors to consider the art and creative craft that goes into making a fustanella and to consider it in a range of styles and settings. Designers have also published spreads in prestigious fashion magazines, such as the Greek *Vogue*.

The Fustanella in the United States

The fustanella has become a recognizable symbol of freedom and identity in Albanian and Greek populations in the United States. Albanian, Greek, and Macedonian immigrants in the United States sometimes wear fustanellas to reflect their heritage and express pride in where they came from. Fustanellas are a common sight at Greek and Albanian heritage festivals across the country.

In May of 2013 Disneyland hosted a Greek festival as one of the features in the "It's a Small World" section of the park. The event featured dance, performances, and Greek food tastings. In the advertisements, Mickey Mouse is wearing a fustanella while he dances with Minnie Mouse, providing further evidence of the strong relationship between the fustanella and ideas of Greek identity.

Influence and Impact

Websites for Greek and Albanian heritage festivals often feature photos of people dancing or marching in fustanellas. Festivals include the Yiasou Greek Festival in Charlotte, North Carolina, and the Massachusetts Albanian Folk Festival in Dorchester, Massachusetts, but there are many festivals, both large and small, that take place across the country every year. These events usually feature food, dancing, performances, children's activities, and crafts. They also provide an opportunity for those who identify with the fustanella to wear it.

These festivals often include performances by groups who regularly use the fustanella as an expression of their own identity and history. The Warriors of Greece are a historical reenactment group that travels across the country making appearances, and the Bashkimi Dance group is one that specializes in Albanian dance in the United States. The Warriors of Greece emphasize the role of the Greeks in forwarding democracy and have made appearances in Fourth of July parades and television programs. These are just two examples, but there are numerous groups across the country that use the fustanella in their programming.

The fustanella has influenced fashion for centuries and continues to do so in current times. The fustanella, like the Scottish kilt, is a skirt designed to show off the strength and athletic prowess of the wearer. Today, however, it remains unusual to see men's skirts in popular fashion trends. While there are some exceptions, and there have been instances of celebrities wearing them, they continue to be largely uncommon. Kanye West wore a black leather kilt in hip-hop performances, and men's skirts have made appearances in metal and punk music, as well as during the 1960s hippie era.

One of the most famous instances of a fustanella-like garment in popular culture was in 1969 when Mick Jagger of the Rolling Stones wore a garment reminiscent of the fustanella during a concert. The memorial show was planned to honor the life and recent loss of bandmate Brian Jones and took place in Hyde Park, London. The outfit created dialogue and some controversy. Many people were unaware of the fustanella and mistakenly believed the outfit was based on a woman's dress.

See also SIBENIK CAP
Compare to JODHPURS; KILT; LEDERHOSEN

Further Reading

"Bashkimi Dance: The Heart and Soul of Albanian Dance in U.S.A." http://bashkimidance.com.
Gen, Doy. "Ptychoseis = Folds + Pleats: Drapery from Ancient Greek Dress to Twenty-First Century Fashion." *Fashion Theory* 9, no. 2 (2005): 251–60.
Skafidas, Michael. "Fabricating Greekness: From Fustanella to the Glossy Page." In *The Fabric of Cultures: Fashion, Identity, and Globalization*, edited by Eugenia Paulicelli and Hazel Clark. New York: Routledge, 2008.

■ CAITLIN TRACEY-MILLER

G

GAUCHO TIE
See BOLO TIE

GELE

"Gele" is the Yoruba word for a female head wrap. The gele is generally made of two yards of brightly colored rectangular fabric formed into an intricate headdress on a woman's head in a variety of fashions. The fabric used is usually stiff but flexible in nature, such as brocade or damask. Ankara cloth, Nigerian wax-resist cloth, is frequently used in the shaping of a gele. However, the most popular material is *aso oke*, a handwoven cloth made of natural Nigerian wild silk and cotton yarns.

The gele fabric is wound twice around the head, tucked on one side, and possibly stuffed to add volume. There is no specific formula for wrapping the gele, resulting in a distinct arrangement each time it is worn. The gele is often made of the same fabric as the rest of the woman's ensemble, or it may be made of an entirely different pattern to create a more unique look.

History

The Yoruba people live in southern Nigeria and are the largest ethnic group south of the Sahara. Yoruba women are known for wearing the extremely elaborate headdresses that may tower several feet off their head. They wear the gele for any assortment of occasions. They are not restricted to purely ritualistic or ceremonial contexts; rather they are often worn when visiting friends, attending parties, or going to the market. The practice of wrapping and decorating the head relates to significant Yoruba beliefs about the sacredness of the head and its role in defining the individual. The beautification of the head is symbolic to the Yoruba people because it is a sign of their respect to the sacred self also found within the physical head.

The Gele in the United States

The United States currently has the third-largest concentration of Nigerians outside of Nigeria. Since the 1970s, Nigerians have been a part of the immigrant pool into the

United States in a quest for Western education, or escaping the sociopolitical situation in Nigeria, the aftermath of the Nigerian civil war, and the military dictatorships of the 1980s and 1990s. Once in the United States they settle in the southern states where the climate is warmer and where education and living costs are generally lower.

Influence and Impact

Because of the extreme importance placed on one's ethnic group, Nigerians will do whatever is necessary to ensure the continuation of their heritage through subsequent generations. They do this out of fear of losing their individual ethnic heritage in the United States, where all black people tend to be classified as one ethnic group. Nigerian-Americans have emphasized the use of dress as a way to express group identity. Despite the pressure to assimilate, traditional Nigerian dress, such as the gele, is a ubiquitous feature of major Nigerian occasions and parties. However, the traditional Nigerian head wrap has undergone a dramatic transformation since Nigerian-American women have turned it into a local fashion statement. In Texas, home to the United States' largest Nigerian-American population, gele have reached astronomical heights, and more and more African-Americans are trying to create and maintain an African identity through the use of African textiles, such as the gele, at their own weddings.

Fati Asibelua, Nigeria's premier fashion designer, frequently creates clothing with a mix of traditional Nigerian design with modern Western aesthetics in her international label Momo and her luxury label Asibelua, which includes contemporary versions of the towering gele. Non-African designers have co-opted the African head wrap for years and walked it down the runways of major international cities. Jean Paul Gaultier is just one of them to be featured in fashion magazines with his rendition of the Nigerian gele.

See also AFRICAN HEAD WRAP; BOUBOU; HAWLI
Compare to CHURCH HAT; DO-RAG

Further Reading

Afolayan, Michael Oladejo, and Betty Wass. "Yoruba Headties." In *Crowning Achievements: African Arts of Dressing the Head*, edited by Mary Jo Arnoldi and Christine Mullen Kreamer, 139–45. Los Angeles: Fowler Museum of Cultural History, 1995.

Bell, Chanelle. "Geles: Crowning Glories of West Africa." *Oakland Post*, July 2012, 7.

Kent, Kate P. *Introducing West African Cloth*. Denver, CO: Denver Museum of Natural History, 1971.

Showalter, Misty. 2010. "Segun Gele: Master of Nigeria's Gravity Defying Headgear." CNN Marketplace Africa, July 16, 2010, http://www.cnn.com/2010/WORLD/africa/07/16/segun.gele.nigeria .headgear/index.html?iref=allsearch (accessed August 5, 2011).

Starke, Barbara, Lillian O. Holloman, and Barbara K. Nordquist. *African American Dress and Adornment: A Cultural Perspective*. Dubuque: Kendal/Hunt Publishing, 1990.

Strübel, Jessica. "Get Your Gele: Nigerian Dress, Diasporic Identity, and Translocalism." *Journal of Pan African Studies* 4, no. 9 (2011): 36–53.

■ JESSICA STRÜBEL

GETA
See FLIP-FLOPS (GETA)

GLOVES
See MOUSQUETAIRE

GOLF CAP
See FLAT CAP

GYPSY SKIRT

The gypsy skirt is derived from a traditional style worn by female members of a nomadic Romani people who migrated from India to Europe in the fourteenth century, referred to as gypsies. The term "gypsy" was derived from Egyptian, as Europeans had mistakenly thought that gypsies had migrated from Egypt. The Romani population is comprised of many subgroups, including the Roma of Central and Eastern Europe.

History

The traditional skirts worn by Roma women inspired the American gypsy skirt. Their traditional attire consists of tight-fitting blouses with low necklines paired with long, full pleated skirts. These skirts are no shorter than mid-calf as the Roma believe women's lower halves are impure due to menstruation and childbirth. This belief ties to the customary Roma punishment of skirt tossing, whereby women render offensive men unclean by lifting or tossing their skirts at them.

By the late 1930s, gypsy skirts were elements of fashionable dress on both sides of the Atlantic. In Paris, designers Elsa Schiaparelli, Jean Patou, Marcel Rochas, and Coco Chanel showed cocktail dresses with low décolletage and full, pleated skirts for summer 1937. These full-skirted dresses were made popular with the revival of the waltz in the late 1930s. By the early 1940s, American department stores, such as Russeks and Macy's, were advertising knee-length gypsy skirts for casual, daytime ensembles.

The Gypsy Skirt in the United States

Gypsy-inspired skirts have been common in the United States since the nineteenth century, when the Roma began migrating to the Americas. Among the earliest adopters of these skirts were the female members of the Women's Dress Reform and the Arts and Crafts Movements in the second half of the nineteenth century. At the time, the fashionable silhouette dictated that women wear corsets, bustles, and other restrictive underpinnings beneath their clothes. These groups encouraged women to adopt loose-fitting, functional garments. They argued that these styles were not only healthier for women but would help them achieve gender equality as well. Although patterns and materials varied, these skirts generally adhered to the shape and length of traditional Roma skirts and were long, full, and pleated.

Gypsy skirts were often elements of romanticized costumes worn by middle- and upper-class women to costume balls in the late nineteenth and early twentieth centuries as well. The *Omaha Daily Bee* reported in their August 26, 1894, issue, "Women attendants [of a local fancy fair] looked their prettiest in their gypsy dress," consisting of "gay plaid skirts, white blouses, red or yellow sashes, and bright handkerchiefs knotted on the head." Although the skirts' silhouettes were not mentioned, the use of plaid reveals the influence of other traditional styles, namely the plaids of Scottish immigrants.

Influence and Impact

Wartime rationing and the rise of the miniskirt curtailed the popularity of gypsy skirts until the late 1960s, when members of the hippie counterculture began to embrace non-Western clothing styles. The skirts' acceptance also coincided with an increase in women working outside the home and a general preference for comfortable, loose-fitting clothing at this time. American designers Norman Norell and Geoffrey Beene featured gypsy-inspired skirts for both day and evening wear in their late 1960s collections, and the French designer Yves Saint Laurent famously adapted the traditional Roma skirt for his 1970s couture collections.

Gypsy-inspired skirts strongly reemerged again in the late 1990s and 2000s. American *Vogue* magazine featured a black lace gypsy skirt by the Italian designers Dolce & Gabbana in its January 2002 issue, hailing it an "optimistic style" with a "joyful swing" in the wake of the 9/11 terrorist attacks. Ten years later, the *New York Times* ran a series of articles that explored the renewed interest in an idealized Roma culture and the spread of gypsy-inspired clothing, including gypsy skirts in bright, clashing colors and patterns in the wake of the country's economic crisis.

See also BOHEMIAN DRESS; PEASANT BLOUSE
Compare to BROOMSTICK SKIRT; CHIMA; DIRNDL

Further Reading

Blum, Dilys E. *Shocking! The Art and Fashion of Elsa Schiaparelli*. New Haven, CT: Yale University Press, 2003.

Bonos, Arlene Helen. "Roumany Rye of Philadelphia." *American Anthropologist* 44, no. 2 (April–June 1942): 257–74.

"Fashion Loosens Up." *Vogue*, January 2002.

"The Gypsy Aesthetic Gains Popularity on Runways and Streets." *New York Times*, July 12, 2012.

"Gypsy Camp and Fancy Fair." *Omaha Daily Bee*, August 26, 1894.

La Ferla, Ruth. "Joining the Gypsy Caravan." *New York Times*, July 11, 2012.

Weyrauch, Walter O., ed. *Gypsy Law: Romani Legal Traditions and Culture*. Berkeley: University of California Press, 2001.

■ LAURA L. CAMERLENGO

HAMMER PANTS

See HAREM PANT (SALWAR); SIRWAL

HANBOK

The hanbok (literally "Korean clothing") is the traditional dress of Korea. It is a flowing, floor-length garment that is gathered at the waist and comes in all kinds of colors. It is also known as *Joseon-ot* because it comes from the Joseon dynasty (1392–1897). It is normally worn on formal occasions and during festivals. In the twentieth century it has undergone several changes. Unlike the Japanese *kosode* (which mutated to become the kimono), the hanbok was not worn in different versions by all echelons of society.

History

The hanbok has its roots in the nomadic peoples of northern Asia around the region of northern Mongolia. Evidence of the garment can be found on murals of Goguryeo dating from before the third century BCE. It was at this time that the basics of the hanbok were established, consisting of the pants (*baji*), the skirt (chima), and the outer jacket (jeogori). It is believed that the migration of Mongolian dress to Korea occurred around the time of the Goryeo dynasty after the peace made with the Mongol Empire in the thirteenth century. This was occasioned by the marriage of Mongol princesses and nobility into Korean houses.

During the Joseon dynasty, the hanbok was worn in a slightly more baggy style. However, in the sixteenth century the jeogori (outer jacket) was shortened to become waist high and tightened, while the chima, or skirt, became fuller. In the eighteenth and nineteenth centuries, the styles became more bell-like, accentuating the hips, mildly reminiscent of the whalebone dresses of the eighteenth century and the bustles of the nineteenth. Clothing reform movements in the twentieth century have tended to make the jeogori longer, although they stayed above the waistline.

In contrast to the various mutations of the women's hanbok, the male version of the jeogori and the *baji* remained virtually unaltered, while the outer coat underwent a major change in the nineteenth century. From at least the sixteenth century, *yangban*, or noblemen, wore a *jungchimak*, a flowing garment with flowing sleeves and two to three splits at the base to accentuate the dramatic flowing movement of the garment while walking.

These were successfully banned, however, by the leading figure of the latter half of the nineteenth century, Daewon-gun. The garment was replaced by *durumagi*, a more fitted garment that dispensed with the splits.

Hanboks came in all manner of fabrics. The upper classes wore them made out of ramie in the colder months and silk in summer, while sumptuary law restricted commoners to wearing only cotton. Children of the nobility wore brighter colors; adults were disinclined to do so. The lower classes were restricted to white but were permitted a small choice of other colors for festive occasions. The colors of the hanbok could be denotive; dark blue, for instance, suggested that a woman had one or more sons. The royal family showed their distinction by wearing gold leaf on richly patterned garments.

In the period after World War II, the hanbok witnessed a decline in popularity with the modernization and Westernization of dress in Korea. But in the 1990s it experienced an aggressive revival. Increasingly worn by politicians and businesswomen to assert their ties to their nation, it became worn as a third option in formal circles to the suit, asserting the presence of Korean rural life.

The story of the hanbok is a little like the kimono insofar as it was a response to outside stimuli before it molded itself into the rhetoric of tradition. The 1990s version is yet another modification of this already recent construction. Retaining only the former shape, it is usually made of cotton instead of silk, is more muted in color, and may use modern fasteners such as zippers. Rebecca Ruhlen in her essay aptly titled "Korean Alterations" concludes that "the new hanbok styles were part of a repertoire for the performance and consumption of national identity, available to all Koreans but used especially by activists." She outlines the extent of the hanbok's involvement as a Korean signifier of both domestic and economic self-assertion, even where the "lifestyle" hanbok is extolled over the unhealthy ostentation of women's Western dress.

Hanbok in the United States

The traditional Hanbok followed along with Korean immigrants to the United States and may be seen among Korean ethnic groups during ceremonial occasions such as a child's first birthday, weddings, and funerals.

Influence and Impact

The silhouette and elegance of the hanbok is also valued by non-Korean women in the United States. Hanbok designs are used as formal evening wear among wealthy Western women because of the garment's ability to combine traditional Korean form with modern aesthetics.

See also CHIMA; JEOGORI; NORIGAE
Compare to HANFU CHINESE ROBES; KIMONO

Further Reading

Geczy, Adam. *Fashion and Orientalism: Dress, Textiles and Culture from the 17th to the 21st Century.* London and New York: Bloomsbury, 2013.
Pfeiffer, Alice. "Traditional Korean Style Gets a Forward Spin." *New York Times*, November 18, 2010.

Ruhlen, Rebecca. "Korean Alterations: Nationalism, Social Consciousness and 'Traditional' Clothing." In *Re-Orienting Fashion*, edited by Sandra Niessen, Ann Marie Leshkowich, and Carla Jones. Oxford and New York: Berg, 2003.

■ ADAM GECZY

HANFU CHINESE ROBES

Chinese hanfu robes are full-length wrapped garments with bell-shaped sleeves extending over the hand. The front left opening is extended to a triangle shape. The robe is wrapped left to right, drawing the left front around the back to the front and tying it with a sash, often supplemented with small, dangling, decorative knots and carvings. Wide bands of contrast edging at the neck, front opening, hem, and sleeves distinguish the hanfu from other robes. When wrapped, the contrast banding creates a dramatic play of line and color. Both men and women wear the hanfu; however, the overlap on the men's style is less extensive. In the Disney film *Mulan*, the title character wears a hanfu to visit the matchmaker.

History

The term "hanfu" means "dress of the Han people." It is based on the two-piece, fitted *shenyi* of the Warring States period (475–221 BCE). *Shenyi* means "deep garment," meaning to wrap the body deep within cloth. According to the Confucian Book of Rites, the robe must be long and spacious enough to completely cover the body, a traditional Chinese ethic. By the Han dynasty (206 BCE–220 CE), the one-piece version emerged as a long voluminous linen or silk robe in vivid, contrasting primary colors. Manchu people from the northeast founded the Qing dynasty (1616–1911 CE). Manchu society was based on the horse, so dress was designed for riding and shooting, featuring jackets with buttons down the center front and trousers. To expunge the Han identity, Qing rulers prohibited Han national dress and required them to wear garments in the Manchu tradition. Han resistance was so severe that the policies were modified. Men, government officials, Confucian scholars, and prostitutes wore the Manchu style; women, errand boys, children, monks, and Taoists were free to wear Han styles. Han dress was also permitted for special occasions such as weddings and funerals.

During the Republic of China period (1911–1949 CE), Euro-American lifestyles and products influenced Chinese dress, representing the shift from dynastic to popular rule. Traditional dress was less interesting than the new choices available. After the revolution in 1949 and the founding of the People's Republic of China, both traditional dress and world dress were rejected in favor of Mao suits and boxy cotton jackets and pants for both men and women. Communist leadership discouraged reference to historical class hierarchies and modern capitalistic values. As a result, traditional Han dress was relegated to ceremonial use.

With the liberalization of the Chinese economy, interest in national dress prompted a search for popular, authentic, and intrinsically Chinese styles. Because the term *han* refers to both the larger Han Chinese identity and the Han dynasty, the term "hanfu" is used to designate all authentic traditional dress of the Han people. Because of its proportions, the hanfu is impractical for everyday dress, but it is worn in China for the Mid-Autumn

Festival and for a newly created coming-of-age ritual. Some favor the hanfu as a proto-type for China's academic regalia. On the other hand, the hanfu resembles the Japanese kimono and Korean hanbok, both based on Chinese robes. Some scholars note that this cultural authentication of styles blurs the geopolitical boundaries of what is authentically Han. Infusion of Chinese-American aesthetics and meanings may further complicate identifying an intrinsically Chinese national dress.

Hanfu in the United States

Han dress arrived in the United States with Chinese immigrants in the nineteenth century. Male laborers tended toward Manchu jackets and pants for work on the pineapple and sugarcane plantations of Hawai'i, in the gold fields of the American West (1848–1855 CE), and on the transcontinental railroad (1863–1869 CE). Over time, their families joined them, bringing traditions such as ceremonial dress.

In the United States, the hanfu is worn as ethnic dress for special occasions throughout the life cycle. Women's hanfu are billowing and fluid, with extended sleeves, trailing ribbons, and swaying dangles. Accessories range from the very traditional to the fashion forward, similar to the trending of other wedding dresses in America. Men's styles are more restrained, but equally elegant.

Influence and Impact

Euro-Americans often identify the hanfu as traditional Chinese dress, inspiring Seventh Avenue, Hollywood, and individuals alike. In addition, when times change, dress is often the stage where the negotiation of cultural values plays out. The hanfu has been that stage, both historically and in the twenty-first century. The hanfu is also used as costuming in cosplay, where tradition and fantasy combine.

See also CHEONGSAM; CHINESE FLATS; CHINESE SILK PAJAMAS; MAO SUIT
Compare to CHIMA; HAORI; JEOGORI; KIMONO

Further Reading

Finnane, Antonia. *Changing Clothes in China: Fashion, History, Nation*. New York: Columbia University Press, 2008.

■ SANDRA LEE EVENSON

HAORI

A haori is a type of Japanese coat usually worn over a kimono. It is worn open at the front and hangs off the shoulders. Its origin may have been earlier jacket-like garments for servants, or alternatively it may have evolved from another type of jacket worn over armor by the samurai for warmth. During the secluded Edo period in Japan from 1603 to 1868, the haori became casual clothing for men but was banned by the sumptuary laws for women as it was considered too masculine. A haori men's coat is typically paired with the *hakama*, a wide trouser-like garment also worn over the kimono. Since the reopening of Japan in the Meiji period from 1868, the haori became formal clothing for men and women and was considered proper street wear. The male haori tended to be shorter, and the sleeves were fully attached to the body, while women's haori were open on the body side similar to kimono sleeves.

Haori

History

Geisha of the Fukagawa area in Edo first wore haori in the late seventeenth century. Geisha and courtesans tended to be trendsetters in the Edo period partly because their profession left them somewhat immune to sumptuary regulation. It was not until the reopening of Japan in the late nineteenth and early twentieth centuries that haori became fashionable and appropriate for ordinary women.

One traditional element of the haori is the occasional inclusion of intricate embroidery, often a figurative scene, in gold and other dramatic colors, but on the inside of a plain-colored haori and thus hidden or only glimpsed during regular wear. This reflected a reaction by the merchant classes to the sumptuary laws imposed on them by the samurai during the Edo period. They were not permitted ostentatious displays of their increasing wealth and thus created an entire aesthetic of subtle display, known as *iki*, or elegant chic, which focused on subtle details.

A haori commonly has up to five family crests, or *mon*, as decoration. Crests are usually placed on the sleeves, on both sides of the front, and somewhat larger at the center of the back below the shoulders. Traditionally only aristocratic families had crests; however, it was part of the project of Japanese modernization that everyone should have a family name, and thus it also became a feature of class aspiration to have a family crest. Virtually all modern Japanese families have a crest, and if not, professional ritual organizers like wedding planners and undertakers offer services to find an appropriate crest. Like the haori itself, family crests were formerly aristocrat elements that became part of mass Japanese culture in the period of modernization. It is thus fitting that they go together today in rituals when tradition is called upon. At weddings, funerals, and times when high formality is required, men and women will wear a haori with a family crest on it.

Haori in the United States

Japanese immigrants to the United States mostly brought haori with them as part of their wedding trousseax. A late nineteenth-century farm girl who went to Hawai'i or California to marry a male Japanese plantation worker who had sent for a Japanese bride once he had saved enough money would usually have sewn her dowry herself, and it would have included a formal haori. Such haori would usually have a family crest, although both the wearing of haori by women and universal crest usage were inventions of the late nineteenth century and reactions to foreign influence in the reopening of Japan.

Influence and Impact

As part of the large-scale reinvention of Japanese traditional clothing that accompanied the introduction and challenge of foreign Euro-American clothing, the longer three-quarter-length woman's haori became an item of bourgeois respectability. The claiming of a masculine item of clothing by women was common in the Meiji period, and other originally male garments, such as the *hakama*, became standard clothing for women. While the *hakama* was associated with women's education, the haori was more of a Japanese reaction to the practicality and formality of Euro-American women's overcoats. Japanese traditional women's kimono-based clothing was drafty in winter, and an extra layer added warmth. As modern urban living increased, there was also a need for a level of formality for walking in the street, and the haori provided this for women. In this way the haori reflects Euro-American ideas of formality filtered through early foreign influences on Japanese male clothing.

See also FLIP-FLOPS (GETA); HAPPI; KIMONO; TABI
Compare to DOLMAN; HANFU CHINESE ROBES

Further Reading

Dalby, Liza. *Kimono: Fashioning Culture*. London: Random House, 1993.
Kawakami, Barbara F. *Japanese Immigrant Clothing in Hawaii, 1885–1941*. Honolulu: University of Hawaiʻi Press, 1993.
Minnich, Helen Benton. *Japanese Costume and the Makers of Its Elegant Tradition*. Tokyo: Tuttle, 1963.
Slade, Toby. *Japanese Fashion: A Cultural History*. Oxford: Berg, 2009.

■ TOBY SLADE

HAPPI

Happi are a type of Japanese haori, a traditional coat-like garment worn over a kimono, commonly worn today by shopkeepers and now primarily associated with Japanese festivals. Happi are loose and open at the front, sometimes with a small tie and sometimes worn with a rope belt. They have straight sleeves and are usually made of indigo or brown cotton and imprinted with a crest, or *mon*.

History

The origin of the Japanese happi was as a garment to easily identify the wearer. Household servants wore happi with the family crest of the household they worked in. Shops and other organizations used happi as a method of identifying livery. They would usually have the crest of the shop and sometimes the name embroidered or printed in Chinese characters. Firefighters, an important and glamorous profession in the Edo period, also wore happi to identify their brigade. There were forty-eight brigades, each identified by one of the forty-eight syllables in the traditional Japanese syllabary. Their happi would have the large syllable character in the center of the back. The huge fires of the dense wooden city of Edo often required amateur help to control, and such uniforms also likely facilitated this.

Traditionally in Japan only aristocratic families had crests, which served as military heraldry. Shops and other organizations began to adopt crests during the peaceful and prosperous Edo period when the role of the warrior classes started to be eclipsed by the urban merchant classes. Today almost all families have adopted a family crest for use at weddings, funerals, or other occasions requiring a reference to traditional formality. The crest of Mitsu is shown in many woodblock prints by Hiroshige and famously later became the emblem for the Mitsukoshi department store. The rules regulating the creation of crests were few and mainly determined by social customs. Apart from prohibitions on using the imperial crests or improperly using a crest used by someone superior, there were no limits to the creation of crests, and thus they were abundantly invented as a form of early corporate logos. Today most traditional crafts and specialty shops have them, as do traditional eateries such as sushi restaurants. The workers in such shops and restaurants commonly wear happi with these crests emblazoned on them.

The Happi in the United States

In the United States the use of happi came to be associated most commonly with the celebration of traditional Japanese festivals by Japanese immigrants, particularly in Hawai'i. The Obon festival is the most important of these and comes from the Buddhist custom to honor the spirit of one's ancestors. It is celebrated in midsummer and traditionally includes a dance called *bon-odori*, which involves dancing around a *yagura*, or purpose-built wooden scaffold or tower.

Dancing in the middle of summer naturally requires a light and festive costume. Before World War II it was common to wear *yukata*, a light and often colorful cotton kimono for the summer, at festivals in Hawai'i. During the war, traditional Japanese customs were largely discontinued in Hawai'i.

Festivals were resumed once again after the war, with most importantly the Obon Festival featuring dancing and other festival events centering around Buddhist temples. After the war, however, instead of *yukata*, many participants began to wear happi with tight black pants. The happi often had the crest of the temple printed on it. The *tenugui*, a soft cotton towel used for bathing, washing, and as a sweatband, also became associated with Obon festivals and were a common accompaniment to the happi, worn around the head as a symbol of the exertion of dancing in the summer. *Tenugui* were given out by temples and had the crest and name of the temple printed on it. Motifs such as dancing figures, lanterns, cherry blossoms, or Buddhist symbols were common themes for their design. Interestingly, in Hawai'i, *obon tenugui* were often sewn together to make happi, as their colorful designs and temple crests made them perfect material for sewing together into a happi.

Influence and Impact

In the United States the happi, mostly only worn at festivals, has become a symbol of a cultural and religious link to the past and to Japan. Its overt symbolism, both directly religious, with its listing of the names of temples, or secular, with its depictions of Japanese motifs, as well as the happi's ability to be worn over either traditional Japanese or Western clothing facilitated its role as a symbolic link to the past and to tradition for Japanese immigrants to the United States.

See also FLIP-FLOPS (GETA); HAORI; KIMONO; TABI
Compare to DOLMAN; HANFU CHINESE ROBES

Further Reading

Dalby, Liza. *Kimono: Fashioning Culture*. London: Random House, 1993.
Kawakami, Barbara F. *Japanese Immigrant Clothing in Hawaii, 1885–1941*. Honolulu: University of Hawai'i Press, 1993.
Minnich, Helen Benton. *Japanese Costume and the Makers of Its Elegant Tradition*. Tokyo: Tuttle, 1963.
Slade, Toby. *Japanese Fashion: A Cultural History*. Oxford: Berg, 2009.

■ TOBY SLADE

HARDANGER

Hardanger is a type of Norwegian embroidery. Working on a fabric with an even warp and weft, the embroiderer counts and pulls out or cuts threads vertically and horizontally to create geometric shapes. The artisan then embroiders the edges of the spaces with satin and other stitches to retain the shape created as well as for decoration. Worked on white fabric, the embroidery is white, black, or multicolored. This embroidery style has been used to decorate traditional Norwegian dress for centuries and got its name from its associations with the folk dress of the Hardanger area in western Norway. Similar examples are found in other Scandinavian traditions, as well as various Mediterranean and other European countries.

History

Of the Scandinavian countries, Norway has the strongest folk-dress traditions. By the turn of the twentieth century, regional outfits had been evolving for many years, the patterns, colors, and embroidery of each representing a certain county. The dress of each region is called a *bunad*, and around the time of liberation from Swedish rule in 1905, the outfit specific to the Hardanger region was adopted as a symbol of national pride; it is still worn on Norwegian National Day (May 17) in both Norway and among the Norwegian diaspora, including in North America. Its main colors, black, red, and white, are heraldic and simple, perfect for use as a symbol of Norway. One of the most recognizable aspects of the Hardanger outfit was the white apron, worn in stark contrast to the dark red and black wool of the outer pieces. Aprons used for special occasions were adorned with what became known as Hardanger embroidery, most often near the hem. The collar and cuffs of the traditional white linen blouse were also adorned with this embroidery technique.

Hardanger in the United States

Norwegian emigration to America began in earnest in 1825. As with immigrants from other countries, especially those who had lived in the countryside, many Norwegians wore their traditional clothing at least for their first few weeks in America. However, many—especially young adults—quickly acquired new American-style clothing so as not to stick out as a newcomer. This was especially true during the late nineteenth century, when the number of immigrants in America exploded. However, folk dress was so attached to holidays and rites of passage that christenings, weddings, and funerals in Norwegian communities in America almost always included the national outfit, if not the regional *bunad*. The embroidered apron, a sign of a special occasion, was an easy way to show identification with Norway on those days; its form did not change with the fashionable silhouette, and it could be added to any outfit.

At the turn of the twentieth century, thin white lingerie dresses with lots of tucks and embroidery were in style; white-on-white Norwegian Hardanger was a popular and fitting decoration. While some traditional garments were handed down, the many copies of these garments made by Norwegian-Americans were often oversimplified, based more on color schemes (black, white, and red) than on traditional materials or silhouette. Hardanger embroidery is a delicate, exacting craft; many reproductions—often copied from postcards until travel to Norway became cheap—were rough approximations made from synthetic materials. Display of ethnic pride was variously celebrated and despised in America during the first half of the twentieth century, and antiethnic sentiment influenced the popularity of items like a Norwegian embroidered apron or folk blouse. However, the embroidery was subtle enough to be added to nontraditional items of clothing to show Norwegian pride, such as on fashionable collars or bonnets. Fashion's interest in vintage lace in the 1970s brought Hardanger back to the forefront, adorning mostly women's clothing.

Influence and Impact

Events such as Norwegian pride celebrations, weddings, funerals, christenings, and confirmations in America still use traditional Norwegian dress, which are more accurate than in earlier decades. More Americans own regional *bunad* outfits, although Norwegian pride is most often shown through the wearing of a sweater knit in a traditional design. Craft and needlework have recently experienced a renaissance in America, and Hardanger has become a popular embroidery style.

See also APRON
Compare to HUIPIL; JILBAB; KOSOVOROTKA; MEXICAN TOURIST/SOUVENIR JACKET

Further Reading
Ciotti, Donatella. *Hardanger Embroidery*. New York: Sterling, 2006.
Colburn, Carol Huset. "Norwegian Folk Dress in America." In *Norwegian Folk Art: The Migration of a Tradition*, edited by Marion Nelson. New York: Abbeville Press, 1995.
Williams, Patricia. "From Folk to Fashion: Dress Adaptations of Norwegian Immigrant Women in the Midwest." In *Dress in American Culture*, edited by Patricia A. Cunningham and Susan Voso Lab. Bowling Green, OH: Bowling Green State University Popular Press, 1993.

■ ARIANNA E. FUNK

HAREM PANT (SALWAR)

The harem pant is a wide-legged, baggy pant confined at the ankle; it is also confined below the knee with folds falling to the ankle. The pant style is not specific to any one culture but is used in the American fashion vernacular to describe a style of pant reminiscent of that worn by women in harems of the Turkish-Ottoman Empire (1299–1922)—a culture of immense Western fascination from the seventeenth to the early twentieth century.

History

The Ottoman Empire was founded at the end of the thirteenth century by Osman I in Anatolia (modern-day Turkey) but was greatly expanded after several successful military campaigns to become a dominant world power. At its height, the empire encompassed much of Asia Minor, southeastern Europe, the Middle East, and northeastern Africa. Increased European trade from the sixteenth century onward spurred subsequent waves of *turquerie*—imitation of Turkish culture and art—across the West.

The origins of the full, wide-legged Turkish pant known as the salvar lie in Central Asia, where Turks resided before migrating to Anatolia in the second century BCE. Like the dress of many nomadic horse-riding tribes, pants were an integral and necessary component of Turkish dress. They prevented chafing while riding and provided an encompassing barrier to the temperate weather of Central Asia. Due to the Ottoman Empire's vast influence, the salvar had many regional variations in style, cut, textile, and name, also known as *shalwar*, *shalvar*, *sirwal*, *salwar*, *chalwar*, and *chalvar*, depending on the culture where it is found.

When the Turks invaded the Byzantine city of Constantinople (present-day Istanbul) in the fifteenth century, they inherited a rich textile tradition that was subsequently infused into their sartorial customs. The Ottoman's luxurious and colorful silk textiles and clothing were a dominant presence in the numerous romanticized depictions of Ottoman harems that flooded the West. The Turkish word "harem" is derived from Arabic *ḥaram* or *ḥarīm*, literally "prohibited place," and was applied to the private household quarters of Ottoman women—a favorite topic in travelers' accounts, literature, music, and paintings across the West. Ottoman women are repeatedly the central motif in the lush, decadent harem interiors and are dressed in ornate ensembles composed of long, layered tunics with full, loose salvars. Though the exact etymology of "harem pant" is unclear, it is likely due to this association that the term came to be applied to the interpretation of similar styles in European, and subsequently American, costume and fashion.

The Harem Pant in the United States

Europeans appropriated many elements of Turkish dress, including the salvar, for the fashionable fancy dress portraits of the eighteenth century. By the early nineteenth century, women were wearing large, baggy pants as sportswear in European sanitariums. In America, the Turkish-inspired pants would surface in woman's clothing in the early

1850s, when the style appeared in the form of "Turkish trousers" or "pantalets" worn by women's rights activists, notably Amelia Bloomer. The voluminous pant was worn under a shortened skirt and offered a comfortable—and controversial—alternative to the prevailing fashions of the time that emphasized a corseted waist and multiple layers of cumbersome, heavy skirts. The dress offended strict societal gender codes that relegated pants to men's wardrobes and was eventually abandoned for more conventional styles by the end of the decade.

A similar, bifurcated style would resurface in the 1890s as acceptable attire for the newly popular sport of bicycle riding. In 1911, it appeared again, this time as a high-fashion alternative for women's at-home wear as promoted by avant-garde French couturier Paul Poiret whose controversial *jupe-culottes* were shocking to polite taste. Dubbed "harem trousers" in the American press, the pants were indicative of both Poiret's passion for Eastern-inspired materials and silhouettes as well as the prevailing Orientalism of the time. The Orientalism that swept Europe and America in this period was due in large part to the huge success of productions by Sergei Diaghilev's Ballet Russes, where the intoxicating and exotic "East" was brought to life in beautiful, brilliant sets and costumes designed by Leon Bakst. The familiar harem-inspired pant was a central motif. American art patron Gertrude Vanderbilt Whitney was one of many members of the artistic avant-garde who adopted the controversial garment. French artist Robert Henri depicts her comfortably lounging in a pair of harem pants in a 1914 portrait.

Influence and Impact

The harem pant has seen subsequent revivals in fashion throughout the twentieth and twenty-first centuries, including the "harem pant" for men popularized by pop artist MC Hammer in the late 1980s, which soon after became known as the aptly named "Hammer pant." Today, the style continues to be reinterpreted and recreated in fashion. The term's perpetual use in relation to such styles speaks to its continued relation to the exotic "East"—even if its cultural origins and associations have been lost.

See also HIP-HOP FASHION; SIRWAL
Compare to BERMUDA SHORTS; CAPRI PANTS; CHINESE SILK PAJAMAS; JODHPURS; LEDERHOSEN

Further Reading

Bloomer, Amelia. "Female Attire." *The Lily, a Ladies' Journal Devoted to Temperance and Literature* 3, no. 2 (February 1851): 13.

Cunningham, Patricia A. *Reforming Women's Fashion, 1850–1920: Politics, Health, and Art.* Kent, OH, and London: Kent State University Press, 2003.

Lewis, Reina. *Rethinking Orientalism: Women, Travel, and the Ottoman Harem.* New Brunswick, NJ: Rutgers University Press, 2004.

"New Gowns for the Maxine and Tango Dances Exhibited at Heimerdinger's." *American Cloak and Suit Review* 7 (January 1914): 326.

Poiret, Paul. *King of Fashion.* London: V&A Publishing, 2009.

"Turkish Costume." *Harper's* 14 (July 1851): 288.

■ CASSIDY ZACHARY

HARRIS TWEED

The term "Harris Tweed" refers to twill cloth that is hand harvested, spun, dyed, and woven by artisans living in the outer islands of Scotland. The hand-dyeing process gives Harris Tweed characteristic variations in color that gives the cloth visual texture and appeal. Though hundreds of patterns have been developed in Harris Tweeds, most often this fabric is created in tartan, herringbone, and houndstooth check patterns. Authentic Harris Tweed is hand inspected in ten-meter lengths and distinguished by the official "Mark of the Orb" trademark.

History

Wool cloth production was a natural by-product of sheep farming in Scotland in the eighteenth century. The cloth was called *clò mór*, which is Gaelic for "the big cloth." The cloth was naturally warm and water resistant, making it ideal for outdoor work on the Scottish moors. Though production was primarily to meet the family's own needs, excess cloth could be used as currency to barter or pay debts. The distinction of Harris Tweed from other Scottish wool products began when the Industrial Revolution came to Scotland. The Scottish mainland quickly adopted mechanized looms for cloth production, but the outer islands of Lewis, Harris, the Uists, Benbecula, and Barra (known as the Outer Hebrides) retained their traditional hand-processing methods.

Around 1830 the cloth came to be known as tweed because of a mistake made in trading. Clò Mór was traditionally woven in a twill pattern, and an invoice to a London merchant from Harwick referred to a shipment as "tweel." The London merchant misinterpreted the handwriting, believing the cloth to be named after the River Tweed that flows through the Scottish borders. The merchant subsequently advertised the cloth as "Tweed," and the name stuck.

In 1836 Alexander Murray, the Sixth Earl of Dunmore, inherited North Harris from his father. After he passed away in 1845, his wife Catherine (née Herbert) took over the estate. In an attempt to protect her people from the ravages of the highland potato famine, she employed crofters to weave the family tartan in the local tweed. She used the cloth to clothe her gamekeepers and gillies (hunting attendants). The superior quality of the fabric soon became apparent to her aristocratic companions, who sought to use it in their own hunting apparel. At the same time, Lady Herbert worked with local craftsmen to standardize and improve production quality and established a market in London. In short order, the famous Harris Tweed became the favored hunting apparel of Queen Victoria and her inner circle. Preference for Harris Tweed hunting jackets spread among the privileged classes and solidified the cloth's reputation.

Harris Tweed

In the twentieth century, the high demand for Harris Tweed inspired the development of Stornoway Tweed, a cheaper-quality, machine-made knockoff. This caused producers from Harris and Lewis to appeal to the Board of Trade for protection for their product. The board agreed, but only if all the Outer Hebrides were included. In 1910, the "Orb Trade Mark" was established and hand stamped onto lengths of authentic Harris Tweed. It was also during this time that the Harris Tweed Association, a voluntary organization committed to protecting the use of the Orb Trade Mark and Harris Tweed cloth, was formed. In 1993, the Scottish parliament passed an official act recognizing the Harris Tweed Authority as the official successors to the Harris Tweed Association. The Harris Tweed Authority continues to protect and promote the cloth and Orb trademark to this day.

Harris Tweed in the United States

The popularity of Harris Tweed in the United States is primarily dependent upon its established European reputation as a high-quality, classic fashion good. In the United States, Harris Tweed is most often used in men and women's suiting, primarily as blazers. Though in the past the Harris Tweed Authority has been disappointed with U.S. sales and imports, they hope improvements to their website and new marketing campaigns will increase American desire for the brand once again.

Influence and Impact

Despite originating in Scotland, Harris Tweed does not have a strong cultural connotation unless woven in historical Scottish tartans. It does carry a slight connotation of gentlemen who would hunt in the English countryside, though wearing a Harris Tweed jacket in America would hardly identify one as a hunter. Archetypically, Harris Tweed blazers are often used to characterize a quiet intellectual with a classic sense of fashion. Though not out of place in the business setting, the tweed jacket with leather elbow patches is often thought of as the stereotypical dress of professors and scholars. The British science-fiction television series *Doctor Who* featured Harris Tweed jackets on actors Patrick Troughton and Matt Smith, the second and eleventh Doctors, respectively. U.S. followers demanded Harris Tweed jackets to emulate the look. Sadly, BBC producers responded to demands for the iconic apparel by exchanging Harris Tweed for a cheaper knockoff cloth and selling replica coats at extravagant prices. Harris Tweed is also the preferred apparel for Dan Brown's iconic character Robert Langdon, protagonist of the novels *Angels and Demons*, *The Da Vinci Code*, *The Lost Symbol*, and *Inferno*. Langdon, a Harvard professor, is specifically described as preferring turtlenecks, khaki pants, and a Harris Tweed jacket. Brown's latest novel, *Inferno*, discusses the history of Harris Tweed and the Orb Trade Mark.

Designers who frequently feature Harris Tweed in their collections include Ralph Lauren, Paul Smith, and Thomas Pink. Prominent companies such as Brooks Brothers, J. Crew, Hugo Boss, and Lands' End also develop specific lines and marketing strategies around the Harris Tweed brand. Footwear companies who use the cloth include Nike, Dr. Martens, Clarks, and others. To a lesser degree, Harris Tweed is featured in home furnishings. In all cases, Harris Tweed is sold at a higher price point than items of similar styling and details. Due to the high-quality craftsmanship and timeless appeal, Harris Tweed will continue to represent a classic in American apparel for years to come.

See also FLAT CAP; WINGTIPS (BROGUE SHOE)
Compare to OXFORD SHIRT; SCOTTISH SWEATER

Further Reading

Harris Tweed Authority. "Harris Tweed/The Cloth" and "Guardians of the Orb." http://www.harris tweed.org (accessed May 27, 2013).

"The History of Harris Tweed." V is for Vintage. http://visforvintage.net/2012/10/21/harris -tweed-history (accessed May 27, 2013).

Lawson, Ian. *From the Land Comes the Cloth*. Ian Lawson Books, 2013.

Platman, Lara. *Harris Tweed: From Land to Street*. London: Frances Lincoln, 2011.

■ LAURA VAN WAARDHUIZEN

HAWAI'IAN SHIRT

See ALOHA SHIRT (HAWAI'IAN SHIRT)

HAWLI

"Hawli" is the Hassaniya dialect word for a long rectangular piece of cloth that is commonly worn as a head wrap or turban by men in Mauritania and Southern Morocco, Mali, Niger, and across North Africa. The hawli protects the wearer from the harsh environmental elements of the Sahara Desert, providing both personal protection and privacy, and is worn in certain social settings to show respect for elders. The hawli is three and a half meters (nearly four yards) long and sixty centimeters wide (about two feet) and is made of lightweight cotton or rayon fabric, usually white, light blue, or black. Winding the long thin piece of cloth around the crown of the head several times makes a turban or head wrap. Depending on the social setting or environmental elements, the face is covered in varying degrees. Worn as part of both the everyday and formal ensemble, the hawli is draped around the neck with long tails ready to be wrapped about the head when needed to protect from the wind and blowing sand.

History

The turban is pre-Islamic in origin and can be traced back for hundreds of years in Southwest Asia. "Turban" is derived from the Persian term *dulband* via the Turkish word *tulbant*. Within the Arab world, the preferred term is *imamah*, meaning headdress, and *litham* is the Hassaniya dialect word for turban or head wrap made from a piece of cloth. Covering the head is seen as a sign of modesty and respect, and Muslim men pray with their head covered. A wide range of head coverings were worn by both men and women in the early Islamic period. During this period the turban did not have direct Islamic significance, but over the centuries, wearing of the turban developed into a badge of Islam (*simaa-Islam*) and became an identifier between Muslim and non-Muslim men. Various types of turbans have developed, some small, neat, and compact while others are elaborate and massive, made from yards of material. The turban, *rezza* in Arabic and *arezziy* in Tamazight, the local Berber language, has a long history in Morocco associated with the Berber people of North Africa. The Almoravid dynasty, a Muslim Berber dynasty that ruled Spain in the eleventh and twelfth centuries, were known for the distinctive way in which they wore their turban covering the lower half of their faces. Today, the people of Northwest Africa are also known as Moutelethimoun, or "the people who wear the head turban that covers the face." Tuareg men commonly wear wrap turbans and face veils called *tagulmust*, and it is considered shameful and undignified to show the mouth. The tagulmust is traditionally made of *aleshu* cloth, a shiny indigo-dyed fabric manufactured in Nigeria that rubs off, dyeing the skin blue. These seminomadic people of North Africa who speak the Berber language Tamazight are known as "the blue men of the Sahara." Among the Tuareg, turbans and face veils symbolize social reserve, respect, and adulthood, and the veil is worn at all times. The veil is thought to protect individuals from the harm of evil spirits or djinns. The veil is adjusted throughout the day in response to shifting moods and the behavioral expectations of others, and a Tuareg man will be judged on how he wears his veil. The wearing of the veil reminds the wearer of the need for caution and self-control in relationships with others. Turbans carry important social meanings symbolizing honor, dignity, and respect. If a man has been dishonored, people may say that his turban has fallen.

The Hawli in the United States

Immigrants living in the United States may wear the hawli as a fashion accessory and symbol of identity when wearing the costume or national dress of their native countries at important social occasions and religious holidays. In the United States today the head wraps and turbans are not commonly worn or understood. Outside of the harsh Saharan environment and far from elders, the hawli is more often draped loosely around the neck, forming large voluminous cowls.

Influence and Impact

Today in the United States scarves are commonly styled and worn in a way that resembles the hawli when it is draped around the neck. Currently, scarves made from long narrow lengths of soft fabric in a great variety fabric types, textures, and colors are an important fashion trend. Scarves accessorize any outfit, provide a degree of warmth, and are relatively inexpensive to purchase. The global recession of 2007–2009 affected the purchasing power of many consumers in the United States. Many consumers suffered long periods of unemployment with limited disposable income for larger fashion purchases. Purchasing a new scarf is a way to update any look for a small price. The "infinity scarf" is a popular version of the long, thin wrapped scarf made from a length of fabric or bulky hand-knit material that is attached at both ends, making a circle of fabric that is looped around the wearer's neck with no tails. Today's college students maintain a striking resemblance to the men of North Africa when wearing the popular "infinity scarf" and the many versions of today's long, thin neck scarf.

See also AFRICAN HEAD WRAP; DJELLABA; TURBAN
Compare to BLANGKON; FEZ; KEFFIYEH; KUFI; RASTA HAT

Further Reading

du Puigaudeau, Odette. *Arts et Coutumes des Maures (Moorish Art and Customs)*. Paris: Ibis Press, 2003.
Loughran, Kristyne. *Art of Being Tuareg: Sahara Nomads in a Modern World*. Los Angeles: UCLA Fowler Museum, 2006.

Rabine, Leslie. *The Global Circulation of African Fashion*. Oxford: Berg, 2002.
Van Offelen, Marion. *Nomads of Niger*. New York: Abrams, 1983.

                                                    ■ VIRGINIA M. NOON

HIJAB

The term "hijab" is most narrowly used in the United States to refer to a veil covering the head and chest worn by adult Muslim women to cover themselves in public and maintain a modest appearance in the presence of adult males from outside their immediate family. As an umbrella term for modest dress, "hijab" is also used in common usage to refer to other body coverings worn by women as an expression of their commitment to Islam and to the maintenance of interpretations of the Qu'ran stressing the importance of modesty in dress for both men and women. Other terms used to refer to full body coverings include "chador" and "burqa."

History

What is noteworthy is that the hijab is not to be understood along conventional lines of clothing or dress, as it is seamless with Muslims' belief and sense of self. It is as much about belief as it is a material item. The literal translation of "hijab" is "curtain" or "partition," but within the United States, "hijab" is most commonly used to refer to commonly worn clothing items that separate women from public view, with a symbolic link to strong Islamic faith.

Hijab

The popular-culture connection of the hijab to religious faith has helped to ignite and maintain a long-standing anxiety over this veiling tradition that was reignited in the United States and in European countries, especially France, after 9/11.

Banning the wearing of the hijab by Muslim women in public in France has a long history. The mixed response of France's law forbidding its public use that came into effect in April 2011 can be traced back to its colonial past. During the Algerian War, the French enforced the unveiling of women, received by the native population as an affront tantamount to rape. It is because of this moment in its history that the veil now has a special place in Algeria and is a symbol of its identity. Veils and the associated measures of covering the body and the face continue to have an ambivalent status in both East and West. For it is not simply a matter of faith; it has to do as much with the distinctions that Islam is at pains to make with the infidel West. When the hijab is worn in the East, there is still a residual understanding of its irritation to Western mores. To the secular Westerner, one does not normally wear one's religion on one's sleeve. Religion is a private affair about which most people remain respectfully discrete. An exception may be Orthodox Jews, but they still wear the Western uniform, the black suit.

The visibility of Islam through dress becomes a problem when the non-Islamic state expects a certain degree of conformity and assimilation from its citizens. The irony is that it is an expectation in Western democracies that clothing reflect freedom. For this reason, veiling of women is perennially the locus where the stark differences between cultural values become apparent. Assimilation usually begins with learning the language. But the ideas of "shared" and "common" values are always liable to experience friction with democratic values of tolerance and multiculturalism.

This came to a head in France in June 2008 when its highest administrative court denied citizenship to a Moroccan woman, Faiza Silmi, who had been living on French soil for the last eight years with four children who were all French citizens. Silmi had recently decided to dress in a head-to-toe veil with only a small slit for the eyes. The court ruled that although the defendant had "a good command of the French language, she has nonetheless adopted a radical practice of her religion incompatible with the essential values of the French community and notably with the principle of equality between the sexes." It was believed that this was not in violation of the other standard of freedom of religious expression. Yet at over five million, Muslims are a populous group in French society. Numerically speaking, observers of Islam are second only to Catholics. All countries have Islamic migrants, but France is a special case because its Muslim population is drawn from places with a particularly high incidence of Islamic fundamentalism. This statistic is critical when applied to the high French thresholds of what it means to assimilate.

The Hijab in the United States

There is a rising interest in "modest fashion" among Muslim women throughout the world, and a growing Internet economy. The Internet has been integral to the circulation and cultivation of a range of styles of hijab, with websites offering wide ranges of fabrics and textile patterns, and tutorials on different styles of draping and wearing the veils. More noticeably than ever, the hijab is not only a religious attribute but also inhabits the separate category of comprising its own specialized fashion system. For the non-Islamic eye that is not attuned to these style variations, one has only to visit the website of a major outlet like the Hijab Shop to see this. This site is an easy-access reminder of the diffusion of styles on a single theme. It gives lie to the belief that hijab style is static and uniform, made by men for imprisoning the female form.

Influence and Impact

The wearing of the hijab by women on college campuses, in the workplace, and in other public venues has created discourse focused on the appropriate role of religion in the public sector. It has also created a stark contrast to the millennium trend toward hyper-sexualization, with some college students arguing that the wearing of a veil is an act of feminism, allowing a Muslim woman to escape the bonds of sexual objectification and be taken seriously as a human being.

See also CHADOR; JILBAB; THAWB
Compare to AFRICAN HEAD WRAP; HAWLI

Further Reading

Geczy, Adam. *Fashion and Orientalism: Dress, Textiles and Culture from the 17th to the 21st Century*. London and New York: Bloomsbury, 2013.

Özdalga, Elisabeth. *The Veiling Issue: Official Secularism and Popular Islam in Modern Turkey*. Richmond, Surrey: Curzon, 1998.

Paxton, Robert. "Can You Really Become French?" *New York Review of Books*, April 2009, 53.

Tarlo, Emma. *Visibly Muslim*. Oxford and New York: Berg, 2010.

■ ADAM GECZY

HIP-HOP FASHION

Hip-hop style emerged out of a music-based subculture of black and Hispanic youth that emerged in the 1970s in the South Bronx neighborhood of New York City. Characterized by baggy oversized jeans, athletic shoes (sneakers), oversized hooded sweatshirts (hoodies), and snapback baseball cap, the style was first adopted by teenage and young adult black and Hispanic males, later trending into mainstream white markets and women's wear.

History

The early hip-hop cultural movement was influenced by Jamaican DJs working in the South Bronx who rapped over instrumental and reggae music in their shows, coupled with Hispanic popular arts including graffiti and break dancing. Tied directly to the economic downturn of the neighborhood as a result of the building of a freeway serving the needs of the wealthy and white, the movement was directly connected to an emergent black/Hispanic masculinity that posed itself in direct contrast to the dominant white culture surrounding it.

Early hip-hop lyrics frequently made direct references to fashion, establishing a mimetic relationship between a performer's music and dress style. An early and influential example of the link between hip-hop musicians and fashion is the case study of Run-D.M.C.'s hit "My Adidas," in which the musicians wore Adidas as a part of live performances, in the promotional music video, and in public appearances. Within one year of the release of the hit, the musicians signed a $1.5 million contract with Adidas to sell Run-D.M.C. sneakers and accessories. This was a turning-point moment for hip-hop fashion as it signaled a transition from rappers' endorsement of existing fashion products to taking a role in designing and developing hip-hop brands, often under the name of existing and well-established companies, such as Adidas. It was also the first extremely lucrative crossover marketing of hip-hop fashion to a white male teen and young adult consumer.

In the 1990s, major menswear companies recognized the economic advantage of having hip-hop artists endorse what was termed street fashion, and starting first with Tommy Hilfiger, mainstream American brands fell in line, including Calvin Klein and Ralph Lauren. Another breakthrough of the 1990s was the entrance of Karl Kani into the hip-hop fashion scene, the first black designer to gain national attention. Making his mark designing a hip-hop-inspired urban version of casual knits and baggy pants, Kani, like Hilfiger, Klein, and Lauren, crossed over and sold his look to white as well as black customers.

Influence and Impact

Def Jam Records started Phat Farm, one of the most culturally influential hip-hop brands, in 1992, focusing its marketing on lifestyle branding. Painting a portrait of a hoodie-wearing hip-hop B-boy as a branding icon, Phat Farm successfully sold apparel through the branding of a racially referenced masculinity appealing to black, Hispanic, and white teen and young adult males. Linked with its brand was a refashioning of black masculinity and Americana, with strong red, white, and blue and masculinity cultural coding within products as well as advertising. Hip-hop fashion looks, while emanating out of an alternative subcultural masculinity, crossed over into women's fashions with the creation of the Baby Phat (the female version of Phat Farm) and Jennifer Lopez's fashion line.

See also BANDANA; DO-RAG; KUFI
Compare to BOHEMIAN DRESS; CHOLO STYLE; JAPANESE STREET FASHION; WESTERN WEAR; ZOOT SUIT

Further Reading

Brunson, James E., III. "Showing, Seeing: Hip-Hop, Visual Culture, and the Show-and-Tell Performance." *Black History Bulletin* 74, no. 1 (2011): 6–12.
Fleetwood, Nicole. "Hip-Hop Fashion, Masculine Anxiety, and the Discourse of Americana." In *Black Cultural Traffic: Crossroads in Global Performance and Popular Culture*, edited by Harry J. Elam and Kennell Jackson. Ann Arbor: University of Michigan Press, 2005.
Hurt, B. "Hip-Hop: Beyond Beats and Rhymes." Educational Media Foundation, 2006.
Romero, Elena. *Free Stylin': How Hip Hop Changed the Fashion Industry*. Santa Barbara, CA: Praeger, 2012.
Sacasa, Edwin P., and Alain K. Mariduena. *Shirt Kings: Pioneers of Hip Hop Fashion*. Arsta, Sweden: Dokument Press, 2013.

■ ANNETTE LYNCH

HUARACHES

Huaraches are handcrafted, lightweight Mexican sandals. It is believed that the word "huarache" is derived from the P'urhépecha term for sandal, *kwarachi*. Traditionally, huaraches have a woven leather upper with leather soles, but the soles can also be created from recycled rubber tires. Huaraches can range from a very simplistic design, with only enough leather straps to keep the soles attached to the wearer's feet (similar in styling to flip-flops), to elaborate woven designs that cover most of the foot and are similar to full shoes. In the case of the latter, however, huaraches are usually distinguished by a distinctive woven design.

History

The design and manufacture of huaraches predate written historical records. They are believed to have been the footwear worn by the indigenous Central American cultures such as the Mayans and Aztecs. Huaraches are made by first cutting a leather sole in the shape of the wearer's foot. Then a long continuous leather strip, called a *correa*, is woven through holes punched in the sides of the sole. Due to their simple, easily accessible materials, huaraches were readily available to all social classes. The intricate weaving on the upper part of the shoes became an art form, a way for craftsmen to express their skill and talent. However, after the Spanish conquistadors invaded Central America and enslaved the indigenous people in the sixteenth century, much of the Aztec way of life was stifled. Huaraches were relegated to peasants and lower social classes for the next few hundred years.

Around the 1930s, huarache design evolved slightly; an additional rubber layer cut from used car tires was added to the sole with tacks or staples. This increased the durability of huaraches while using materials that are readily accessible for little to no cost.

Most recently, much interest has turned to the Tarahumara Indian society, a tribe in northern Mexico who retreated to hillside labyrinths when Spanish conquistadors invaded and therefore remained largely unchanged by Western influence until the present age. What is remarkable about the Tarahumara Indians is their long-distance running; some are known to run up to two hundred miles over two days in one stretch. Their footwear of choice is handcrafted huaraches. Despite running incredible distances in the most minimal of foot covering, the Tarahumara Indians rarely suffer "running injuries" that plague modern athletes.

Huaraches in the United States

It is presumed that the huarache style migrated to the United States with Mexican immigrants as they moved into the southwestern states. Additionally, starting in the 1950s American tourists to Mexico would bring them back for summer wear. Within the last five years, huaraches have been introduced to runners as a way to get more out of their workout and avoid running injuries. This idea has been promoted by American journalist Christopher McDougall in his book *Born to Run: A Hidden Tribe, Superathletes, and the Greatest Race the World Has Never Seen.*

Influence and Impact

Despite their strong cultural influence and history, huaraches are not a required element of traditional Mexican dress. Huaraches are classic warm-weather footwear for many Americans. They have made appearances in novels such as Jack Kerouac's *On the Road,* Kathryn Stockett's *The Help,* and hit songs like the Beach Boys' "Surfin' USA."

Athletes who wear huaraches identify themselves as "barefoot" or "natural" runners and share their experiences in online communities like www.borntorun.org. Abebe Bikila, Zola Budd, and Bruce Tulloh are Olympic athletes who have participated "barefoot." Companies such as Luna Sandals sell foam-based "running" huaraches, while Xero Shoes will sell kits or create custom footwear for customers that send in a foot scan. Scientific evidence on "barefoot" running is inconclusive, and it remains to be seen if the style will take off with runners at large. Steven Sashen, owner of Xero Shoes, appeared on ABC's show *Shark Tank* but was ultimately unable to convince the "sharks" that selling shoes that people could make themselves was a truly marketable idea.

The popularity of huaraches created a market for the manufacture of factory-produced, cheaper knockoffs. Even though the cost of an authentic, handcrafted pair of huaraches is moderate at $30 to $60, the widespread availability of knockoffs is pushing *huaracheros* (craftsmen who create huaraches) out of business. Interest in the native market is not enough to support the business either, as most Mexicans would prefer brand-name footwear at that price point. Grassroots movements like huaracheblog.wordpress.com are attempting to bring public awareness to the art of huaraches to keep the craft alive. The influence of the woven sandal look can be seen in many American designers' collections. Most recently, Dolce & Gabbana featured them prominently in their spring/summer 2013 menswear collection. Even though the future of huaracheros is unknown, the huarache style will continue to appear as a classic in summer footwear.

See also HUIPIL; PONCHO; SERAPE; SOMBRERO
Compare to BIRKENSTOCKS; CLOGS; ESPADRILLES; JELLIES; TABI

Further Reading

Kennett, Frances, and Caroline MacDonald-Haig. *Ethnic Dress*. New York: Facts on File, 1995.
Kittner, Marcus. "A Quick Introduction to Mexican Huarache Sandals." http://huaracheblog.word press.com (accessed May 2, 2013).
Pendergast, Sara, and Tom Pendergast. *Fashion, Costume, and Culture: Clothing, Headwear, Body Decorations, and Footwear through the Ages.* Vol. 2, *Early Cultures across the Globe.* Edited by Sarah Hermse. Detroit, MI: UXL, 2004.

■ LAURA VAN WAARDHUIZEN

HUIPIL

The traditional blouses called huipil worn by indigenous women in Mexico and Central America are typically colorful and intricately patterned. Many are embroidered or hand woven, with a variety of geometric, floral, animal, human, or religious images. They are typically made from cotton, but wool, acrylic, and silk have also been used. Seemingly subtle characteristics of the dress, ranging from the color scheme or motifs within the cloth to the garment shape or wrapping technique, can signal the wearer's ethnicity, geographic origin, marital status, socioeconomic status, community organization membership, age cohort, ceremonial roles, and personality.

In southeastern Mexico and Guatemala, these blouses are known as huipiles, from a word in Nahuatl, the language of the Aztecs. They are usually large and rectangular, constructed from one to three panels, with a central opening for the head. Where the panels are joined, they often feature decorative ribbons or embroidery to cover the seams. The sides may be sewn with space for the armholes or may be open and wrapped around the body. Huipiles often have religious significance: the neck opening may represent the sun, at the center of the four cardinal directions. The designs also frequently reference Mayan religious beliefs about nature, which are sometimes combined with Catholic imagery. The number of panels, the shape of the garment, woven or embroidered patterns, and the color scheme vary by town and the ability of the weaver. Weavers express their individual personalities within traditional community-based aesthetic genres through their choices of style, pattern, and color. While blouses and huipiles identify their wearers to

Huipil

their towns of origin, indigenous women may choose to wear the blouse from another region for fashion's sake or to express an affiliation with that town. Ceremonial huipiles, which are the most richly decorated, are used for special occasions, such as weddings, burials, and religious processions.

History

Blouses and huipiles are part of an ancient textile tradition predating the arrival of Spanish conquistadores. Evidence from codices, pottery, murals, and stelae suggests that the forms of *traje*, or traditional dress, have changed little from pre-Columbian times. Following the Mayan goddess of weaving, Ixchel, women wove and embroidered blouses and fabrics for their own families, and the best weavers used their craft to gain status in their communities and earn extra income. When the Mayans fell under Aztec rule in the fifteenth century, they paid tribute in huipiles and other weavings.

The skill of back-strap weaving is highly gendered and passed from mother to daughter. Girls learn to weave by watching their mothers spin yarn, prepare the warp, warp the loom, and weave, and gradually joined in on the more basic steps. They usually begin weaving on their own around the age of ten to learn the skills they will need to create their own households. While the majority of indigenous men have adopted Western dress, many indigenous women maintain their traje. These traditions may have been conserved through the link between dress and identity, which is particularly strong in this region. Since the 1970s, younger women have been turning to lighter commercial blouses or huipiles and reserving the traditional huipiles for formal occasions.

The Huipil in the United States

Mexican and Central American blouses became popular in the United States through the counterculture revolution that began in the 1950s. Reacting against the sleek styles of mainstream fashion, the Beat Generation turned to "peasant" and folk looks. They expressed their sense of marginality within society by appropriating forms of dress they viewed as exotic and primitive, combining a variety of styles from indigenous communities around the world.

These folk and Beat styles evolved into the hippie movement of the 1960s. The ethnic aesthetic represented by Mexican and Central American blouses fit with the "flower power" image of the new youth movement, which protested against war and materialism. For hippies, ethnic fashion indicated their close connection to the earth and their rejection of consumerism.

Influence and Impact

Over time, these peasant and ethnic styles fused and gave rise to the "folklore look" of the 1970s, which spread from the fringes to mainstream society and influenced high fashion as well as low. In the mid-1970s, ethnic patterns became accessible for home sewers through the California-based pattern company Folkwear. After the 1970s, the popularity of these blouses waned, but they continued to inspire fashion designers such as Jean Paul Gaultier, who entitled his Mexican-themed collection "Homage to Frida Kahlo" in 1998.

See also BOHEMIAN DRESS; BRICOLAGE; PEASANT BLOUSE
Compare to CH'ULLU; DIRNDL; HARDANGER

Further Reading

Anawalt, Patricia Rieff. *Indian Clothing before Cortes.* Norman: University of Oklahoma Press, 1981.
Cordry, Donald, and Dorothy Cordry. *Mexican Indian Costumes.* Austin and London: University of Texas Press, 1968.
Craik, Jennifer. *The Face of Fashion: Cultural Studies in Fashion.* London and New York: Routledge, 1994.
Schevill, Margot Blum, Janet Catherine Berlo, and Edward B. Dwyer, eds. *Textile Traditions of Mesoamerica and the Andes: An Anthology.* Austin: University of Texas Press, 1996.

■ REBECCA NELSON JACOBS

IKET
See BLANGKON

INVERNESS COAT

The Inverness coat, also referred to as an Inverness cape, is a topcoat that was popular during the mid-nineteenth century. It featured sleeves covered by a long cape, which reached the entire length of the sleeve. The Inverness coat transformed into the Inverness cape in the 1880s, when the sleeves were completely removed and the armholes were cut away beneath the cape, leaving the topcoat and cape together as one. The Inverness coat was first popularized between the 1850s and 1870s and was reminiscent of the curricle coats of the 1840s due to the attached cape. However, the Inverness was a much looser-fitting coat than the curricle and featured wider sleeves.

History

While it is unclear how the Inverness coat got its name, it may be linked to the city of Inverness, located in the northwestern Scottish Highlands. Due to cold temperatures, residents of Inverness require warm garments throughout the year. "Inverness" translates to "Mouth of the River Ness," referring to the River Ness, which flows nearby. Inverness is an important center for bagpipe players and enthusiasts, as the Northern Meeting Highland Games are hosted there every September. The Northern Meeting Highland Games attract large numbers of bagpipe players and fans who often wear Inverness coats. While the Inverness cape is not necessarily manufactured in Inverness, the garment is still worn as rain gear by Scottish bagpipers.

Inverness Coat in the United States

Near the end of the nineteenth century, the Inverness cape made its way stateside in the form of day wear that consisted of a topcoat reaching mid-calf and an elbow-length shoulder cape. Throughout the early twentieth century, the Inverness cape remained a part of the male wardrobe because it provided extra warmth. Around the same time, the Inverness cape was worn as a topcoat over a dress suit and was a popular option for formal functions. The Inverness cape was best made of the finest materials available, which includes a lower cape and an upper cape. The hem of the lower cape reaches the knee of the wearer, and the upper cape falls to the knuckles.

The Inverness cape could be worn for multiple occasions, either for more casual day wear or formal events. If worn for day wear, the cape was finished without lapels and featured a simple collar. For more formal events, the cape was designed with short lapels, and the upper and lower capes were set behind them to display this formal detail. While the formal Inverness cape was sophisticated and elegant, the more casual Inverness cape was favored by coachmen and cabdrivers as they required the ability to move their arms freely throughout the day, a concern met by the Inverness cape.

Sidney Paget (1860–1908), a British illustrator best known for his illustrations of Arthur Conan Doyle's (1859–1930) Sherlock Holmes stories for *The Strand* magazine forever linked the fictional detective with the Inverness cape and the deerstalker hat in his illustrations in 1891. Despite the strong connection between Arthur Conan Doyle's character and the Inverness cape, Doyle never mentioned a cape or a deerstalker hat in the sixty Sherlock Holmes stories he wrote beginning in 1887. The association of Sherlock Holmes with the Inverness cape and deerstalker hat can be attributed to Paget's illustrations as well as actor Basil Rathbone (1892–1967), who played Sherlock Holmes in fourteen Hollywood films produced between 1939 and 1946. In his portrayal of Holmes, Rathbone commonly wore an Inverness cape and a deerstalker hat, further sealing the connection between the garments and the fictional detective. In the 1970s, the third doctor in the long-running British television series *Doctor Who*, Jon Pertwee (1919–1996), frequently wore an Inverness cape over his fancy attire, bringing the Inverness cape into modern times.

Influence and Impact

In the twenty-first century, remnants of the Inverness coat can be found in the stylistic choices of followers of steampunk, a subgenre of science fiction inspired by the industrialization of Western civilization in the nineteenth century. A mixture of neo-Victorian, Edwardian, and military styles, the sartorial choices of steampunk followers are sometimes accessorized with brass goggles, harnesses, and clockwork pendants. Female steampunk fashion favors the inclusion of corsets, bustles, crinolines, and parasols, while male steampunk fashion advocates the integration of clothing that recalls the personalization and tailoring of nineteenth-century haberdashery. This often includes structured coats like the Inverness coat, which can be purchased from online retailers and specialty stores. For both men and women, steampunk also incorporates contemporary clothing by the designers Nicolas Ghesquiere, Alexander McQueen, and the more traditional Ralph Lauren. With sartorial influence from the goth and punk movements, steampunk first appeared in the late 1980s and early 1990s and gained momentum around 2008.

See also KILT
Compare to BURNOUS; DOLMAN; DUSTER; PELISSE; SERAPE; TRENCH COAT

Further Reading

Davis, Ronald. *Men's Garments, 1830–1900: A Guide to Pattern Cutting and Tailoring.* StudioCity: Players Press, 1996.

Flusser, Alan. *Dressing the Man: Mastering the Art of Permanent Fashion.* New York: HarperCollins, 2002.

Peacock, John. *Men's Fashion: The Complete Sourcebook.* London: Thames & Hudson, 1996.

■ JESSICA SCHWARTZ

JAPANESE STREET FASHION

Japanese street fashion is a general title referring to multiple distinct styles of dress that originated in Japan's Harajuku shopping district in the 1980s.

History

Harajuku is in the Shibuya district of Tokyo. Historically, Harajuku was a market district and became a pedestrian-only shopping area after the end of World War II. U.S. military troops and their families stationed in Tokyo took up residence and opened shops in this area, and the influence of Western culture on Japanese young people began here. Harajuku was a place for young people of different backgrounds to spend time socializing and shopping. Over time it became a center for youth culture in Tokyo. The Laforet shopping center opened in 1978 as a center for new businesses marketed toward the youth fashion scene.

During the 1980s in Japan, economic prosperity enabled young people living at home to have jobs, which gave them disposable income to spend on fashion and entertainment. The economic crash of the 1990s forced Japanese consumers to begin buying local products rather than importing from the West and provided an environment for new Japanese designers to set up businesses.

All Japanese street fashion shares a high attention to detail and a focus on personalization. There are four main styles of Japanese street fashion, each with multiple substyles included in each group: *kawaii* (English translation = "cute"), gothic lolita, cyber punk, and *uru hara*. Gothic lolita is the most famous of Japanese street style, originating from Osaka in the Kansai region of southwestern Japan. Gothic lolita style developed from the New Romantic fashion and music movement founded in Britain in the 1980s. Bands such as Duran Duran, Spandau Ballet, and Japan (David Sylvian) toured throughout Japan and successfully gained a large fan base. Japanese bands began to emulate British bands and were given the name "visual kei," which came to represent bands with a strong visual element to their performances. The Japanese theater tradition of Kabuki, with men being costumed and performing as women, can be clearly seen in the performances of visual kei bands such as Malice Mizer. The lead singer of Malice Mizer, Mana, came to define the gothic lolita style by dressing in a feminine, Victorian doll style. Over time, fans of

Japanese Street Fashion

visual kei bands copied the clothing style of the performers, and gothic lolita emerged as the dominant style of Japanese street fashion familiar in the United States.

Japanese Street Fashion in the United States

The influence of Japanese street fashion in the United States can most readily be seen in varying forms of media and consumer product design. Since the economic and technology boom in the 1980s, Japanese cartoons, video games, fashion, and media technology have been in demand, and this demand is still increasing. The increase in global consumerism made possible by the rise of the World Wide Web has made it possible for consumers in the United States and Japan to freely share ideas and products. In the United States, top fashion houses such as Donna Karan, Calvin Klein, and Marc Jacobs are recruiting young Japanese designers in order to influence the aesthetics of their seasonal collections.

The most widely adopted forms of Japanese street fashion in the United States are gothic lolita style and anime/cosplay characters. Both styles are worn by young, creative people involved in a subcultural social network interested in Japanese comics and video games. Followers of both styles create their own DIY costumes to emulate their favorite characters or images they see in publications such as *Fruits* and *Gothic Lolita Bible*. The name "gothic lolita" being used in the United States is somewhat misleading to the average American, since the term "gothic" has a very different interpretation in U.S. culture. In the West, "gothic" fashion is associated with bondage and S&M lifestyles, whereas in Japanese culture, abstinence, girlishness, and virginity are implied and reflect the original interpretation that is neither sexual nor threatening. The reference to the term "gothic" in gothic lolita style is due to the predominance of black that is worn by followers of the style.

Influence and Impact

In 1998, Kera created a new magazine devoted to gothic lolita fashion called *Gothic & Lolita Bible*, and in December 2000 it was imported to the United States to meet the demands of the increasing market interest overseas. Mana (Malice Mizer) began designing his own clothing line in 1999 called Moi-meme-Moitia, followed on with h.NAOTO in 2000. His labels have expanded internationally thanks to celebrities in the alternative music scene, such as Marilyn Manson and Amy Lee of Evanescence, who wear his designs.

One of the most visible examples of the influence of Japanese street fashion in the United States is Gwen Stefani's Harajuku Lovers clothing and perfume line from 2004. Stefani dressed her backup dancers in gothic lolita style during her Harajuku Lovers tour, and the companion merchandise and marketing also reflected the singer's fascination with Japanese street fashion. As the lead singer of the successful California band No Doubt,

Stefani's established fame and popularity exposed Japanese street fashion to a wider audience than it previously had. In more recent years, *Fruits* magazine reports new trends in Japanese street fashion from Harajuku and is widely subscribed to by many top U.S. fashion brands.

Critics of Japanese street fashion accuse followers of focusing on consumerism and abandoning traditional morals of religion, humility, and conformity. The biggest contrast between street fashion in the United States and Japan is the context. In the United States, street fashion is political and often subcultural. It confronts issues of race, economics, gender, and lifestyle. Street fashion in Japan is pop culture; it's not considered art, nor is high quality important to those who wear it. There is no subcultural context implied in Japanese street fashion—it is not a lifestyle; it is purely fashion for fashion's sake.

See also KIMONO; OBI

Compare to BOHEMIAN DRESS; CHOLO STYLE; HIP-HOP FASHION; ZOOT SUIT

Further Reading

Godoy, Tiffany. *Tokyo Street Style: Fashion in Harajuku*. London: Thames & Hudson, 2007.
Shoichi, Aoki. *Fruits*. New York: Phaidon Press, 2001.
Steele, Valerie. *Japan Fashion Now*. New Haven, CT: Yale University Press, 2010.
Various. *Gothic & Lolita Bible*. Northridge, CA: Tokyopop, 2000–2009.

■ JENNIFER ROTHROCK

JELLIES

Jellies are colorful plastic shoes that were very popular in the 1980s in mainly Europe and the United States. Women and children of all classes wore them because they were fun, easy-to-care-for summer footwear that was relatively inexpensive. They were available in many different colors, textures, and styles, from slip-ons to sandals. Although jellies were the most prevalent during the 1980s, they come back into style every few years.

History

The true origins of jellies are not known, but there are a few theories as to why they were created. Jellies are made by a process called injection molding. Some believe the first plastic shoes completely molded were created in the 1960s and were not meant to be fashionable. Their original target customer was a Third World worker because the shoes were inexpensive to produce since they are made completely by machine. Another proposition is that the shortage of leather after World War II caused a manufacturer in France to produce plastic shoes. However, Elizabeth Semmelhack, curator of Toronto's Bata Shoe Museum, believes fashion designers started using plastic in their products in the 1950s and 1960s when the new material was becoming popular. She considers jellies a creation born out of curiosity instead of need. Regardless of how they came to be, they eventually made their way to the United States.

Jellies in the United States

There are two men held responsible for bringing jellies to the United States—Andrew Geller and Preston Haag Sr. Geller was inspired to design jellies because of plastic oxfords he saw Greek hotel employees wearing. He brought a similar style back to New York in 1980, and his shoes were very popular in stores like Saks. Preston Haag Sr. traveled to Brazil, where he noticed the bright shoes that the young women were wearing. They were designed by Dorothee Bis, Fiorucci, Thierry Muglar, and Jean Paul Gaultier. The company Grendene was manufacturing them, so Haag negotiated with them to export their plastic shoes to the southeastern United States. They combined their names to make Grendha. Haag's family introduced jellies in Brazil's lot at the 1982 World's Fair in Knoxville, Tennessee. The comfortable summer shoes fared well there. That next year, the Grendha jellies gained national attention at a shoe exposition in Chicago. A Bloomingdale's New York representative ordered 2,400 pairs, and they were featured in their catalog and main floor of the store. Because of the European designers, the frequent change of design, and the quality of stores jellies were sold in, the Haag family strove to keep the shoes high fashion. However, cheap imitations were inevitably created.

Influence and Impact

Grendene is still the number-one manufacturer of jellies. They started in 1971 making plastic wine-bottle covers, expanding to produce different plastic parts, such as soles and heels for shoes, and then changed to plastic sandals. Plastic shoes are still being designed under the Melissa brand, which was created in 1979 to make high-fashion, designer jellies. Melissa is working with Judy Blame, Edson Matsuo, Alexandre Herchcovitch, and Fernando and Humberto Campana to design jellies for the international fashion market. Over the years, they have also teamed up with designers such as Vivienne Westwood, Isabela Capeto, and Karim Rashid.

Jellies had a big comeback in 2003 with designs coming from companies ranging from Burberry to Old Navy. Also, in 2009, top designers reinvented plastic shoes after Crocs made it more socially acceptable to wear plastic shoes again. Advancements have been made over time to make them more comfortable and less sweaty. Plastic designer shoes have successful sales because they can come in styles ranging from flats to high heels, are eco-friendly, and are fairly inexpensive. Throughout the years, jellies have retained a solid image and target market. They started as fun, careless, inexpensive shoes for all ages and classes, and remain so whenever they come back in style.

See also CHINESE FLATS; FLIP-FLOPS (GETA)
Compare to BIRKENSTOCKS; CLOGS; HUARACHES; MOCCASINS

Further Reading

Baker, Steve. "Jelly Shoes Make Success Story." *Ocala Star-Banner*, March 10, 1985, sec. 4, p. E. http://news.google.com/newspapers?id=uisaAAAAIBAJ&sjid=pg4EAAAAIBAJ&pg=4045,5922226.
Walford, Jonathan. *The Seductive Shoe*. London: Thames & Hudson, 2007.
———. *Shoes A-Z*. New York: Thames & Hudson, 2010.

■ SABRINA SKERSTON AND ELLEN C. MCKINNEY

JEOGORI

The jeogori is one of the main items of the hanbok, traditional Korean attire. A jeogori is worn with a matching chima (skirt) for women or matching *baji* (pants) for men. The men's jeogori is longer and wider than the women's jeogori, and the shapes of the sleeves and hemlines are flatter. The jeogori is made in two dimensions, and its added straps and ties fit the shape of the body, creating the unique beauty of curvy, soft lines with sharp points and edges. A jeogori consists of a *dongjung* (a removable white layer on the collar following the neckline), a *git* (a band covering the collar), and a *kutdong* (another colored layer on the cuffs). The *gorum* is a coat tie, and the *belle* is the width of the sleeves.

History

In the period of the Three Kingdoms of Korea, Goguryeo (37 BCE), *yoo*, the original shape of a jeogori, was a long wrapped top style covering the hip with a belt to hold it. In the unified Shilla period (57 BCE), men and women wore *pho-yui*, an outer layer; only women wore an additional top called *dan-yui* between the underwear and the outer layer. At this time, women layered skirts over the *dan-yui*, and the top was shorter than in previous periods. In Goryeo (918–1392), there were differences in garment styles among social strata, especially for women. The queen wore a red-colored, gilded top. Found in relics from noble ladies in Goryeo, their tops had ties and *dongjung* at the necklines with smaller sleeve widths than in previous periods. During the Chosun dynasty (1392–1910), men wore jeogori that fell below the waistline, inside of *dopyo* and *durumagi*, which are long outerwear. In the early Chosun dynasty, the length of jeogori was long and wide. After the middle of the Chosun dynasty, the width of the collar and the length and width of jeogori were smaller. In the middle age of the Korean Chosun dynasty, after 1580, the length of the jeogori became shorter until the 1920s. The jeogori become longer and wider; in particular, the length of the jeogori kept changing from short to long, back and forth. After the 1930s, it became about ten inches or longer, and after the 1950s, the length of jeogori shortened to the bustline. In modern times, the lengths of jeogori and their designs are varied.

The Jeogori in the United States

Since 1903, Korean immigrants have come to the United States, and many Korean-Americans immigrated after 1968 when the Immigration Act of 1965 was in full effect. Immigrants brought hanbok, including jeogori and chima, to the United States. After the 1980s, designers modernized traditional Korean jeogori, varying the designs and presenting them at fashion shows in the United States. Nowadays, people can purchase hanbok in stores or through online websites in the United States with various price ranges.

Influence and Impact

In the United States, hanbok is worn mostly at special events—such as a Korean wedding, a baby's first birthday, a sixty-plus birthday, and during holidays such as New Year's Day and Korean Thanksgiving Day. White jeogori are worn for funerals; currently, women sometimes wear black jeogori. The jeogori was mostly worn by Korean immigrants, their descendants in the United States, and other Americans. Sometimes, if there are events related to Korea and Korean culture, jeogori are worn with matching chima and *baji* to create traditional outfits. Hanbok jeogori represent the Korean culture and a heritage transmitted through the centuries. Jeogori represent the identity and roots of Korean-American families' history and also indicate understanding of and an interest in Korean cultures.

Many designers from Korea and the United States are inspired by the hanbok jeogori as an ensemble that can create the unique beauty of hanbok. Modernized jeogori was created in simple shapes and comfortable materials, and jeogori for special events was made decorative through gilting.

See also CHIMA; HANBOK; NORIGAE
Compare to BOLERO JACKET; DOLMAN; HANFU CHINESE ROBES; PELISSE

Further Reading

"The Korean Hanbok." Asianinfo.org. http://www.asianinfo.org/asianinfo/korea/cel/hanbok.htm.
Lee, Seoung-ah. "Hanbok: Hidden Stories in Hanbok History." June 14, 2012. http://www.mcst.go.kr/
    english/issue/issueView.jsp?pSeq=2427.

■ HELEN KOO

JILBAB

"Jilbab," or *jilbaab*, is the Arabic word for garment, dress, gown, or veil and is used to describe any long, flowing, and loose-fitting overcoat. A jilbab is the overgarment or cloak traditionally worn by Muslim women in public. Usually made from solid-color opaque fabrics, the gown is worn to maintain modesty and conceal the shape and contours of the body and is worn over normal clothing when going out. The modern jilbab is a balance

Jilbab

of style and modest clothing, covering the entire body except for the hands, face, and head. The head is covered with a separate scarf, the hijab, and sometimes an additional face veil, the *niqab*. The jilbab is worn by Muslim women around the world as a religious identifier, symbolizing cultural identity as well as a renewal of traditional ideals and values. Styling and names given to this traditional outer garment may vary regionally, reflecting both cultural and environmental factors of the country where it is worn. It should be noted that in Indonesia, the word "jilbab" refers to a head scarf rather than a long baggy overgarment. In Somalia the jilbab ensemble consists of a skirt, a close-fitting head wrap, and a second head covering that frames the face and drapes down over the torso, very similar to the habit worn by Catholic nuns. Contemporary jilbabs can be very basic, often in solid black or dark colors, or from a range of lighter colors as well as highly embellished with embroidery and ornamentation around the center front, neckline, and sleeves of the garment.

History

Islam, one of the major monotheistic religions of the world, was founded in the early seventh century CE in the region that now comprises Saudi Arabia. The Islamic religion brought with it concepts of what was and was not acceptable in all aspects of life, including dress. During the pre-Islamic period, easygoing attitudes toward nudity existed; however, the arrival of Islam ushered in a new modesty code. Early Muslim traditions recommended modesty and austerity in dress and avoidance of extravagance. Islam holds a moralistic view on the purpose of clothing and dress in general, and dress has played an important role in the history of the Islamic world. During the medieval period, Islamic dress consisted of garments worn in three or more layers composed of under, middle, and outer garments that covered and concealed the shape of the wearer's body. The number of layers and garments varied depending on a person's wealth. Garments worn outdoors by women were meant to further conceal the body, and men's clothing was intended to be modest and not ostentatious. Over time with the expansion of Islam throughout Southwest Asia and northern Africa, three styles of dress prevailed, creating what is known today as the Islamic vestimentary system, or Islamic style of dress. The three styles included (1) loose, flowing, and untailored garments, suitable for living in hot dry climates and conditions; (2) Greco-Roman tunics and wraps of various kinds that included cut and sewn garments; and (3) cut and shaped Irano-Turkic garments with tailored forms emphasizing the shape of the human body. It is important to note that many variations in style of dress have existed over time and continue to exist today.

The Jilbab in the United States

Islamic dress as it has come to be known today came into common usage in the mid-1970s. In response to the secularization of society, college students in Egypt began to appear in what was called "Islamic dress." For women, emphasis is on hijab or covering, always with some type of head veil and loose-fitting and floor-length outer garment. Initially, austere forms of Islamic dress emerged, displaying a strong antifashion stance. Over time the basic styling has been elaborated and reworked into what is known today in the literature and the market as "Islamic fashion."

The outer garment worn by many Muslim women today is currently under transformation. In today's globalized world and with the advent of the Internet, Muslim women around the world now have an opportunity to purchase garments online from a wide range of sources. The wearing of the jilbab is a story of immigration of ethnic groups to the United States, and the garment is worn wherever Muslim women live and work. Traditional garments from the Middle East can be purchased at Islamic shops in mosques or at shops that sell Middle Eastern products in urban centers, and they are sometimes hand carried or sent by relatives or friends from home countries. Recently several British and American designers have emerged offering modest, contemporary styles of dress reflecting both modernity and traditional Islamic beliefs and values. The arrival of Islamic fashion companies is traced to the lack of suitable styling for the modern Muslim woman, and many of today's prominent designers began by sewing garments at home for personal use. The major outlet for designers is online sales, with jilbabs as a major category of garments offered. The styling observed on websites offering Islamic fashion represents variations on the common theme of a loose-fitting, one-piece, and long-sleeved floor-length garment.

Influence and Impact

The general styling of the jilbab is most similar to styling in the United States of the floor-length, zip-front bathrobe, and heavier jilbabs for colder climates are similar in styling to the maxicoat, the floor-length winter coat made popular in the United States during the early 1970s. Styling for the modern jilbab in the West draws on Islamic fashions elsewhere around the world and the rapidly expanding Muslim media that includes television, lifestyle magazines, fashion blogs, and discussion forums catering to the Muslim lifestyle. In addition, massive annual fairs such as IslamExpo and Global Peace and Unity (GPU) held in London attract Muslims from around the world to celebrate and trade all things Islamic. These fairs showcase a broad range of products including the latest fashions and offer the opportunity to spot up-and-coming trends. Muslim women in the United States are now beginning to have a much broader range of styling to choose from when purchasing a jilbab, allowing a woman to dress both fashionably and modern as well as faithful and modest.

See also CHADOR; HIJAB
Compare to BOUBOU; DASHIKI; DJELLABA; KEBAYA AND SKIRT; THAWB

Further Reading

Moors, Annelies. "Fashionable Muslims: Notions of Self, Religion and Society in San'a." *Fashion Theory* 11, nos. 2–3 (2007): 319–47.
Moors, Annelies, and Emma Tarlo. "Introduction." Special double issue of *Fashion Theory* 11, nos. 2–3 (2007): 133–42. doi:10.2752/136270407X202718.
Stillman, Yedida. *Arab Dress: A Short History from the Dawn of Islam to Modern Time*. Leiden: Brill, 2000.

■ VIRGINIA M. NOON

JODHPURS

Jodhpurs are a pantaloon-style trouser typically cut fuller in the thigh and billowing slightly outward, creating a half-moon shape. The original utilitarian trouser was designed for playing competitive polo. With the development of new fibers and stretch fabrication technologies, the jodhpur style has gradually become more tailored so as to create a skin-tight look from thigh to toe. Some jodhpurs have stirrups, with a material cuff underfoot. Leather patches for reinforcing protection at the knees as featured by the "Maharajah of Jodhpur" are still favored. The trouser is often khaki/tan in color, with earth tones and black being other popular style choices.

History

Jodhpurs were developed for the playing of polo, one of the oldest organized sports, which is believed to have originated in Persia over 2,500 years ago. During the 1850s, British tea planters were introduced to polo in Manipur, India. They became enamored of the sport and in 1862 founded the "Calcutta Club," Silchar, the oldest club in the world. Polo requires robust and healthy horses to play, necessitating its general requisite as a game favored by the elite. Around 1890 the Maharajah Sir Pritap Singh of Jodhpur began wearing specially adapted riding "breeches" whose overall style is still favored to the present day. By the 1920s when the Indian Jodhpur polo team retained their success, women also sported jodhpurs. It is thought that jodhpurs entered the United States in the late 1800s. Similar traditional-style pants can still be seen in parts of the Indian community as contemporary everyday dress in the United States.

Jodhpurs in the United States

The jodhpur remains foremost a riding garment, and quintessentially seen as British despite its Indian origins. Its look has been adapted slightly, according to considerations such as country, climate, economy, cultural history, and fashion trends. "Breeches," a tight-fitting pant similar to jodhpurs, were in use in the United States by the military in 1893 and the first pair worn in the 1840s (and noted in the American Army Museum system). Sky-blue color in wool, and slightly pegged in style, these infantry and cavalry pants were not utilized for riding but were influenced by the jodhpur style. Inspired by Parisian designer Coco Chanel introducing "pants for women" in the 1920s, aviator Amelia Earhart in the 1930s wore jodhpur-type trousers on numerous flights.

With the introduction of materials such as jersey being made into riding breeches in the early 1900s, and later in the 1940s with nylon and other synthetic stretchy fabrics, such radical postwar sportswear became revolutionary. Adapted into related styles like capris and ski pants with stirrups in the 1950s, these figure-hugging pants retain a similar style today as fashion and riding wear. In the 1970s and 1980s, new colors and materials such as stretch denim emerged and were fashionably radical in the riding world. In Kentucky jodhpurs, used for "saddle seat" riding in the United States, while longer in length and slightly wider, the "bell-bottom" style is reflected in the flared fashion trouser seen in contemporary casual street wear.

Ralph Lauren's Polo brand launched in the 1970s purveyed an aspirational lifestyle that grew to encompass notions of British gentry combined with classic all-American style. The jodhpur, with its strong British riding-culture history, was a key element of equestrian attire used by Ralph Lauren in his advertising and as a part of his collections to capture the British landed gentry lifestyle that he sold through his brand to American consumers.

Influence and Impact

British designers such as John Galliano, whose interpretations, especially for men, have a dandyesque quality, acknowledge "Victorian gents in jodhpurs." Equally, collections from Vivienne Westwood and Alexander McQueen encapsulate similar scenarios and styles. Various street-wear styles such as skinny jeans and leggings are descendants of the jodhpur, and similar qualities are apparent in the functional spandex.

Popular-culture musicians have used the jodhpur and its coded messages of class and sexuality in stage costuming. Though highly exaggerated versions, rock music of the 1970s and 1980s included musicians such as David Bowie, who wore styles with a nod to the jodhpur. Madonna in the 1990s, and more recently OutKast and Lady Gaga, with their several costume and persona transformations, display similarly appropriated riding clothing. The tight-fitting and formal/"restrictive" character of the garment hints at suggestions of a sexual nature.

See also BRITISH RIDING BOOTS
Compare to BERMUDA SHORTS; CAPRI PANTS; SIRWAL; WESTERN WEAR

Further Reading

Bolton, Andrew. *Anglomania*. New York: Metropolitan Museum of Art, 2006.
Smith, Ron. Society of the Military Horse. http://www.militaryhorse.org/forum/viewtopic.php.
Tomerlin Lee, Sarah. *American Fashion*. London: Andre Deutsch, 1976.
Whitaker, Julie, and Ian Whitelaw. *The Horse*. East Sussex: Ivy Press, 2008.

■ WENDY ROSIE SCOTT

K

KAFTAN
See CAFTAN

KANGA
Kanga (or *khanga*) can also be called *kitenge* or *chitenge*. The kanga is a piece of cotton measuring three feet by two feet that can be worn for modesty, decorative purposes, and protection from the elements. The kanga is worn traditionally in East Africa around the head and waist. Kangas often have a contrasting border around a central motif. The border of the kanga is called *pindo* (in Swahili); the center motif, *mji*, differs in design from the border. Some designs on the kanga include writings in Swahili that promote communication by way of slogans, aphorisms, metaphors, poetic phrases, or proverbs.

History
The kanga cloth is largely associated with East Africa, especially the Swahili culture at the coast. Kanga comes from the old Bantu (Kiswahili) verb *ku-kanga*, to wrap or close. The origins of the kanga are often disputed, but it is believed the kanga was created in Mombasa or Zanzibar in the mid-nineteenth century. Colorful cotton handkerchiefs, called *lesos*, were brought to Africa by Portuguese traders. Some women from Zanzibar got the idea by buying the fabric in lengths of six from bolts of cotton cloth from which they were cut off and sold singly. The fabric of six lengths was then cut into two lengths of three and sewn together along one side to make a three-by-two sheet. Early kangas had a border with black and white spots on a dark background. The kanga got its name after the noisy sociable guinea fowl that has elegant black and white colors on its body and plumage. Due to the influence of Indian and Arab traders, Kanga designs have evolved over the years from spotted prints to include a variety of simple and intricate patterns, numerous colors, and motifs. Writing on the kanga appeared around 1910. Since writing was added to the kanga, the fabric has been used to send messages by the wearer.

The Kanga in the United States

Worn throughout East Africa by women, the kanga is often sold in pairs called *doti*. One piece is wrapped around the head and upper torso while the other is wrapped around the waist and tied like a skirt. Kangas are worn on beaches as a bathing-suit cover-up or bathing suit. Recently, kanga cloths have been imported into the United States and used by some American fashion designers to create bright, colorful, and exotic clothing from high fashion to department store markets. Fashion designers from the United States visiting Kenya and Tanzania have been inspired by kanga designs. These fabrics are being incorporated into American fashion collections, joining the mainstream in international interest in ethnic fashion. The most notable fashion house that has helped to give the fabric global exposure is SUNO. American fashion designer Max Osterweis, part of the design team, incorporates the kanga in the women's apparel collection. Founded in 2008, the New York–based fashion house has made kanga garments a high-end product.

Influence and Impact

In the East African fashion industry, kangas are used as a medium to express personal, political, social, and religious ideas and aspirations. Kangas are often traded or purchased for friends and family for the sheer beauty of the cloth, and to communicate messages implied by the phrase on the cloth. This message can be a message of love, comfort, education, or gratitude. These garments are an expression of the wearer, at times commemorating iconic figures or social or political events. These beautiful garments are a popular and useful part of East African dress and culture.

See also BANDANA; KIMONO
Compare to BOUBOU; CAFTAN; CHIMA; HAORI; JILBAB; KEBAYA AND SKIRT; MUʻUMUʻU

Further Reading

Beck, Rose-Marie. "Ambiguous Signs: The Role of the 'Kanga' as a Medium of Communication." *Afrikanistische Arbeitspapiere* 68 (2001): 157–69.
Hanby, Jeannette. *Kanga 101 Uses.* Nairobi: Ines May Publicity, 1984.
Hongoke, Christine J. *The Effects of Khanga Inscription as a Communication Vehicle in Tanzania.* Research Report 19. Dar es Salaam: Women's Research and Documentation Project, 1993.
Linnebuhr, E. "Kanga: Popular Cloths with Messages." In *Sokomoko: Popular Culture in East Africa,* edited by Werner Graebner, 81–90. Matatu, vol. 9. Amsterdam: Rodopi, 1992.
Parkin, David. "Textile as Commodity, Dress as Text: Swahili *Kanga* and Women's Statements." In *Textiles in Indian Ocean Societies,* edited by Ruth Barnes, 46–67. London and New York: Routledge, 2004.

■ KAREN J. GILMER

KEBAYA AND SKIRT

The kebaya is a traditional Indonesian and Malaysian female blouse. The term "kebaya" is derived from the Arabic word *kaba*, meaning clothing. The Portuguese introduced the transition of the word *kaba* into "kebaya." The traditional use of the kebaya is to be paired with a skirt in the form of *kain* (uncut cloth) or a *sarung* (sarong). The kebaya and skirt became the Indonesian national dress and one of Malaysia's ethnic costumes. The skirt that is paired with the kebaya depends on the area where the garment is worn. In Indonesia the skirt that is worn with the kebaya is called *kain* (cloth). *Kain* is an uncut textile that encircles and wraps around a woman's waist and falls to her ankles. This differs from the sarong, which in an Indonesian context refers to a tubular sewn skirt. In Malaysia, kebaya are usually paired with a sarong skirt.

History

The Javanese and Malaccan first wore the kebaya during the fifteenth and sixteenth centuries, concurrently with the emergence of Islam in both areas. The occurrence of the kebaya and skirt as the traditional costume was part of Islamic convention. The blouse style of the Indonesian and Malaysian kebaya originated from the integration of styles of the Chinese Ming dynasty, the Arab Muslim, and the Portuguese. Thus, there are various styles of kebaya, each named after its wearer, location, or modification. Kebaya Nyonya (Malaysia), also known as Kebaya Encim (Indonesia) has multiple hook closures at the front and is usually embellished with decorative embroideries. This style was named after its user, the Nyonya or Encim, meaning the Chinese descendant wife. Kebaya Kartini describes a style named after the Indonesian heroine Kartini, who is often portrayed in historical photographs wearing a typical classic blouse fastened with brooches. Kebaya Bali (Bali) is usually worn together with a traditional textile belt on the hip. Kebaya Labuh, also known as kebaya *panjang* (long kebaya), is strongly influenced by Arab Muslims. It falls to the ankles and is often worn by Malaysian Muslims. Kebaya modern refers to a garment that has been modified with contemporary design. Today, the use of kebaya and skirt in Indonesia and Malaysia ranges from wedding ceremonies to formal occasions, cultural celebrations, and casual wear.

The Kebaya and Skirt in the United States

The kebaya is thought to have entered the United States in the 1950s and 1960s through Dutch-Indonesian migration after the Second World War, as well as from the Indonesian migration to the United States in the 1960s and from the migration of Chinese-Malay (*peranakan*) people to the United States. When introduced to the United States, kebaya and skirts were intended for wear at special cultural and formal occasions. The continued wearing of kebaya for formal events contributes to the upholding of tradition for Indonesian and Malay cultures in the United States. Currently, various designs of kebaya and skirts are available widely in the United States in stores and online.

Influence and Impact

As wearing a kebaya and skirt represents nationalism and the cultural identity of Indonesians, Malaysians, and their descendants, the use of the kebaya as cultural costumes often appears at formal occasions such as seminars, Independence Day celebrations, conferences, and other special events held in Indonesian and Malaysian diplomatic offices. As kebaya and skirt are linked to the culture of Indonesia, nowadays the kebaya and skirt are also worn as the uniform of musicians in U.S.-based gamelan music groups. The Indonesian bride or brides in Indonesian-style wedding ceremonies held in the United States often wear the kebaya and skirt. Furthermore, the modification of kebaya and skirt using lace fabric is sometimes worn as a modern wedding gown or party blouse in the United States. Originally worn as a cultural costume for attending formal occasions, today the use of kebaya and skirt in the United States is not only limited to formal and cultural events but is also worn as casual and day wear; for example, kebaya made from cotton and silk fabric are often paired with denim trousers or Western-style skirts. Modern skirts that cross over the traditional-style sarong with modern Western-style skirts are also available in the United States. The traditional kebaya and skirt that are worn in the United States are mostly imported from Indonesia; however some designers are based in the United States and produce modern versions of the costume.

The kebaya and skirt influences many fashion designers in United States. Today, the silhouette of the kebaya style in the United States appears in many variations, from evening lace blouses to red carpet gowns and loose summer tops paired with denim. The *kain* and sarong has also inspired the style of modern wrap skirts in the United States.

See also KIMONO; SARONG
Compare to BOUBOU; CAFTAN; CHIMA; HAORI; JILBAB; MU'UMU'U

Further Reading

Cattoni, Victoria. "Behind 'Through the Kebaya.'" *Artery*, May 2005, 12–13.
———. "Reading the Kebaya." In *15th Biennial Conference of the Asian Studies Association of Australia*. Canberra: Asian Studies Association of Australia, 2004.
Kim, Lee Su. *Kebaya Tales: Of Matriarchs, Maidens, Mistresses and Matchmakers*. Kuala Lumpur: Marshal Cavendish, 2011.
Mahmood, Datin Seri Endon. *The Nyonya Kebaya: A Century of Straits Chinese Costume*. Singapore: Periplus, 2004.

■ APRINA MURWANTI

KEFFIYEH

The keffiyeh is a head cloth that originated from the Arabic tradition in the Middle East. A cotton rectangle, 33 by 133 centimeters, woven with a bicolor pattern, usually white with black or red, it can be held in place by the *agal*, a cord or group of cords.

History

Farmers and peasants from the Arabian subcontinent originally wore the keffiyeh for protection. This piece of cloth mainly served as a shield against the sweltering heat, the freezing cold, and the severe sandstorms of the desert. Predominantly white scarves were usually used in summer and colored ones in winter. During the Palestinian strikes of the 1930s, rural peasants and Bedouin wore the keffiyeh, and this colorful head covering became a symbol of resistance. During the mid-twentieth century, the keffiyeh spread to

Palestinian cities where its utilitarian value was transformed into a vehicle for personal expression. The distinct pattern of the keffiyeh gained global recognition in the 1960s when the Palestinian leader Yasser Arafat adopted the black and white keffiyeh as a personal trademark, transforming the keffiyeh into a symbol of Palestinian national identity.

Keffiyeh in the United States

As early as the 1980s, adventuresome American tourists, having spent time in Europe, wore the keffiyeh when back home more for its aesthetic value than to make a political statement; however, when mainstream fashion companies attempted to commercialize the look, the backlash was palpable. In January of 2007, Urban Outfitters began to carry an "antiwar woven scarf"; however, within a few months the company deleted the product from its assortment due to pressure from the media. Despite the controversy, in 2008 the keffiyeh became a fashion trend, meshing political symbolism and marketing strategies at a level rarely attained. True to the "trickle-up" theory of fashion, John Galliano's keffiyeh-inspired designs even found their way into luxury fashion and formal wear. Trickling back down to the mainstream, keffiyeh motifs were strong in summer 2011 ready-to-wear collections in items such as sun hats, scarves, and women's printed dresses reflecting a desert style in pale neutrals.

Influence and Impact

The keffiyeh was introduced to the United States by subcultures beginning in the 1960s, and attempts were made at commercializing the pattern to the mainstream population by the end of the twentieth century. The American public became more familiar with the keffiyeh during the decades surrounding the turn of the twentieth to the twenty-first century when a wide range of celebrities either wore the keffiyeh or garments with the keffiyeh design integrated into them, including pop singer Ricky Martin, Oscar-winning director Quentin Tarantino, actress Kirsten Dunst, celebrity cook Rachel Ray, and actor Colin Farrell. Wearing the keffiyeh can create a highly charged political statement that influences the public's perception, as former Vermont governor and U.S. presidential candidate Howard Dean saw when a photograph of him in 2004 wearing a keffiyeh scarf caused nationwide speculation of anti-Israeli sentiment.

The keffiyeh has morphed from a simple, functional scarf into a symbol of the Palestinian pursuit of civil liberties and freedom, and while it is difficult to separate the keffiyeh's symbolism from its purely aesthetic characteristics, the keffiyeh is on its way to becoming part of the fashion designer's repertoire. Commercializing the keffiyeh in any form requires designers to be aware of the symbolism behind the keffiyeh pattern. While the use of the symbolism around the keffiyeh pattern might be part of a strategic marketing plan, the majority of American consumers will more than likely not be aware of the sensitive nature and history that the keffiyeh carries. As the distinctive keffiyeh pattern becomes more and more ubiquitous in the repertoire of fashionable Western styles, an unaware public may just adopt it for the aesthetic value and ignore the keffiyeh's highly charged symbolic nature.

See also BANDANA
Compare to HAWLI

Further Reading

Anonymous. "Stitch in Time." *New Statesman* 139 (2010): 26.

Janardhan, M. "Mideast: Arafat's Headgear Finds New Fans among Arab Youth." Global Information Network. 2002.

Kawar, W. K., and T. Nasir. "The Traditional Palestinian Costume." *Journal of Palestine Studies* 10, no. 1 (1980): 118–29.

Mitnick, J. "Radical Wrap," *New York Jewish Week*, 2007, 1, 33.

■ MARY RUPPERT-STROESCU AND REBECCA VANG

KENTE CLOTH

The kente is a handwoven strip cloth that originated among the Ashante in Southern Ghana and the Ewe from the border of Ghana and Togo. "Kente" is not the traditional term used by the weavers in either ethnic group, but Ghanaians and Togolese now also use the Ashante term to describe the popular strip cloth. The origin of the term "kente" is uncertain, but researchers believe that it may be a derivative of the Fante word for basket. The Fante are another ethnolinguistic group to the south of the Ashante in Ghana. Fante traders used the term "kente" to describe the handwoven textiles they bought in the Ashante cultural capital, Kumase, to resell on the coast.

Kente Cloth Apparel

Traditionally, men weave kente cloth, and the skill is passed down from father to son or from uncle to nephew. Legend says that women do not have the mental capacity needed to complete the complicated kente designs. Both the Ashante and the Ewe groups use warp striping and supplementary weft floats in their weaving. However, the Ewe are known for using weft-faced inlay motifs, such as lizards and birds, on their cloths. The strips of cloth are made on multiple heddle strip looms made by the weavers themselves. Linear designs are woven into distinct patterns along the length of each narrow strip of approximately 2.5 to 4.5 inches wide. The narrow strips are then sewn together into the legendary cloth. The yarns used by the weavers come in various types. Silk yarns are the most valued and are used to make the most prestigious cloths, worn originally by chiefs and kings. Cotton yarns are used for general-use kente cloth.

Kente is a visual representation of history, oral literature, religion, society, or underlying proverbial meaning. For example, a black and white striped cloth means the "lion catcher" and is said to symbolize courage and bravery. Color is just as symbolic to kente cloth as the design. Gender traditionally dictated the color of cloth one wore, but today individuals choose cloth based on individual preference. Red is associated with blood and suggests life. It is often worn to represent spirituality and sacrifice. Because of green's association with vegetation, it symbolizes growth and fertility. Royalty and people of high status often wear gold due to the color's association with precious metal.

Kente cloth is never sewn into a form-fitting garment. Men generally wear one piece of kente cloth draped over the body like a toga. The cloth is usually twelve feet long, or twenty-four strips. Older women of high standing will also wear the toga-like garment, but most women commonly wear kente cloth as a long skirt made of fewer strips than men.

History

Historical accounts trace the origin of kente cloth to various early weaving traditions in the ancient West African kingdom prior to the seventeenth century and the formation of the Ashante kingdom. Legend holds that a man named Ota Karaban and his friend Kwaku Ameyaw, who learned the art of weaving from observing a spider weaving its web, created what is now recognized as Kente cloth. After presenting their new cloth to their Ashante chief, he reserved it for royalty and limited its use to special occasions. Historians have linked a blue and white strip cloth from the eleventh century in sub-Saharan Africa to the origins of kente cloth because of similar technical and aesthetic features. The sub-Saharan cloth was used in burial ceremonies in Ghana.

According to Ashante tradition and early, precolonial sumptuary laws, common people were not allowed to wear the clothing of richer individuals. Therefore kente cloth soon became a symbol of prestige. The most elaborate kente was made of silk yarns obtained by unraveling imported silk clothes and fabrics from European traders in the eighteenth century. While kente cloth remains a symbol of status among the Ashante, the Ewe have a more democratic approach to the cloth. When an Ewe has the financial ability to pay for the cloth, he or she can wear it regardless of sociopolitical standing.

Kente Cloth in the United States

In 1958 and 1960, Kwame Nkrumah, then president of Ghana, was dressed in kente when he visited the United Nations in Washington during the Eisenhower presidency. The image of the first president of Ghana adorned in the relatively unknown kente cloth appeared on the cover of many magazines and newspapers, such as the *New York Times*, *Ebony*, and *Life* magazine, catching the attention of African-Americans. Mr. Nkrumah then donated a piece of the cloth to the United Nations where it remained in the lobby of the General Assembly. The cloth has since been replaced several times by the Ghanaian government. Kente once again captured the attention of the general public when W. E. B. DuBois wore a kente academic gown in 1963 to receive his honorary degree at the University of Ghana, Legon.

Since the early 1990s, West African style has inspired dress among Americans of African descent. By 1991, kente was a flourishing business in the United States. Kente was selling out of Harlem shops as early as the 1960s, helping it to become one of the most popular symbols of black identity and black power in the United States. Kente serves as an identifier of ethnic origin and a linkage to African history that is misunderstood or simply unknown to most African-Americans. In the United States, the cloth has become an integral part of the lives of African-Americans, being adapted for occasions like Kwanzaa celebrations, Martin Luther King Day, Black History Month, and graduations.

Kente is found everywhere today as clothing, backpacks, ties, and even key chains. Most of the kente cloths available in American shops are Ewe. Because of their democratic views on the use of kente, the Ewe weave most of the cloth for the external market, whereas Ashante fabrics are reserved for local markets rather than exportation. Despite the widespread production of machine-printed kente spin-offs in the Far East (primarily China), authentic forms of the cloth are still regarded as exclusive symbols of social prestige, wealth, and noble sophistication.

Influence and Impact

Kente cloth is yet another localized product being copied and mass produced in China and other Asian countries without any compensation to the originators of the design. Intellectual property laws adopted by Ghana are meant to protect kente labeling. Ghana introduced a copyright law in 1985 on geographical indication that sought to protect kente, among other products, from imitation, such as artwork and folklore.

Despite the fights by the Ghanaian government to protect the legitimacy of its traditional cloth, kente has become a fundamental part of popular culture in the United States and beyond. Everyone from Muhammad Ali and Michael Jackson to dignitaries such as Bill Clinton and Nelson Mandela have all worn kente cloth. Ali wore kente during a visit to Africa in 1964. Michael Jackson was presented with kente during his enthronement as prince of the Kingdom of Sanwi (Ivory Coast) in 1992. Bill Clinton and his wife, Hillary, both draped themselves in kente in 1998 during a visit to Africa, while Mandela wore kente on the cover of *Time* magazine in 1990 when he was freed from prison.

Stoles of kente are not only commonplace at graduations for African-American students wishing to demonstrate their heritage, but Latino students also have been known to wear kente stoles at graduation ceremonies. Minority usage of the traditional cloth has also turned into controversy over the years. In 1995, two high school students from Muskogee, Oklahoma, had their diplomas withheld for wearing kente stoles during their graduation ceremony. Several other high schools and universities have been known to debate the appropriateness of wearing the kente stole by minority students at graduation ceremonies. Even without direct ties to Africa, for many minority students the kente stole represents a sense of accomplishment and solidarity among their minority classmates in white-majority schools.

Despite its pop-cultural assimilation, kente cloth remains a respected cultural artifact that has been the subject of several museum exhibitions. In 2001, Ghanaian fashion designer Francis Selorm Seshie held a fashion show in Copenhagen, Denmark, that was intended to showcase Ghanaian cultural heritage through the use of kente fashion. Seshie has been credited with turning kente into an art form. "Wrapped in Pride: Ghanaian Kente and African American Identity" was a popular installation that explored the history and tradition of Ghanaian kente cloth at Newark Museum and at the National Museum of African Art in the late 1990s.

See also DASHIKI

Compare to BATIK CLOTH APPAREL; CALICO AND CHINTZ; CHAMBRAY; HARRIS TWEED; KANGA; TIE-DYED APPAREL

Further Reading

Boateng, Boatema. *The Copyright Thing Doesn't Work Here: Adinkra and Kente Cloth and Intellectual Property in Ghana*. Minneapolis: University of Minnesota, 2010.

Cole, H. M. "Kente." *American Visions* 5, no. 5 (1990): 18–23.

Hernandez, Sandra. "Exhibiting a Pattern of Pride." *Black Issues in Higher Education* 15, no. 26 (1999): 46–50.

Picton, John, and John Mack. *African Textiles*. London: British Museum Publications, 1989.

Tranberg-Hansen, Karen, and D. Soyini Madison. *African Dress: Fashion, Agency, Performance*. London: Bloomsbury, 2013.

Yamaguchi, Precious, and Frankline Nii Yartay. "Kente Cloth and Adinkra in the Global Market." In *Cyberculture and the Subaltern: Weaving of the Virtual and Real*, edited by Radhika Gajjala, 135–153. Lanham, MD: Lexington Books, 2012.

■ JESSICA STRÜBEL

KHANGA

See KANGA

KILT

Modern kilts or small kilts are pleated, knee-length garments, similar to skirts. They are usually made of woolen fabric in a tartan plaid pattern that may or may not have symbolic meaning to the wearer. Kilts began as masculine garments, but women have adopted them in the name of fashion. Traditional kilts possess deep pleats across the skirt back and a flat double layer of fabric in the front. The overlapping front flaps are secured with leather tabs and buckles, and the kilt is belted. A leather or fur sporran, or pouch, hangs in front of the kilt.

History

Kilts originated with the men and boys of the Scottish Highlands. The oldest identified reference to a kilt-like garment was made in the late sixteenth century in an Irish annal referenced as *The Life of Hugh Roe O'Donnell*. The author described the Scottish clothing: "Their exterior dress was mottled cloaks of many colours with a fringe to their shins and calves, their belts were over their loins outside their cloaks."

Great kilts or belted plaids were the earliest forms of kilts and functioned as clothing and bedding for men. A great kilt was constructed of seven to nine yards of woolen fabric in a tartan plaid pattern. The common phrase "the whole nine yards" means the full amount of something. This may have referred to the yardage needed to create a great kilt. The kilt was fashioned around the body by temporarily pleating a portion of the fabric and securing the pleats to a man's waist with a belt. While there are multiple ways to fold and wear a pleated kilt, the wearer often draped the excess length over his shoulders to serve as a cape. When removed from the body, the flat fabric functioned as a blanket.

In addition to the original functions of a kilt, the garment has symbolic meanings. Although kilts began as clothing for men living in the Scottish Highlands, the kilt has since become a symbol of the entire country of Scotland. The unique plaid patterns of the tartan fabrics represent specific clan names, such as Campbell or Mackenzie.

The Kilt in the United States

Many Scottish immigrants entered the United States through Ellis Island, New York, in the late eighteenth and early nineteenth centuries. The records show that 75,000 Scots relocated to America prior to 1790. By 1820, the number of Scotch-Irish immigrants had increased to 225,000. Just as the immigrants brought their own dialect, they also brought their native costume, the kilt. People with Scottish ancestors may research a plaid pattern and colors registered to their family name. In 1998, the U.S. Senate designated each April 6 as National Tartan Day, giving Americans of Scottish heritage an opportunity to organize cultural events featuring the wearing of the traditional kilt.

Influence and Impact

While gender symbols may vary across cultures, garments that resemble skirts, like kilts, are considered a feminine-gender sign in the United States. Women more readily adopt menswear, but strong social taboos prevent U.S. males from wearing styles that are closely linked to their female counterparts. To date, most American males perceive kilts as women's skirts and have no desire to wear the style. American rapper musician Kanye West wore a black leather designer kilt for his performance at a concert in 2012 and was ridiculed.

The influence of kilts can be summarized as occasional fashion popularity, special events, and school uniforms. Occasionally a fashion designer presents a fall/winter fashion lineup that includes a pleated, plaid, wrap skirt, loosely resembling a kilt. The hemline length varies depending on the fashion of the day. On National Tartan Day, some men wear kilts as a symbol of their Scottish heritage. Kilt-like garments are seen on a daily basis in some private and parochial schools where female students are required to wear pleated plaid skirts that closely resemble kilts.

See also HARRIS TWEED; INVERNESS COAT; TAM-O'-SHANTER
Compare to FUSTANELLA; LEDERHOSEN; SIRWAL

Further Reading

Berthoff, R. "Under the Kilt: Variations on the Scottish-American Ground." *Journal of American Ethnic History* 1, no. 2 (1982): 5–34.
Bray, G. "History and Culture of the Scots . . . The Great Kilt." St. James Lutheran Church for Cultural Connections. 2007.
Ellis Island Foundation. "The Peopling of America." ellisisland.org (accessed June 18, 2013).
Koch, J., ed. *Celtic Culture: A Historical Encyclopedia.* Vol. 3. Santa Barbara, CA: ABC-CLIO, 2006.

Ray, R. C. *Highland Heritage: Scottish Americans in the American South.* Chapel Hill, NC: University of North Carolina Press, 2001.

Walsh, P. "Historical Criticism of the Life of Hugh Roe O'Donnell." *Irish Historical Studies* 1, no. 3 (1939): 229–50.

■CELIA STALL-MEADOWS

KIMONO

The kimono is a T-shaped loose-fitting robe with a V-neck opening, *eri* (detachable collar), and *sode* (straight-cut wide sleeves). The distinguishing feature of the kimono is the obi, a long wide sash wrapped tightly several times around the midriff and a little higher to cover the ribs. "Kimono" is a generic term for clothing meaning "a thing to wear." It is the traditional national dress of Japan. During its thousand-year history, the kimono has evolved and been refined, but it predominantly retains its traditional shape.

History

Japanese culture was class conscious and highly formalized. The type of clothes worn defined a citizen's identity and status. The style, color, and pattern of the kimono defined the level of formality, rank, sex, age, marital status, and seasons of the year. The long-sleeved colorful *furisode* (swinging sleeves) was reserved for young women of marriageable age. The *tomesode* (short-sleeved), a dark-colored kimono with fewer patterns, was reserved for married women.

Sumptuary laws were passed governing the art of dressing and how the kimono should be worn. It was to be folded left to right and secured with the obi. Styles ranged from multilayered imperial court robes to an informal lightweight *yukata*, an unlined cotton housecoat or bathrobe. Construction was simple and economical, made from a bolt of cloth (*tan*) measuring approximately twelve to fourteen yards long and twelve to sixteen inches wide. Decorative patterns were derived from the natural world.

The kimono's origins date back to the multilayered imperial court robes of the Heian period (794–1185). It evolved from *kosode*, a plain white narrow-sleeved undergarment worn by Heian court nobility. Heian women of the aristocracy wore the silk *junihitoe*, a twelve-layered robe often increasing to twenty layers. During the Kamakura period (1185–1333), the *kosode* evolved into a colorful outer robe and became standard dress for women of the nobility until the nineteenth century.

Kimono

The Kimono in the United States

The opening of Japan to international trade in 1854 by U.S. naval officer Commodore Matthew Calbraith Perry (1794–1858) created a craze for all things Japanese. Shiploads of Japanese goods flooded the European and American market. International world fairs or expositions such as the 1867 Paris Exposition impacted significantly on the West and drew attention to Japanese culture and the kimono.

The kimono's entry into American popular culture coincided with the 1876 Exposition held in Philadelphia. For the first time, millions of ordinary American citizens had the opportunity to view Japanese goods on a grand scale on their own soil. The Japanese Pavilion with teahouse and geishas serving tea at the 1905 St. Louis Exposition held in Missouri gave visitors a real opportunity to witness Japanese traditions and customs.

During the late nineteenth and early twentieth centuries, kimonos came to America as souvenirs by artists, photographers, soldiers returning from war, and avid travelers. Japanese ukiyo-e (woodblock prints), depicting courtesans attired in a kimono, hand-tinted photographs, geisha postcards, and photographic mementos of American travelers attired in the kimono, generated a craze for all things Japanese, and the kimono became a recognizable object in American popular culture.

Publications such as *Glimpses of Unfamiliar Japan* (1894); *La Japon Artistique* (1838–1891); *Bric-a-Brac: An Artist's Letters from Japan* (1897); *Etoffes Japonaises: Tissees et Brochees* (1910), a portfolio of Japanese textiles; and *hinagata-bon* (kimono pattern books) helped to educate Americans about Japanese culture and the kimono.

For American women in the first half of the twentieth century, the kimono became a much-admired exotic object. By the second half of the century, it evolved into a comfortable loose-fitting robe that offered freedom of movement and easily slipped on or off the body.

The kimono became associated with exoticism, avant-garde sensibilities, intimate interiors, and fashionable at-home robes. Women wore the kimono as a negligee, dressing gown, or lounge robe. For American women it exemplified wealth and luxury, a sense of style and sophisticated taste, social distinction, liberty, the spirit of independence, and a newfound freedom of expression.

Theater and movie personalities and middle- and upper-class women of economic means wore the kimono. Noted examples include actress Lotta Crabtree (1847–1924), choreographer Ruth St. Denis (1879–1968), society hostess Elsie Whelen Goelet Clews (1880–1959), and First Daughter Alice Roosevelt Longworth (1884–1980).

Influence and Impact

Japanese woodblock prints had a significant influence on artists and fashion designers at the turn of the century, dramatically changing the course of Western art and fashion. European and American artists such as Edward Manet (1832–1883), Mary Cassatt (1844–1926), and James McNeil Whistler (1834–1903) depicted Western women in intimate interiors attired in kimonos.

The visually arresting splendor of Japanese theater and opera costumes, set designs from Gilbert and Sullivan's *Mikado*, Kabuki and Noh singing and dancing dramas, Puccini's *Madame Butterfly*, and Ballets Rousse's Paris debut in 1909 enchanted the West and perpetuated interest in the kimono.

Haute couture designers such as Paul Poiret (1879–1944), Charles Fredrick Worth (1826–1895), Mariano Fortuny (1871–1949), Madeleine Vionnet (1876–1975), Jean Paquin (1869–1936), and Elsa Schiaparelli (1883–1971) assimilated kimono elements into Western-style fashion. Typical elements included kimono sleeves; a straight-cut, loose-fitting silhouette; a V neckline; *fuki* (wadded lining at the hem); a *hikisuso* (long train); *date-mon* (family crests); a *nukiemon* (dropped collar); *yuzen* (polychrome stencil prints); an *obi-jime* (silk twisted and tasseled cord); a *datejime* (wide sash); *shibori* (resist dyeing); and a pillow-shaped wadded collar. Art to Wear artists adopted the kimono for their studio-based practice. The two-dimensional, flat, canvas-like quality of the kimono with simple rectangular construction appealed to their artistic sensibilities. Art to Wear became a potent vehicle for personal iconography, political statements, and feminist ideologies.

See also FLIP-FLOPS (GETA); HAORI; HAPPI; JAPANESE STREET FASHION; OBI; TABI
Compare to ALOHA SHIRT (HAWAI'IAN SHIRT); CHEONGSAM; CHIMA; HANBOK; HANFU CHINESE ROBES; JILBAB; KEBAYA AND SKIRT; MU'UMU'U; SARONG

Further Reading

Dalby, Liza. *Kimono: Fashioning Culture*. London: Vintage, 2001.
Fukai, Akiko. *Fashion: A History from the 18th to 20th Century; the Collection of the Kyoto Costume Institute*. Kyoto: Taschen, 2002.
Honour, Hugh, and John Fleming. *A World History of Art*. London: Macmillan, 1982.
Munsterberg, Hugo. *Images of Asia: The Japanese Kimono*. New York: Oxford University Press, 1996.
Schafler Dale, Julie. *Art to Wear*. New York: Abbeville, 1986.
Sittenfeld, Michael, ed. *Five Centuries of Japanese Kimono*. Chicago: Art Institute of Chicago Museum Studies, 1992.
Stevens, Rebecca A.T., and Yoshiko I. Wada, eds. *The Kimono Inspiration: Art and Art-to-Wear in America*. The Textile Museum, Washington, DC. San Francisco: Pomegranate, 1996.

■ VISHNA COLLINS

KITENGE
See KANGA

KOLPIK
See SHTREIMEL

KOSOVOROTKA

Kosovorotka is a traditional long-sleeved shirt of mid-hip length worn by Russian farmers from the sixteenth to the mid-twentieth century. Kosovorotka is a peasant's version of an ancient Russian *rubaha* (a tunic-like man's outfit). The distinguishing feature of the kosovorotka is the noncentered placement of a front cut ("noncentered" sounds like "kosoi" in Russian, so "kosovorotka" means "a shirt with a noncentered front cut").

History

Men of any age, wealth, family, and social status wore kosovorotka. At the same time, color, decoration, and type of cloth used worked as identification, signifying age group, social status, and even place of living of a wearer. For instance, young bachelors wore white and bright red kosovorotkas made of expensive and fancy-looking fabrics, whereas respectable married men preferred white, dark red, and dark blue woolen and linen shirts. Everyday kosovorotkas were sewn of "motley" (home-woven cloth made of mixed thread—linen, wool, hemp) and, later, of cheap machine-made cotton. In contrast, silk and bleached linen decorated with golden trim, river pearls, and appliqué were used for festive kosovorotkas, with only white home-woven linen allowed for ritual shirts.

For villagers, kosovorotka was not only a clothing item, but also a spiritual "armor" shielding a wearer from any supernatural danger. Three specific details of decoration served this "protective" purpose. The first one was a "magical" needlepoint-covered kosovorotka's chest part, and also encircled sleeve cuts and a hemline. Designs used differed in accordance with age, family status, and usage of an item. Everyday and festive shirts carried only basic "protective" symbols (to the end of the nineteenth century, people started substituting everyday kosovorotkas' embroidery with colorful trim and/or appliqué). Ritual kosovorotkas had heavily decorated chest "shields" embroidered with "sacred" signs of sun, fire, fertility, good luck, and the like.

The second "magic" element of a kosovorotka's decoration was a red trim placed around the neck hole or along the front cut, the sleeve cuts, and the hemline. This trim was comprehended as "fire edges" that burned out evil spirits that came close to a wearer. *Lastovica* (red armpits) were the third "protective" detail. They were supposed to defend a wearer's arms and actions performed by the arms. *Lastovica* and "fire edges" appeared to be the most persistent elements of traditional clothing "magic." Even in the 1950s people still used them, whereas "magical" embroidery designs were almost forgotten at that time.

Tradition required wearing kosovorotka with a waistband or a belt. A waistband signified that a wearer was a human being, not a spirit or a ghost. In contrast, when using a kosovorotka as grave clothes, a waistband was strictly prohibited. Embroidery for a "grave shirt" was modest and made with the hair of the wearer.

The Kosovorotka in the United States

The kosovorotka was introduced in the United States in three waves. For the first time, it appeared at the beginning of the nineteenth century as part of the wardrobe of village-born settlers of Sitka (Alaska) and Fort Ross (California). Soldiers, workers, and hunters brought their native clothes to keep a connection with their motherland. The second appearance of the kosovorotka occurred in the 1960s, when groups of Russians established a settlement at Woodburn, Oregon. For them, wearing kosovorotkas was believed to be part of a traditional lifestyle that they proudly maintained despite the hostile environment of an "outside" world. The third wave is happening right now. Highly educated immigrants from Russia (those who are ethnically Russian) sew and wear kosovorotkas as a token of national identity. People study their family history and order (or make for themselves) kosovorotkas of exactly that fashion their ancestors wore.

Mostly men put on kosovorotkas for Russian traditional festivals (like Maslenitsa, the spring celebration; Kupalo, the summer solstice; and others); however, some of them wear kosovorotkas as an everyday outfit as well. In addition, it became popular among Russian-Americans to celebrate important family events such as weddings and birthdays in accordance with Russian village tradition that required, inter alia, wearing a traditional outfit.

Influence and Impact

A real kosovorotka continues to be a strictly traditional outfit. Some theater costume designers create stage versions of kosovorotkas; however, with the Russian immigrant community, these are considered costumes-by-idea, not copies or replicas of a traditional Russian outfit.

See also ALOHA SHIRT (HAWAI'IAN SHIRT); BARONG TAGALOG; RUBAHA
Compare to BUSSERULL (NORWEGIAN WORK SHIRT); CHAMBRAY; OXFORD SHIRT

Further Reading

Aleshina, Tat'iana S. *History of Russian Costume from the Eleventh to the Twentieth Century.* New York: Metropolitan Museum of Art, 1977.
Vucinich, Wayne S. *The Peasant in Nineteenth-Century Russia.* Stanford, CA: Stanford University Press, 1968.

■ IRINA ZHOUKOVA PETROVA

KUFI

"Kufi" is a term for a brimless round cap originating in West Africa. In the West African Yoruba language, *kufi* is translated as "crown." This men's hat is made with a thin band of fabric that stands up from the forehead with a rounded or crown-shaped top. It is most often made of traditional African cloth such as kente cloth, mudcloth, or *aso oke* cloth.

History

As part of traditional West African dress, the kufi is worn with a dashiki or an *agbada*. The dashiki is a loose-fitting pullover that features a V neck and covers the top half of the body. It is often brightly colored and features embroidery on the neck and sleeves. Worn with *sokoto* (drawstring trousers), the dashiki, kufi, and *sokoto* compose the three pieces of a dashiki suit. The *agbada* are brightly colored, loose robes that extend to the ankles. They can be open or stitched at the sides.

The Kufi in the United States

During the 1960s and 1970s, the black nationalism movement inspired many African-Americans to find their cultural roots. One manifestation of this search for identity was the search for traditional African apparel, including the kufi, to express cultural identity and pride. Beginning first as retail operations specializing in imported West African dress items and fabrics, the opening of the Internet to commerce substantially expanded the ability of African-Americans to purchase West African apparel items.

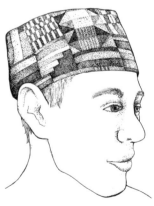

Kufi

African-American men usually wear the kufi for special events or to express national pride. As a result, marketing and sales of kufi hats always experience an increase during Black History Month. African-American women can also wear kufis but do so to a lesser degree, preferring the more traditional tied head wrap or turban. Kufis can also be worn with mainstreamed Western apparel to mark dual identity. Some tuxedos marketed toward African-Americans feature the typical black suit coat and trousers but have an African print on the vest and cummerbund and are completed with a coordinating kufi.

Influence and Impact

The kufi is now a well-recognized symbol in the United States for African heritage and pride. Many prominent African-American celebrities, musicians, and politicians have worn kufis, giving credibility to the style. Being a symbol of identity, some rappers have used the wearing of a kufi as a way to challenge rivals whom they feel are "posers" in the African-American community. To "kufi smack" or "kufi slap" someone is to expose them as a fake. The common usage of these popular-culture idioms underscores the central importance of the kufi as a cultural icon. During a time when African-Americans were searching for a collective identity and heritage, the kufi arose to become an undeniable symbol of black style and pride.

See also DASHIKI
Compare to BERET; BLANGKON; FEZ; FLAT CAP; RASTA HAT; SIBENIK CAP; TAM-O'-SHANTER; TAQIYA

Further Reading

Leventon, Melissa. *What People Wore When: A Complete Illustrated History of Costume from Ancient Times to the Nineteenth Century for Every Level of Society*. New York: St. Martin's Griffin, 2008.
National Museum of African Art. "Hats Off! A Salute to African Headwear." Smithsonian National Museum of African Art. http://www.nmafa.si.edu/exhibits/hatssite/nonflash/hats.htm (accessed May 28, 2013).
Pendergast, Sara, and Tom Pendergast. *Fashion, Costume, and Culture: Clothing, Headwear, Body Decorations, and Footwear through the Ages*. Vol. 2, *Early Cultures across the Globe*. Edited by Sarah Hermse. Detroit, MI: UXL, 2004.
Tulloch, Carol. *Black Style*. London: V&A Publications, 2004.

■ LAURA VAN WAARDHUIZEN

L

LEDERHOSEN

Lederhosen (literally "leather pants") are not pants as such but shorts that are supported by their own integrated suspenders that flank a decorative leather band across the chest. This band is decorated by heraldic or folk motifs relative to a region which, as the name indicates, derive from the Germanophone states of Europe. They are considered particular to the Tyrol region and Bavaria. Lederhosen are also worn, but less commonly, in states that once belonged to the Austro-Hungarian Empire such as Slovenia and the Czech Republic. They were particularly worn in the Alpine regions. They continue to be worn as folk and traditional dress during festivals and fêtes, much the same as the kilt in Scotland. The longer variants are known as *bundhosen*. They are not generally worn in southwestern Germany or in Switzerland.

History

While not strictly the national dress, lederhosen retain strong links to the rural past of Germanic Europe. Farmers originally wore lederhosen since they were more durable than fabric, but harder to clean. While the time of their origin remains obscure, they probably began to be worn in the late Middle Ages.

The popularity of lederhosen dropped considerably in the nineteenth century with the increasing migration of many from rural to industrialized and urban areas, whereupon the style came to be thought of as the clothing of rural peasants. This was unfortunate, as forms of lederhosen and *bundhosen* had been worn for hundreds of years by members of the nobility as well for activities such as hunting. Often highly decorated, historical examples of lederhosen are a rich source of knowledge of local folk design.

Lederhosen in the United States

This perception altered at the end of the century, particularly in Munich, in which there was a renewed interest in traditional forms of dress. It was perhaps because of this that lederhosen maintain the strongest association with Bavaria and for over a century continue to be worn on festive occasions, most famously during the beer festival Oktoberfest. It is in facsimiles of such festivals in the United States that they are mainly worn. Unless the person hails from Germany, they are worn more self-consciously as costume and as a promotional exercise. Commercial offshoots such as these help to propagate the notion that lederhosen are quintessentially Bavarian. Outside of Bavaria, lederhosen continue to be linked to the robust country dweller. In addition to festivals, lederhosen are worn by German and even French youths as Boy Scout uniforms.

Influence and Impact

Today lederhosen are firmly cemented within the Central European folk tradition and are marketed as such. They enjoy their own firm niche popularity in Europe and the United States. Their female counterpart is the dirndl, with which they are characteristically paired in specialist shops and in online purchasing.

Beyond traditional wear, lederhosen are seen influencing more contemporary fashions. For example, there have been recent spates of celebrities wearing leather shorts, which are directly linked to the lederhosen tradition. Designers such as Thakoon and Helmut Lang have created lederhosen-influenced garments for the women's marketplace, and the popular retail house Zara recently marketed a collection of leather shorts for women.

See also DIRNDL
Compare to FUSTANELLA; KILT; SIRWAL

Further Reading

Adams, William L. "Lederhosen Chic: From the Alps to the Catwalk." *Time*, May 5, 2010. http://www
    .time.com/time/world/article/0,8599,1986417,00.html.
Hintz, Katie. "Are Lederhosen the New Jeggings? Say It Ain't So." *New York Magazine*, April 22, 2010.
    http://nymag.com/thecut/2010/04/are_lederhosen_the_new_jegging.html.

■ ADAM GECZY

LEOTARD

A leotard is a torso-covering garment that is stepped into and pulled up that encompasses a range of styles including sleeveless, long sleeve, short sleeve, high necks, low backs, straps, lace inserts, and so forth. The leotard is named after its French originator, Jules Leotard (1842–1870), who designed the garment for trapeze performance. The garment was originally called a maillot, which means "tight-fitting clothing" in French. It was designed for two specific purposes: to enable him to move freely without getting caught in the ropes and to show off his well-developed muscles.

History

Jules Leotard's father was a gymnastics teacher in France and taught him the skills that he would eventually transfer to the trapeze bar. His family ran a swimming pool, which led Jules to hang a trapeze over the pool, allowing him to build his talent and precision. He made his debut on the trapeze in 1859, becoming the first person to ever use multiple trapeze bars simultaneously. He was the main aerialist in the Cirque Franconi in Paris, along with the Alhambra in London. Jules had two great legacies—he performed on five trapezes, somersaulting between each of them, and he invented the maillot, later adopting the name of the leotard.

At that time of its first development, the leotard was a knitted suit that provided freedom of movement. The performer did not have to worry about any part of the garment getting caught in any of the trapeze mechanisms or ropes. Another side benefit to the garment was how it displayed Jules's athleticism and masculine physique. Ballet studios in Paris were the first non-circus performers to adopt the leotard as their choice garment, but that did not occur until over a decade after Jules Leotard's death. In 1886 the name "leotard" was used for the garment that Jules Leotard always referred to as the maillot. Transformation into women's leotards resulted in a leotard style with a tighter crotch area and higher leg opening that was optimal for dancers. In 1867 a British music hall performer, George Leybourne, sang a song about the famous trapeze artist titled "The Daring Young Man on the Flying Trapeze" that is still well known today.

The Leotard in the United States

Throughout the years, leotards have always remained as a type of uniform in ballet. A large influencer of new trends has been the continual advancement of materials. Lycra, spandex, and cotton blends are typical fabrics used in athletic wear. High-performance stretch and moisture-wicking materials continue to enhance the ability of the leotard to serve this consuming audience. In practice, leotards allow teachers to accurately critique movements. Today the leotard has multiple uses in the United States. Most athletes that require precision of movements, artistry, and muscular form embrace this type of garment for their performances. It allows the audience to pay particular attention to the movement of the body and allows the performer full body flexibility.

In the 1970s, women in the United States began wearing leotards and snap-fasten-crotch bodysuits under pants or skirts in everyday outfits. More colorful variations of the standard leotard colors appeared, which led to the emergence of leotards in nightclubs. During the 1980s, aerobics exercise enthusiasts adopted leotards as a staple garment. The latter part of the decade saw a decline in the usage of leotards for exercise and some types of dance as sports bras and boy shorts gained in popularity.

Influence and Impact

The impact of the leotard has been substantial. A garment that was specifically designed to help a trapeze artist move more freely has crossed over into many other performing arts and sports including multiple forms of dance, ice skating, gymnastics, weightlifting, and wrestling. Some of the sports call it a singlet, while others retain the name leotard. Professional stage performers, including showgirls and burlesque dancers, also used a form of leotard on stage. Interestingly, showgirls normally wore colored leotards that had a stronger stage presence, whereas burlesque dancers wore flesh-colored leotards, giving the illusion of being nude. Ironically, the leotard was invented by a man and was primarily worn by men during its early history. Through the years it transformed into a garment predominantly worn by women. During the 1920s and 1930s, leotards were the design inspiration for swimwear, and its influence is evident when looking at historical pictures of the era. A significant shift in gender wearing patterns occurred in the 1930s when men were allowed to be bare chested at swimming pools and beaches, thus eliminating the need for a man to cover his upper body with a leotard-style garment.

See also BRICOLAGE
Compare to BUCKSKIN

Further Reading

Harder, Kelsie B. "Leotards and 'Tightsomania.'" *American Speech* 35, no. 2 (May 1960): 101–4.

■ LUANNE MAYORGA

MADRAS CLOTH

Indian madras refers to a brightly colored, lightweight, breathable, handwoven cotton fabric that is yarn-dyed in checks, plaid, or stripes, which originated in Chennai (formerly called Madras), a city in South India. The cloth has also been identified by its colloquial name, madrasi checks. Although "Madras" is the name of a place, in this context it is used as an adjective and not as a proper noun. Real madras had pure cotton yarns that were colored by homemade vegetable dyes and were hand woven. The resultant fabrics were known to "bleed" and fade when washed, thus rendering a unique, "washed-out" appearance to the fabric, commonly known as bleeding madras. In the present day, not all madras bleeds. A distinguishing feature of real madras is that it has the same pattern on both sides. A stitched assemblage of four to six different patterns of cloth is known as patchwork madras. Some madras fabrics have a characteristic texture and luster. Other variants employ basket weave, seersucker fabric, and may occasionally be blended with polyester. By the twentieth century, it was documented that real Indian madras could be differentiated from other Indian trade cottons based on twelve characteristics, namely color, dyes, fiber content, fabric width, length, unique odor, motif, repeat, format, yarn count, weave, and distinctive fold.

History

Cloth historians say that the first handwoven cloth in Madras was made of yarn from the tip skin of ancient trees, called *karvelem patta*. The earliest form of Indian madras, called Guinea stuffs, was a grouping of cotton textiles produced along the Coromandel Coast in colors such as indigo blue, madder red, off-white, yellow, shades of green, brown, and lavender.

The Portuguese recognized that the Kalabari merchants in West Africa would appreciate the aesthetic of Indian textiles. The European East India companies traded these for commodities from West Africa (Guinea Coast) and the Middle East. Kerchiefs and head scarves, particularly in hues of red, were worn by slave women in West Africa as a mark of their social status. It is believed that the Indian native hand weavers took design inspiration from the tartan patterns worn by Scottish regiments and reinterpreted them in their local color palettes in the 1800s.

Madras Cloth in the United States

Indian madras was imported from India, via London, to the United States from 1784 until 1816 when an import tariff was imposed. The Industrial Revolution saw the emergence of imitation Indian madras, which was characterized by the use of colorfast synthetic dyes and power looms. This imitation Indian madras was introduced by companies such as Brooks Brothers and Hathaway Shirts in the 1920s and 1930s. Bleeding madras was popularized in the United States in the 1950s and 1960s, where these were marketed with a guarantee to fade. In the 1980s, madras became synonymous with the identity of the preppies, who were known for their education in elite institutions, their athletic interests in sports such as tennis and golf, and their memberships in country clubs.

Influence and Impact

Madras is popularly worn in the United States during spring and summer owing to its soft hand, its light-to-medium weight, and its nonclinginess to the body. It renders an urban casual look and has become a quintessential staple for the American classic wardrobe. Ralph Lauren, O'Connell, and J. Crew have used Madras to create the iconic preppy look. American novelist S. E. Hinton describes madras as preferred by rich children in her book *The Outsiders*. Hollywood celebrities have also popularized madras in movies. Madras plaids or madras checks are used as shirts, blouses, beach shorts, sports jackets, blazers, skirts, aprons, ties, quilts, handkerchiefs, and footwear by men and women alike. Since it has a busy pattern, it is usually worn in combination with subdued solid colors such as white and icy blue.

Madras has been reinventing itself stylistically over the years. The print, however, has not undergone any drastic change. Anyone can wear madras, regardless of age and gender. The fabric is also symbolic of preppy crowds seen in the city of Madras, especially during summer. Major markets for madras are in the United States, where it is evocative of the preppy lifestyle and affluence, and in West Africa, where it uniquely identifies the ethnicity of tribes such as the Kalabari. It is said that the Kalabari involve their physical senses in identifying the authenticity of madras by way of appearance, tactile nature, and sometimes even by taste.

See also CALICO AND CHINTZ
Compare to BATIK CLOTH APPAREL; CHAMBRAY; KENTE CLOTH; TIE-DYED APPAREL

Further Reading

Evenson, Sandra. "Indian Madras Plaids as Real India." In *Dress Sense: Emotional and Sensory Experiences of the Body and Clothes*, edited by Donald Clay Johnson and Helen Bradley Foster. Oxford: Berg, 2007.
Milcetich, Jessica. "The Meaning of Madras." *Morning Call*, June 14, 2006. http://articles.mcall.com/2006-07-14/features/3690236_1_fashion-consultant-washed-fabric.

■ HARINI RAMASWAMY

MANCHU JACKET
See HANFU CHINESE ROBES

MAO SUIT

The Mao suit, known in China as "Zhongshan zhuang" after Sun Yat-sen, is a loosely fitted jacket featuring a five-button enclosure, four symmetrical patch pockets (breast pockets smaller than the waist pockets), three cuff buttons, and a high, turned-down collar. The jacket is usually worn with matching pants that fasten in the front. The suit was typically made of cotton and polyester during Mao's era (1949–1977). Wool or wool-blend materials were more desirable but harder to come by. The Mao suit was a popular male dress form during the Mao era and well into the 1980s in Mainland China. Even today, it is still worn by a large segment of the older generation. Celebrities and fashionable youth adopted slimmer or modified versions in China.

History

The progenitor of the Mao suit was originally designed in the early years of the fledgling Chinese Republic (1912–1949), with input from Sun Yat-sen, who sought to establish a form of national dress that was not associated with the Qing court but that was also distinct from purely Western dress forms. The original form did not have patch pockets, it typically had seven buttons along the front closure instead of five, and the collar was high-standing instead of turned down. Some claim that the original form is based on a Japanese cadet uniform, while others maintain that student uniforms worn in Hong Kong in the early twentieth century influenced it. The colors of the Mao suit are typically blue, gray, or black, and sometimes military green, with each color having different social and political implications.

The sartorial details of the Mao suit are often described as having symbolic meaning. The four front patch pockets are said to represent the Four Cardinal Principles of the Guanzi (Book of Changes): courtesy (*li*), righteousness (*yi*), integrity (*lian*), and the sense of shame (*chi*). The five buttons on the front closure are said to symbolize the five branches (*yuan*) of government codified in Sun Yat-sen's five-power constitution (executive, legislative, judicial, control, and examination). And the three cuff buttons are supposed to represent Sun's Three Principles of the People (nationalism, democracy, and people's livelihood).

In the early years of the Chinese republic, military officers initially wore the suit, but by 1929 it had become the official uniform for civil servants under the newly formed Nationalist government. Mao Zedong also adopted the suit, and it eventually became the military attire of soldiers in the Red Army. Slight changes were implemented to the early form of the suit, such as increasing the size of the collar fall and sharpening the collar corner so the jacket would better fit Mao personally. By the years of the Cultural Revolution (1966–1976), the Mao suit had become the de facto national dress of the People's Republic of China. Mao Zedong and other leaders of the Communist Party wore the Mao suit on various formal and informal occasions, including at the founding ceremony on October 1, 1949.

Mao Suit

It was also widely adopted by the masses and became what was known as one of the "three old styles" of the Mao era, along with the *qingnian zhuang* (youth jacket) and the *jun bianzhuang* (casual army jacket). But a variety of simplified and modified versions of the Mao suit existed at this time due to economic constraints. The extensive popularity of the Mao suit in China during the Mao era made it a highly recognizable symbol of China, especially to outsiders. However, in part it was also because of the suit's strong association with Mao and China's turn inward during the early decades of the PRC that it gradually lost ground to various Western dress forms as China opened up to the outside world after Deng Xiaoping's ascent to power in 1978, with the Western business suit becoming standard business attire by the late 1980s.

The Mao Suit in the United States

By the early 1970s, modified versions of the Mao suit were making an appearance on the streets of New York. In 1971, Halston designed a modified silk version for women, while simple cotton versions of the Mao suit were being sold in department stores such as Bloomingdale's. U.S. newspapers claimed that the Mao jacket had become a fashion craze for both genders, fueled by the announcement of President Nixon's visit to China. By the late 1970s and early 1980s, the Mao suit was featured on the cover of UK and Australian *Vogue*, its antifashion utilitarianism and association with Maoist China transformed into an exotic fashion statement.

Influence and Impact

The symbolic meaning of the Mao suit has undergone several changes reflecting changes in the political and social climate in China. During the Republic era, the Mao suit came to symbolize Sun Yat-sen's political outlook and governmental structure. During the Mao era, the Mao suit spoke the language of egalitarianism, frugality, and proletarian revolutionary enthusiasm. After the implementation of economic reforms in the late 1970s—and especially today—the Mao suit has become a symbol of patriotism and political leftism. Choosing to don the Mao suit or a Western suit by any Communist Party leader is often interpreted as a sign of socialist or reformist leanings. However, the role of the wearer also gives different meanings to the Mao suit. For example, a Chinese pop star can still turn the Mao suit into an innovative fashion statement that serves to mark Chinese identity.

See also Hanfu Chinese Robes
Compare to Mariachi Suit; Nehru Jacket; Waistcoat; Zoot Suit

Further Reading

Bao, Mingxin, Wu Juanjuan, Ma Li, Yang Shu, and Wu Di. *Zhongguo qipao* [Chinese *qipao*]. Shanghai: Shanghai Wenhua Chubanshe, 1998.

Clark, Hazel. *The Cheongsam*. New York: Oxford University Press, 2000.

Finnane, Antonia. *Changing Clothes in China: Fashion, History, Nation*. New York: Columbia University Press, 2008.

Garrett, Valery M. *Chinese Dress: From the Qing Dynasty to the Present.* Rutland, VT: Tuttle, 2007.
Steele, Valerie, and John Major. *China Chic: East Meets West.* New Haven, CT: Yale University Press, 1999.
Wu, Juanjuan. *Chinese Fashion from Mao to Now.* Oxford: Berg, 2009.

■ JUANJUAN WU

MARIACHI SUIT

"Mariachi suit" refers to the costume worn by a group of Mexican musicians that plays a traditional-style folk music. Originally the mariachi suit was very humble as the roaming bands wore the traditional clothing of a laborer in Mexico. Most members had very little money, so they wore sombreros, white pants and shirts, and either boots or sandals. The costume now associated with the term emerged after the Mexican Revolution, when musicians started to dress to express national pride in the style of a *charro* horseman. As their popularity continued to rise, they began wearing costumes that are still influential today. The suit consists of a small jacket with silver buttons, a sombrero, a shirt, an embroidered belt, a wide bow tie, pants, a cummerbund, and cowboy boots. The suits have become very elaborate and colorful, with sombreros that perfectly match the clothing. Female members of the mariachi band are normally in long skirts with the same ornamentation and colors as the male members.

History

Charro-style dress originated in Spain and was worn by Spanish hacienda owners and horsemen who immigrated into Mexico. The wealthier a person was, the more embroidered or ornate was their costuming. *Charros* dressed to ride in short tailored jackets with leather chaps, boots, and spurs. *Charros* became known throughout Mexico as adept horsemen who often took part in rodeo-style competitions similar to the western cowboy. During and after the revolution, this style of dress became a statement of Mexico's liberation and democracy.

The Mariachi Suit in the United States

As Mexican immigrants came into the United States, so did the folk music and dress styles of the mariachis. In the 1930s, mariachi music and costuming began being featured in films, including *Alla en el Rancho Grande*, and radio broadcasts. It continued to grow in popularity during the 1950s and 1960s. Mariachi music is very popular in the Southwest region of the United States and is most often performed while wearing the traditional mariachi dress style.

Influence and Impact

Charro Days are a featured annual event in some Texas towns such as Brownsville. Dating back to 1938, the Brownsville festival bills itself as a binational celebration, and community members and visitors are encouraged to wear the authentic costumes of Mexico whenever possible. With some community members boasting trunks of *charro*-style dress collected throughout the years, the community dresses up for the festival days. To the delight of students enrolled in the public schools in Brownsville, sometimes teachers arrive to class dressed in *charro*-inspired apparel.

Mariachi bands dressed in *charro*-inspired apparel are frequent performers throughout the southwestern part of the United States. You can find them year-round playing at Mexican restaurants, festivals, and special events. Singer Linda Ronstadt created an album in 1988 that further popularized the ethnic sounds of the mariachi band. It was titled *Songs of My Father*, saluting her Mexican heritage.

See also MEXICAN POINTY BOOTS; MEXICAN TOURIST/SOUVENIR JACKET; SOMBRERO
Compare to BOLERO JACKET; CHOLO STYLE; MAO SUIT; WESTERN WEAR; ZOOT SUIT

Further Reading

Clark, Sylvia. "Mariachi Music as a Symbol of Mexican Culture in the United States." *International Journal of Music Education* 23 (December 2005): 227–37.

■ LUANNE MAYORGA

MELHFA

"Melhfa," or *malahfa*, is a dialect word stemming from the Arabic word *lahfa*, meaning to cover or envelop. It refers to an item of women's clothing and is a single piece of fabric three and a half by one and a half meters (thirteen by five feet) that is draped around the body. An age-old garment commonly worn in the Atlantic Sahara since the eleventh century, it continues to be worn today from the south of Morocco to the Anti-Atlas, the Senegal River, and Mauritania. Made from a variety of lightweight fabrics, the melhfa is wrapped around the body, tied at the shoulder, and then draped again around the shoulder and head. The melhfa symbolizes feminine elegance, poise, and refinement in Atlantic Saharan culture.

History

Until the middle of the twentieth century, the melhfa was made from cotton cloth dyed a very dark indigo blue called *nila*. The fabric was heavily impregnated with indigo and when new had a sheen to it similar to a chintz finish. The people of the Sahara called the fabric *chandor* after the Indian village where the fabric originated on the western shores of Hindustan. The fabric made its way to the region traveling across Persia and Syria from east to west in Saharan caravans with the spread of Islam during medieval times. The Europeans referred to all cotton fabric traveling by caravan from the South (Sudanese Guinea) as Guinea and referred to the garment as "Guinea veil." The *chandor* fabric was soft and draped nicely on the body, creating soft pleats and folds as it wrapped and covered women from head to toe. The indigo dye would rub off onto the wearer's skin, discoloring and dyeing the skin a blue purple color and providing protection to the wearer against the sun's rays. Once the fabric stopped dyeing the skin, it became less valuable, and the lady of the house would discard the garment, often handing it down to a servant. The fabric was highly sought after and a status symbol and was said to be one of the most precious gifts a man could give to a woman.

Today the wraps are selected from many kinds and qualities of cloth and in a range of shimmering and vibrant colors. Hand-dyed melhfas are produced locally from inexpensive imported cotton fabrics from China and India. Each piece is dyed by hand in a solid color or a unique tie-dyed design, with no two melhfas being the same. Price varies according to the amount and quality of design detail; the more complex the design, the more expensive it is. Melhfas are also fashioned from a broad range of commercially produced fabrics. Unique and more expensive silk, polyester, and rayon fabrics with ever-changing prints and textile designs drive fashion trends in urban centers. Many inexpensive commercially dyed and printed cotton and rayon fabrics are also widely available at a low cost in local markets. Melhfas at all quality levels are coordinated with the latest shoes and handbags, watches, and jewelry following European and global fashion trends.

The Melhfa in the United States

Traditional hand-dyed melhfas produced locally in Mauritania are exported throughout the region, including Morocco, Mali, and Niger, and are found in communities wherever women from this region live across the globe. The total coverage provided by the melhfa makes for an extremely functional garment for women living a traditional nomadic life in the hot Saharan climate. The draped layers of lightweight cloth protect from severe heat, sun, and wind. In Mauritania, traditional ideals of noble feminine beauty emphasize corpulence, coverage of the body, and carefully selected adornment. The degree of body coverage provided by the melhfa allows for gestures of coquetry and playful revealing and concealing of fabric and for adjustments to allure and capture the attention of men.

Influence and Impact

In the United States today, the melhfa is not a widely known or understood garment. There is more of an influence in Europe due to its close geographic proximity to the region, the French colonial ties with Mauritania, and the large number of French tourists who travel regularly to the region. American Peace Corp volunteers may also be familiar with the melhfa, and most are fascinated with the unique and beautiful textile designs; some may fashion the melhfa into window coverings, scarves, or other items of dress. In the United States today there are several large immigrant communities in Kentucky and Ohio where the melhfa is widely worn by Mauritanian women who have immigrated to the United States, for whom the melhfa is the preferred item of dress for all occasions.

See also CAFTAN; CHADOR; DJELLABA; HIJAB; JILBAB
Compare to BOUBOU; CHEONGSAM; HANBOK; HANFU CHINESE ROBES; HAORI; KIMONO

Further Reading

du Puigaudeau, Odette. *Arts et Coutumes des Maures* [Moorish art and customs]. Paris: Ibis Press, 2003.
———. "Costumes feminins." *Hesperis Tamuda* 11 (1970): 5–48.
———. "La Vie materielle." *Hesperis Tamuda* 9 (1968): 329–427.

Mitatre, Laiire C., and Herve Negre. *El Melhfa, Drapes Feminin du Maroc Saharien* [The melhfa, draping for women of Saharan Morocco]. Casablanca: Malika Publications, 2013.
Tauzin, Aline. *Figures du Feminine dans las Societe Maure*. Paris: Karthala, 2001.

■ VIRGINIA M. NOON

MEXICAN POINTY BOOTS

Mexican pointy boots, or in Spanish, *botas picudas*, are cowboy boots with toes so long they curl up toward the knees. Some are only inches longer than traditional cowboy boots, while others are elongated by up to five feet. The initial trendsetters of Monterrey, Mexico, fabricated the boots themselves using plastic garden hoses for the curved sole extensions of the pointy toes. To date, the longest pair of boots measures seven feet in length. The boots are not only characterized by their exaggerated length, but also by lavish decoration. The boots are often made in very colorful leather with flashy cutouts, logos, sequins, belt buckles, and even flashing lights and disco balls. Anything that will draw attention to the wearer is added to the boots. The more extravagant the design, the better the boots.

History

Mexicans have been wearing boots for a long time because of their cultural legacy, which is closely tied to their ranching and agricultural backgrounds. Boots were a quintessential *charro* uniform of the 1800s in Mexico. The Mexican cowboy paired simple utilitarian boots with his suit of silver buttons during a period of banditry. The costume became a symbol of manliness and a connotation of dignity. The common vaqueros also wore boots as they displayed their equestrian skills required in cattle ranching. By the mid-nineteenth century the *charro* image was combined with ideas of power and manhood.

The Mexican pointy boot originated in late 2009 in Matehuala, Mexico, the fourth-largest city in the Mexican state of San Luis Potosi. The most common origin story of the boots begins with a man known as "Cesar of Huizache" who walked into a cobbler's shop in Matehuala, Mexico. He asked Dario Calderon, the owner, to make him a pair of custom-made sequined boots modeled after a photo of a pair he had on his cell phone with long, pointy tips. No one knows exactly where the image Cesar had came from, but it did catch on quickly once it became associated with intricate footwork and dance contests set to house music known as tribal *guarachero*.

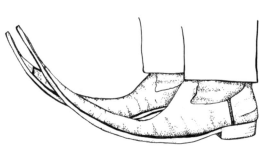

Mexican Pointy Boots

In Mexico City in 2005, Ricardo Reyna and Eric Rincón introduced a new style of music, an odd mixture of ancient indigenous chants, Colombian *cumbias*, and thumpy techno beats. The sound was labeled tribal *guarachero*. The new genre of music quickly flowed out of Mexico City into the rest of Mexico. It soon became synonymous with a recognized sartorial style, like most music scenes. The quintessential piece of the tribal *guarachero* look is exaggerated Mexican pointy boots, which emerged out of San Luis Potosi. The craze spread throughout Monterrey in late 2009 in nightclubs and at rodeos but reached its peak of popularity with the emerging tribal *guarachero* music.

Mexican Pointy Boots in the United States

In the second decade of the millennium, the pointy-boot phenomenon has infiltrated the United States in border states and other areas where large groups of Mexican immigrants reside. Dallas, Texas, with its large population of immigrants from the state of San Luis Potosi, popularized yet another trend. Young men created dance crews and entered dance contests where they showed off their intricate footwork, cheaply made outfits, and of course their pointy boots. Today the most acclaimed tribal events actually take place outside of Mexico, and Dallas is home to one of the biggest tribal *guarachero* scenes.

The pointy-boot trend has created a unique consumer market for custom-made boots with matching accouterments, such as belts, cowboy hats, and matching feathers. This trend is restricted to only young males who have recently immigrated to the United States. These young men are frequently made fun of and called *nacos* (a pejorative term associated with lower-class, ill-mannered people) by non-Mexicans and more assimilated Mexicans for their careful attention to meticulous dress and peacocking for women that is reminiscent of the exquisitely fashionable (and feminized) dandies of the nineteenth century.

Influence and Impact

The pointy-boot phenomenon is believed to have trended in the early 2000s and has fallen out of style in favor of the lower-heeled, square-toed roper-style boots, according to DJs at rodeo-themed nightclubs. However, all-male dance troops sporting the pointy Aladdin-style boots are still hired for weddings, *quinceañeras*, rodeos, and TV appearances across Dallas and Houston.

See also MARIACHI SUIT; MEXICAN TOURIST/SOUVENIR JACKET; SOMBRERO
Compare to BLUNDSTONE BOOTS; BRITISH RIDING BOOTS; UGG FOOTWEAR

Further Reading

Carone, Angela. "Mexican Pointy Boots Have Me Speechless." KPBS.org, 2011. http://www.kpbs .org/news/2011/may/16/mexican-pointy-shoes-have-me-speechless (accessed November 1, 2012).

Najera-Ramirez, Olga. "Engendering Nationalism: Identity, Discourse, and the Mexican Charro." *Anthropological Quarterly* 67 (January 1994): 1–14.

Rodriguez, O. R. "Matehuala, Mexico's Mutant Pointy Boots Create a Style Craze." *Huffington Post*, May 16, 2011. http://www.huffingtonpost.com/2011/05/16/mexico-pointy-boots_n_862617 .html#s279330 (accessed November 1, 2012).

Steinmetz, K. 2011. "Ridiculously Pointy-Toed Boots: So Hot in Mexico Right Now." *Time*, May 18, 2011. http://newsfeed.time.com/2011/05/18/ridiculously-pointy-toed-boots-so-hot-in-mexico -right-now (accessed November 1, 2012).

■ JESSICA STRÜBEL

MEXICAN TOURIST/SOUVENIR JACKET

The Mexican tourist jacket originated as a souvenir of Mexico and gained popularity among girls and women during the mid-twentieth century. The striking feature of the Mexican souvenir jacket consisted of colorful wool appliqué and yarn embroidery. Machine sewn of brushed, plain-weave wool fabric, jackets were available in solid black, white, or primary colors. Back and front pieces hung straight from the shoulders, and a plain collar, patch pockets, and set-in sleeves completed the boxy shape. Coarse embroidery, often blanket or running stitch with finished raw edges, attached appliqué to the underlying fabric. Embroidery stitches often incorporated sequins and included herringbone, feather, detached chain, bullion, stem, and back stitch. Motifs depicted such iconic Mexican symbols as serapes, sombreros, ceramic jugs, desert fauna, and dancing couples.

History of the Appliqué Symbols

The dancing couple is among the most common appliqué symbols represented on the backs of tourist jackets. To the Mexican eye this is no ordinary couple, but the emblematic national *duo el charro* and *la china poblana*. In the twentieth century, the male partner, dressed as *el charro*, had become internationally recognized in association with mariachis, a band of musicians suited in monochrome matching pants and jackets, often black or white. The mariachi jackets are buttoned up to the neck and end in Nehru collars, and the fitted pants are decorated on the sides with silver chains and buttons. *El charro* is said to have evolved during the colonial era in Mexico but gained the greatest importance during the nineteenth century. Its name is derived from the Salamanca region of Spain, and a recognizable influence is received from the horsemen of Andalucía and Navarra. An enthusiasm for riding reaches back to the arrival of the conquistadors, but after Mexico's independence, riding remained the chief amusement of Creole and mestizo landowners. When riding, they wore clothing often so loaded down with adornments that the term *charro* became synonymous with the adjectives "loud" and "flashy."

The *china poblana*, too, became a national figure and represented the mestizo ideal of femininity in towns and some country regions. It is not known how the name originated, although exotic tales abound that focus on the arrival in Puebla de Los Angeles of an Oriental princess during the seventeenth century. Frances Toors explains that "china" meant not only "Chinese" but also "maid servant" and was extended at the end of the colonial period to describe the colorfully dressed girls who sold refreshments in town plazas. The term *poblana* derives from "pueblo" (village); thus these women were from the working class. The distinctive costume associated with the *china poblana* is thought to have developed during the late eighteenth or early nineteenth century, inspired by the Spanish peasant styles from Andalucia and Lagartera in the province of Toledo.

The *china poblana* attire is a Mexican variation of European peasant dress: replacing the native skirt, *enredo* (wraparound), one sees the influence of European tailoring in a skirt gathered into a waistband, called a *de corte* (cut length). It consists of a full wool skirt and deep upper section of lighter material gathered into a waistband for pleating, a white embroidered blouse, a bead necklace, and a silk rebozo. The silk rebozo, made using a *jaspe* technique that existed before the conquest, possibly also shows an Asian influence.

Some of the silk shawls have many Chinese-style embroidered flowers, almost certainly derived from the *mantón de Manila* (shawl made in China), a trade item that would have arrived via the Manila galleons. As a nationalist reaction to the Porfiriate's French influence, national symbols, red and green satin, and a sequin eagle became standard as the *china poblana* made the transition from dress to costume. The twentieth century also saw the *china poblana* appearing in popular contexts. In 1919, Ana Pavlova dressed in the *china poblana* costume and danced the *Jarabe tapatio* (the Mexican hat dance), which is considered to be a typical Mexican dance and in which the male costume is that of the *charro*. From the 1930s on, there has been a consensus that the *china poblana* is the most typical, appropriate, and representative attire for Mexican women in the popular milieu, including advertising, movies, fiestas, parties, family celebrations, postcards, tourism, and so forth, promoting *Mexicanidad*.

Tourist Jackets in Mexico and the United States

Tourist jackets date back to the early 1940s and emerged within the context of a developing tourism industry in Mexico and a strengthened relationship with the United States. Once the United States entered World War II in the 1940s, Mexico's natural resources, agriculture, and labor became valuable to the war effort, which caused a warming of relations between the countries and an end to a serious economic slump in Mexico. The first "bracero" program gave permission to more than 300,000 Mexican laborers to come to the United States to offset the labor shortage. American Airlines received permission to begin flights to Mexico City in 1943, attracting business as well as vacation travelers. By 1941, Mexican tourism offices existed in New York, San Antonio, Los Angeles, and Tucson. In 1949, 176,000 tourists arrived. In 1951, their numbers increased to 400,000. The arrival of American Airlines, and one of its first tourist publications, "Make Friends with Mexico," coincided with the greatly improved relationship between the two countries.

While tourism also served to improve relations between Mexico and the United States, especially during World War II, both governments encouraged American travel to Mexico as early as the 1930s as a way to build friendship between the nations. Since the formal founding of a modern Mexican tourism industry in the late 1920s, efforts to frame tourism as something that served a broader purpose than mere profit can be found in magazines, official documents, and organized trips to Mexico. Among the cultural perceptions of Mexico that arose from this industry was that of an exotic and foreign land, yet amenable and only "a step away." With the backdrop of the Good Neighbor Policy, propaganda during wartime contributed to the promotion of tourism as a form of diplomacy. Not only was it affordable and accessible to travel to Mexico during wartime, but it was also "patriotic to vacation in Mexico." However, this seemingly benevolent cultural exchange through tourism was not equitable; it was unbalanced because Mexico had to prove itself worthy and familiar to prospective U.S. tourists, who associated the country with banditry, backwardness, and tumult. Transforming its image was tantamount to asserting its national identity, especially through its representative symbols.

The majority of vintage tourist jackets on the collectors' market today are dated back to the 1940s and 1950s, and their authenticity is traced to their fabrication in Mexico. These jackets reflect the constant and amenable transit between the United States and

Mexico in the first half of the twentieth century. Nine prolific textile manufacturers or retailers have been identified among collector items, all from Mexico: Berty, Casa Cruz, Garcia Leal Hermanos, Lab-Mex Trabajos Típicos, López, La Mexicana-Fábrica de Ropa, Presidente, Ramírez, and the House of Oppenheim. While most of these jacket labels display a generic "Hecho en México" (Made in Mexico) tag, about half display northern or border town sites, such as Nogales (Sonora), Ciudad Juarez (Chihuahua), and Nuevo León (Monterrey), which confirms the souvenir exchange of this product among American tourists traveling near or across the Mexican-U.S. border. Very little public and current information is found on these manufacturers, except that the House of Oppenheim has been identified as a department store founded in 1892 in Ciudad Juarez. It specialized in a large assortment of leather goods, perfumes, sterling silver, and all types of Mexican handcraft.

Mexican souvenir jackets entered the U.S. fashion market as a casual, playful trend during the late 1940s and early 1950s. Little girls and adult women who wore the jackets reinforced cultural perceptions of Mexico as exotic and foreign, and yet a familiar neighbor. Interestingly, by the late 1940s and early 1950s, *McCall's Needlework* advertised patterns for readers to create their own Mexican jackets with "gay fiesta peasant scenes" stitched with wool yarn and easy embroidery stitches. Patterns called for wool felt or flannel fabric, and sizes ranged from toddler to adult. Advertising headlines that read "Here We Go to Mexico" and "Mexican Mood" linked the homemade jackets to their origins as souvenirs of Mexico. Stereotypical Mexican motifs mimicked those of the Mexican souvenirs. The Kresge Company advertised felt by the yard for sewing Mexican jackets. In addition, for several years *McCall's Needlework* published photographs of Mexican jackets made by their readers, documenting the appeal of Mexican jackets among home needleworkers.

The current status of the Mexican souvenir jacket lies in the vintage collectibles market. Museum and private collections include extant souvenir jackets, and dealers sell jackets online or in antique malls at prices typically less than $100. A cultural creative may wear a Mexican souvenir jacket as a statement of interest in unique vintage textiles.

See also MARIACHI SUIT; MEXICAN POINTY BOOTS; POLLERA; SOMBRERO
Compare to ALOHA SHIRT (HAWAI'IAN SHIRT); BARONG TAGALOG

Further Reading

Berger, Dina, and Andrew Grant Wood, eds. *Holiday in Mexico: Critical Reflections on Tourism and Tourist Encounters.* Durham, NC: Duke University Press, 2010.

Boardman, Andrea. *Destination México: "A Foreign Land a Step Away": U.S. Tourism to Mexico, 1880s–1950s.* Dallas, TX: DeGolyer Library, Southern Methodist University, 2001.

Sayer, Chloë. *Mexican Textiles.* London: British Museum Publications, 1990.

Schevill, Margot, and E. M. Franquemont, eds. *Costume as Communication: Ethnographic Costumes and Textiles from Middle America and the Central Andes of South America in the Collections of the Haffenreffer Museum of Anthropology, Brown University, Bristol, Rhode Island.* Bristol, RI: The Museum, 1986

■ SUSAN M. STRAWN

MISSONI KNITS

Missoni knits are known worldwide for their unique and colorful designs along with the use of luxurious fabrics in their designs. In the United States, the Missoni brand became a household name in the late 1960s following publicity in *Vogue* and other American magazines. The company was founded in 1953 in Gallarate, a small town north of Milan, Italy, by husband and wife duo Ottavio Missoni (1921–2013) and Rosita Jelmini (1932–). Both Ottavio, known as Tai, and Rosita previously worked in the fashion and textile businesses; Tai owned a firm that manufactured tracksuits, and Rosita worked for her family's textile company. The company began with a few knitting machines, and the couple produced knitwear in the basement of their home, which they then sold to other designers.

History

When their dresses began to appear in magazines in the 1960s, Missoni received a boost in publicity from Diana Vreeland, then editor in chief of American *Vogue*. Rosita claimed Vreeland was her fairy godmother because she provided the fashion house with access to retailers in the United States. Missoni knitwear appeared in the United States as early as 1968 when the fashion house opened an in-store boutique in Bloomingdale's in New York City. By the 1970s the company was manufacturing unique knitwear in bold patterns and designs that catered to an international clientele. As a design team, Missoni cleverly blended colors in knit sweaters, suits, jackets, coats, and dresses and is credited with changing the fashion world's attitude toward knitwear. Missoni won the prestigious Neiman Marcus Award in 1973 for their work to extend the boundaries of traditional knitwear as well as their attempts to explore new color relationships in their clothes. In the twenty-first century, Missoni diversified into home goods and furnishings, including a diffusion line with mass retailer Target in the United States in 2011.

Missoni Knits

Originally industrial artists, Rosita and Tai began the design process with colored yarns of silk, cotton, linen, wool, rayon, and mohair, which Tai then worked into complex patterns. Inspired by the blurred stripes seen in the work of applied artists of the mid-twentieth century, early Missoni knits featured bold colors and shades. Rosita and Tai were also inspired by ancient Egyptian, Guatemalan, and Incan textiles, Central European folk themes, and the colorations used by the Impressionists. These sources mixed with the Missonis' own cultural heritage to provide inspiration for their knitwear. While Missoni knitwear features bright colors and intricate patterns, the silhouettes are generally classic and serve to highlight the patterns and colors.

Missoni Knits in the United States

In December 1970, journalist Bill Cunningham of the *Chicago Tribune* wrote the following about Missoni knitwear: "Sensational knitwear in Italy. Colors that are a revelation of natural beauty . . . in an absolutely unexpected mix which grasps the free atmosphere of today's fashion" (Missoni). Ellen Saltzman, the fashion director of Saks Fifth Avenue during the 1970s, claimed the Missonis transformed the knit industry from dowdy and old to young and energetic through their design philosophy that "bold is better." In February 1975, American *Vogue* included the Missonis among their list of the ten most influential European designers in America. In October 1979 the company continued to grow as they presented the first men's collection in Florence, Italy.

In 1994, pieces of Missoni knitwear were featured in numerous museum exhibitions, including *Italian Metamorphosis 1943–1968* at the Guggenheim Museum in New York City and *Missonologia* at the Pitti Palace in Florence, Italy. Near the end of 1998, Missoni opened a flagship store at 1009 Madison Avenue, where it remains today. In the same year, Missoni presented a new line for men and women called M Missoni, which featured innovative and colorful knitwear for a younger clientele at a more affordable price. On the fiftieth anniversary of the founding of the fashion house in 2003, Missoni created a large-scale retrospective show, which featured over one hundred items chosen from the Missoni archives. The retrospective traveled to the Mode Museum of Antwerp, Belgium (MOMU); the Victoria and Albert Museum (V&A) in London; and the Yoyogi Stadium in Tokyo. In the twenty-first century, the Missoni fashion house continues to produce timeless knits with distinctive colors and patterns that are popular in the United States and internationally. Missoni is now run by Tai and Rosita's daughter, Angela Missoni (1958–), who took over design responsibilities in 1996.

Influence and Impact

In 2011, Missoni partnered with mass retailer Target in the United States to develop a diffusion line. The diffusion line, which launched on September 13, 2011, featured a wide range of products, including clothing, accessories, home goods, athletic equipment, luggage, and more, totaling four hundred pieces in all. The partnership between the Missoni fashion house and Target proved to be a savvy business decision for both sides, as the launch caused a complete crash of the Target website and resulted in sold-out inventory across the country. The Missoni for Target line is a great example of the mainstreaming of a luxury brand to meet the desires of pragmatic fashion followers. Following the success of the Missoni for Target diffusion line, other luxury brands such as Prabal Gurung, Jason Wu, and most recently Philip Lim have partnered with Target and experienced their own success.

Compare to ALPACA SWEATER; ARAN SWEATER; NORWEGIAN SWEATER; SCOTTISH SWEATER

Further Reading

Missoni. "History." http://www.missoni.com (accessed October 2, 2012).
Mohammadi, Kamin. "Missoni: A Family Always in Fashion." *Guardian*, August 14, 2010, http://www.guardian.co.uk/lifeandstyle/2010/aug/14/missoni–italian–fashion (accessed October 16, 2012).
Steele, Valerie. *Fashion: Italian Style*. New York: Fashion Institute of Technology, 2003.

■ JESSICA SCHWARTZ

MOCCASINS

Moccasins are the traditional soft leather footwear worn by generations of indigenous people throughout the area that became the United States. A basic moccasin is constructed of a single piece of leather placed under the foot, brought up around it, and joined with seams at the top of the foot and heel. The back portion typically extends to form a flap that is either folded down as an ankle cuff or worn up, though there are also taller boot and legging styles. Some moccasins have a second inset piece covering the top of the foot while those made for wear on rough terrain have harder soles reinforced with rawhide. American Indian moccasins range from simple and utilitarian to elaborate versions made for special occasions and ceremonial wear.

History

Initially derived from the resources at hand as protection against the elements, moccasins reflect the diversity and creativity of Native American people. The distinctive styles they developed reveal regional environments in their materials and also indicate group identities through aesthetic norms of construction and embellishment. Women traditionally used bone needles and sinew to sew moccasins from tanned hides of deer, elk, moose, buffalo, and other large animals. Skilled tanners produced supple leather in a range of colors from light brown to nearly black depending upon the time allowed for smoking the hides and the selection of wood. Early moccasins were variously finished with self-fringe, fur, shells, and tassels of hair or feathers and were sometimes tinted with pigments or embroidered with dyed porcupine quills in a range of wrapped, plaited, overlaid, and folded techniques.

The arrival of Europeans beginning in the late fifteenth century gave Native people access to novel materials with a host of creative possibilities. American Indians incorporated the newcomers into established trade networks and, with the emergence of the fur trade, bartered for an array of luxury items, including glass beads, sewing thread, steel needles, scissors, and thimbles. Over the centuries, the availability of trade goods, the increasing presence of Europeans, further encroachment by Euro-Americans, and later confinement to reservations had profound and complex effects on American Indians and their material culture. During periods of relative affluence, American Indians embellished their moccasins and finery with exuberance. During harsh periods, unassuming needlework helped maintain cultural ties, whether women made items for family and friends or for sale beyond the community.

American Indian women generally embraced imported ornaments and used them on moccasins in an array of pleasing ways. Though they did not entirely supplant preparation-intensive quills in embroidery, beads made an indelible impact. Whether applied with restraint in delicate picot-like edgings to early nineteenth-century moccasin flaps in the Northeast, in profusion to completely cover the surfaces and soles on some later nineteenth-century plains examples, or somewhere in between, beads were employed almost universally. Tribal styles can be discerned through designs, colors, and needlework techniques, and also by subtle variations of stitching, fringe, heel construction, and finish.

Moccasins in the United States

Regional historic moccasin styles are appreciable but useful only as an introduction, since such generalizations overlook the heterogeneity of American Indian culture, the distinct histories of each group, and individual creative impulses. Throughout the eastern woodlands, Native Americans traditionally made deerskin moccasins with front seams and beaded designs in overlaid stitch. Those created by southeastern tribes are often characterized by semicircular cuffs and beadwork in lively, abstract asymmetric designs. In the Northeast, double-curve motifs are frequently associated with Iroquois moccasins while their exquisite moose-hair-embroidered floral designs and models with raised beadwork in graduated shades were popular with Victorian travelers. Moccasins from the Great Lakes area are often identified with puckered toes and floral beadwork, though notable exceptions include a distinctive style with oversized flaps extending from the top of the foot to the upper toes worn by Winnebago women.

Moccasins made farther west and south are characterized by hard soles for protection from prairie grasses, sharp rocks, and cacti. Styles from the plains and plateau regions usually have plain leather flaps and front ties securing a rectangular or split tongue. Northern plains moccasins often feature bold abstract geometric patterns in the so-called lazy or lane stitch. On the southern plains, moccasins often feature color-stained hides, use comparatively fewer beads, and have fringe, particularly at the heel, with legging moccasins common for women. Historical plateau moccasins are typically embellished with stylized floral and abstract geometric designs in overlaid stitch. Great Basin moccasins usually feature lane-stitch beadwork in geometric designs, sometimes in combination with overlaid abstract motifs. In the desert Southwest, tall moccasins are common, and those worn by Pueblo women often have white leggings and limited adornment. Extended turned-up toes are associated with Apaches but were worn by others as well. Traditional Navajo-style moccasins are distinctive for their side overlap and silver button closures.

In the wake of European contact, Native Americans carried on traditions connecting them to previous and future generations. Despite ever-changing contexts, new moccasin expressions have flourished. Although relatively few American Indians currently wear moccasins on a daily basis, they remain a vital component of ritual ceremonial wear and dance regalia worn at powwows. For many Native Americans, moccasins are visual shorthand for endurance and tradition.

Influence and Impact

Moccasins have long been popular souvenirs at sightseeing destinations where generations of tourists have found them as appealing as the earlier fur traders and settlers who sometimes adopted them for their practicality, comfort, and beauty. Although souvenir moccasins are usually worn as house slippers, the footwear has made episodic appearances in mainstream fashion, often in the context of broader ethnic trends.

The enduring Minnetonka Moccasins brand, founded in Minnesota in 1946 as an outgrowth of the tourist trade, became popular throughout the United States in the mid-1960s. In the late 1960s and early 1970s, male and female hippies wore moccasins as part of their natural, earth-friendly style. The strong presence of moccasins and moccasin-inspired sandals, shoes, and boots in early twenty-first century women's fashion may also relate to eco-conscious attitudes; however, the trend is more likely an aesthetic choice as a foil for shorter skirts, skinny jeans, and shorts. Fringed styles in various heights have gained popularity, as have moccasins with small beaded designs or metal conchos.

A specialized form of the soft-soled indigenous footwear is the driving moccasin, which enables the driver of a car to feel its pedals. Typically worn by men and women without socks, driving moccasins are identifiable by rubber nubs on the soles and heels and are a casual staple of many luxury brands. The Car Shoe brand patented a moccasin with rubber studs in 1963 for added ease behind the wheel. Whether they choose "drivers" or other fashionable moccasin styles, members of the general public invariably identify comfort as a major factor in their appeal. Non-Native people usually wear moccasins to make a fashion statement rather than as a means of connecting with American Indians and their heritage.

See also BUCKSKIN; POWWOW ACCESSORIES; WESTERN WEAR
Compare to BIRKENSTOCKS; CLOGS; HUARACHES

Further Reading

Brasser, Theodore. *Native American Clothing: An Illustrated History*. Buffalo, NY: Firefly Books, 2009.

National Museum of the American Indian Collections (footwear). http://www.americanindian .si.edu/searchcollections/results.aspx?catids=0&objtypeid=Clothing%2fGarments%3a+Foot wear&src=1-4 (accessed January 2, 2013).

Phillips, Ruth B. *Trading Identities: The Souvenir in Native North American Art from the Northeast, 1700– 1900*. Seattle: University of Washington Press, 1998.

Splendid Heritage. *Treasures of Native America Catalogue* (moccasins). http://www.splendidheritage.com/ nindex.html (accessed January 2, 2013).

West, W. Richard, Jr., ed. *All Roads Are Good: Native Voices on Life and Culture*. Washington, DC: Smithsonian Institution Press, 1994.

■ SUSAN NEILL

MOO MOO
See MUʻUMUʻU

MOUSQUETAIRE

Opera or evening gloves had been in existence since the latter part of the sixteenth century but became more fashionable during the Napoleon/Regency era and reached their height of fashion during the Edwardian era. Throughout these periods, upper-class men and women's hands were routinely covered throughout the day and evening. *Mousquetaire* is French for a special type of opera glove that opens at the wrist and has a fastener to close the gloves for a tighter fit. A button was typically used, ranging from one to three buttons for the closure, and the wrist opening was approximately three inches in length. Opera gloves are routinely measured in "buttons" due to their extended length. A sixteen-button glove can almost reach the shoulder, whereas an eight-button glove will reach the area of the elbow. All of this is dependent on the size of the wearer.

History

The original influence of the mousquetaire gloves was the French musketeers in the latter part of the fifteenth and early part of the sixteenth centuries. Gauntlets were used by the body guards of the French kings. Their longer style allowed ample coverage and protection in duels.

By the mid–1800s, etiquette rules increased placing rules on occasions in which gloves should be worn. During this time period in America, there were a number of men who made their fortunes in the advancement of industrial technology and business. Social mobility grew in prominence instead of family lineage being the determinant of your place in society. Therefore etiquette books became more widely adapted to assist those who were attending events to do so in proper fashion. The most important component of the glove was its tight fit—not the embroidery, quality of leather, or country it was made in. Most gloves were made of leather, although some were silk or cotton, which tended to be used during the warmer months. Cotton gloves were predominantly white, and some featured colored silk embroidery. Caution had to be exercised when determining the color of the gloves as it was not acceptable to choose a color that did not blend with the dress. Light tints of color were common, as a dark or bright color was considered vulgar. In the early 1800s, brightly colored gloves had a brief tenure as being fashionable. Tan gloves were most common during the day, as the color effectively hid any noticeable soil. In the evening, white gloves were used for formal occasions.

The reason for the popularity of the mousquetaire is that a woman was able to open the wrist area and take out her hand without needing to remove the entire glove. Once the fingers of the glove were tucked back inside the glove, the woman was able to eat easier than with the gloves fully on. Removing the entire glove gracefully was challenging and was referred to as improperly alluring because of how tight the gloves fit. Etiquette rules stipulated that a woman should never remove her gloves in public; removing only the hand was acceptable. One has to understand that propriety was paramount in the nineteenth century; even physical contact outside of private circumstances was considered distasteful.

The Mousquetaire in the United States

A French-born actress by the name of Sarah Bernhardt is credited with introducing the mousquetaire gloves to the United States in the 1870s. She was a well-known vaudeville actress and enjoyed wearing the gloves to help conceal her arms, which were considered very thin. Another influence of the gloves is said to be Lillian Russell, who was an American opera singer and later a vaudeville performer. Many Hollywood starlets have also been photographed with opera gloves throughout the years, particularly in the 1940s and 1950s.

Influence and Impact

Evening gloves continue to wax and wane in popular fashion in the United States and around the world. Most recently haute couture collections in the late 2000s featured evening gloves.

Compare to NORWEGIAN KNITTED MITTENS AND GLOVES

Further Reading

Collins, C. Cody. *Love of a Glove*. New York: Fairchild, 1945.

■ LUANNE MAYORGA

MUUMUU
See MU'UMU'U

MU'UMU'U (MUUMUU)

The mu'umu'u is a loose dress, worn since 1820 in Hawai'i and on the mainland United States since the mid-twentieth century. It has come to be known as a comfortable dress made in brightly printed tropical fabrics.

History

The history of the mu'umu'u is as complex as the history of the Hawai'ian Islands. These Polynesian islands developed as a monarchy without Western intervention until the late eighteenth century. Once missionaries arrived in 1820, rapid changes occurred throughout the nineteenth century. The Hawai'ian Islands continued as a kingdom until American business interests overthrew the monarchy and the Hawai'ian queen was imprisoned in her palace. In 1898 Hawai'i became an American territory, and in 1959 it became the fiftieth American state. This political history is quite relevant to the development of material culture in Hawai'i, as the textile history reflects the sociocultural changes as they occurred.

The Mu'umu'u in the United States

The origins of the mu'umu'u are in the early nineteenth century when Hawai'i was a kingdom. It was originally a chemise, introduced by American missionary women in 1820. At that time, Hawai'ian women wore wrapped skirts made of bark cloth (*kapa*) with the upper body exposed. When the missionaries arrived in empire-style dresses, Queen Dowager Kalakua was enchanted and demanded a gown for herself. However the typical Hawai'ian woman was more than twice the size of an American woman, and this presented a design challenge. In order to fit larger women, and to adapt to the hot, humid environment, the missionaries adapted their high-waisted style for a loose, comfortable fit, replacing their high waistline with an above-the-bust yoke. The end result was a basic design that was simply a full, straight skirt attached to a yoke with a high neck and tight sleeves. The garment was flattering and comfortable. It was eventually called the *holoku*. In addition, the missionary wives provided a simple chemise to be worn as an undergarment with the *holoku*. This became known as the mu'umu'u. It was originally a short-sleeved, knee-length underdress. Hawai'ian royalty who converted to Christianity initially wore the garments, and then by the end of the century most women wore the *holoku* and mu'umu'u; however the function of the mu'umu'u had changed. Due to the hot, humid climate, two layers of clothing made no sense to the Hawai'ians who rarely wore it as an undergarment. The mu'umu'u quickly replaced *kapa* (bark cloth)

Mu'umu'u

skirts as everyday wear for the home and was worn for sleeping and swimming during the nineteenth century. Most mu'umu'us were then made of calico, but in the 1850s laborers from Asia arrived to work on the plantations. The women adapted their traditional costume for the tropics and made mu'umu'us from their traditional textiles (such as kimono fabrics). During this time Hawai'i became a multiethnic society, and this would become important to textile production.

After the overthrow of the Hawai'ian monarchy in 1898, Hawai'i became an American territory, and more Americans arrived in the islands. Western-styled clothing was favored by Americans and Europeans in Hawai'i. In the early twentieth century, women's apparel in Hawai'i was either home sewn or produced by Chinese or Japanese tailors, using fabric primarily imported from Japan. The majority of fabric was intended for kimonos but primarily was used for mu'umu'us and *holoku*. One of the favorite fabrics was Japanese *kabe* crepe. These fabrics were very brightly printed designs intended for use in little girls' kimonos. With the introduction of bright prints on the mu'umu'u, the dress left home. It was now considered an appropriate day dress and became the standard dress for women born and raised in Hawai'i.

In the 1920s *holoku* became formal garments, and mu'umu'us became daytime dresses. Textiles and cut differentiated the two dress styles. Mu'umu'us were beginning to be made of fabric designed and made in bright tropical colors. The first Hawai'ian designs were small linoleum block prints, then later large silk-screened prints. The designs favored sea life and tropical flora and fauna. At about the same time, very large tropical motifs were roller printed onto heavy cotton drapery fabric in the United States and imported into Hawai'i for draperies and slipcovers. The boldly printed designs were so popular that they were scaled down and screen-printed onto lighter-weight cottons for mu'umu'us and *holoku*. While tourists rapidly adopted the Hawai'ian prints, the local residents of Hawai'i were not as accepting until imports of fabric and apparel into Hawai'i ceased during World War II. Local artists began producing textile designs that drew from Hawai'ian and Polynesian culture for design motifs and imagery. Even after World War II, textile production continued in Hawai'i because manufacturers wanted smaller runs of fabric that had multiple colors and found that there were many advantages to producing it locally.

In the 1950s, Hawai'ian textiles became the backbone of the Hawai'ian apparel industry that grew from mom-and-pop shops to major manufacturing facilities by the time that Hawai'i became a U.S. state in 1959. By the 1960s and the influx of people from the mainland United States, the trend in Hawai'ian textiles had shifted from large, realistic, brightly colored tropical prints on rayon to abstract prints on fine cottons throughout the 1960s. The dramatic prints were used for mu'umu'us in long as well as short shift styles. Both styles were worn frequently for both daytime and dressy occasions and were worn by women of all ethnicities in Hawai'i. As the shift became an important fashion in the U.S. mainland, Hawai'ian designers such as Alfred Shaheen used the flat front as a sort of canvas for very large panel prints.

Westernization has been the focus of Hawai'ian design from the 1960s forward as Hawai'i has become more Americanized. Hawai'ian styles follow the style lines of designers from Los Angeles and New York; the main difference that sets mu'umu'us apart is the focus on tropical print designs and that there is no waistline (so that the dress is cool to wear). As body-conscious dressing took hold from the 1980s on, the mu'umu'u has fallen out of favor and is no longer a common form of dress today, especially for young women.

Influence and Impact

After statehood in 1959, Hawai'i was all the rage on the U.S. mainland. Tourism became the dominant industry in Hawai'i. People brought aloha attire home. Male celebrities embraced aloha shirts, and some key women favored mu'umu'us. America's First Lady, Jacqueline Kennedy, spoke of the need to wear American styles and was photographed in a velvet mu'umu'u. Hawai'ian luaus and tiki parties were fashionable all over the United States and mu'umu'us were essential. While this clothing was made in Hawai'i, it was exported to major department stores in New York, Los Angeles, and Miami, and aloha attire became fashionable in the larger United States. It became a badge of a carefree attitude toward life. While the key feature of the mu'umu'u is that it is a loose dress, that concept is antithetical to today's body-conscious styles. However, it gave rise to a new form of aloha attire in the 1990s called "island style dresses"; this refers to close-fitting shift dresses, often made with bias cuts or knit fabrics, always with bold tropical prints. These dresses are intended for the influential resort market and are seen in resorts and warm-weather locales all over the country, and the world.

See also ALOHA SHIRT (HAWAI'IAN SHIRT); CALICO AND CHINTZ; KIMONO
Compare to BOUBOU; CHEONGSAM; HANBOK; HANFU CHINESE ROBES; HAORI; SARONG

Further Reading

Arthur, Linda. *Aloha Attire: Hawaiian Dress in the Twentieth Century.* Atglen, PA: Schiffer Publications, 2000.

———. "Cultural Authentication Refined: The Case of the Hawaiian Holoku." *Clothing and Textiles Research Journal* 15, no. 3 (1997): 129–39.

McClellan, E. "Holoku and Mu'umu'u." *Forecast Magazine*, 1950, 12.

■ LINDA ARTHUR BRADLEY

N

NEHRU JACKET

The Nehru jacket is a single-breasted fitted suit coat ending at hip length. Its collar is a short stand-up-style collar, either cut straight or rounded at the edges. The collar may or may not overlap at the front. The coat is made from typical suit materials and can be in subtle or bright colors, and it may or may not match the trousers with which it is paired.

History

The name Nehru comes from Jawaharlal Nehru, first prime minister of India from 1947 to 1964. He was known for wearing ethnic Indian clothing instead of Western dress as India moved into independence after World War II. A common article of clothing he wore was called the *sherwani*, a long coat-like garment or jacket with a short stand-up collar. He and many others who helped usher in India's independence believed that wearing clothing in the style of their native land made the statement that Indians should support their own fabric industries and their own native styles to create a feeling of Indian nationalism.

In the 1960s, many influential Westerners, rock stars, wealthy philanthropists, and rich playboys traveled to India and other Eastern countries. They brought back to the West not only interest in Eastern religions and practices, but also an interest in Eastern clothing styles. Pierre Cardin was one of the first designers who adopted the basic style of the jacket worn by Nehru, adding his own Western tailoring. Other designers across the West followed with similar designs.

The Nehru Jacket in the United States

In the early 1960s, modern style focused on simplicity and clean lines. The style of Nehru and his contemporaries' clothing captured the imagination of early Western menswear designers. The first James Bond movie in 1962 featured the villain in a Nehru jacket. The storyline also placed Bond's character in the same jacket. In 1965, the Beatles performed in Shea Stadium wearing Nehru jackets with military details. The immense popularity of the group, along with the Monkees and lounge singer Sammy Davis Jr., continued to help launch the tailored short collar style into mainstream designs for the American man. The same jackets were used in casual dress with a wide variety of colors and in formal evening wear as an alternative to the traditional tuxedo styling. The style in various forms remained in fashion for men into the early 1970s.

The original elements of the Nehru jacket were meant to inspire Indian nationalism, setting the wearers apart from the Western dress of the colonial masters of a previous era. In the late 1950s in Western society, the mod style promoted simple lines and minimal cuts. Designers liked the elements of the original Indian clothing and created shorter, slim jackets with simple stand-up collars to carry the mod idea further into the 1960s. Use of the style in movies, television, and by popular rock bands, most especially the Beatles, helped to make it popular for mainstream menswear. Ready-to-wear stores carried the styles in the 1960s and early 1970s. The style gained popularity at first with the youth set, but as it was worn by older celebrities such as Sammy Davis Jr., it grew to be acceptable for older men to wear in everyday or formal situations. The style crossed most social classes and could be had by anyone interested in a sleek modern look.

Influence and Impact

Nehru probably never imagined that his clothing could become a fashion statement in the United States. By the 1960s, the meaning of the cut of the jacket was lost on Westerners. Their choice in the style was driven by designers fascinated with Eastern dress themes and elements or designers with an interest in creating a futuristic feel in clothing trends. The style was so popular, patterns for men and boy's Nehru jackets could be purchased throughout the 1960s and into the 1970s for at-home seamstresses to make for their family members. Women wore a similar style with a more flared hem at the bottom of the jacket, paired with flared trousers, but the Nehru jacket stayed mainly as an icon of menswear in the 1960s.

See also BOUBOU; CHOLI; MADRAS CLOTH
Compare to MAO SUIT; THAWB

Further Reading

Colaiacomo, Paolo, and Vittoria C. Caratozzolo. "The Impact of Traditional Indian Clothing on Italian Fashion Design from Germana Marucelli to Gianni Versace." *Fashion Theory* 14 (June 2010): 183–214. doi:10.2752/175174110X12665093381586.

Fashion Bank. "Pierre Cardin." http://www.my-fashionbank.com/articles/article34.html (accessed May 29, 2013).

Tarlo, Emma. *Clothing Matters: Dress and Identity in India.* Chicago: University of Chicago Press, 1996.

■ JENNIFER VAN HAAFTEN

NORIGAE

A norigae is a Korean woman's traditional accessory. Women hang norigae on a top (jeogori) or on a skirt (chima). A norigae consists of five parts: *ddidon*, a top ring to hook on garments; *dahui*, strings made of various materials to connect all components; *juche*, the main decorative ornaments such as jewelry; *maedeup*, knots using various colors of cords;

and *youso*, various kinds of tassels that are usually placed at the end of the norigae. There are various kinds of norigae depending on their colors, jewelry, and materials—and even norigae used as perfume pockets, needle cases, and pockets for medicine and for small knives as protection. The pockets were decorated with embroidery and cloisonné work. The jewelry and materials are gold, silver, jade, pearl, amber, or coral. If there is jewelry, it is called *danjak norigae*; if there are three types of jewelry, it is called *samjak norigae*. The ornament shapes are usually animals, such as turtles, butterflies, and carp; Korean traditional imaginary characters called *haetae*; plants such as eggplant, red pepper, grapes, peaches, and lotus flowers; and music instruments. These ornaments have many meanings such as long life, healthy life, and wealth.

History

During the Chosun dynasty (1392–1910), women wore different sizes and types of jewelry and tassels, depending on the occasion. The types of norigae represented status or social rank. Royal family and noble ladies usually wore more decorative norigae with various decorative ornaments, while average women citizens wore simpler norigae such as that made of silver. Queens wore *samjak norigae* for special events. Especially on a wedding day, the queen wore *dae-samjak norigae*, which was more than twelve inches and contained three big coral jewelry pieces, meaning success. Jade butterflies indicated a happy married life, and Buddha's hands made of amber indicated his mercy, with large tassels in three colors. Only the queen could wear *samchunju norigae* decorated with three big pearls, meaning a long life. In addition, close friends gave norigae as presents. There are differences among ages: young women wore brightly colored norigae, and older women wore darker-colored norigae. Seasonal differences also influenced the use of ornaments in size, materials, and wearing areas. For example, women wore dark-colored jade on Chuseok, Korean Thanksgiving Day, and yellow-gold norigae in the fall. Nowadays, norigae have varied designs in terms of size, colors, and materials and in various price ranges.

Norigae in the United States

Norigae came to the United States with hanbok traditional Korean attire in the early 1990s with immigrants and visitors. They passed norigae to their descendants. After the 1980s, Korean visitors and traders increased. People gave norigae as presents to their friends and family in the United States. With wide price ranges of norigae, they became souvenirs, and American visitors bought norigae when visiting Korea, such as in Insadong where there are historic streets with many traditional Korean souvenir shops.

In the Chosun dynasty and until the mid-1900s, norigae—an expensive accessory—were used more on special days than in daily life. Now, Korean women immigrants and their female descendants usually wear hanbok for special events or holidays, and norigae are also worn on those days. Norigae are hung either on *goreum* coat strings or on a jeogori top or as waist strings of a chima skirt. By passing the strings through the ring of norigae *ddidon* and tying them, a norigae can be secured on a hanbok. Norigae connect the colors and design lines between jeogori and chima, creating balance and harmony of design. Further, norigae are not only for decoration but also function to easily store and carry small objects.

Influence and Impact

Norigae were also modernized and added Korean beauty to their designs with various materials and techniques not used previously by designers. Sometimes norigae are even used as interior décor, for example, hung on walls when they are received as presents or bought as souvenirs.

See also CHIMA; JEOGORI
Compare to ETHNIC JEWELRY

Further Reading

Lee, Kying Ja. *Norigae: Splendor of the Korean Costume.* Vol. 2. Seoul, Korea: Ewha Womans University Press, 2005.
Kim, Hee-Jin. *Maedeup: The Art of Traditional Korean Knots.* Elizabeth, NJ: Hollym International, 2006.
Kyŏng-ja Yi, Na-yŏng Hong, Suk-hwan Chang, and Mi-ryang Yi. *Traditional Korean Costume.* Boston, MA: Global Oriental, 2005.
Yoo, H., and M. Kim. *The History of Korean Costume.* Seoul, South Korea: Kyo Mun Sa, 2004.

■ HELEN KOO

NORWEGIAN KNITTED MITTENS AND GLOVES

Norwegian knitted mittens and gloves are hand coverings characterized by such motifs as the dancing couple, reindeer, birds, *selburose*, and other figures inspired by nature. The typical Norwegian mitten or glove is knitted in the round with wool yarn and a "Norwegian" thumb gusset; the palm side is knitted in a simpler geometric pattern than the more figurative back. The mitten is tapered at the top, as are individual fingers on gloves. Historically, natural black and white wool was most available for Norwegian knitters, with red, blue, and green yarn used when obtainable. Interlooping yarn using two or more needles creates knitted fabric, a textile that stretches for ease of fit and comfort. Knitting with different colors of yarn delineates motifs within the fabric.

History

Motifs associated with Norwegian mittens and gloves originated in different nations using various textile techniques long before knitting appeared in Norway. These motifs served as symbols for visual language associated with folk beliefs in preliterate societies and were later adapted into the printed pattern books. The association of these motifs with Norway traces to nineteenth- and twentieth-century Scandinavian politics and economics. When Denmark ceded Norway to Sweden in 1814, Norwegians gained national pride and identity by using Norwegian resources instead of imported goods to meet basic needs, and new laws allowed Norwegian knitters outside the guild system to sell garments knitted using their own wool. Knitted mittens and gloves were also traditional gifts for wedding guests. During the mid- to late nineteenth century, regional Norwegian design traditions developed, including the Selbu knitting tradition named for the district of Selbu near Trondheim. Marit Gulsetbrua Emstad (1841–1921) receives credit as the first knitter to incorporate the best-known and most common Selbu motif, the *selburose*, or eight-pointed star, into knitted mittens using natural white and black wool yarn. More designs followed, either adapted from cross-stitch embroidery designs or invented by individual knitters. After dissolution from Sweden in 1905, Norway sought culturally unique national symbols, and the government hired artist Annichen Sibbern to travel the nation and collect knitted designs found in Norway at the time. In 1929, Sibbern published *Norwegian Knitting Patterns* in Norwegian (published in English in 1952), which featured Selbu and other regional designs. Selbu knitting gained international recognition when Husflid, a Norwegian home crafts organization, provided supplies and a marketplace for artisans in economic need. An estimated two thousand knitters found employment with Husflid and other home industries, which exported more than one hundred thousand Norwegian mittens and gloves.

Norwegian Mittens and Gloves in the United States

The United States imported thousands of Norwegian mittens and gloves between the two world wars, and the style proved so popular that in 1927 *Needlecraft: The Home Arts Magazine* published a knitting pattern for Norwegian mittens. Although Norwegian immigrants had introduced skiing to the United States in the mid-nineteenth century, Norwegian mittens and gloves gained a close association with skiing only during the 1930s with the development of the ski industry in the American West. At the invitation of ethnic Norwegians in the Pacific Northwest, Olympic skiers and members of the royal family arrived from Norway to publicize the fledgling ski industry in the West. These celebrities wore Husflid mittens and gloves to promote their sale to U.S. consumers.

Ski industry periodicals and movies set in ski resorts promoted Norwegian mittens and gloves as warm, practical skiwear well suited for skiing and other outdoor sports—and well connected with Scandinavian culture. Such knitwear manufacturers as the Jantzen Corporation of Portland, Oregon, mimicked Norwegian designs in outerwear as early as the 1930s, and Norwegian motifs appeared on everyday garments by the 1950s. Publication of Sibbern's *Norwegian Knitting Patterns* in English and its distribution in the United States contributed to the strong association between Norway and characteristic Norwegian knitted motifs.

Influence and Impact

The *selburose* and other nature-inspired motifs that characterize Norwegian knitted mittens and gloves remain closely identified with outdoor sports, especially skiing, although high-technology fabrics have largely replaced wool in ski and other outdoor wear. Industrially produced sweaters continue to copy Norwegian motifs, and designers incorporate Norwegian designs into fashion lines. Traditional Norwegian designs intrigue hand-knitting enthusiasts, and Norwegian mitten and glove patterns appear in knitting books. Norwegian mittens and gloves are collected as material culture in Scandinavian heritage museums.

See also Busserull (Norwegian Work Shirt); Norwegian Sweater
Compare to Mousquetaire

Further Reading

Bøhn, A. S. *Norwegian Knitting Designs*. Oslo, Norway: Grøndahl & Son, 1965.
Pagoldh, S. *Nordic Knitting: Thirty-One Patterns in the Scandinavian Tradition*. Loveland, CO: Interweave Press, 1987.
Shea, T. *Selbuvotter: Biography of a Knitting Tradition*. Seattle, WA: Spinningwheel, 2007.
Strawn, S. M. "Nordic Knitting Designs as Icon for Developing the American Ski Industry." *Proceedings of the Costume Society of America Midwest Region Annual Meeting and Symposium*, 2012.
Sundbø, A. *Norwegian Mittens and Gloves*. North Pomfret, VT: Trafalgar Square, 2011.

■ SUSAN M. STRAWN

NORWEGIAN SWEATER

In America, boldly patterned Norwegian sweaters are worn for winter outdoor activities or to identify with Norwegian-American heritage in social settings. Norwegians wear sweaters for practical everyday use regardless of the season, and they also use distinct sweater patterns as a means to identify with specific cultural regions of Norway.

Norwegian sweaters may be hand knit or industrially produced. Regardless of manufacture, they fulfill the same functional and cultural purposes. There are key components to understanding the Norwegian sweater. As a wool-producing country, high-quality wool is the preferred material for sweaters. Multicolored patterns created by two-color knitting emphasize design while providing additional warmth. For hand knitters, the body and sleeves are knitted entirely "in the round." Circular knitting assists the knitter in creating a pattern, as it is always in view. Norwegian hand knitters are known for their inventive use of pattern, built upon traditional motifs yet incorporating a personal design.

History

In the mid-nineteenth century, pullover sweaters were a visible underlayer of everyday men's clothing. Distinctive sweaters evolved regionally, resulting in identifiable styles such as the lice-patterned sweater from the southern mountain valley of Setesdal, and the Fana sweater named after a coastal community near Bergen. The Setesdal sweater has white dots on a black field, geometric patterning across the shoulders, and embroidery finishing the neckline and cuffs. The

Norwegian Sweater

Fana sweater includes horizontal stripes, star motifs, and woven bands at the front edge. Cardigan styles and many design variations developed as sweaters became souvenir items for tourists to Norway. The northern community of Selbu, famous for cottage production of hand-knit souvenir sweaters, featured a wide variety of motifs including snowflake, flower, and reindeer patterns. The Home Art and Craft Association was founded in 1891 to preserve and promote Norwegian handcraft. It continues today, supplying high-quality materials to handcrafters and marketing regional handcrafts.

Leading up to independence from Sweden in 1905, Norwegian sweaters became increasingly symbolic of national identity. This symbolism was internationally recognized when Norway became prominent in ski competitions. The Marius sweater, a 1950s variation on the Setesdal sweater, was first knitted in the Norwegian flag colors of red, white, and blue. When modeled by ski champion Stein Ericksen and his brother, World War II hero Marius, the style became famous internationally. Manufactured reproductions and patterns for hand knitting this sweater are still widely available for men, women, and children. For the 1994 Winter Olympics in Lillehammer, Norway, the yarn and knitwear company Dale of Norway designed a Norwegian ski team commemorative pattern. They continue to design such patterns for each of the Winter Olympic locations.

The Norwegian Sweater in the United States

Handcraft traditions came with Norwegian immigrants to the United States from 1825 until well into the twentieth century. Artifacts, letters, and family lore describe warm knitwear that was made to sustain immigrant families. As knitting became a leisure activity, strong connections with Norway encouraged the continuance of traditional handcrafts. In the 1960s when downhill skiing became popular in America, *Woman's Day* magazine published a version of the Marius design adapted for American knitting techniques. Norwegian patterns for ski sweaters have became classic, and instructions for Norwegian sweaters are now translated for English-speaking knitters. A design for the American Birkebeiner was created in 2010 by designer Allison Snopek Barta. The design combines traditional Norwegian motifs with figures depicting this Wisconsin event.

Today in America, high-tech outdoor gear has largely replaced woolen sweaters for skiwear. Instead of the strong association with sport, authentic Norwegian sweaters are treasured for their beautiful design. They are worn for casual wear, family holidays, or at Norwegian-American gatherings. To Americans, traditional regionally based sweaters and modern variations are all emblematic of Norway. The international clothing marketplace includes inexpensive cotton and synthetic sweaters with Norwegian motifs, attesting to the continued fascination with Norwegian design.

Influence and Impact

Since the 1980s, aesthetic aspects of Norwegian sweater design have found expression in high-end international fashion. Paris-based Norwegian fashion designer Per Spook's 1990s women's wear collections *From Paris to the Arctic Circle* and *Nordic Fairytales* included new interpretations of traditional Norwegian sweaters. Solveig Hisdal's designs incorporate colors and motifs inspired by historical sources and are produced and marketed widely by the Norwegian knitwear company Oleana. Whether for outdoor wear or for fashion, the bold patterns of Norwegian sweaters continue to appear in contemporary American dress.

See also BUSSERULL (NORWEGIAN WORK SHIRT); NORWEGIAN KNITTED MITTENS AND GLOVES *Compare to* ALPACA SWEATER; ANORAK/PARKA; ARAN SWEATER; MISSONI KNITS; SCOTTISH SWEATER

Further Reading

Flanders, Sue, and Janine Kosel. *Norwegian Handknits: Heirloom Designs from Vesterheim Museum*. Minneapolis, MN: Voyageur Press, 2009.

Sundbø, Annemor. *Everyday Knitting—Treasures from a Ragpile*. Kristiansand, Norway: Torridal Tweed, 2000.

Vesterheim: The Norwegian-American Museum. Decorah, Iowa.

■ CAROL ANN COLBURN

NORWEGIAN WORK SHIRT

See BUSSERULL (NORWEGIAN WORK SHIRT)

O

OBI

The obi is a long, wide panel of fabric, wrapped around the waist and tied in a decorative style. The direct translation of *obi* to English is "sash." In Japan, the obi is one component of a formal style of traditional dress with a kimono.

History

The obi was originally developed as a method of closing the kimono. The design of the kimono determined the development of the obi. Early kimonos had sleeves that were fully attached to the body of the garment, which would only accommodate a narrow obi. Over time the sleeve of the kimono became partially unattached from the body of the garment, allowing a wider obi to be worn without limiting the movement of the arms. Over time, obis became wider and resembled the current style of four inches wide for men and up to twelve inches wide for women. Obis were originally tied in front, but as they grew in complexity and size the knot was moved to the side and then the back for practical reasons. The correct length of the obi is determined by the height of the woman wearing it and is tied according to visually correct proportions. There are multiple ways of tying the obi and multiple styles of completed obis.

Textiles are an important signifier in Japanese culture and ritual customs such as weddings and funerals. More elaborate obis are for unmarried women or brides. Casual obis are narrower, shorter, and have a simplified textile design. The wider and longer the obi is, the more formal the occasion. Obis were originally designed according to sumptuary laws based on rank and class. Modern obis still perform this function; obis can cost as much as the kimono itself and are considered valuable and collectible.

Early in Japanese history, obis were narrow for everyday wear at around three inches, and men's and women's obis were of a similar size being made from ribbon. Shizuka Gozen (1165–1211) was a court dancer and mistress of Minamoto no Yoshitsune, a romantic idol of the age and brother of Yoritomo, shogun of the Kamakura era. She is one of the first women appearing in the written history of Japan, and her story gives us information about how the obi was worn in her time. Obis worn by Shizuka Gozen grew to two to three inches wide, were made from linen and brocade, and were tied in front with two short hanging ends. This style is similar to the costume worn by Noh dancers in modern-day performances and religious festivals. Actors, geisha, and courtesans directly influenced trends in the design of the obi during this period. Courtesans were distinguished by the extravagant material and exaggerated size of their obis. It has been stated that courtesans continued to tie their obis in front in order to be easily recognized by fellow citizens, but this has not proven to be true in all cases.

In the middle period, court obis were two inches wide and made of heavy black silk brocaded with designs in gold thread. Obis began to have a paper lining inserted to stiffen the fabric and were not tied. Instead, the ends were tucked into one side. Later, in the Edo era, heavier, stiff fabric originally used for the kimono was replaced with softer fabric, and the stiff silks were transferred to the obi.

The great fire of Edo Meireki (1657) had an unexpected influence on the obi and changed its design and development going forward. Before the great fire, obis were tucked or loosely tied.

During the fire, as people were trying to escape with their lives and possessions, the obi came undone, forcing people to leave their possessions behind in order to keep themselves dressed. After the fire it was determined that the obi would always be securely tied. The loss of personal clothing and textiles during the fire was so great that when replacements were ordered they had to be of a simplified design for ease and speed of manufacturing. Now known as *kambun* designs, the kimono is tied with a narrow cord and tied at the side with a simple butterfly knot, with the obi wrapped and tied over it. In later eras, obis became much wider, increasing from six to eight inches up to twelve inches. During the Genroku era, the increase in the width of the obi required the overall design of the kimono to take into account the design of the obi as one garment.

The Obi in the United States

Antique kimonos and obis are now regarded as collectible art in the United States. Specialist textile sellers and museums import and collect kimonos and obis for sale and display to the general public. There has been an increased interest in textile printing methods used to create the patterns on kimonos and obis, and textile designers are taking inspiration from the simplicity and detail in the print designs.

In the United States, kimonos and obis are worn by Japanese and Japanese-Americans only on formal occasions such as births, weddings, and funerals. Non-Japanese people occasionally wear kimonos and obis for Halloween and fancy-dress theme parties, but they are not a fashion readily seen on American streets. Kimonos and obis are the most widely recognized visual representations of Japanese culture in the United States, and many Americans see these garments as representative of Asian culture as a whole, even though this view is culturally incorrect.

Influence and Impact

The first American exposure to Japanese culture occurred in 1876 at the Philadelphia Centennial Exposition. The aesthetic style of Art Nouveau in the later eighteenth and early nineteenth centuries was heavily inspired by Japanese decorative arts motifs and embellishment. For the founders of the aesthetic dress movement of the same period, the kimono and obi were adopted as a reaction to the restrictive dress and corsetry of the previous century. From the 1920s forward, the shape and simplicity of kimonos and obis can be seen in designs for lounge and nightwear and are clearly visible in common robes for both men and women. Interest in Japanese culture and decorative arts was negatively affected by the Japanese involvement in World War II, and for a time was seen as neither valuable nor desirable. Since the end of World War II, interest in and appreciation of Japanese culture, decorative arts, and textiles has steadily flourished.

In our time, interest in world culture and the globalization of fashion has increased the fascination with Japanese fashion. Japanese designers such as Mamechiyo Modern have embraced their native culture and added current fashion trends to the kimono and obi. This new category of gothic and lolita style, called Japanese lolita, is currently on long-term display at the Victoria and Albert Museum in London, settled among traditional Japanese decorative art. Western designers, such as Louis Vuitton and Marc Jacobs, regularly borrow design inspiration from Japanese traditional dress and replicate the obi as a fashion accessory. In 2011, obi-styled belts were seen as the top trend in fashion accessories shown on catwalks in New York, Paris, London, and Milan.

See also JAPANESE STREET FASHION; KIMONO; TABI
Compare to CAFTAN; DOLMAN; HANFU CHINESE ROBES; NORIGAE

Further Reading

Kennedy, Alan. *Japanese Costume: History and Tradition.* Paris: Editions Adam, 1990.
Minnich, Helen Benton. *Japanese Costume and the Makers of Its Elegant Tradition.* Rutland, VT: Tuttle, 1963.

■ JENNIFER ROTHROCK

OXFORD SHIRT

The oxford shirt, so named because the original was made with oxford cloth, is a dress shirt with collar points that attach to the shirt body with small buttons. Oxford cloth is a plain-weave variation, with the warp threads weaving in pairs against a single weft thread. This weave is sometimes referred to as a partial basket weave. When the warp threads are

dyed, which is often the case, the fabric can be referred to as an oxford chambray. This cloth is thought to have originated in Great Britain or Scotland, with some believing the name derived directly from Oxford University. Although not all button-down shirts are oxford cloth, the name "oxford" has become a common term for many shirts with button-down collar points. Generally, the oxford shirt is mass produced, has a looser cut than its bespoke precursors, and features a long sleeve with one button on a barrel cuff. Some have a so-called locker loop at the center back of the yoke, which the clothier Gant is said to have innovated.

Oxford Shirt

History

While most men in Britain and the United States wore stiff, uncomfortable detachable collars at the turn of the twentieth century, clothing worn while playing sports was often more relaxed, with looser fit and softer materials to allow for a range of motion or other needs specific to each sport. Polo players in the United Kingdom, for example, wore dress shirts with attached soft collars that buttoned at the collar points to keep them from flipping up in their faces as they rode their horses. As with sneakers and bifurcated garments for women, the button-down oxford shirt was a practical measure used for sports that gradually made its way into mainstream fashion. Edward VIII of England (1894–1972), later the Duke of Windsor, was an important fashion influencer in the early twentieth century. His banishment of starches and linings in his wardrobe and use of sports clothing for nonsporting occasions inspired a generation of British and American men to wear soft collars and plus-fours.

The Oxford Shirt in the United States

Beginning in the first two decades of the twentieth century, American men began to sartorially distance themselves from their staid British counterparts. Many American men favored the sack suit, an inexpensive mass-produced suit with a loose, relaxed shape that could be worn throughout the day, rather than the multiple fitted, bespoke suits that proper British societal rules required. Brooks Brothers, which by the turn of the century was considered a classic American clothier, had introduced a successful sack suit in the 1850s but were also known for their excellent bespoke tailoring. In addition to suits, the company offered traditional items from the United Kingdom with an American twist, such as the Fair Isle Sweater. They introduced their "button-down polo shirt" in 1896, inspired by the garment's practicality and encouraged by the relaxed attitudes of the American populace. They used cotton oxford cloth in solid white or in thin balanced stripes of white and blue, pink, or yellow.

The simple button-down collar changed the way men dressed; removable starched collars were uncomfortable and had to be separately laundered or often replaced, and attached soft collars had to be held down by stays, pins, or bars. The "new" oxford button-down shirt subtly streamlined the average man's wardrobe. After World War I, during which many had worn uniforms with soft-collared, button-down shirts, most American men abandoned the stiff collars of their fathers and grandfathers for good. While their fathers had looked to Savile Row for fashion inspiration, many young Americans of the 1930s and 1940s looked to the wild styles of Oxford and Cambridge students.

By the 1940s, fashionable young women were wearing clothing taken directly from menswear. The Brooks Brothers oxford shirt was a popular example, but women were forced to buy the boys' version if they wanted in on the trend. Brooks Brothers finally began offering women's clothing in 1949, and their pink Oxford shirt for women was an instant hit. It was so popular that it was featured in the August 1949 issue of *Vogue* and even on the cover of *Life* magazine. Sometimes these shirts were basically copies of the men's version cut for a woman's form, but they might also feature more feminine details, such as a rounded Peter Pan collar.

At the mid-twentieth century, American style was dominated by the Ivy League look, supplied by clothiers such as Brooks Brothers, McMullen, and J. Press. The style was born at the eponymous group of colleges and universities, such as Harvard, Yale, and Princeton. With a student population mostly consisting of young, rich, white men, the privileged sports popular with their fathers and grandfathers were an important part of college life. Athletic ability and youth had long since been considered the pinnacle of beauty, and the styles these young men adopted in their college years often became a "uniform" of sorts, an identifier of Ivy League education in the workplace that was worn throughout one's life and considered appropriate for most occasions. The white oxford shirt was one of these staples, along with a smart suit in neutral colors, loafers, and a subtle silk tie.

The Kennedy family glamorized Ivy style for many middle- and upper-class Americans. Much like the Duke of Windsor, Jack Kennedy (1917–1963) understood the importance of his public sartorial persona but preferred a looser, untucked outfit in his free time. Pictures of then-President Kennedy on vacation in the early 1960s with the tails of his oxford shirt hanging out and pants rolled up gave the buttoned-down Ivy League look a new insouciance. The word "preppy" came into use in the 1980s, and many preppy young men dressed as their Ivy League fathers had, the Oxford shirt considered a wardrobe staple, but by that decade it could be in solid blue, yellow, or pink for men, in addition to the previous choices; bright colors were all the rage for 1980s preps.

The oxford shirt is still prevalent, perceived by many to be dressy or business attire. Labels such as Brooks Brothers, Tommy Hilfiger, J. Crew, and many others have replaced a traditional left-side chest monogram (originally used for distinguishing one's clothing at the laundry) with their logo or icon, and oxford shirts are produced at all price levels and in many different qualities and types of cloth. The term "oxford shirt" is essentially synonymous with "button-down," used to describe shirts that button down the center front, although both terms are often misused.

See also CHAMBRAY; HARRIS TWEED; WINGTIPS (BROGUE SHOE)
Compare to ALOHA SHIRT (HAWAI'IAN SHIRT); BARONG TAGALOG; BUSSERULL (NORWEGIAN WORK SHIRT); DASHIKI; POLO SHIRT

Further Reading

Banks, Jeffrey, and Doria de la Chappelle. *Preppy: Cultivating Ivy Style*. New York: Rizzoli, 2011.
Chenoune, Farid. *A History of Men's Fashion*. Translated by Deke Dusinberre. Paris: Flammarion, 1993.
Uggolini, Laura. *Men and Menswear: Sartorial Consumption in Britain, 1880–1939*. Hampshire, UK: Ashgate, 2007.

■ ARIANNA E. FUNK

PAJ NTAUB (HMONG FLOWER CLOTH)

Paj ntaub (pronounced "pan-dow") is Hmong for "flower cloth" and is a traditional form of Hmong textile work that combines embroidery and reverse appliqué techniques. These were used to form geometric patterns in fabric that have had specific symbolic meanings.

History

In Laos, brightly ornamented clothing was hand sewn by Hmong women and girls and worn for both everyday and ritual events. Young girls were trained in the techniques of reverse appliqué, appliqué, embroidery, and batik, in addition to the cultivation of hemp, spinning, bleaching, and weaving. While all women were educated in the needle arts, the best sewers used bright silks obtained in trade in combination with their own hand-produced fabrics to create striking designs in bright colors with invisible stitches, precise patterning, and straight, even borders. Girls were also educated in the traditional symbolism embedded in the needlework, thus using these bright portable arts to sustain and disseminate the culture of their ethnic group.

Reverse appliqué belts, aprons, and other apparel items dating in design back to the beginning of the twentieth century are now worn by Hmong-American women and girls as emblems of ethnicity during the annual New Year's public festival and for ceremonial occasions such as weddings. First designed by sewers living in the hills of China, paj ntaub apparel designs were originally strongly influenced by contact with Chinese merchants who supplied the early Hmong designers with silk materials in bright pinks, reds, greens, yellows, and violets, colors they were not able to achieve using their own natural dye methods. Portable symbols of ethnic identity such as these belts were carried by the seminomadic Hmong as they made their way from the hills of central China to northern Vietnam, Laos, and Thailand.

Paj Ntaub in the United States

The forced relocation of the Lao Hmong to the United States in the aftermath of the Vietnam War brought these bright symbols of continuity and identity into America. Within the United States, paj ntaub apparel items are most commonly produced by specialized sewers within the community or in some cases are imported from Laos. Young

Hmong American girls are not uniformly taught the needle arts, and many rely on older relatives and/or the marketplace to provide Hmong belts to wear to the New Year or to a wedding.

The most important time period for the wearing of Hmong traditional dress styles in the United States is the annual Hmong New Year festival. The New Year is historically celebrated at the end of the growing season, with a focus on the community coming together to mark the end of the growing season and the beginning of a new agricultural season. In communities throughout the United States with large Hmong populations, the annual New Year is a fall community festival with staggered dates to allow Hmong Americans to travel around the country to attend family reunions. Festivals are typically held in large community centers and include the playing of a traditional ball-toss courtship game, dance and beauty contests, and also volley ball and soccer tournaments in warmer parts of the United States.

Within the United States, gendered patterns of dress emerged, with women charged with the wearing of paj ntaub to the annual New Year celebration and to family events such as weddings to express commitment to cultural history and tradition. In contrast, men and boys commonly attend the festival wearing Western apparel to signal their comfort with and commitment to success within their new country. Textile traditions that within Laos and China marked different subgroups within the larger Hmong ethnic group have been melded into a more general paj ntaub style marking a more unified Hmong ethnic population within the United States. Ideals of feminine beauty within the Hmong American community have been influenced by American standards of appearance, with a thinner body type and a less heavily layered waist more common in the millennium, in contrast with the heavier ideals and heavy waist belting that tended to dominate at the earlier Hmong New Year celebrations in the 1980s.

Influence and Impact

By and large, paj ntaub is still mostly worn within the Hmong American community to mark ethnicity and pride at the New Year. Hmong belts have made it into the American online and retail market as handcrafted clothing. Within that arena they are marketed as accessories that can be added to a fashionable ensemble as a decorative accent.

See also BATIK CLOTH APPAREL
Compare to CALICO AND CHINTZ; ETHNIC JEWELRY; KENTE CLOTH; MADRAS CLOTH; TIE-DYED APPAREL

Further Reading

Lee, Gary Yia, and Nicholas Tapp. *Culture and Customs of the Hmong.* Westport, CT: Greenwood Press, 2010.
Lynch, Annette. *Dress, Gender and Cultural Change.* Oxford and New York: Bloomsbury Academic, 1999.
———. "Hmong American New Year's Dress: The Display of Ethnicity." In *Dress and Ethnicity: Change across Space and Time,* edited by Joanne B. Eicher, 255–68. Oxford and Washington, DC: Berg, 1995.

■ ANNETTE LYNCH

PANAMA HAT

A panama is a lightweight, strong, flexible, cream- or white-colored hat originally made in Ecuador. The classic panama has a relatively wide brim woven from a special palm straw, *paja toquilla* or *carludovica palmata*. A *sombrero de paja toquilla*, *jipijapa*, or *montecristi* are additional reference terms. The term *toquilla* is a derivative of the Spanish word *toque*, which was a hat worn during the time of conquest. Jipijapa is the town where the hats are believed to have originated. The highest-quality panamas are made in Montecristi, a small town near Manta. The selection of the straw, the fineness of the weave, and the regularity of the brim determine the quality of a panama and its price. The highest grade of hat, the *montecristi superfino*, takes several months to make, while cheaper versions are completed in about a week. The final classic touch is the addition of a simple band of black cloth.

History

The coastal Ecuadorian provinces of Guayas and Manabí are where the artisanal production of the hats is thought to have begun in the 1630s. It was the mid-nineteenth century, however, when production and exportation exploded. In 1835, Manuel Alfaro, a Spanish entrepreneur, arrived in Ecuador, settled in Montecristi, and set up an export business that shipped straw hats, pearls, and cacao throughout Panama and out into the world. Alfaro is considered one of the first major hat exporters who organized weavers and perfected a consistent and smooth production system. Soon after, the elites in the province of Azuay, particularly Cuenca and Azogues, used their power to foster a new straw-hat cottage industry in the region. In 1844, their city councils decreed that children should learn to weave along with their schoolwork. Prisoners were forced to weave, and learning how to weave became compulsory for adults and children upon threat of prison time if they refused. Production in Cuenca became so economically important that it outstripped the coast, and hats woven in the region became known as Cuencas. By 1850, the United States was buying 200,000 hats, and exports more than doubled by 1863.

Panama Hats in the United States

While these straw hats are originally from Ecuador, it was in Panama where the world discovered them and they acquired their name, much to the chagrin of Ecuadorian authorities. In the 1850s, gold miners heading through the Isthmus on their way to California picked up the lightweight hats as protection against the sun. The construction of the Panama Canal added to the hat's popularity as workers found it indispensible, and visiting dignitaries, such as Theodore Roosevelt, were seen wearing it. By 1910, panamas were being exported to Europe, North America, and South and Central America, with the United States the principal buyer.

The panama hat's surge in popularity was related to the fineness of its construction and its association with the tropics. By the end of the nineteenth century, it became a staple of casual, yet elegant, menswear of the upper class and aristocracy for wearing with light summer suits during trips to the seashore and lake resorts. The wearing of straw hats such as the panama was restricted to their "proper season," from Straw Hat Day until Felt Hat

Day, September 15 after 1908. Straw Hat Day became a marketing ploy of the hat trade to encourage seasonal purchases. While it first appeared in June, the day shifted toward Easter depending on the arrival of spring in particular areas of the country. Politicians proclaimed particular days as the "official" Straw Hat Day in their regions, and advertisements promoting the arrival of the buying season sported beautiful women. While the beginning of the proper season to wear straw hats was flexible, the end date was not. Men who wore their straw hats after or even on Felt Hat Day did so at their own peril. A straw-hat smashing orgy that broke out in 1922 lasted for three days as young thugs roamed neighborhoods ripping hats off pedestrians, smashing them, and beating up those who resisted. Instances such as these contributed to the shift away from hat wearing attributed to the later 1920s.

Influence and Impact

The height of the panama hat trade was in the 1940s when 250,000 children and adults were involved in the market and market value reached $4.7 million. After World War II, the market collapsed because of the importation of cheaper versions and the decline in hat wearing overall. Internet searches return a plethora of sites that advertise panamas for sale; prices range from twenty dollars to thousands of dollars. China exports inexpensive imitation panamas made from paper or raffia. The finest panama hats continue to be woven of straw in Montecristi, Ecuador. Like many hand-produced products, mass production, the historic role of intermediaries, and more lucrative economic opportunities have threatened the sustainability of panama-hat weaving in Ecuador. However, companies such as the fashion free-trade company Pachacuti and dealer Brent Black draw upon the panama's reputation as the symbol of classic elegance and fair-trade practices to improve the quality of weavers' lives and foster a sustainable market for artisanal quality. Moreover, the panama hat continues to enjoy a following because choosing the "right" panama hat signals to the world a sense of power and recognition of the importance of one's image.

See also FEDORA; SOMBRERO; SLOUCH HAT (AUSTRALIAN)
Compare to TOQUE

Further Reading

Buchet, Martine. *Panama: A Legendary Hat*. Paris: Editions Assouline, 1995.
Kyle, David. "The Panama Hat Trail from Azuay." In *Transnational Peasants: Migrations, Networks and Ethnicity in Andean Ecuador*, 45–80. Baltimore, MD: Johns Hopkins University Press, 2000.
Miller, Tom. *The Panama Hat Trail*. New York: Vintage, 1988.
Sadler, Richard. *Hats: A History of Fashion in Headwear*. Letchworth: Garden City Press, 1974.

■ BLAIRE O. GAGNON

PARKA
See ANORAK/PARKA

PASHMINA SHAWL AND SCARF

The pashmina shawl is a multipurpose, oblong piece of woven fabric that is used most often as a dress accessory for women. The yarn is made out of *pashm*, or fine wool, carefully combed from *changra*, or domestic Asian mountain goats, usually after winter has passed. The harvested wool goes through dehairing, scouring, and bleaching before it is hand spun or machine woven to produce the pashmina textile. Shawls made from hand-spun yarn are superior in quality, feel (softness), and life span when compared with those created from machine-spun yarn. The fine yarn is often woven from the delicate fiber using plain, twill, or diamond weave and is dyed using natural (e.g., vegetable or saffron flower) and chemical dyes. Pashmina textiles are created in different lengths based on their use as a scarf, wrap/stole, or shawl. The edges of the textile are finished by seams, tassels, or fringes (knots, twists, or braids). While most pashminas are solid colors, usually pastels, some shawls have painstakingly block printed or embroidered designs of delicate nature motifs along the borders or through the entire pashmina.

History

Skilled artisans in Kashmir (a North Indian region) process *pashm* from neighboring Ladakh in Tibet into beautiful, soft, luxurious "cashmere" shawls. Seventeenth-century colonial trade introduced the Kashmir shawl to Britain and France, where it enjoyed popularity and prompted imitation. Pashmina fabric was also exported from India and Iran to Russia, Armenia, and Egypt. Futile attempts to rear the *changra* goats in other parts of the world have established the Ladakh and Kashmir region as the main producers of the fine pashmina. While other imitation shawls use cotton, silk, or viscose blends to meet consumer demand, an original pashmina is a unique piece of art and a time-consuming labor of love. A pashmina was a status symbol coveted and patronized by royalty in the sixteenth and seventeenth centuries. French empress Josephine, a collector of more than four hundred shawls, declared them "ugly and very expensive, but light and warm." The pashmina was also used as a floor or wall covering near thrones, and rare "shawl maps" commissioned by royals (now museum artifacts) are powerful narratives of their times. Shawls continue to be precious heirlooms handed down for generations during weddings and baptisms, worn by both men and women.

Pashmina Shawls/Scarves in the United States

Early accounts of pashminas in the United States can be found in 1861. A wave of South Asian immigrants in the 1970s might also have contributed to the pashmina presence in the United States as they brought their heirloom or personal pashminas with them. However, the greatest demand for pashmina shawls/scarves in the United States was in the late 1990s.

Pashmina shawls are very versatile accessories; videos on popular video-sharing websites demonstrate more than twenty ways of wearing a pashmina. Pashminas are traditionally draped over or wrapped around the shoulders by both men and women. In the United States, immigrants and naturalized citizens from South Asia continue to wear the pashmina traditionally. They are also used (mostly by women) as an accent (for example, with a black dress), draped around the arms (for example, with a prom dress), wrapped around the arms like a bolero, draped over the shoulders, or worn with a belt around the waist. A pashmina scarf can also be worn as a hair band or to cover the head and neck as a hijab. Hijab wearers also find many ways to fashion a pashmina into creative coverings secured with brooches and pins. A longer pashmina effectively conceals the neck and head while framing the face with soft luxury. More recently, cancer patients use pashmina scarves and shawls as protective head covering when experiencing treatment-induced hair loss. A pashmina is a favorite of those travelers who pack light because it takes such little space when folded, yet provides for multiple looks due to its versatility. Even though very lightweight, a pashmina shawl can provide great warmth, substituting for bulky coats while traveling.

Influence and Impact

The word "pashmina" evokes luxury, softness, warmth, and care. For example, a recent cancer awareness project that serves economically disadvantaged South Asian women immigrants and refugees in the midwestern United States is called the "Pink Pashmina Project." In the United States, pashmina products enjoyed high popularity in the late 1990s—"shawl parties" similar to Tupperware parties were held for interested consumers. Despite its synonymy with specialness, there are everyday implications of the worldwide demand for pashminas. Extreme cold in the Tibetan mountains is affecting the lives of the mountain goats from whom the *pashm* is combed and the livelihood of the nomadic Changpa people who care for the goats. Imitation pashminas also threaten the subsistence of the indigenous artisans and craftspeople. The changes, however, are accompanied by innovations in obtaining and creating the yarn and the pashminas—using steel combs instead of yak-horn combs, creating dehairing machines, and using new dyes. The pashmina is also viewed as an ecological choice because wool is a renewable resource, and *pashm* in particular is harvested with care and without harm to the goats.

See also CHOLI; SARI; SHAWL
Compare to SERAPE; TALLIT; TZITZIT

Further Reading

Ahmed, Monisha. "Changra and Changpa: Pashmina Goats and Their Herders." *Marg, a Magazine of the Arts*, March 2009, 12.
Housego, Jenny. "Kashmiri Embroidery." *Marg, a Magazine of the Arts*, June 2007, 32.
Raja, A. "Extraction of Natural Dye from Saffron Flower Waste and Its Application on Pashmina Fabric." *Advances in Applied Science Research* 3, no. 1 (2012): 156–61.
Sharrad, P. "Following the Map: A Postcolonial Unpacking of a Kashmir Shawl." *Textile* 2, no. 1 (2004): 64–79.
Yaqoob, I. "Pashmina Shawl: A Traditional Way of Making in Kashmir." *Indian Journal of Traditional Knowledge* 11, no. 2 (April 2012): 329–33.

■ GOWRI BETRABET GULWADI

PEASANT BLOUSE

A peasant blouse is a sleeved upper-body garment—usually white with embroidered details—that slips on over the head. It has either short puffed or long raglan sleeves. The neckline may be gathered, have a drawstring closure, or a small collar. This blouse is a shortened version of the chemise or shift, a garment that for centuries constituted the primary washable layer of female garb throughout Europe. It was originally worn with a long skirt and vest or a jumper-like overdress that revealed the embroidery.

History

The word "peasant" has a pejorative connotation in modern times, but in previous centuries it meant someone who lived in a rural community and farmed the land, often for a large landowner. A peasant was part of a socioeconomic system that developed during Europe's Middle Ages. On Sundays and holidays, peasants donned festive clothing that resembled styles worn in neighboring villages but differed from that of more distant places. In this way, peasant dress—also known as folk, ethnic, local, regional, or national dress—helped link an individual to a place or an ethnic group. Linen blouses thrived as part of local festival dress in Eastern Europe, the Balkans, the Baltic countries, and Scandinavia. Those with the most intricate embroideries came from Eastern European countries.

An authentic peasant blouse was made from locally grown cellulosic fibers, either flax or hemp, that grew readily in Europe's moist, temperate climate. The fibers were removed from the plants and then spun into yarns of varying fineness and woven into cloth. Sun bleaching whitened the fabrics. Shirts and blouses sewn from rectangular pieces did not waste any of the precious handmade cloth.

As early as the fifteenth century, fine linen shirts with embellished edges became the norm among the nobility. This fashion spread to nearby villages; however, sumptuary laws often prohibited the lower ranks from wearing certain styles or materials. Villagers could not afford professionally made fabrics, but their wives could embellish homespun linen with needle and thread. Scholars claim that European folk dress, including the peasant blouse, reached its golden age in the late eighteenth century.

When the Industrial Revolution made factory-produced cloth available to rural communities in the early nineteenth century, cotton replaced linen as the fabric of choice for peasant blouses. Gradually, villagers abandoned local dress in favor of international fashion. Around the same time, intellectuals promoting nationalism found inspiration in "folk" traditions and began collecting songs, tales, dances, and costumes. Curators at national museums wrote books about their country's peasant dress, typically accompanied by color illustrations. Such books reflect the shifting politics in Europe for which regional dress helped to solidify a nation's identity.

Peasant Blouse

The Peasant Blouse in the United States

Immigrants from Europe who arrived in the United States in the late nineteenth and early twentieth centuries sometimes brought peasant blouses with them. Augustus F. Sherman, a clerk at Ellis Island and an amateur photographer, asked detainees to pose for him in their national costumes. Several of his photographs portray women in peasant blouses. Once these women arrived on shore, however, they packed away their local costumes in favor of American ready-to-wear clothing, specifically white shirtwaists and black skirts.

Many immigrants settled in the Lower East Side of New York City. In nearby Greenwich Village, around the time of World War I, young bohemian intellectuals donned the peasant blouses and shirts so recently cast off by the immigrants. Soon enough, Manhattan's ready-to-wear manufacturers picked up on the trend and began producing peasant blouses for sale throughout the country. Their popularity accelerated when leading Parisian fashion designer Coco Chanel featured Russian peasant blouses in her couture collection in 1922. Travelers to Eastern Europe sometimes brought back peasant blouses, which had become a cottage industry in countries such as Romania.

Peasant blouses have been in and out of fashion ever since. A number of Hollywood actresses posed in peasant blouses from the 1940s through the 1960s, often pairing them with ruffled gypsy-like skirts for an earthy, sexy look. The Mexican peasant blouse, a new entry in the bohemian wardrobe, appeared between the wars on creative persons such as artist Frida Kahlo. Unlike European peasant blouses, Mexican blouses have short sleeves and square necklines with front and back bodice sections gathered to a yoke. They feature colorful embroidery on a white cotton ground.

The hippies of the 1960s embraced the peasant blouse and wore it with Levi's, cutoff jeans, and long ruffled skirts. Its symbolic ties to Old World farmers and Mexican peasants coalesced with their back-to-the-land yearnings. By the 1980s, fashion designers such as Yves Saint Laurent co-opted the look and recreated it in luxurious materials. Now a recurrent style, the peasant blouse is often described as "boho chic." Produced in a wide range of fabrics—sometimes printed, sometimes embroidered—its original features are often simplified, such as elasticizing the neckline.

Influence and Impact

The peasant blouse has had several cultural meanings over time. As noted above, one of these is nationalism. Another ties the peasant blouse to subcultures such as Greenwich Village bohemians and countercultural hippies, whose members demonstrated liberal political leanings including solidarity with the downtrodden as well as oneness with the earth. Finally, a peasant blouse worn with the neckline open, or off the shoulders, is revealing of the female body and signals earthiness and sexuality.

See also BOHEMIAN DRESS; CHEMISE; GYPSY SKIRT
Compare to DIRNDL; HUIPIL

Further Reading

Kennett, Frances. *Ethnic Dress*. New York: Facts on File, 1995.
Saville, Deborah. "Freud, Flappers and Bohemians: The Influence of Modern Psychological Thought and Social Ideology on Dress, 1910–1923." *Dress* 30 (2003): 63–79.

Sherman, Augustus. *Augustus F. Sherman: Ellis Island Portraits, 1905–1920*. New York: Aperture, 2005.

Welters, Linda, ed. *Folk Dress in Europe and Anatolia: Beliefs about Protection and Fertility*. Oxford and New York: Berg, 1999.

———. "The Natural Look: American Style in the 1970s." *Fashion Theory* 12, no. 4 (2008): 489–510.

■ LINDA WELTERS

PELISSE

A pelisse is a type of outerwear that was worn from the mid-1700s and continued in some form through the mid-1800s. Its military iteration was in the form of a sleeved fur-lined or trimmed jacket cut to the waist and worn by Hussars (light cavalry units of Europe) of the mid- to late 1700s over their dolman in the winter. During summer months, the jacket was worn off the shoulder of the dolman like a cloak for parade dress. For women, it was originally a style similar to a short cloak, coming to mid-thigh, lined with wool or fur. There usually were slits in the cloak for the woman to put her hands through and an attached hood. In the early 1800s, the pelisse became a shaped overcoat with sleeves and a wide collar, also fur lined or trimmed.

History

Hungarian mercenary cavalry, called Hussars, were the inspiration for light cavalry groups in Europe at the turn of the nineteenth century, both in tactics and in uniform. Their uniforms included a short, heavily braided, wool-lined, fur-trimmed coat slung over the shoulder like a cape. Napoleonic Hussars at the turn of the nineteenth century helped popularize this style, which they called a pelisse, which was also adopted by other European countries who also developed their own Hussar units. More fitted overcoats with fur lining or fur trim spread into women's fashion at the turn of the nineteenth century, appropriating the name pelisse from earlier unfitted cloaks. They were longer than the men's styles but did not fully cover the dress they were worn over. Women's pelisses carried some elements of the military style in the beginning. The pelisse changed through the 1830s and 1840s, becoming a pelisse robe, which was a full outerwear coat that covered the entire dress.

The Pelisse in the United States

The United States did not have Hussar military units, and the men's style of uniform did not penetrate the U.S. military. However, American fashions took their cue from European fashions. In the early years of the U.S. republic, women wore the same styles as European women, bringing the pelisse into their fashion repertoire as well.

Despite American independence won through revolution, citizens of the United States looked to England and Europe for fashion cues. The style of the Regency, copying details from classical Greek and Roman shapes, suited the ideals of democracy for the new U.S. republic. However, the thin fabrics used to create the flowing, body-hugging shapes were not suited to the colder climates of some areas of the United States. Upper-class women were more likely to go to extremes in their choice of thin fabrics for dress, but even printed cottons required an overgarment that kept out the cold. The pelisse followed the same Empire waistline but was made of wools with fur trim or lining for the wealthy.

It retained some of its military beginnings, decorated with frogs and braid down the front. Eventually the pelisse evolved into a heavier full-covering outer dress. As skirts continued to widen in the 1850s, the fitted style of the pelisse was abandoned for circular cloaks and large shawls that could accommodate the hoop skirt.

Influence and Impact

Military dress styles influenced high fashion for women as much as women added personal touches to military dress in Europe. The pelisse is an example of a coat that evolved from a basic round cloak, to a fur-lined coat for a light cavalryman who wore it like a cloak over his shoulder, to a tighter-fitted coat for women as well. European women's fashion at the beginning of the nineteenth century was still looked to by the wealthy and influential in the United States. Elements of the classical style and the military look appealed to the citizens of a new democracy touting republican ideals and military might in one outfit for a lady. Women of more practical needs may not have been as decorative in their clothing but were still interested in following the shape of the style leaders, and they co-opted the practical elements of the pelisse to stay warm in portions of the U.S. climate.

See also DOLMAN; SHAWL
Compare to BURNOUS; CHADOR; INVERNESS COAT; JEOGORI; TRENCH COAT

Further Reading

Hennessy, Kathryn, ed. *Fashion: The Definitive History of Costume and Style*. New York: Dorling Kindersley, 2012.
Leonard, Neil. *Wellington's Army Recreated in Colour Photographs*. London: Windrow & Greene, 1994.
"Making a Short Cloak." *The Hive Online*. http://www.thehiveonline.org/short-cloaks.htm (accessed May 30, 2013).

■ JENNIFER VAN HAAFTEN

PINAFORE

The pinafore was a protective garment worn to keep children's clothes clean that evolved out of the apron or pin cloth, originally pinned to the front of a frock or worn over a garment to keep the wearer clean. Derived from the action of wearing, "pin afore" meaning to pin on the front, synonyms include "pin cloth" and "pinner," or "jumper" in American English. Eighteenth-century working-class pinafores were made from a single piece of cloth meeting at the center back with slits for the arms and a drawstring at the neck and later developed sashes and waistbands in the nineteenth century, which were popular for upper-class children. Pinafores could also be worn alone in the summer or over a frock in the winter in order to save more expensive garments from wear and were generally made of holland, printed cotton, muslin, or diaper-weave linen.

History

The pinafore originated as an English form of dress but was also seen elsewhere in continental Europe. Pinafores mainly functioned as work or play clothes, similar to a smock or apron. As soon as children were able to walk, they began wearing pinafores over their frocks to protect their clothes and keep them clean. Pinafores were used by both working and gentry classes and were differentiated by quality of fabric as universal children's wear in Britain.

The pinafore served as a children's uniform in British culture as early as the second half of the eighteenth century, and children living in orphanages or hospitals often wore pinafores up until puberty as a practical and affordable institutional dress. Pinafores also functioned as school uniforms in Britain and America for girls up to the 1970s. Examples of pinafores as school uniforms can also be documented in the British colonies of New Zealand and Australia in the nineteenth century.

Pinafores (or Jumpers) in the United States

Once the pinafore entered the United States through British colonial diffusion, school uniform traditions, and the need for economical and practical children's clothes, it varied in name between the British pinafore and the American jumper. A jumper is defined as a sleeveless overdress usually worn with a shirt underneath, which dates as early as 1908 in the United States and is a derivation of the French *juppe*, meaning skirt, and the Arabic *(d)jibbah*, meaning overdress.

Within the United States, pinafores were repopularized, and jumpers further developed during and after World War II due to fabric shortages and ration coupons. Jumpers were emphasized as an economical way to stretch the life of textiles by reusing adult garments and continued to be worn through the 1960s and 1970s as casual clothing and school uniforms in the United States. The pinafore or jumper represents a functional, simple, and economical form of dress for keeping children clean and comfortable at work or play. Furthermore, it represents a uniform for childhood in school or family life and has served as an adaptable design that can be recycled during times where resourcefulness is required.

Influence and Impact

In modern-day fashion the pinafore or jumper is no longer worn as an overdress or protective garment but as a dress in its own right. Jumpers are most often worn by children and are now worn with blouses, T-shirts, or sleeved tops underneath rather than frocks. Jumpers are not commonly worn by women, but the apron represents a branch off of the traditional British pinafore still worn by adult women today.

See also APRON; DIRNDL
Compare to CAFTAN; CHIMA; POLLERA

Further Reading

Brooke, Iris. *English Children's Costume since 1775*. London: A. & C. Black, 1930.
Buck, Anne. *Clothes and the Child: A Handbook of Children's Dress in England, 1500–1900*. New York: Holmes & Meier Publishers, 1996.
Collard, Eileen. *From Toddler to Teens: An Outline of Children's Clothing circa 1780 to 1930*. Burlington, Ontario: Collard, 1973.
Guppy, Alice. *Children's Clothes, 1939–1970: The Advent of Fashion*. Poole: Blandford Press for the Pasold Research Fund, 1978.

■ ELLEN HLOZAN

POLLERA

The pollera is a garment originating in Latin America during colonial times and generally refers to a long, voluminous skirt but can also mean a full ensemble. It is unclear whether the pollera derived from the cone-shaped silhouette of the farthingale or verdugado, a Spanish fashion worn by the aristocracy during this period, or if it originated with the lower classes, servants and wet nurses, who wore a white version for their daily work. Both styles reflect the preference for a conical style that was gathered at the waist and full around the hips.

History

This style skirt gained popularity during the sixteenth-century Spanish conquest of Latin America and was worn through the nineteenth century by the indigenous peoples of Peru, Colombia, Bolivia, and especially Panama. In Panama, the national dress continues to be called pollera and is worn by women of all backgrounds on feast days. This special-occasion pollera, called a *pollera de gala*, consists of full gathered skirts, petticoats, and ruffled blouses, which are complemented by hair ornaments, jewelry, and accessories. It is especially noted for its intricate embroidery, usually consisting of flowers, butterflies, fruits, or birds, which line its borders. The entire ensemble is made by hand using traditional techniques such as *talco al sol*, which combines appliqué and openwork embroidery. An everyday pollera or *pollera montuna* resembles styles worn elsewhere in Latin America, which shared a common shape and the use of multiple petticoats to achieve the desired fullness.

Pollera in the United States

The pollera was most likely first seen in the United States at nineteenth-century fancy dress balls, where attendees came dressed up in costume. An interest in Spanish culture flourished in this period that saw the first production of George Bizet's *Carmen*, the Spanish-American War, and the construction of the Panama Canal. Americans living in the Canal Zone may have been among the first to introduce the pollera in the United States. References to "Spanish dancer" costumes for fancy dress balls could be found into the 1920s, and it was not until the 1930s that Latin American dress aesthetics made their way into mainstream American fashion.

With the advent of American sportswear in the 1930s came the popularization of so-called peasant styles that shared similarities with the South American pollera. These styles were especially popular among designers like Louella Ballerino in California, where the climate and the Hollywood lifestyle allowed for more laidback fashions. Ballerino's first major fashion success was a peasant skirt and matching shawl made of serape, a South American fabric. Shortly afterward, during World War II, Californian designers were acclaimed for their innovative use of ethnic clothing sources in the face of material regulations. Deriving inspiration from the styles of Guatemala, Peru, and Chile, they designed skirts that resembled the pollera's deep flounces and puff-sleeve blouses with low scoop necklines. Similarly inspired accessories completed the look.

As Dior's New Look pervaded in the postwar period, however, the peasant skirt was relegated to the bohemian counterculture. Beatnik women wore the style as a symbol of their association with society's artists, writers, and others who made their home in places like New York's Greenwich Village. Yet, while the skirt retained its conical shape, the overall look was more Eastern European than South American. It was not until the 1960s that hippies revived the pollera-inspired skirt, with its tiered, full styling. The natural look that defined much of America's youth fashion in the late 1960s and 1970s was often derived from traditional Latin American clothing, which was seen to signify a closer connection to the earth and a simpler life.

Influence and Impact

The pollera-style skirt made its way back into American mainstream fashion in the 2000s. During the summer of 2005 the skirt became immensely popular on account of its ability to adapt to an array of occasions and body types. That same summer, however, it was dubbed the "Skirt with No Name" by the Global Language Monitor because, despite its success, retailers had not decided on a single identifier. The same style skirt, full through the hips, with or without tiers but always with a conical shape, was referred to as peasant, tiered, gypsy, flouncy, boho, and more. Nevertheless, the success of the Americanized pollera signaled the return of all skirts to the average woman's wardrobe, a change that is still relevant today.

See also BOHEMIAN DRESS; HUIPIL; MEXICAN TOURIST/SOUVENIR JACKET; PEASANT BLOUSE
Compare to BROOMSTICK SKIRT; DIRNDL; GYPSY SKIRT

Further Reading

Mendes, Valerie D., and Amy de la Haye. *Fashion since 1900*. London: Thames & Hudson, 2010.
Milbank, Caroline. *New York Fashion: The Evolution of American Style*. New York: Abrams, 1989.
Root, Regina A. *The Latin American Fashion Reader*. Oxford: Berg, 2005.

■ MARCELLA MILIO

POLO BOOTS
See BRITISH RIDING BOOTS

POLO SHIRT

The polo shirt, a casual tennis shirt, was first introduced in the late 1920s by René Lacoste (1904–1996), a notable French tennis player. Lacoste originally had the shirt made for his own personal use on the tennis court. The shirts were ideal for perspiration on court, as they were manufactured from comfortable, breathable knit cotton. The polo shirt enabled Lacoste to cope better with the heat he endured while playing tennis in the hot and humid American summers. While the shirts initially experienced popularity, the French Tennis Federation dubbed the shirts indecent on the court due to their slim fit.

History

In the early 1930s, Lacoste teamed up with France's largest knitwear company, André Gillier, to establish a clothing manufacturing company. In conjunction with the company, Lacoste designed the first polo shirt, which featured a crocodile logo. The crocodile logo refers to Lacoste's nickname, "the Crocodile," which he received during his tennis career. Lacoste's loose-fitting and lightweight design was radical for the time because it was more functional than the typically starched, long-sleeved tennis shirts that were commonly worn on the court. The lightweight knit fabric used to create the shirt along with the short sleeves, ribbed collar, and longer shirttails increased mobility for players. The movement-inducing characteristics of the polo shirt made it one of the first pieces of performance sportswear ever produced. The polo shirt Lacoste designed with the crocodile emblem over the left breast also marked the first time a logo appeared on the outside of a garment.

Polo Shirt in the United States

During the 1950s, the popularity of the shirt rose to the point of enabling Lacoste to export garments to Italy and the United States. The sportswear manufacturer David Crystal Inc. imported the shirts into the United States and sold them under the label Jack Izod in the 1950s. During the 1960s, the Lacoste polo shirt remained a specialty product and experienced global popularity. By the 1970s, exclusive retailers in the United States, such as Bloomingdale's and Brooks Brothers, were carrying the shirt, which resulted in prestige and exclusivity for the brand. In the same decade, the polo shirt reached the height of its popularity due to the preppy trend that swept through the United States. In the early 1970s, General Mills acquired the U.S. manufacturing license for the Lacoste polo shirt, and by the 1980s the company began manufacturing the product in the Far East to increase profits. Due to this decision and others, such as overmarketing the crocodile logo, the reputation of the Lacoste polo shirt declined and resulted in decreased popularity of the shirt. Throughout the 1990s, the Lacoste company worked to resurrect its reputation, and in 1992 the company regained control of its licenses in the United States, Canada, and the Caribbean. In recent years the Lacoste brand has experienced revitalization in its prestige, and in the early 2000s the polo shirt regained popularity following the renewed preppy trend in the United States.

During the 1930s, physical fitness and sun worshipping reached cult proportions in the United States and Europe. As a result, active sportswear that enabled maximum movement was necessary. The Lacoste polo shirt achieved this goal and became a staple in the modern man's wardrobe. Lacoste himself was the biggest promoter of the polo shirt and can be attributed with achieving initial fame for the design. Lacoste's son, Bernard, ran the company for more than four decades and is credited with building it into a global sports brand. During the late 1950s, President Dwight D. Eisenhower (1890–1969) was photographed wearing a Lacoste polo shirt during a game of golf. Once the president of the United States was viewed wearing the crocodile emblem, the polo shirt became extremely popular in the United States, and copies of the knit polo shirt soon appeared.

Influence and Impact

Originally, the Lacoste polo shirt was designed in white, made of woven cotton, featured a turn-over collar with two or three buttons to the neck, and short sleeves. The polo shirt was eventually manufactured in many different colors, and consumers were given the additional option of long or short sleeves. The polo shirt was often paired with casual pant styles and over time became the preferred shirt for casual business attire.

See also HARRIS TWEED; OXFORD SHIRT
Compare to ALOHA SHIRT (HAWAI'IAN SHIRT); BARONG TAGALOG; BUSSERULL (NORWEGIAN WORK SHIRT); DASHIKI; KOSOVOROTKA

Further Reading

Costantino, Maria. *Men's Fashion in the Twentieth Century: From Frock Coats to Intelligent Fibres.* New York: Costume & Fashion Press, 1997.
Fleishman, Sue. "Champions in the Sun." *California History* 63 (1984): 80–83.

■ JESSICA SCHWARTZ

PONCHO

The poncho is a South American Indian garment that originated in the Andes mountain range, which covers modern parts of Peru, Chile, and Bolivia. It is a rectangular garment generally measuring five feet square with an opening in the center for the wearer's head. It hangs from the shoulders, covering the entire torso. Some versions of the poncho, called *ponchillo* or *calamaco*, are short with rounded borders and originated in the Peruvian highlands in the nineteenth century. An especially large poncho, resembling a chasuble and called a *balandrán*, was originally used in the pampas and is worn in contemporary Argentina.

History

Despite the Spanish conquest and their insistence on the adoption of Hispanic peasant dress, the poncho's use spread throughout South America, making it one of the most common outer garments for Indian men from the sixteenth century onward. The Spanish recognized the utility of this garment, especially for cavalry, and adopted it for their own use, spreading it throughout South America and beyond. As the poncho reached various regions of South America, it appropriated their colors, traditional motifs, fabrics, and weaving techniques, enabling the wearer to identify and be identified by this singular garment. In colder climates the poncho would be hand woven of alpaca, vicuña (originally for Incan royalty only), guanaco, llama, or sheep wool, while in tropical regions silk, linen, or cotton yarns were used.

Poncho

The woven textile was rarely decorated with embroidery but did feature geometric motifs such as the fret, a serpent motif in Mexico and the Andean world that related to beliefs about the ascent to the afterlife. Since ponchos were often part of mourning dress in the Andean region, this particular motif was perfectly suited to this purpose.

In addition to its use as an outer garment, the poncho was used as a source of protection, a bed, a pillow, and sometimes even as a shelter, a shield, or an agricultural tool. Its rectangular design made the poncho an exceptionally practical and useful item for its wearers. For example, the gaucho, or Argentinian cowboy, often possessed nothing more than one or two ponchos that did double duty as sleeping quarters and could be used as a shield by wrapping it around the arm during a duel of daggers. In Argentinian literature, after the implementation of fenced-in ranches in the nineteenth century, the poncho-wearing gaucho became a symbol of a lost traditional way of life. Since spun alpaca was an especially strong yarn, however, the poncho experienced a longer life span in other regions. For example, indigenous farmers continued to use their alpaca ponchos as a means to collect and transport produce from the fields.

The Poncho in the United States

Though it is unclear how the poncho made its way to the United States, it is likely it was introduced by travelers who recognized the utility of this versatile garment and had appropriated it for their own use. Randolph B. Marcy's book *The Prairie Traveler* lists the poncho as one of the few essential items an explorer might need in the American West. The poncho was also highly valued as a military garment for similar reasons. During the nineteenth-century wars of independence against Spain in South America, the poncho's popularity grew among both the indigenous populations and the criollos, or New World–born Spaniards. All criollo generals wore large ponchos that provided protection both for themselves and their horses. Similarly, by the 1850s the American military also began using the poncho for outerwear and issued ponchos made of gutta-percha, an early form of latex, which rendered the garment waterproof. The poncho continues to be a standard issue for American soldiers and is used in many of the same ways it had been traditionally: as a bed, a shelter, or for protection.

The poncho became an American fashion item in the 1960s and 1970s with the rise of the natural look and was popularized as part of the hippie style. Followers of this movement did not follow fashion, and they avoided spending money on their appearance as a manifestation of their disapproval of the American mainstream. They adopted traditional costumes like ponchos in opposition to the pressed and polished look of suited businessmen and girdled women. Inspired by ethnic items of dress, hippies also sought to revive handcrafts such as weaving and embroidery in an effort to connect to a simpler way of life. In 1976, anthropologist-turned-entrepreneur Annie Hurlbut started a company importing South American indigenous garments for sale in the United States called Peruvian Connection. Other merchants began to recognize the value of the natural look and marketed to the hippies' interest in earthy tones and ethnic styles. Popular culture afforded the poncho a place in movies, as seen on Clint Eastwood in the spaghetti western trilogy, in music like "Camarillo Brillo" by Frank Zappa, and on TV where Susan Dey undoubtedly started a poncho trend as Laurie on *The Partridge Family*. As a result, the poncho shifted in use from being a traditionally male garment to one used in western fashion primarily by women.

Influence and Impact

While the poncho's place in popular fashion subsided by the 1980s, it was revived in the 2000s. In the fall of 2004, the poncho could be found in mainstream women's wear stores such as Ann Taylor, the Gap, J.C. Penney, and Macy's as well as on the pages of high-fashion magazines like *Vogue* and *Harper's Bazaar*. Celebrities, from the high-fashion Kate Moss to the girl-next-door Jennifer Aniston, could all be found wearing the poncho. Gone were the traditional motifs of indigenous South Americans that adorned the hippies' ponchos. The modern incarnation of this centuries-old outerwear was made of synthetic fabrics like rayon, nylon, and acrylic and came in a variety of colors, shapes, and sizes. Since its revival in the early 2000s, the poncho has continued to come in and out of fashion. More recently in the fall of 2011, generic "Indian"-style clothing gained popularity, and with it the poncho. Though these examples made an attempt at a more authentic model than the styles of the first decade of the 2000s, they failed to replicate the value of handwoven or knit ponchos from early times.

See also SERAPE
Compare to ANORAK/PARKA; SHAWL; WESTERN WEAR

Further Reading

Anawalt, Patricia Rieff. *The Worldwide History of Dress.* New York: Thames & Hudson, 2007.
Root, Regina A. *The Latin American Fashion Reader.* Oxford: Berg, 2005.
Welters, Linda. "The Natural Look: American Style in the 1970s." *Fashion Theory: The Journal of Dress, Body & Culture* 12, no. 4 (December 2008): 489–510.

■ MARCELLA MILIO

PORCUPINE ROACH

The porcupine roach is a crested headdress made of porcupine guard hair topped by one or two feathers and worn by male American Indian dancers. The stiff brown hair stands upright from a base that is either round or, more often, round with an elongated drop at the back; both styles are edged with shorter, natural white or dyed deer-tail hair. Long versions of the roach extend fifteen to twenty-four inches or more in length and are tied with porcupine hair tapering from about eight inches tall at the front to four inches toward the back. A flat roach spreader worn on top fans the hair out and also serves to attach the feathers. In action, the porcupine roach quivers with every movement of the dancer.

History

Although the origins of the porcupine roach are unknown, early versions may have represented special spiritual or protective relationships between the animal and certain individuals.

The headdress has also been identified with warrior society membership, but evidence for this is limited. Despite the uncertainties of its early use, by the era of the fur trade the headdress was worn in a vast region related to the habitat of the North American porcupine, extending from the Northeast throughout much of the western half of the United States.

The Porcupine Roach in the United States

Due to the organic nature of their materials, porcupine roaches made before 1800 do not survive. Visual data can be derived from numerous paintings produced in the early and mid-nineteenth century depicting Native Americans arrayed in their finery. Euro-American and European artists typically identified their subjects by name and tribal affiliation. Portrayals of imposing warriors and chiefs wearing the porcupine roach described as Blackfoot, Fox, Iowa, Kansas, Mesquakie, Oto, Pawnee, Sauk, and Sac affirm its use among tribes in the western Great Lakes and plains regions. Photographs from the late nineteenth century provide further evidence. Images of Arapahoe, Assiniboine, Crow, Kiowa, Omaha, and Ponca men show the persistence of both round and elongated-style roaches, even as they incorporated more European-style clothing into their formal dress.

The prominence of the color red in historical depictions of American Indians reflects its significance as medicine and as paint. Roaches in these portraits are shown in red and brown, with the brown areas presumably representing porcupine hair and the red depicting dyed deer hair. This interpretation is supported by examples from the late nineteenth and early twentieth centuries in museums and private collections. Extant historic porcupine roaches are typically made of natural porcupine hair and deer hair dyed red, although some examples incorporate deer hair in other colors or in alternating stripes of two colors. Similar surviving roaches are made from turkey beard, which is the small cluster of long hair-like feathers that grows from the chest of male turkeys. Today, porcupine hair remains the preferred material for roaches, but more affordable fibers including horsehair are also used. The contrasting deer hair in contemporary porcupine roaches ranges from traditional red or natural white to almost any vibrant color, including neons and even multicolored arrangements. Traditionally, the roach was secured with a small braid of hair passed through a bone spreader; contemporary roach spreaders are often metal, and the headdress itself usually ties to the head.

Porcupine Roach

Many American Indian men and boys wear the distinctive porcupine roach as part of their dance regalia, which relates to their specific dance style and is comprised of multiple garments and numerous accessories. Dancers in the southern straight tradition are typically identified by their single-feather roach, ribbon shirt, bandoliers, and a large ornamented drop at their back. Traditional dancers wear roaches with two feathers along with a breastplate, aprons, and a large feather bustle. Grass dancers usually wear roaches with two feather fluffs atop wires, a yarn-trimmed or fringed cape, matching aprons, and ankle bells. Dancers in the fancy category customarily wear roaches with two feathers that rotate or rock, two large feather bustles at the upper and lower back, smaller arm bustles, aprons, side panels, and bells below the knees. As part of elaborate performance dress, the porcupine roach expresses individual identity and the vitality of Native American culture. It connects its wearers to their ancestors and is an iconic marker of American Indian male identity.

Influence and Impact

With the notable exception of headpieces shown by Jean Paul Gaultier in his women's haute couture collection for spring/summer 2011, the porcupine roach has had little direct influence on Western fashion. The roach is, however, visually referenced by Mohawk and fauxhawk hairstyles. The Mohawk is achieved by shaving the sides of the head and leaving a strip down the middle from the forehead to nape; the hair is typically styled to stand out stiffly from the scalp in a crest and is often vividly dyed in one or more colors. The menacing hairstyle gained popularity among followers of the antiestablishment punk movement that emerged from the music scene in New York and London in the mid-1970s. Its name is actually a misnomer, since men of many northeastern tribes, including Mohawks, traditionally removed hair from the front, sides, and back of the head, leaving a three- to four-inch round or square lock at the crown. Similar to the Mohawk but shorter and lacking shaved sides, the fauxhawk became popular in the early twenty-first century. The fauxhawk is similarly styled with a noticeable ridge in the middle. Wearers of Mohawks and, to a lesser extent fauxhawks, gravitate to the attention-getting styles for their countercultural associations, power, and toughness and are essentially unaware of any resemblance to the porcupine roach.

See also Bolo Tie; Concho Belt; Moccasins; Powwow Accessories
Compare to Cholo Style; Keffiyeh; Zoot Suit

Further Reading

Hartman, Sheryl. *Indian Clothing of the Great Lakes: 1740–1840.* Liberty, UT: Eagle's View Publishing, 1988.

McNeil, Legs, and Gillian McCain. *Please Kill Me: The Uncensored Oral History of Punk.* New York: Grove Press, 1996.

"Pow Wow Terminology." http://library.thinkquest.org/3081/terms.htm (accessed January 11, 2013).

Splendid Heritage. *Treasures of Native America Catalogue* (hair ornament). http://www.splendidheritage .com/nindex.html (accessed January 11, 2013).

West, W. Richard, Jr., ed. *Creation's Journey: Native American Identity and Belief.* Washington, DC: Smithsonian Institution Press, 1994.

■ SUSAN NEILL

POWWOW ACCESSORIES

A powwow is a social event where Native American and non-Native people come together to celebrate and honor American Indian culture through music and dance. The elaborate ensembles worn by American Indian dancers are known as regalia and typically consist of several garments, jewelry, paint or makeup, and numerous personal items. The regalia of an individual reflects their dance style and emphasizes its postures and movements. From headdress to moccasins, a dancer is arrayed with intricate creations. Whether wearing the spectacular twin feather bustles of the male fancy dancer, a traditional female dress with its waterfall of buckskin fringe, or the outfit of another dance style, almost every participant displays elements of ribbonwork, beadwork, yokes, leggings, moccasins, bags, belts, hair ornaments, shawls, and other accessories.

History

The rich customs of American Indian dress stretch back countless generations. Depending on the climate, people wore garments of animal skin or plant fiber and enhanced their bodies with paint and tattoos. Everyday clothing was frequently embellished, but ritual celebrations and formal occasions were recognized with more elaborate dress and adornment. Over time, distinct styles developed that reflected group identities through aesthetic norms of construction and embellishment. Garments and accessories were finished with fringe, fur, and beads of shell, bone, or stone. Women also applied designs with pigments or dyed porcupine quills embroidered in a range of wrapped, plaited, overlaid, and folded techniques.

Powwow Accessories in the United States

After the arrival of Europeans in the late fifteenth century, Native people bartered for imported materials that fueled their creativity. Some needleworkers adopted colorful glass beads for embroidery in place of preparation-intensive quills; others stitched rows of silk ribbons and developed the unique art of ribbonwork. These new techniques elaborated on established styles in visually exciting ways.

Traditional ribbonwork highlights contrasts of texture and color by juxtaposing panels of light-reflecting silk ribbons with soft tanned leather or wool broadcloth. Its simplest form is a sawtooth border made by placing one length of ribbon on top of another, snipping the upper layer, folding the raw edges under, and stitching them together. Elaborate shingled designs are created by repeating this technique with numerous ribbons. Other continuous, often curvilinear patterns are usually mirrored in adjacent panels and finished with herringbone hand stitching. The current tradition is dominated by ribbon appliqué, in which discrete designs are cut out of fabric widths (rather than ribbons) and sewn by machine. Both the ribbon appliqué and shingled ribbonwork worn at contemporary powwows feature striking color contrasts in shiny fabrics such as synthetic taffetas and satins.

Another showy aspect of powwow regalia is beadwork. American Indians have embraced glass beads for their ease and limitless potential in embellishment. Czech glass beads—actually made in north Bohemia—became widely available in the nineteenth century after the development of molded and pressed technology, which enabled thousands of identical beads to be produced cheaply.

Over the centuries, coarser "pony" and finer seed beads across the color spectrum have been used to produce myriad effects. Curved designs are often executed with the spot or overlaid stitch in which beads are strung and laid atop the surface and secured with a second thread at intervals between beads. In the so-called lazy or lane stitch often used for abstract geometric designs, multiple beads are strung onto a needle and secured with a tight stitch, then repeated in parallel adjacent rows; the slight arc of each row adds dimension echoed in subsequent bands. Gourd stitch creates both flat and round shapes well suited for jewelry, fan handles, and dance sticks while the grid-like bands produced in loom weaving are used on bags and as garters, headbands, and jewelry.

Regalia is highly personal and may combine inherited or gifted objects with those made specifically by or for the wearer. Accessories often carry additional layers of meaning in motifs and colors while those made with traditional methods further reinforce cultural ties. Professor, scholar, and powwow dancer Tara Browner asserts that the contemporary powwow grew out of warrior society dances, reservation-era intertribal dances, exhibitions including Wild West shows, and postwar homecoming celebrations. This complex history is reflected in the regalia of its participants, which simultaneously expresses individual identity, cultural continuity, and adaptation. The exuberant garments and accessories worn by powwow dancers communicate the vitality of American Indian culture within the community and to the world beyond.

Influence and Impact

Some Native Americans wear personal items resembling smaller, basic powwow accessories as part of their everyday dress. Silver or beaded jewelry, hair accessories, belts, small bags or pouches, moccasins, and even ribbon shirts can express individual identity and signify heritage on a daily basis. Members of the general population also adopt many of these items. More often than not, such wear demonstrates an appreciation of American Indian craftsmanship, and their purchase supports traditional artisans. On the other hand, most American Indians consider the appropriation of their dress for wear as Halloween costumes and at popular music festivals culturally insensitive, if not overtly racist. Recently, public figures and corporations have encountered backlash for perpetuating stereotypes and cultural appropriation. In 2012 alone, the Navajo Nation sued retailer Urban Outfitters for using its name in products, the band No Doubt pulled a music video portraying its lead singer as an "Indian princess," and Victoria's Secret issued an apology for featuring a feather headdress in a lingerie fashion show. These actions confirm the importance of powwow regalia as markers of Native American identity and culture.

See also BOLO TIE; BUCKSKIN; CONCHO BELT; MOCCASINS; PORCUPINE ROACH
Compare to ETHNIC JEWELRY; WESTERN WEAR

Further Reading

Berlo, Janet Catherine, and Ruth B. Phillips. *Native North American Art.* New York: Oxford University Press, 1998.
Browner, Tara. *Heartbeat of the People: Music and Dance of the Northern Pow-Wow.* Chicago: University of Illinois Press, 2002.
Her Many Horses, Emil, ed. *Identity by Design: Tradition, Change, and Celebration in Native Women's Dresses.* New York: Collins, 2007.

■ SUSAN NEILL

POWWOW T-SHIRTS

Powwow T-shirts are a subcultural form of the classic T-shirt category. According to the *Oxford English Dictionary*, the term "T-shirt" appeared in the United States in the 1920s and describes a simple garment typically made of a knitted cotton fabric that forms a T shape when laid flat. The term "powwow T-shirt," as used in this article, describes a T-shirt form that incorporates a plethora of applied images and phrases that reference and/or are sold at Native North American gatherings called powwows.

History

The etymology of the term "powwow" has been traced to proto-Algonquian, and it referenced a shaman or healer as well as a gathering of practitioners. Today, the word "powwow" references Native North American gatherings centered on dance, drumming, food, and the selling of arts and crafts. The powwow form familiar to participants and attendees today developed in the 1930s from traditional dances of the southern plains such as the sun and war dance and popular Wild West and traveling carnival shows such as Buffalo Bill Cody's. Native traditional dances were banned in the late nineteenth century because they were seen as a detriment to the "civilizing" programs of the federal government and missionaries. In this hostile environment, the traveling shows offered an opportunity for Indian dances and identities to be preserved and reproduced in relation to the dominant society. In the early twentieth century, Native peoples found the sociopolitical space to challenge the dance bans of the previous century and to promote self-determination. The powwow became an important public, performative, and intertribal venue where Indian communities and identities could be asserted and negotiated in relation to non-Natives. Today, the powwow is considered one of the most popular, visible, and dynamic forces in Indian country. Spaces such as the powwow that purposely bring together multiple Native groups as well as non-Natives are important venues where social injustices and ethnocentric stereotypes can be resignified.

Powwow T-Shirts in the United States

The creation and marketing of logoed T-shirts as well as buttons, bumper stickers, and baseball caps by powwow organizing committees was evident by the 1970s. Like concert T-shirts and travel souvenirs, they are collected as cultural capital forms. The production of cultural forms for the souvenir market allows aboriginal people to assert their right to represent their past and the current political context. After two important political incidents in Canada, a powwow was held on the Kahnawake reserve in 1991 to promote healing, bring Natives and non-Natives together, and provide a venue where Native people could produce their own narrative. Central to this process was the production and marketing of particular T-shirt forms that promoted positive messages of the Mohawk. One popular T-shirt sported the inscription, "Kahnawake—Echoes of a Proud Nation."

Today, entrepreneurs, powwow committees, and nonprofits market and sell powwow T-shirts to Natives and non-Natives at events and on the Internet. They come in a multitude of styles and sizes for all ages and genders. Important categories of powwow

T-shirts include the event-specific designs marketed by organizations that sponsor individual powwow events, culturally coded shirts, and those that incorporate obvious political statements. Today's event T-shirt designs are usually original artworks commissioned by powwow organizing committees. Powwow T-shirts also include culturally coded images—drums, eagles, turtles, wings, or a circle divided into the colors white, yellow, red, and black—and phrases: "Got Frybread?" "NDN," "Proud to be [Apache, Chippewa, Sioux]," or "Frybread Power," a slogan made famous in the film *Smoke Signals*.

Another important category of powwow T-shirts draws upon a sense of humor found in Indian country that is often pointedly political. For example, a common powwow T-shirt design incorporates a historical image by C. S. Fly of four Apache warriors holding guns that includes Geronimo and his son. The most common caption to the image reads, "Homeland Security: Fighting Terrorism since 1492." The T-shirt design appeared soon after the September 11, 2001, attacks and became, at times, a topic of heated discussion in the media. Celebrities such as Bill Cosby and Johnny Depp have been photographed wearing it. The T-shirt slogan also has a Facebook page associated with the website www .westwindworld.com that claims authorship of the original design. The ability of powwow T-shirts to index and engage contemporary issues continues; in 2012, a T-shirt with the slogan "Pow Wow the Vote" appeared to encourage Wisconsin Native peoples to make their voices heard during the 2012 elections.

Influence and Impact

Powwow T-shirts are functional souvenir forms that incorporate visual representations of culture that become part of a discourse of empowerment. Participants purchase these T-shirts to financially support organizing committees and memorialize their attendance. Moreover, one's powwow T-shirt collection does not just remind one of good times. When worn to powwow events or in Native contexts, powwow T-shirts, particularly event-related shirts that incorporate the year, event anniversary, and location, signal one's allegiance to powwow culture through time and space. Powwow culture participants recognize and comment on the powwow participation of others because of the powwow T-shirts they wear. Adopting the T-shirt form for aboriginal empowerment challenges exoticized interpretations of difference by providing a more sophisticated way to represent contemporary realities.

See also POWWOW ACCESSORIES
Compare to MEXICAN TOURIST/SOUVENIR JACKET

Further Reading

Blundell, Valda. "Aboriginal Empowerment and Souvenir Trade in Canada." *Annals of Tourism Research* 20 (1993): 64–87.

Ellis, Clyde, Luke Eric Lassiter, and Gary H. Dunham, eds. *Powwow*. Lincoln: University of Nebraska Press, 2005.

Gelo, Daniel J. "Powwow Patter: Indian Emcee Discourse on Power and Identity." *Journal of American Folklore* 112, no. 443 (1999): 40–57.

Mattern, Mark. "The Powwow as a Public Arena for Negotiating Unity and Diversity in American Indian Life." *American Indian Culture and Research Journal* 20, no. 4 (1996): 183–201.

Shea Murphy, Jacqueline. *The People Have Never Stopped Dancing: Native American Dance Histories*. Minneapolis: University of Minnesota Press, 2007.

■ BLAIRE O. GAGNON

PRESSING CAP

See DO-RAG

Q

QUECHUA
See CH'ULLU

R

RASTA HAT

The Rasta hat, also known as the Rasta cap, is a distinctive form of headdress among many members of the Rastafarian movement. The Rasta hat is simple in style and diverse in size. It varies from brightly colored caps to knitted or crocheted woolen tams. Rasta hats are usually constructed similarly to a toque, a round, close-fitting hat squared off at the top, and occasionally stylized with a narrow brim in front to shade the eyes. The hat is large and malleable enough to cover long dreadlocked hair. Although the origin of the design is not clear, it has become popular in some communities around the world and is worn by both Rastas and non-Rastas. The Rasta hat is worn primarily by men, while Rasta women don the African-inspired head wrap or turban. Some Rastafarian men, such as the Bobo Shanti, a sect within the movement, prefer instead to wear tightly wrapped turbans around their dreadlocked hair.

History

The Rastafarian (Rastafari or Rasta) movement emerged in Kingston, Jamaica, during the early 1930s as a political, social, and philosophical movement. Followers of the movement are called Rastas, Rastafari, Rastafarians, or Ras Tafarians. In Jamaica, Rastas are sometimes referred to as Natty Dread due to their thick dreadlocked hair. The movement developed in the poor areas of the Jamaican capital during a period of colonial oppression, widespread poverty, racism, and economic depression. Rastafarianism was born out of the prophesy of Jamaican black nationalist and Pan-Africanist Marcus Garvey (1887–1940), who prophesied in 1927, "Look to Africa for the crowning of a black king, he shall be your redeemer and deliverer." On November 2, 1930, when an Ethiopian prince, Ras Tafari Makonnen, was crowned emperor of Ethiopia, many of Garvey's followers believed that the emperor was the messiah that had been predicted and soon began to worship Selassie as a god (Jah) on earth. The emperor took the throne name of Haile Selassie (Might of the Trinity) and is often referred to as Jah Rastafari by Rastafarian followers. The movement takes its name from Ras Tafari, the preregnal title of Haile Selassie. As the movement took shape, it fostered a distinct language, dress, diet, music, and philosophy. Although the movement is loosely organized with distinct sects, all members believe in the divine status of Haile Selassie. In 1974 the emperor was overthrown and later killed by his captors; nonetheless, he remains a king and god for Rastafarians.

The Rastafarians sought to liberate oppressed Jamaicans and black people from the clutches of colonial elitism and the intolerance of the established Christian church. From its inception, the Rastafarian movement was influenced by Ethiopianism, and it dedicated itself to the ideals of black supremacy, black freedom, and black dignity. Rastafarians embraced and appropriated the symbols and colors of imperial Ethiopia in their dress. These symbols had complex meanings that were incorporated in their worship of Ras Tafari. The Rasta hat and Ethiopian-inspired dress represented not only Rasta resentment at the dominant social and religious order, but also their rejection of their subordinate status and their struggle for social justice and reform.

Rasta Hat

The Rasta colors of black, red, green, and gold along with the popular emblem of the male lion were adapted from the Ethiopian imperial flag and fashioned into brightly colored flowing robes, knitted tams, and head wraps to cover dreadlocked hair. The red represents the blood of martyrs who died for black liberation, green for the beauty and lushness of Ethiopia, gold for the wealth of Africa, and black represents the people. The use of these colors in Rastafarian hats and dress reflects Rastas' loyalty and devotion to Ethiopia, which many viewed as Zion, a type of ultimate paradise, particularly during the reign of Selassie.

The Rasta hat serves many functions. It adorns and protects the head, and it differentiates and identifies those who belong to the movement. In the formative years of the movement, Rastas were persecuted by Jamaican authorities because of their appearance, their teachings, and their use of cannabis or marijuana (ganja, sinsemilla) in their rituals. Among some people, the Rasta hat is worn to make a political statement and can be viewed by some citizens as highly radical or extreme, subversive, and even disruptive. Rasta hats served both secular and religious functions. For others it is a fashion statement, an accessory, or an expedient form of head covering, especially for those who work in the health and food services and for safety reasons around heavy machinery.

Rasta Hat in the United States

A few Rastafarian immigrants first introduced Rasta hats into the United States around the 1950s from the Caribbean. The fashion remained primarily within the immigrant black community. By the 1960s and 1970s this changed, with increased immigration and travel between the United States and Jamaica giving rise to small Rastafarian communities in large metropolitan cities in the United States such as Miami, Chicago, New York, and Philadelphia. These Rasta communities maintained the dress customs, and Rasta hats were soon copied and adapted by non-Rastafarians, including community activists who found the symbols and philosophy of the movement appealing.

Influence and Impact

In the mid-1970s, Rasta hats became popular due to the role of Jamaican reggae superstars, like Bob Marley and Peter Tosh, who wore Rasta hats and used their music to propel Rasta philosophy into the international consciousness. Reggae deeply impacted U.S. culture, and some youth activists wore Rasta hats to show their solidarity with the movement's messages. Audiences in the United States were introduced to the colorful Rastafarian dress and hats through the media, popular culture, and films like *The Harder They Come.* As reggae was eclipsed by new musical genres such as dance hall and hip-hop, Rasta hats became less popular in the United States and more readily available in costume shops as a novelty or souvenir for American tourists visiting Jamaica. Despite this, the Rasta hat remains popular in Jamaica and in some black communities around the world. For many people it continues to serve as a symbol of black pride and dignity, as well as a celebration of their African identity.

See also Tam-o'-shanter; Toque
Compare to African Head Wrap; Beret; Do-Rag; Fez; Kufi; Sibenik Cap; Snood

Further Reading

Akel, Jah. *Rasta: Emperor Haile Selassie and the Rastafarians.* Chicago: Lushen Books, 1999.
Barnett, Leonard. *The Rastafarians.* Boston: Beacon, 1977.
Buckridge, Steeve. *The Language of Dress: Resistance and Accommodation in Jamaica, 1760–1890.* Kingston, Jamaica: University of the West Indies Press, 2004.
Campbell, Horace. *Rasta and Resistance: From Marcus Garvey to Walter Rodney.* Trenton, NJ: Africa World Press, 1990.
Owens, Joseph. *Dread.* London: Sangsters, 1984.
Potash, Chris. *Reggae, Rasta, Revolution: Jamaican Music from Ska to Dub.* London: Schrimer Books, 1997.

■ STEEVE O. BUCKRIDGE

RUBAHA

The rubaha, or Russian folk tunic, is a traditional Russian ankle-length, long-sleeved women's clothing usually worn under a sarafan dress or a *poneva* skirt (in the manner of an underdress).

History

Historically, a rubaha ("a piece of cloth" in ancient Slavic) was the first and only type of clothing for Slavic people, for both men and women. Later, men's rubaha became shorter and started to be worn with pants. Women's rubaha kept its full length until the 1890s, when it was shortened to the waist in some regions of Russia.

Until the 1700s, a rubaha was worn by any Russian woman, regardless of her social or family status. Later, when the tsar Peter the Great forbade wearing traditional clothes by nobility, a rubaha became mandatory for village women only. A woman wore a rubaha for her entire life. Children did not put anything on top of their rubahas. Teenagers and adolescent girls added a sarafan to their outfit (except in Northern Russia, where only married women covered their rubahas with a sarafan and an apron). Senior women, again, took off any upper clothing and kept wearing only rubahas, similar to children.

A traditional Russian rubaha has a very simple cut. It consists of six rectangular pieces of cloth (front, back, two sleeves, and two *lastovica*—armpits) plus two more parts (*paliki*—shoulders), which could be either rectangular or triangular, depending on the region of the country.

Mythologically, a rubaha was comprehended as another skin and was supposed to defend a wearer from supernatural danger of any kind. To fulfill this purpose, a rubaha bore a lot of talismans. The mandatory talisman was a red trim placed around the neck hole, the front cut, the wrists, and the hemline of the rubaha. It was thought of as a "fire edge" that burned any evil spirit that appeared near a wearer to ash.

Another type of talisman was embroidered patterns that decorated a rubaha. Spiritually, the most important symbols should be placed on the *paliki* (shoulders). The paliki's designs differed not only from one region to another, but even each village kept its own designs (they were remains of tribal identification signs of ancient times). Also, embroidery covered sleeves and cuffs (for the festive rubahas of young women), and the hemline and belly (for ritual rubahas).

Everyday rubahas were sewn of nonexpensive materials: home-woven linen, hemp, and "motley"—a cloth made of a mixed fiber. Festive rubahas applied any expensive and fancy-looking fabric people could find and afford: silk, bleached linen, fabric-woven cotton. At the same time, only home-woven linen was thought to be "pure enough" for ritual rubahas.

In some regions, festive and ritual rubahas could have extremely long sleeves (up to three meters). Such sleeves symbolized that these rubahas were not made for work but for celebration/rite purposes only.

The Rubaha in the United States

As a part of an actual traditional Russian woman's outfit, a rubaha was introduced to the United States in the 1960s, when groups of Russian Old Believers established a settlement at Woodburn, Oregon. For them, wearing rubahas was believed to be part of a traditional lifestyle they proudly maintained despite a hostile environment of an "outside" world. Before the 1960s, people occasionally brought pseudo-traditional tunics as part of a "Russian" costume for costume parties. And sometimes a particular family's heritage could include a rubaha, but it was kept as a museum item instead of using it as an everyday item of clothing.

Since the mid-1990s, highly educated immigrants from Russia (these who are ethnically Russian) have started sewing and wearing traditional rubahas (not as an everyday outfit, but as a traditional costume for special occasions: Russian festivals, traditional family celebrations, etc.). People study their family history, find embroidery patterns worn by their ancestors, and make replicas of their grandparents' traditional dress.

Influence and Impact

So, from an everyday clothing item, the Russian folk tunic—the rubaha—became a of national identity. Being an underdress, a rubaha has never been used as a model modern outfit, neither in the United States nor in Russia.

See also Kosovorotka; Sarafan
Compare to Bohemian Dress; Chemise; Peasant Blouse

Further Reading

Aleshina, Tat'iana S. *History of Russian Costume from the Eleventh to the Twentieth Century*. New York: Metropolitan Museum of Art, 1977.
Vucinich, Wayne S. *The Peasant in Nineteenth-Century Russia*. Stanford, CA: Stanford University Press, 1968.

■ IRINA ZHOUKOVA PETROVA

RUMBA DRESS

The Cuban rumba dress, or bata Cubana, is a synthesis of Spanish, African, and indigenous dress customs in the Caribbean. It is a princess-cut gown in bright colors with a ruffled skirt edged in contrasting trim. African-style head wraps or creative headdresses are often worn, especially for carnivals, fiestas, or special occasions. Some rumba dresses are floor length with tiers of ruffles falling from the waist. Others are styled closer to their Spanish flamenco roots, with ruffles falling from the knee and flowing into a train. Dresses may be sleeveless or have long sleeves with ruffles from the elbow. Traditional bata Cubana are often red with black or white trim or red with white polka dots. Men wear a matching shirt with billowing ruffled sleeves.

History

The Cuban rumba dress originated with the Spanish flamenco dress. The North African Moors conquered Spain in 408 CE and introduced sericulture, silk weaving, and color-fast dyes. Brilliant reds and deep blacks were favored by the Spanish and still inform the Spanish aesthetic today. Gold and silver from the New World became part of mainstream fashion, and the well-to-do wore brightly colored silk garments trimmed in precious metals. These garments evolved into the ethnic dress of Andalusia called flamenco and are associated with music of the same name. The Roma, sometimes called "gypsies," added their own aesthetic with polka-dot fabrics and low-cut necklines. Flamenco choreography features quick turns and dramatic movements, emphasized by the ruffles and exaggerated by the contrasting edging. When the Spanish colonized the Caribbean, flamenco came with them.

Even after the abolition of slavery in Cuba in 1865, the African head wrap remained popular for women. When worn with the bata Cubana for fiestas and entertainment, the head wrap could be suggestively erotic. In addition, an important musical genre called rumba grew out of the rhythms of Africa and Cuba, along with influences from the Spanish rumba. Music, dance, and costume came together in the Cuban rumba dress.

The Cuban Rumba Dress in the United States

The Cuban rumba dress arrived in the United States in the early twentieth century when yachting culture among the American wealthy emerged. The Caribbean was close by, warm, and exotic, generating a long-running fashion for all things Latin American from the 1930s into the 1960s when Hollywood, Broadway, and television had a significant influence on fashion. For example, Carmen Miranda was a popular singer during this period. She was Brazilian but drew from across the Caribbean and Latin America for her music and costumes. She was best known as the "Lady in the Tutti Frutti Hat" because of her spectacular headdresses and head wraps featuring fruit, flowers, and tropical birds. In her 1941 film *Week-End in Havana*, her costumes included the styling of the bata Cubana. The cross-dressing character of Klinger, in the television series *M*A*S*H*, carried on her legacy to a new generation when he donned a bata Cubana ensemble to bid farewell to his commanding officer. When young Puerto Rican women sang "America" in the 1957 musical and 1961 film *West Side Story*, their costumes and choreography were inspired by flamenco and rumba. The television series *I Love Lucy* starred a Cuban-born bandleader whose musicians sported the ruffle-sleeved shirt version of the bata Cubana.

Influence and Impact

In the twenty-first century, the Cuban rumba dress appears in three forms. As ethnic dress, it is worn for heritage festivals, family occasions, and holidays. Cuban contestants may wear it in pageants and international competitions. The Cuban salsa singer Celia Cruz preferred the bata Cubana when performing to highlight her ethnicity. Style elements regularly inspire designers. Balenciaga (1895–1972) and Antonio Canovas del Castillo (1913–1984) were famous for their flamenco-inspired dresses, and their influence continues in designers such as Cuban José Arteaga. In everyday dress, infants and toddlers are often fitted out with "rumba panties"—diaper covers or underpants with rows of ruffles along the bottom and visible when the baby crawls. In competitive ballroom dance, the rumba is a specific style in the Latin Dances division. The mood of the rumba is strong, sexy, and decisive. As such, the costume is styled after the Cuban rumba dress, though it is short and reveals more skin than its ancestor.

The Cuban rumba dress is a joyful, sensual, lively style. Colors are happy or dramatic, edging is playful and eye catching, and ruffles are fun to shimmy. Designers turn to the rumba dress when the zeitgeist calls for these characteristics.

See also AFRICAN HEAD WRAP
Compare to CHEONGSAM; KIMONO; POLLERA; SARONG

Further Reading

Daniel, Yvone. *Rumba: Dance and Social Change in Contemporary Cuba (Blacks in the Diaspora)*. Bloomington: Indian University Press, 1995.

■ SANDRA LEE EVENSON

RUSSIAN FOLK TUNIC
See RUBAHA

S

SALVAR

See HAREM PANT (SALWAR)

SARAFAN

The sarafan is a traditional Russian sleeveless, ankle-long dress worn on top of a rubaha (long-sleeved underdress), originally worn by men and later adopted by women.

History

Visitors from Sweden and Norway around the thirteenth century introduced the sarafan to Russia. Originally it was a nobleman's clothing: a long-sleeved coat made of wool or brocade. Russian chronicles of that period of time mention "Great Princes and boyars wearing Sarafans."

Gradually the sarafan switched to a woman's outfit (the transformation was fully complete by the sixteenth century). The sarafan underwent a dramatic change in cut and fashion as it was transformed from a man's to woman's garment. The sleeves were at first narrowed, then became an ornamental detail, and at last disappeared completely. The back and shoulders diminished, turned into a narrow and short back detail, and evolved into shoulder stripes. Finally the front cut was closed—first from neck to waist, then from neck to hips, and finally from neck to hemline. Some of these details persisted as decorative elements. Even in the 1890s village girls attached mock sleeves made of a veil-like cloth to their festive dresses. Metal buttons along a false front cut were a mandatory decoration of a sarafan until the 1920s.

As any traditional outfit does, the sarafan functioned not only as clothing but also as a social identifier. Coded symbols included in the design signified age group, family status, place of living, and even (in some regions) quantity and gender of the wearer's children. It is interesting that in different parts of Russia different social groups were allowed to wear sarafans. In northern Russia, a sarafan was exclusively the dress of a married woman. In contrast, in the southern regions, a sarafan was a dress of adolescent girls only, with married women switching their clothing style to a *poneva*—a skirt of a specific cut. In central Russia and Siberia, a sarafan was forbidden just for spinsters and senior women. Any woman except these two categories had to wear a sarafan in this region.

Traditional sarafans were made of a range of fabrics. Nobles, who wore sarafans before the eighteenth century, applied golden brocade decorated with gemstones and golden threads to their outfit. In contrast, village people used an expensive cloth (silk, brocade, or fine-woven wool) for festive dresses only. Everyday farmers' sarafans were sewn of home-woven linen, wool, and "motley" (a cloth made of a mixed fiber—linen, hemp, or wool).

The continued evolution of the sarafan style within Russia led in the 1930s to the invention of a contemporary city-style sarafan: a light summer dress for girls and young women made of any type of fiber—thin cotton, silk, or synthetic. A city-style sarafan was significantly shorter than the traditional style, ranging from knee length to above the knee. Of course, the dress style lost any symbolic or "identity card" function linked to the traditional sarafan.

The Sarafan in the United States

It is hard to ascertain exactly when a sarafan was introduced to the United States for the first time. The only thing known for sure is that Russian Old Believers who immigrated to the United States in the 1960s brought their traditional outfit (including sarafans) with them. Therefore, the Old Believers' settlement in Woodburn, Oregon, could be counted as the first place in the United States where Russian people wore traditional sarafans as their everyday clothes.

Highly educated immigrants from Russia with ethnic backgrounds from the homeland sew and wear traditional Russian outfits, including sarafans, for special occasions: Russian festivals, rites of passage, and family celebrations. Russian immigrants to the United States study their family history, find particular styles and silhouettes worn by their ancestors, and make replicas of their grandparents' clothing. Their intention is "to dress up as it really was, not as Russian dancers do." In the United States, many designers use traditional sarafans as a model for creating stage costumes, especially for Russian operas and performances.

See also KOSOVOROTKA; RUBAHA
Compare to DIRNDL; PINAFORE

Further Reading

Aleshina, Tat'iana S., *History of Russian Costume from the Eleventh to the Twentieth Century.* New York: Metropolitan Museum of Art, 1977.
Vucinich, Wayne S., *The Peasant in Nineteenth-Century Russia.* Stanford, CA: Stanford University Press, 1968.

■ IRINA ZHOUKOVA PETROVA

SARI

The Indian sari is a traditional yet modern, conservative yet sensual, and revealing yet concealing garment. It is a timeless legend. The sari is a rectangular piece of fabric measuring fourteen to twenty-nine feet by approximately four feet. It is usually worn by draping, wrapping, folding, and pleating to form fit according to the body. The wearer's ability to move and adjust the fabric makes it dynamic and versatile. The sari yardage has three distinct parts—the *pallu* (end piece), the longitudinal border, and the field. Although merging boundaries may occur in the design of the sari, it is essential to keep these parts distinct to maintain the design integrity and function of the garment. The style of draping utilizes all three parts creatively to enhance the fit on the wearer and attract the gaze of the viewer to the aesthetically defining details of the garment. In addition to modern and creative panaches, there are over one hundred different traditional styles for draping a sari. Traditional styles represent regional differences in the art of draping, whereas the modern look is contingent toward the ingenuity of the individual wearer or designer. The sari has evolved with a variety of fibers, woven fabrications, and styles based on social, political, economic, geographical, and international influences.

History

The earliest evidence of the sari in historical manifestation is from the Gandaharan civilization (50 BCE–300 CE) and the Ajanta caves (late fifth century CE) in western India. During that era, saris were showcased on goddesses and signified elite status and royalty. Over numerous centuries, the sari has transformed into its current form. In this particular form, the sari is paired with a choli (blouse) and is worn over a foundation garment known as a petticoat (skirt). The petticoat is a garment that derived from the *ghagra* (a decorative skirt). It is almost always a solid-colored skirt with no embellishments. The choli is a fitted top that has the tendency to reveal by exposing the midriff section. However, the sari's fabric conceals the midriff partially. Although most common in India, women in many other countries such as Bangladesh, Nepal, and Sri Lanka wear saris as well.

The Sari in the United States

The sari has crossed national borders through different manners, including but not limited to international travel, migration, and fashion designers' quest for inspiration. With the advent of globalization and the transnational movement of individuals, the world has become a place of cultural redisposition. Within this new arrangement, the cultural groups that share similar ethnic heritages reconcile and constantly seek ways to maintain their respective identities. Various designers have presented saris and sari-inspired designs in the United States. Saris as well as sari-inspired clothing can be purchased online at the convenience of the individual or in stores. Several websites sell saris to locations throughout the world. These saris could be of traditional style or costume pieces. Indian saris are also popular on auction sites such as eBay, and women have started to "pin" sari-inspired looks on Pinterest. Furthermore, the influence of Indian sari designs and styles can also be seen in items ranging from designer gowns on the red carpet to fast-fashion items at mass retail stores in the typical American mall. The newest trend of summer crop tops paired with skirts emulates the foundation choli and petticoat garments that are worn under a sari. This traditional Indian garment has permeated the pop-culture aspect of American life and dress in a number of ways.

The Indian community across the United States wears a sari as a symbol of ethnic identity, culture, beauty, and respect for heritage. Cultural and religious events, temple gatherings, and other festivities within the ethnic group or family provide women an opportunity to wear their fanciest sari and be a part of this tradition. The sari is a garment that unifies Indian subcultures, pluralistic American culture, generations, and people. Besides Indian women, other women from this melting pot of nations and cultures also have become admirers of the long, draping, and flowy designs of the sari. Women from other cultures wear the traditional sari as tourists in India, attending Indian gatherings in the United States, or even as their own fashion statement to show their admiration for this garment and respect for the culture.

Influence and Impact

The Indian sari has had a significant impact on American markets. Women in the West have shown much enjoyment in wearing saris or sari-inspired garments. The sari can be seen on celebrities and on women from all classes incorporating this renowned style of dress into their everyday lives. Saris have made a remarkable impact on American designers, international designers, and famous brands. These designers have incorporated the draping, the embellishment, and the color from saris in their work. Some key designers and brands that have done this include Marc Jacobs, Alexander McQueen, Dolce & Gabbana, Valentino, Armani, Marchesa, Elsa Schiaparelli, Germana Marucelli, Mingolini-Gugganheim, Madame Grès, Marcel Rochas, Gianni Versace, Hermes, Jean Paul Gautier, and Carolina Herrera. Marc Jacobs in collaboration with Louis Vuitton released a sari-inspired line of dresses recently in 2010. This line was created from vintage sari material sourced from India. Jacobs brought an appealing twist on the Indian sari that garnered attention from women all over the world. Similarly, this influence has also been rendered on the red carpet. At the 2012 Academy Awards, Jessica Chastain wore an Indian sari-inspired Alexander McQueen black dress with intricate gold embroidery and detailing. Other sari-inspired dresses that have adorned actresses include Natalie Portman's Rodarte dress and Scarlett Johansson's Dolce & Gabbana dress, both of which were inspired by the elaborate decorative details of the sari and were unmistakable crowd-pleasers. Elizabeth Hurley is known for wearing saris to record numbers of prestigious events, including breast cancer awareness dinners and award galas.

The beauty of the sari is its ornate form. It creates a mystical essence with the color, embellishment, and art of draping as an enigma. The color in the sari is stirred from an endless palette to suit not only the occasion but personal preference as well. With embellishment ranging from woven, print, embroidered, sequined, and beaded along with the mixed-technique design, the grace and sensuality of the sari give designers a fabulous, adaptable medium for creative expression.

See also CHOLI
Compare to CHEONGSAM; JILBAB; KIMONO; POLLERA; SARONG

Further Reading

Banerjee, Mukulika, and Daniel Miller. *The Sari*. New York: Berg, 2003.
Lynton, Linda. *The Sari*. London: Thames & Hudson, 1995.

■ ANUPAMA PASRICHA

SARONG

The sarong (or *sarung*, Indonesian and Malay for "sheath") is a large swath of cloth, usually of bright colors and striking patterns, that is worn wrapped around the waist by both men and women of Indonesia and Malaysia. But it is not confined to these countries, being worn throughout Southeast Asia, India, Sri Lanka, the Arab Peninsula, the Horn of Africa, and the Pacific Islands. It is also occasionally utilized by beach culture on the northern coasts of Australia and the coasts of the United States.

Normally made from cotton, it is traditionally decorated with batik or ikat dyeing. The width of the cloth can be up to a meter wide and over two and a half meters long. The center is usually marked by a contrasting panel of about a foot (30 centimeters) wide known as the "head," or *kepala*. This piece of cloth is an extra panel that forms a tube that the wearer steps into, after which the excess fabric is folded to the front center, all of which is secured through rolling the top. Today Malay men largely wear checks and women wear batik patterns.

History

The origins of the sarong are uncertain, but the simplicity of its design suggests it has persisted since ancient times. The development of its textile designs occurred visibly from the fifteenth century onward with growing trade between the Asia-Pacific region and India. The exchange of Indian textiles and Indonesian, particularly Javanese and Balinese, spices enjoyed long life, lasting well into the eighteenth century. It was over these centuries that hundreds of thousands of meters of Indian cotton and silk were exported to the Indonesian archipelago. Islamic sailors as well as Dutch, English, Portuguese, and French traders conducted such trade.

Thus the traditional batik designs in Indonesian and Malay sarongs have to be seen together with the strong influence of the Indian designs, together with the conventional sari, although the sari, around six meters, is normally much longer than the sarong. Indian textiles were not only decorated by batik, but by tie-dyeing and block printing, which also persists in Indonesia. Both in the past and today, textiles in Indonesia under the influence of Buddhism and Hinduism continue to exhibit motifs taken from Indian religious and cosmological imagery, such as the mandala. In the fifteenth to seventeenth centuries, the most highly valued textiles across Indonesia were the double ikat *patola*. These were sari-length silk textiles in brilliant colors that were produced exclusively in Gujarat, West India. These textiles are characterized by separately tying and dyeing the weft and the warp threads into intricate designs after weaving.

But the development of batik appears to have developed more out of Indian chintz rather than *patola*. The ready supply of spices to India meant a steady influx of both cloth and chemical dyes to Indonesia. The Indian-influenced designs and techniques were readily embraced by commercial workshops on the Indonesian north coast. In turn, Indonesian interpretations of erstwhile Indian designs began to appear back on Indian shores.

Sarongs are worn in Yemen and in Saudi Arabia, where they are known as *izar* or *izaar*. Designs vary from checks to stripes to flowing designs. Double plaid patterns that are popular show the continued influence of Indonesian design. Tribal groups in Yemen have their own particular version that involves tassels and fringes, known as the *fāṭah*. This is said to resemble the tribal *izaar* of pre-Islamic times. In India, sarongs are referred to as *mundu* if white or black and *lungi* or *kaili* if in color. The dhoti is worn on more formal occasions.

Sarongs are also the common dress in Somalia and the Horn of Africa. Both nomadic and urban Somali men have worn the garment for centuries. However a more recent development is the *macawiis* sarong introduced from Southeast Asia and India. First being from cotton, they can now be made of silk and synthetics such as polyester and nylon. *Macawiis* are largely of high-key colors, black varieties being rare. As opposed to the Indonesian and Malay variety, the Somali sarong is sold presewn and worn wrapped several times around the waist.

In Sri Lanka the sarong is worn exclusively by men. The female equivalent is known as a *redda*. The sarong is worn mostly in rural areas and by working classes; however other classes will wear it indoors and as sleepwear. Overall, wearing the sarong is decreasing in Sri Lanka, since it is seen as lower-class clothing and not modern.

The Sarong in the United States

American audiences became familiar with sarongs when viewing a spate of motion pictures in the 1930s and 1940s that were romantic dramas taking place in the South Pacific. The American actress starring in those films was Dorothy Lamour. Consequently she is most associated with the sarong. Her sarongs were designed by Edith Head.

Influence and Impact

The sarong is not commonly worn in the United States, except in Hawai'i and occasionally on the West Coast and in Florida as part of surf and holiday culture. Its prevalence was greater in the 1970s when the hippie generation introduced all manner of Asian influences in their clothing. Since then, its use has declined. In the United States and Australia the sarong is more often worn by women as a wraparound over a bikini after sunbathing, which can double up as a surface to be laid on the sand for reclining and sunbathing.

See also BATIK CLOTH APPAREL; CALICO AND CHINTZ; SARI
Compare to CHEONGSAM; JILBAB; KIMONO; POLLERA

Further Reading

Barnes, Ruth. *The Ikat Textiles of Lamalera*. Leiden: Brill, 1989.
Gittinger, Mattiebelle. *Splendid Symbols: Textiles and Tradition in Indonesia*. Singapore: Oxford University Press, 1985.
Maxwell, Robyn, and Mattiebelle Gittinger. *Textiles of Southeast Asia: Tradition, Trade and Transformation*. Rev. ed. Singapore: Periplus, 2003.
Ramseyer, Urs. *The Art and Culture of Bali*. Oxford: Oxford University Press, 1977.

■ ADAM GECZY

SCARF

See PASHMINA SHAWL AND SCARF

SCOTTISH SWEATER

Scottish sweaters fall into four major styles made common by their knit structure and wool fiber content. The following will be a brief discussion of each sweater separately and then considered in whole as they were adopted in the United States.

History

Fair Isle sweaters refer to a particular knitting style with colorful, alternating geometric patterns that change or repeat every few rows. Knit with circular needles, the sweaters contain variations of colorful patterns of Xs (crosses) and Os (lozenges). Knitters create each row using only two colors, and when a color is not needed for the surface pattern, it is stranded across the back of the fabric. Traditional colors include deep reds and indigo blues, but a variety of other colors are often used in the sweaters.

Scotland's Fair Isle is known for this colorful stranded knitting technique that dates to the 1850s. Edward, the Prince of Wales, popularized Fair Isle sweaters in the 1920s when he was photographed wearing a tank top sweater in the Fair Isle pattern while golfing in Scotland. Since then, the popularity of Fair Isle sweaters has waned and waxed, but the pattern name maintains its association with Scotland. While some sweaters are still hand knitted, machines can produce patterns that resemble the beauty of the original Fair Isle sweaters.

A Shetland yoke sweater refers to a sweater with a patterned yoke and a solid lower body. The decorative yoke extends across the shoulder area, while the lower body of the sweater is a solid color to speed production. Fine wool from the Shetland sheep breed may be used to create a soft feel or hand, but this style of sweater can be produced in other fibers, such as acrylic or cotton.

Shetland yoke sweaters emerged in the mid-1900s and are economical adaptations of the Fair Isle sweaters. The fine-textured wool used in Fair Isle and Shetland yoke sweaters originally came from the indigenous sheep raised on Scotland's Shetland Islands, which are about one hundred miles north of the country's coast. Shetland wool is a favorite of hand knitters because of the fine staples and the broad range of natural colors, from creamy white to dark neutrals. Shetland sheep are now raised in other locations, including the UK mainland and Canada.

Dark, medium, and light-colored diamonds overlaid with plaid patterns characterize argyle sweaters. While the term "argyle" refers to the unique diamond pattern, the sweaters vary in style and fiber content. An intarsia knitting technique creates an argyle pattern across the sweater front, while the back is a solid color.

Argyle sweaters date to menswear in the 1930s, but the pattern was adapted from the centuries-old tartan plaid. Historically, the Scottish argyle stockings or leggings that were worn with kilts were created from plaid-woven fabrics cut diagonally or on the bias to allow for more form-fitting shapes. The plaid rectangles became diamonds when the fabric was turned on the bias. When knitted stockings replaced bias-cut stockings, the diamond pattern was replicated and called argyle.

The fisherman's Guernsey sweater is a close-fitting, collared pullover that is knitted in the round with juxtaposed knit and purl stitches that give the sweater a heavily textured pattern. These sweaters are highly functional, including shortened sleeve lengths to prevent saturation with water and gusseted sleeves to be replaced when damaged. The five-ply yarns are so tightly spun or twisted they have been called seamen's irons. The overall effect is a thick and durable garment that affords protection from the wind and sea. While waterproof jackets have largely replaced the need for these sweaters, the fisherman's Guernsey style remains an icon.

Fishermen's Guernsey or Jersey sweaters date to the late seventeenth century and bear the name of two islands located in the English Channel. This popular sweater style stretched along Britain's coastline and north to the Shetland Isles. Depending on the coastal area, the Guernsey sweater may also be called the *gansey, gansy,* or *ganzy.* Historically, it was frequently dyed an indigo blue, representing the sea and sky. Hand-knitted sweater patterns were unique for each fisherman and were handed down for generations as family secrets. It has been said that drowned fishermen whose bodies washed ashore were identified by the unique patterns of their one-of-a-kind Guernsey sweaters.

Scottish Sweaters in the United States

The Fair Isle sweater prints first became popular in men's sportswear in the 1920s, but they now occur more often in women's fashions. Shetland yoke sweaters have frequent associations with snow-skiing apparel and were highly popular winter sportswear in the 1960s for men and women. Argyle sweaters also experience periods of popularity in women's fashion, but the print remains a classic in men's hosiery and sportswear, like golf apparel. The iconic fisherman's sweater was popularized in a 1957 photograph of author Ernest Hemingway wearing a cream-colored cable-knit fisherman's sweater with a heavy rolled collar.

Many Americans assign prestige to anything from the British Isles. They are fascinated with the British aristocracy, although ruling lineage based on bloodlines has no place in U.S. history. Fashion designers such as Ralph Lauren have capitalized on consumers' desires to portray themselves as privileged gentry, if only through their clothing. U.S. consumers consider Scottish sweater styles to be classic symbols of a group of people who were born into privilege. By wearing these styles, Americans conspicuously associate with this elite group.

Influence and Impact

The origin of these sweaters may be traced back to the British Isles, but the beauty of the designs has charmed U.S. consumers for decades. Sometimes one of these sweater fashions has a widespread fashion impact for a season, such as the argyle prints in 2009. At other times, only a limited group, such as golfers or snow skiers, wears the styles. Even so, they are recognizable designs even when they are dormant in the fashion life cycle.

See also ALPACA SWEATER; ARAN SWEATER; KILT; NORWEGIAN SWEATER; SCOTTISH SWEATER; TAM-O'-SHANTER
Compare to MISSONI KNITS; PASHMINA SHAWL AND SCARF; SHAWL

Further Reading

Compton, Rae. *The Complete Book of Traditional Knitting*. London: B. T. Batsford, 1983.
Feitelson, Ann. *The Art of Fair Isle Knitting: History, Technique, Color and Patterns*. Kent, England: Interweave Press, 2007.
McGregor, Sheila. *The Complete Book of Traditional Fair Isle Knitting*. New York: Dover, 1981.
Starmore, Alice. *Book of Fair Isle Knitting*. Newtown, CT: Taunton Press, 1988.

■ CELIA STALL-MEADOWS

SERAPE

Serapes, or *sarapes*, are the most recognizable element of traditional male dress in Mexico and, less commonly, some of the colder regions in the highlands of Central America. The serape is a brightly colored, wool-fringed poncho, often knee length, that can be worn open as a poncho or folded and draped over one shoulder as a shoulder blanket. The fabric is usually woven on a foot-operated treadle loom, with cotton warps crossed by a wool weft. A serape is constructed from two matching rectangles sewn together lengthwise, with an opening left in the middle for the head.

History

The likely antecedents of the serape are the long capes, or *tilmas*, worn by noblemen in the pre-Columbian era, which were tied at the shoulder. At this time, they were made on back-strap looms warped with cotton and woven with maguey (agave) fiber. Modern serapes are at least in part the product of Spanish colonialism, which introduced sheep and foot-treadle-loom technology to Mexico.

Given that the exact origins of the serape are unclear, the hybrid garment probably reflects the variety of traditions that gave rise to it, containing elements of indigenous capes or ponchos; the Spanish manta, a rough-textured blanket used in Spanish America; and Arabic kilim fabric, a form of geometrically patterned tapestry weaving. The patterns often draw from Middle Eastern motifs, such as diamond patterns. The distinctive designs link the wearer to a family, hometown, and social status. Symbolically, the garment represents the universe, and the four sides of its rectangular shape represent the four cardinal directions. When a wearer puts it on as a poncho, he places himself at the center of the universe, with his head pointed toward the heavens and his feet anchored to the earth. The best-known serapes come from Saltillo; one of these fine serapes could take up to twelve months to produce, even with the aid of a printed pattern board. The serape is traditionally worn with a sombrero. The sombrero is a wide-brimmed hat made of straw, palm, felt, or leather, often featuring an elaborately decorated hatband made from ribbon or handwoven fabric. Some of these hats have a low, flat crown and stiff brim, while others have a tall crown and floppy brim. Bandanas (neckerchiefs) or handwoven head cloths are sometimes worn under the hats.

The Serape in the United States

The textile industry that produced serapes was passed from the Pueblo Indians of Mexico to the Navajo Indians of the United States in the late seventeenth century when Mexicans fled north to escape retribution for the Pueblo Rebellion of 1680. The two weaving traditions developed side by side in what is now the borderland between Mexico and the United States; the Navajo serapes developed into an important handicraft industry that now includes tapestry rugs as well as blankets. In the early colonial period, indigenous Mexicans began wearing wool shoulder blankets over light shirts and loose-fitting trousers. Commercial serape production emerged in the nineteenth century, and the popularity of the garment spread.

While serapes were originally identified with indigenous culture, they were adopted by vaqueros (cowboys) and other mestizos (people of mixed Spanish and indigenous heritage) from rural areas. Serapes served vaqueros and cowboys as outerwear, bedding, and saddle pads. During cattle roundups, vaqueros would flap serapes in the air to get the cattle moving. When Mexico gained its independence from Spain in 1821, vaqueros were idealized as national heroes, and the serape became a symbol for the new nation. Serapes were initially popularized among the lower classes, but wealthy ranchers and hacienda owners from the north and central regions of Mexico began co-opting the garment to express the populist ideals of the early republican period. As they were adopted by the upper classes, elaborate, finely woven serapes began to serve as status symbols.

Influence and Impact

The weaving style of the Navajo Indians, which was strongly influenced by serape weaving, is a tradition that has attained iconic status in the Southwest. The influence of Mexican and Central American men's dress on the "cowboy style" of the American Southwest is its most important impact on material culture in the United States.

See also BANDANA; PONCHO
Compare to POWWOW ACCESSORIES; SHAWL; WESTERN WEAR

Further Reading

Cisneros, José. *Riders across the Centuries: Horsemen of the Spanish Borderlands*. El Paso: University of Texas, 1984.

Phoebe A. Hearst Museum, University of California–Berkeley. *Tesoros Escondidos: Hidden Treasures from the Mexican Collections*. http://hearstmuseum.berkeley.edu/exhibitions/mexico2.

Slatta, Richard. *Cowboys of the Americas*. New Haven, CT: Yale University Press, 1990.

Wilson, Laurel. "American Cowboy Dress: Function to Fashion." *Dress* 28 (2002): 40–52.

Wroth, William. *The Mexican Sarape: A History*. St. Louis, MO: Saint Louis Art Museum, 1999.

■ REBECCA JACOBS

SHAWL

The simplicity of the shawl suggests that it is a timeless and ancient garment: a large bolt of fabric slung around the shoulders for warmth or protection from sand or sun.

History

Early examples of the shawl were in Bactria and Gandhara, but it is also said to have hailed from Persia and Central Asia, the word coming from the Persian *chal* or *shaal*. It is perhaps vain to conjecture too far, given that it is such a simple, if not self-evident, piece of clothing. The shawl's evolution from the understated and generic to one of sartorial significance took place in the late eighteenth century with the European "discovery" of cashmere wool. At this time the word "cashmere" was often given preference to the word "shawl" in order to distinguish itself from the garment's nondescript origins. By the mid-nineteenth century, a cashmere shawl was the sine qua non of women's fashion. If there had to be one item that summed up the nineteenth century in women's fashion in France, it was the cashmere shawl. It was coveted not only for its agreeable texture, but also for its relative rareness and costliness, thus making it a symbol of class and status. By the 1830s it was something that any woman of substance had to own and went from curiosity to ubiquity. It was the fabric of excellence, what to the nineteenth century silk had been in past ages.

As an item of imperialism, the cashmere shawl was the result of mixed fortunes. European efforts to import the goats from which the wool came met with poor success, while the British colonization of the design used on the shawls, the *buta*, was repossessed in the name "paisley," named after the Scottish town of the same name where shawls were woven and new, richer variants of the well-known tear-drop motif were conceived. Because shawls were more accessories that articles of clothing, they complemented a wide range of fashions. Shawls quickly became sublimated into the European mind as something more than a piece of clothing; they articulated the beauty and profits of colonization. Thus shawls went well beyond the category of admirable apparel: they stretched to be a dramatic social and even political phenomenon. In the mid-nineteenth century, the shawl was the principal article by which Britain was able to visualize its Indian colony, and possessing one was literally to partake in empire.

France also managed to co-opt the shawl into its own colonial narrative. The period when France was most gripped by "cashmere fever" was associated first with the Egyptian campaign and then conveniently with the conquest of Algeria three decades hence. In their courtship, Josephine was bombarded with cashmere shawls from Napoleon while he was away in Egypt; an 1806 inventory lists forty-five shawls. This was an exceptional number for the time in France, as there was an embargo on their importation because of the blockade of trade with Britain. When Napoleon married Marie-Louise he included seventeen shawls in her *corbeille de noces* ("wedding basket"). This was not just lip service to fashion; it had special importance of reminding his wife that he was a conqueror of distant lands. Its symbolic resonance did not just survive more than three regime changes; it escalated, for the reason that it was associated with the imperial might of what France had been and what it might be again.

European attempts to break the back of the Eastern monopoly also bear an uncanny resemblance to the difficulties encountered in the sixth century in securing its own silk supply. Spurred on by the insatiable demand in Europe for cashmere, during a trans-Himalayan trip in 1812, the veterinary surgeon and superintendent of the East Asia Company, William Moorcroft, secured the possession of fifty mountain goats, but only the males reached Europe due to a shipwreck. French efforts proved just as unsuccessful, since the Pyrenees were inadequate to sustain the goats, which were only used to the Himalayan climate. Thus the regions of Ladakh and Kurdistan maintained their hold on cashmere production, forbidding the export of untreated fiber.

The beginnings of the Kashmiri shawl industry remain obscure. A popular account is that it appeared during the Moghul conquest during the rule of Zain ul'Abdin (1420–70). But only a century later, during the reign of Emperor Akbar after his conquest of the Kashmir Valley, did the garment come into its own. Esteemed by the emperor himself, shawls were the benchmark of artisanal craftsmanship and of the power of personal patronage in India, and they were objects of trade. They were also used as bribes, as described by the English envoy to the Moghul court in 1616, who reported that he had formally rejected one. In 1739 the emperor of Constantinople accepted a huge trove of shawls presented on behalf of Nadir Shah, the Persian invader of India.

Kashmir had a mystique rooted in the frustratingly inalienable fact that their geographic and demographic conditions were the secret to a product that could not be replicated. But this only made the challenge greater. Kashmir and its shawls circulated in the mid-nineteenth-century British imagination with talismanic mystique. Perhaps more than any other article, it also showed how Victorian Britain used commodities to experience and reflect on its empire, its subdivisions classified according to what was produced and what could be gained (as opposed to the people deployed to produce them), with Kashmiri shawls at the apex, at least in terms of aesthetic allure.

Factories in Paisley (the town near Glasgow), Norwich, Edinburgh, and Lyon began to imitate Indian shawls. With respect to these imitations, Norwich led the standard, having begun in the 1780s with block-printed patterns. Together with Edinburgh, it took up soon after weaving the patterns on draw looms that included pattern harnesses as well as regular loom harnesses. Comparing British and French textile production at the middle of the nineteenth century is no contest, at least with respect to quantity. In 1848, British production dwarfed that of the French, as they possessed twice as many automatic looms (675,000) as France (328,000); however Lyon continued to be a leader in variety and quality. Soon after France began their production in 1804 and thanks to the invention of the "harness" and the Jacquard loom (the latter only becoming recognized in the 1820s), weavers were able to mechanically imitate designs that were painted or embroidered by hand. Fabrics were either wool or silk, but not cashmere, in which India still had the monopoly. But this was no deterrent. Lyon labeled the shawls generically as "cashmeres" in their exports to America, which presumably was too remote from India to know the difference. These shawls were produced in all manner of materials, from damask and chenille to *barège*. The widening of styles with improvements in dyeing and printing caused the magazine *Belle Assemblée* in November 1838 to comment, "There is really quite a mania for shawls, besides those of Cashmere, which still maintain their ground, we have velvet shawls, satin, and *peluche* ones, and a great variety of fancy shawls." The ample availability of choice did not quell manufacturers' desire to find a serviceable alternative to cashmere, which by the 1830s was already commanding astronomical prices. The most notable figure to do so was Titus Salt, whose life span (1803–1876) roughly straddles the time when shawls were most in vogue. In 1836 he fell upon some bales of Alpaca wool in Liverpool. He made his fortune with the alpaca spinner, thus creating "alpaca," which became a popular alternative to both silk and cashmere. In 1980 there were as many as twenty thousand registered alpacas in England.

The Shawl in the United States

As with most other women's fashions of the time, the adoption of the shawl in the United States was directly influenced by European fashion. In fact the "shawl period" in the United States coincided with that in Europe and spanned the time between 1800 and the 1870s.

Influence and Impact

During the "shawl period" in the United States, the shawl was worn primarily as a fashion item, but also functionally to provide warmth to the wearer. Shawls, as true for other fashion items, could serve as a symbol of status. Though not considered an essential garment in contemporary fashion, the shawl continues today to exist as a dress accessory.

See also PASHMINA SHAWL AND SCARF; PONCHO; SERAPE
Compare to PELISSE; POWWOW ACCESSORIES; TALLIT; TZITZIT

Further Reading

Geczy, Adam. *Fashion and Orientalism: Dress, Textiles and Culture from the 17th to the 21st Century*. London and New York: Bloomsbury, 2013.

Hiner, Susan. "'Cashmere Fever': Virtue and the Domestification of the Exotic." In *Accessories to Modernity: Fashion and the Feminine in Nineteenth-Century France*. Philadelphia and Oxford: Pennsylvania University Press, 2010.

Mathur, Saloni. *India by Design: Colonial History and Cultural Display*. Berkeley and London: University of California Press, 2007.

Zutshi, Chitralekha. "'Designed for Eternity': Kasmiri Shawls, Empire, and Cultures of Production and Consumption in Mid-Victorian Britain." *Journal of British Studies* 48 (2009): 422–23.

■ ADAM GECZY

SHEARLING

Shearling is the hide of a lamb with pulled wool kept at an even length of under half an inch. Known for its warmth and durability, shearling is generally used for cold-weather outerwear. It has leather on one side and shorn wool on the other; the latter is customarily on the inside of the garment or boot.

History

The definitive origins of shearling are unclear, as the practice of sheep husbandry has been present for centuries throughout most of the world. The emergence of similar textiles has been recorded over several millennia and regions—for example, third-millennium BCE Sumer (in Mesopotamia) and eighth-century Scandinavia. Today's definition of "shearling" can be traced back to England, however, with its long history of shearling lamb trade, the evidence of which having been documented since the Middle Ages.

In the nineteenth century, Glastonbury was at the center of the sheepskin industry in England. The first shearling slippers were produced there in 1825, and in 1870, John Morland opened a nearby tannery; his company, Morlands, has since been credited with the beginnings of the shearling look known today. The firm introduced shearling boots in the 1930s and by 1940 distributed shearling jackets and boots as part of the uniform of Royal Air Force pilots, many of whom fought in the Battle of Britain. Even decades later, the shearling-clad aviator look remains iconic the world over.

Shearling in the United States

Shearling is a choice material for jackets, coats, hats, boots, and slippers; its warmth is especially appreciated during cold winters. Over the decades, whether in battle or the great outdoors, shearling outerwear has lent Americans an aura of bravery and adventure.

In the United States, shearling is best known for its use in jackets and coats. In 1934, the U.S. military introduced the B-3 jacket, adding shearling to the famous flight jackets issued in World War I and also popular with British, French, and Belgian forces. Shearling became invaluable for World War II aviators who flew over Europe in freezing, unpressurized cabins. Despite its discontinuation in 1944, the B-3 is to this day recognized as the quintessential bomber jacket, though the latter garment in its many styles was usually not limited to bomber crews. The success of this style incited the U.S. Navy to produce a similar and still popular jacket, the M-44.

A number of both historical and fictional American heroes of the 1930s and 1940s have donned shearling bomber jackets, thus sparking a trend with civilians, for whom additional pockets were added. Amelia Earhart often wore one on her journeys, and General George S. Patton wore his B-3 in the Battle of the Bulge in 1944. In Hollywood, shearling bomber jackets were prominent costumes in World War II movies, sported by stars such as William Holden in Billy Wilder's *Stalag 17* (1953) and Gregory Peck in *Twelve o'Clock High* (1949). Shearling coats have also been immortalized in American cinema, thanks to actors such as Steve McQueen in *The War Lover* (1962), Dennis Hopper in *Easy Rider* (1969), and Robert Redford in *Jeremiah Johnson* (1972).

Influence and Impact

With regard to the shearling uniform pieces worn by American, British, French, and Belgian forces in World Wars I and II, the textile's insulating qualities helped keep troops warm, whether in air or on land. American fashion, whether for women or men, recurrently relies on military details, the bomber jacket being no exception, and styles frequently seek to convey hardworking and adventurous attitudes through clothing.

Wartime-era jackets are a popular vintage item, sought after by history and fashion fans alike, and the garments are regularly discussed, traded, and sold in online vintage, battle recreation, and war history forums.

Another example of shearling in popular media is the advertising figure of the Marlboro Man, sometimes seen in campaigns exploring the American West in a shearling coat. The rugged cowboy image was key in selling cigarettes in the United States from 1954 to 1999 and became a symbol of American masculinity.

Shearling producers occasionally receive criticism for slaughtering lambs (which are sheep no older than twelve months) for the sole purpose of using their hide. While shearling is in fact made of both hide and wool, many manufacturers insist that these lambs are primarily raised for meat and that shearling is a by-product of the current meat industry.

See also UGG FOOTWEAR; WESTERN WEAR
Compare to DUSTER; TRENCH COAT

Further Reading

Rottman, Gordon L. "Flying Clothes." In *US Army Air Force (1)*. Oxford: Osprey Publishing, 1993.
Sims, Josh. "The Bomber Jacket." In *Icons of Men's Style*. London: Laurence King Publishing, 2011.
Studenroth, Jenny. "The Way We Wear: Shearling." *Wall Street Journal*, October 21, 2010, http://magazine.wsj.com/fashion/the-way-we-wear/shearling.

■ MARIE-CLAIRE EYLOTT

SHERWANI
See NEHRU JACKET

SHOESTRING TIE
See BOLO TIE

SHTREIMEL

The shtreimel, also known as a kolpik, is a fur hat worn by many married Hasidic men on Shabbat (the Sabbath), Jewish holidays, and other festive celebrations, such as one's wedding. It is never worn during the weekday. The bride's father usually purchases the shtreimel for the groom on his wedding day, and it becomes the most costly garment in his wardrobe. A shtreimel ranges in price from several hundreds of dollars to several thousands. A high-quality shtreimel is made of the tail of the sable, marten, fisher, or silver fox. A lower-quality shtreimel may be made of badger or raccoon fur. Some men even own one made of synthetic fur for days when the costly, real fur shtreimel may be damaged by stormy weather.

The shtreimel is generally worn only by Hasidic men once they marry, but some younger boys from other Jewish communities are wearing them after their Bar Mitzvah (the Jewish rite of passage marking the transition into adulthood). While the shtreimel is

Shtreimel

suggested to be a "god-like" garment, there is no religious significance to this hat. Therefore, a yarmulke is always worn under the shtreimel in accordance with the custom of the Jewish male to always cover his head.

History

Since the thirteenth century, Jews in Poland and Russia were required to distinguish themselves from Christians through their dress. In the beginning, it was simply by a red badge, but by the sixteenth century, Jews were obliged to wear a special caftan and fur hat. The fur hat was believed to be a symbol of persecution during the eighteenth century when all Jews were forced to wear the tail of an animal on the Sabbath to show that they were not working. To wear the rest of the animal skin was forbidden by the Polish king. The animal tail custom quickly spread throughout Eastern Europe, but the production was perfected and tailored by the Jews and the fur hat soon resembled the fur hats worn by Russian and Polish nobility. The saucer-shaped fur hat known as the shtreimel was a variation of the fur hat that came out of Galicia reserved for rabbis.

The Shtreimel in the United States

Like other Jewish garments, the shtreimel came to the United States through a successive wave of immigration resulting from persecution in Russia and Poland beginning in 1880. The largest populations of Hasidic Jews are living in New York in distinctly immigrant neighborhoods, where their dress has remained relatively unchanged since the eighteenth century.

Because of its high value, the shtreimel is often viewed as a prestige garment among Hasidic Jews. A wealthy man may own more than one shtreimel, which is also an indicator of his social position in the Hasidic community. However, there is a growing trend to adopt synthetic fur shtreimlach (plural of "shtreimel") among a small group of Hasidim who see showing off one's wealth as frivolous when compared to the inhumane treatment of animals.

Influence and Impact

In 1993 Jean Paul Gaultier shook the fashion world with his controversial collection *Chic Rabbis*, which he said was inspired by a group of rabbis observed on a trip to New York. Several of his models walked the runway wearing his trendy interpretation of the furry headgear.

Korean-born designer Gunhyo Kim, in his provocative 2008 collection, *Hot Hasidim*, was inspired by Antwerp's Hasidic community. The Il Galantuomo label coupled the shtreimel with a sleek sharkskin suit on a clean-shaven male model who paraded the creation down the catwalk in Barcelona. The desecration of religious iconography conjured up much criticism from the Hasidic community and the fashion world alike. However, others reacted more positively, feeling flattered that Kim, an assistant to designer Dries Van Noten, would use the traditional attire as an inspiration for his line.

See also FEDORA; SNOOD; TALLIT; TZITZIT; YARMULKE (KIPPAH)
Compare to BLANGKON; COONSKIN CAP; HAWLI; TAQIYA; TURBAN

Further Reading

Boyarin, I. "Voices around the Text: The Ethnography of Reading at Mesivita Tifereth Jerusalem." *Cultural Anthropology* 4, no. 4 (1999): 399–421.
Koutsoukis, Jason. "Blessed Be the Shtreimel Makers, Despite Fur Fury." *Sydney Morning Herald*, June 27, 2009, http://www.rickross.com/reference/ultra-orthodox/ultra102.html (accessed December 1, 2012).
Poll, Solomon. "The Hasidic Community." In *Dress and Identity*, edited by Mary Ellen Roach-Higgins, Joanne B. Eicher, and Kim K. P. Johnson, 224–38. New York: Fairchild, 1995.
Rubens, Alfred. *A History of Jewish Costume*. London: Peter Owen, 1981.

■ JESSICA STRÜBEL

SIBENIK CAP

The Sibenik cap is a distinctive orange cap with black embroidery and a circular shape. It is unique to the town of Sibenik, Croatia, and has become a recognizable symbol of Croatian identity. Red caps are worn throughout the Balkans, but orange caps with a black silk design are specific to Sibenik and the Dalmatia region. The top of the cap is flat rather than pointed, and the style does not include dangling ornaments or additional pieces.

History

Sibenik is the oldest Croatian city and was not originally Greek, Roman, or Byzantine, as many other cities in the region once were. It first appears in records in 1066, and at times it has been a part of Croatia-Hungary, Italy, the Austro-Hungarian Empire, and the Kingdom of the Serbs, Croats, and Slovenes. Throughout these transitions, it has maintained a strong identity and heritage, and Croatian folk dress often includes embroidered designs that reflect some of the stories, landscape, and history of the region.

The Sibenik cap developed over time, but today's cap can be linked to the work of nineteenth-century seamstresses and craftsmen who began to use sewing machines to manufacture large numbers of uniform caps. The caps were worn across the region and grew in popularity, particularly after World War I. Before it became a part of the cap's image, the orange color may have been the result of a manufacturing process that was different from the traditional hand dyeing.

Today, Sibenik is a tourist destination and the home of the Cathedral of St. James, a UNESCO World Heritage site. People who visit the area may purchase a Sibenik cap as a souvenir of their time there, and caps can now be seen around the world.

The Sibenik Cap in the United States

People in the United States who wish to associate with Croatian history and culture wear the Sibenik cap. Hats can serve as a signifier of identity and heritage, and the Sibenik cap is one cap among several that wearers associate with Croatia. Many hats are manufactured with images of the Croatian flag or patriotic colors. Other Croatian hats include the Lika, which is somewhat similar to the Sibenik cap but is red and black with tassels. The Lika is also associated with Serbia. The Montenegrin cap has a similar style but is worn by those who associate with the Serbians of Montenegro.

The political and military conflicts that dominated the Balkans during the 1990s led to a large number of refugees leaving the region. Some Croatian immigrants came to the United States, joining in a long history of Croatian immigration to the United States. Croatian heritage festivals celebrating Croatian culture take place across the country every year. These celebrations include the Houston Slavic Heritage Festival in Texas, which features dancing and traditional costume, and the International Pittsburgh Folk Festival. Croatian immigrants in the late nineteenth and early twentieth centuries participated in large-scale industrial projects and factory work and have a long-standing presence in many of America's steel towns.

Influence and Impact

The Sibenik cap can serve as a signifier of Croatian identity and heritage. Wearing the hat is one way to represent pride and solidarity with a particular region of the Balkans, including during recent conflicts. The Sibenik cap is one example of a culturally significant Balkan cap, and it plays a role in Croatian festivals and events. While these hats are traditionally worn by men, today they are sometimes worn by women as well. The Sibenik cap is an example of a much larger hat trend. Hats are often intended as a symbol of identity with a particular group or way of thinking. For anyone who recognizes it, the Sibenik cap represents Sibenik and its long history.

See also FUSTANELLA
Compare to BERET; BOWLER HAT; FEZ; FLAT CAP; KUFI; RASTA HAT; TAM-O'-SHANTER; TAQIYA

Further Reading

"Croatia: Small Country Has Big Impact on Pittsburgh." *Popular Pittsburgh.* http://www.popularpitts
    burgh.com/pittsburgh-info/pittsburgh-culture/pittsburgh-nationalities/pittsburghcroatiancommu
    nity.aspx.
Cvitanic, Marilyn. *Culture and Customs of Croatia.* Denver, CO: Greenwood Press, 2011.
Radovinovic, Radovan, ed. *The Croatian Adriatic: Features of Cultural and Natural Interest.* Tourist guide.
    Zagreb: Zednko Ljevak, 2001.
Ware, Carolyn. "Croatians in Southeastern Louisiana: Overview." *Louisiana Living Traditions.* http://
    www.louisianafolklife.org/LT/Articles_Essays/main_misc_croatians_s_la.html.

■ CAITLIN TRACEY-MILLER

SILHAM

See BURNOUS

SIRWAL

"Sirwal" is the Arabic word for waist covering and commonly refers to loose baggy cotton trousers traditionally worn as undergarments by men and women across North Africa

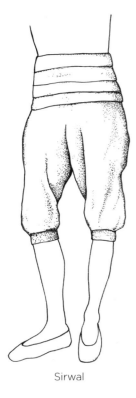

Sirwal

and the Arabian Peninsula in predominantly Muslim countries. The traditional garment ties with a drawstring and can be worn at waist or hip level. Styling varies regionally, but the sirwal is characterized as being loose fitting and wide in the seat.

History

Traditionally the sirwal was made of percale or *chandora*, called Guinea fabric by the Europeans. The people of the Sahara called the fabric Chandora after the Indian village of Chandor where the fabric originated on the western shores of Hindustan. The fabric made its way to the region traveling across Persia and Syria from east to west in Saharan caravans with the spread of Islam during medieval times. The Europeans referred to all cotton fabric traveling by caravan from the South (Sudanese Guinea) as Guinea. The Chandora fabric was soft and draped nicely and was always a blue violet color. The sirwal is believed to have come from Persia by, at the latest, the sixth century CE and was adopted by many Arab communities. By the medieval period, a great variety of styling existed, including knee-length, calf-length, and ankle-length; baggy or closer fitting; and high or low crotch. Each style of sirwal had a different name and group of people that wore the style. Both men and women wore the pant in both urban and rural settings at all times, and this tradition continues today in many Islamic countries.

Today the trousers are more often worn by men and may be long, reaching to the floor, or short, reaching to just below the knee, and are worn to conceal the body when worn under the thawb (ankle-length gown or tunic) or boubou (long flowing ankle-length robe). The sirwal is considered men's underwear and is only partially visible at and below the knee from underneath the long robes. The traditional sirwal never goes below the knee and is a simple rectangle shape cut from three to four panels of fabric with an extremely wide center panel twice the length of the out seam. A simple construction, with encased waist, closed bottom panel, and side leg openings, men wear the sirwal with a leather belt gathered through a casing that meets at the center front and hangs between the legs. The width of the center panel varies, with the very wide and full sirwal demanding a higher price. The sirwal with its wide center panel that drapes between the legs when worn is an extremely functional design providing a degree of modesty, ease of movement, and padding in the saddle when riding a camel or horse. Regular pants with a close-to-the-body fit would not function in the same way.

The Sirwal in the United States

A broad variety of styling exists today of this basic undergarment and it has evolved to be an important influence on pant and trouser stylings for both men and women in Europe and the United States. The encased waistband that was traditionally gathered with a belt or cord now has deep front and back pleats and a three- to four-inch-wide (about eight centimeters) fixed waist band with fly front opening and front button closure along with wide belt loops. The wide center panel and very low, droopy seat is a characteristic feature of this garment. Out seam lengths continue to vary, but the most commonly worn styles end at mid-calf or just below the knee and may have elaborate embroidery that matches the robe or tunic it is worn with. This style of sirwal continues to be worn today across North Africa from Morocco to Egypt. In the Arabian Gulf countries, a pant styling also called sirwal resembles men's baggy pajama bottoms and is generally ankle length, with loose-fitting draw-string or elastic-waist pants.

Influence and Impact

Today in the United States, versions of the traditional sirwal appear and reappear in both men's and women's fashion from time to time. The distinguishing feature that relates back to the traditional sirwal is the dropped crotch seam. The style received its broadest exposure when MC Hammer, a popular American rapper and entertainment celebrity, popularized a similar style of pants in the 1980s and 1990s. Now known as Hammer pants, the modern version Hammer wore was a combination of the sirwal and harem pant and were voluminous, ankle-length trousers with a pronounced dropped seat made from flowing, flashy, often metallic fabrics.

See also BOUBOU; TAQIYA; THAWB
Compare to KILT; LEDERHOSEN

Further Reading

du Puigaudeau, Odette. *Arts et Coutumes des Maures (Moorish Art and Customs)*. Paris: Ibis Press, 2003.
El Gundi, Fadwa. "Private Reflections." *International Journal of Middle East Studies* 39 (2007): 172–73.
Loughran, Kristyne. "The Idea of Africa in European High Fashion: Global Dialogues." *Fashion Theory* 13, no. 2 (2009): 243–72. doi:10.2752/175174109x414277.
Rabine, Leslie. *The Global Circulation of African Fashion*. Oxford: Berg, 2002.

■ VIRGINIA M. NOON

SLOUCH HAT (AUSTRALIAN)

The Australian slouch hat is a low-crowned, wide-brimmed felt hat with one side of the brim turned up. It has been associated with Australian-based military since 1885, when the hat's introduction is ascribed to Colonel Tom Price of the Victorian Mounted Rifles.

A number of elements pinpoint the Australian slouch hat. Firstly it is traditionally made of rabbit fur. Secondly its color has been fixed since World War II as the jungle-green variant of khaki that clothed the Australian army. Thirdly there are some specific styling details that identify the Australian slouch hat from all others: the dented crown at right angles to the face, the pleated linen puggaree (hatband), and the rising sun badge. The form of the puggaree was standardized in the 1930s, ensuring that the hat was well established in its format by the Second World War. The inclusion of the puggaree itself indicates the British imperial inheritance of the slouch hat; its etymology comes from *pagri*, a Hindu word for "veil," and its folds echo the traditional Indian head wrapping, here used as protection from the sun. A true slouch hat has seven pleats in its band, one for each state of Australia and one for the Northern Territory. The royal military college Duntroon adds an eighth pleat to represent regional graduates of the Australian army officer corps such as New Zealanders. The hats are easy to buy with pastiche military badges for civilians and are worn overseas by Australians or taken home by departing tourists. While there have been as many as two hundred companies making hats for the Australian army at different times, they are now closely associated with the internationally renowned Australian hatters Akubra.

History

The slouch hat was originally a specifically military variation of the brimmed felt hat and was associated with companies of soldiers armed with early firearms such as harquebuses and smooth-bored muskets. One side was turned up to ensure that early long-barreled weapons did not get entangled with head wear, especially during drill commands that involved raising and lowering the weapon above the shoulder and past the face. Even at this early date, more flamboyant companies such as British royalists, various mercenaries, and especially officers would decorate the hats with plumes. Bicorne and tricorne hats worn widely in the eighteenth century were more formalized iterations of these early turned-up brims.

The slouch hat was standard with infantry in the Imperial Australian army during the Napoleonic period and early nineteenth century. The son of Colonel Tom Price of the Victorian Mounted Rifles, the first Australian regiment to adopt the slouch hat in 1885, believed that his father had adopted the hat from the Burmese Native Police. By about 1889, New South Wales soldiers are photographed with slouch hats and a conference of various military commanders from across the Australian continent in 1890 affirmed soft felt hats as the most suitable head wear for local armies. Various colonial forces took up the slouch hat in different colors and also pinned up brims in both right and left orientations.

The Second Anglo-Boer War (1899–1902) marked a high-water mark for the universality of soft felt hats not only among the British imperial forces and their opponents, but also in other countries, including the North American Rough Riders (First U.S. Volunteer Cavalry) and German regiments in East Africa. Whereas Britain increasingly abandoned felt hats from 1905 onward, they were retained by the Australian Commonwealth military forces at their formation in 1903, and by World War I they had attained iconic status among Australians as a national symbol.

When the slouch became outmoded for military use because of its nonprotective aspect, its retention by the Australian army during World War II suddenly became a standout point of distinction, and it has retained this identity-marking role ever since. Within Australia the hat had been the feature of innumerable postcards and patriotic folk art in World War I, and in 1942 it was celebrated in a popular marching song, "Just an Old Slouch Hat with the Side Turned Up."

The Australian Slouch Hat in the United States

The slouch hat communicates an unmistakable and immediate Australian identity. Yet concurrently the long and not specifically Australian backstory of the hat indicates how modern ethnographic and nationalist icons can be contrary, shifting, and arbitrary. Equally, the hat demonstrates how short and lightly rooted—even fantastical and confected—are core elements of public memory and public culture that are supposedly constitutive of the spirit of any given people or race. It could be linked to Kwanzaa or folk dance companies as an invented icon.

While North Americans would have seen slouch hats in World War II and Korea, the Vietnam War is crucial to the hat's familiarity in U.S. culture. Not only did U.S. military personnel become aware of Australian traditions due to very close contact and cooperation with Australians, but the greater protection offered by the slouch hat against the sun made it desirable as much as quaint. Hats were traded or bought from Australians not only as souvenirs but as practical wear in a hot, steamy climate. The demand was such that interarmy trading could not meet it. Americans were also kept supplied with slouch hats by pastiches made by local tailors in Vietnam from cast-off parachutes and other surplus textiles. Many Australian slouch hats were brought back to the United States.

This back exchange is ironic considering that the Australian infantry hat, complete with plume and hard blocking of the crown, which was the ultimate source for the Australian slouch hat, had already been widely worn in mid-nineteenth-century America in the guise of the Hardee hat used by the U.S. Army in the 1850s and 1860s. A lighter, less structured slouch hat was de rigueur for both Confederate and Union cavalry during the Civil War and was also frequently worn by officers of other branches of service during that conflict. While the traditional genealogy of the Australian slouch emphasizes the British imperial origins of late colonial military uniforms, drawings and paintings of the period indicate that some nineteenth-century mounted Australian units prior to the standardization of uniforms from the 1890s onward also looked somewhat like Western-theater Civil War cavalry, especially the irregulars, guerrillas, and Confederates. Mid-nineteenth-century Australia's extreme but superficial fascination with the Civil War as entertainment spectacle and boys' own fun as evidenced by the lengthy copying of any random press accounts in the early 1860s and Leigh Astbury's claim that nineteenth-century Australian bush dress was actually drawn from illustrations of North American miners and cowboys would provide a general context of plausibility.

Influence and Impact

The international popularity of Australian historical films in the 1970s and 1980s also exposed a global audience to the slouch hat in films such as *Gallipoli*, *Breaker Morant*, and *The Lighthorsemen*, as much as it made the Drizabone coat and the bush hat popular.

See also SHEARLING; TRENCH COAT; UGG FOOTWEAR
Compare to BERET; BOWLER HAT; FEDORA; SOMBRERO; WESTERN WEAR

Further Reading

Craik, J. "Is Australian Fashion and Dress Distinctly Australian?" *Fashion Theory: The Journal of Dress, Body & Culture* 13, no. 4 (2009): 409–42.

■ JULIETTE PEERS

Snood

SNOOD

A snood is a type of head wear. It resembles netting, constructed of knotted, crocheted, or knitted yarn. Worn by women, it is placed around the hair that hangs from the back of the head. The front of the snood sits just behind the hairline and extends either just in front of or behind the ears and down under the nape of the neck. The netting hangs from this line like a small sack. Usually the mass of hair can be seen through the netted yarn, though sometimes a liner is placed inside the netting to cover the hair completely. Snoods in the modern era can also be made of solid fabrics.

History

Netting worn on the hair can be seen in images beginning in medieval times. The word "snood" has been in use in the English language since the eighth century for many types of hair coverings. The snood as a bag shape for holding hair came into being sometime in the 1500s in European countries. In the United States, as well as Europe, the snood returned as a netted bag hair accessory in the 1860s. After a brief fashion run, the snood did not appear again until the 1940s when it was considered a stylish way to hold longer hair back from machinery and mechanic work.

The Snood in the United States

In the late 1850s and early 1860s, using netting to decorate the hair came into fashion. *Godey's Lady's Book* carried instructions for creating hair netting out of chenille, braid, velvet, crocheted or knitted lace, or netted yarn. The word "snood" was not used in the United States but was used in Europe for the same fashion. In the 1940s, the snood returned to the everyday woman's fashion scene. Its practicality for holding the hair back was valued by working women. After the war, it fell out of mainstream fashion. In the late twentieth and early twenty-first centuries, Orthodox Jewish women have found its shape practical for covering the hair.

During the 1860s, when the snood (or netting, as it was called in the United States) was a stylish accessory, it was deemed most appropriate for young women. The accessory fell out of fashion by the 1870s. When it was revived in the 1940s, women who worked in industry found it practical for keeping long hair enclosed, while adding color and interest to a woman's wardrobe. When women returned to care for the home after the war, the snood fell out of favor again.

Married Orthodox Jewish women who cover their hair for religious reasons of modesty, called *tzniut*, have revived the snood as one style choice for covering. Snoods for sale on Jewish modesty sites are made entirely of fabric, netted material lined with fabric, or netted material without the extra lining. Women who wear snoods in the twenty-first century are usually covering their hair for religious reasons.

Influence and Impact

Netted hair coverings have gone in and out of style for thousands of years. In the nine-teenth century, women's fashions were heavily influenced by what was known to be worn on the continent. The snood transferred to the United States as hair netting just as the Civil War started. Directions for creating your own versions were found in women's mag-azines through the early part of the 1860s, but were well out of fashion in the magazines by mid-decade. Elsa Schiaparelli added a netted bag to hold hair to hat designs, bringing the snood back into mainstream America by the start of World War II. Women in factories and plants assisting with the war effort but still being extolled to remain feminine found the snood to be a pretty but practical adornment while working. It fell out of favor with mainstream fashion.

The snood has made a comeback in Orthodox Jewish circles. In the quest for a variety of hair coverings that are acceptable or can be made acceptable, the snood, along with scarves, berets, wigs, and even baseball caps, has joined the ranks of items needed to create a modest look according to Jewish law.

See also FEDORA; SHTREIMEL; TALLIT; TZITZIT; YARMULKE (KIPPAH)
Compare to BATTENBERG LACE; BERET; RASTA HAT

Further Reading

Hennessy, Kathryn, ed. *Fashion: The Definitive History of Costume and Style*. New York: Dorling Kindersley, 2012.
"Obsolete Fashion: All Good in the Snood?" *ModCloth*, March 29, 2010, http://blog.modcloth .com/2010/03/29/all-good-in-the-snood (accessed May 31, 2013).
Schiller, Mayer. "The Obligation of Married Women to Cover Their Hair." *Journal of Halacha and Con-temporary Society* 30 (Fall 1995): 81–108.

■ JENNIFER VAN HAAFTEN

SOMBRERO

The Spanish translation of the word "sombrero" is "hat." It is a derivative of the word *sombra*, which means "shade." Sombrero is a type of head wear that has a wide brim and was primarily worn in farming communities or on ranches. They featured a round crown that varied in height. Some of the crowns were quite short, while others were incredi-bly tall and became pointed toward the top. The width of the brim ranged from four to eight inches, which provided protection to wearers from the elements. There are some sombreros with a more exaggerated brim that can be up to two feet wide! Sombreros usually have one side that is turned up.

Through the years, sombreros also took on an alternative function as a way to provide shade while a siesta, or midday nap, was taken. These hats have strong influences tied to Mexico, and it is interesting to note that there has been very little change in the design or style of the sombrero over several hundred years.

History

Mestizos, who were rural farmworkers and peasants in Mexico, traditionally wore these specialized types of hat made out of straw. Typically they were created out of raw materials that the workers found locally. The style was created for utilitarian purposes as it provided good coverage of the head and neck, thereby protecting individuals from the elements. Bandanas were often worn underneath the sombrero to absorb perspiration, as the straw would not wick the moisture away. For field use, the hats are generally very plain since they get dirty and sweaty. Wealthier individuals had sombreros made out of felt.

The Sombrero in the United States

The sombrero came into the United States through Texas as many of the Mexican horsemen wore the wide-brimmed hat. History illustrates horsemen wearing these types of hat as far back as the thirteenth century. Sombreros always have a chin strap to ensure that the hat will stay in place and not blow away. This makes them very useful in all types of situations, including riding horses.

It is speculated that the sombrero was the original influencer of the American cowboy hat. This theory makes perfect sense since sombreros were made popular by horsemen on Texas ranches. Some variations of the sombrero have the same indentation in the crown that cowboy hats do. Obviously the main difference between the two types of head wear is the width of the brim. The fabrication used for both types of hat is even similar. Cowboy hats for workers, especially on ranches, are made of straw, whereas the more formal cowboy hat is made out of felt. The original cowboy hat was created by John Stetson in 1865.

Influence and Impact

The sombrero is a strong representative of Mexican culture and heritage. Tourists often purchase elaborate versions of the headdress while visiting Mexico as a remembrance of their trip. Many Mexican-Americans also have sombreros for special occasions or decorative purposes such as Charro Days in Texas.

See also HUARACHES; MARIACHI SUIT; MEXICAN TOURIST/SOUVENIR JACKET; PONCHO; SERAPE; WESTERN WEAR
Compare to CONICAL ASIAN HAT; FEDORA; SLOUCH HAT (AUSTRALIAN); TAM-O'-SHANTER

Further Reading

Bender, Texan Bix. *Hats & the Cowboys Who Wear Them.* Layton, UT: Gibbs Smith, 2002.
Carlson, Paul Howard. *The Cowboy Way: An Exploration of History and Culture.* Lubbock, TX: Texas Tech University Press.

■ LUANNE MAYORGA

T

TABI

Tabi are a traditional Japanese sock-like form of footwear, usually ankle high and having a separation between the big toe and the other toes. Unlike socks, they are not elastically fitted but rather sewn from cloth cut to shape. Because of this they are open at the back to be slipped on and then fastened with a clasp or button closure. Traditionally this was done with a *kohaze*, a coin-shaped clasp, but later buttons were used.

History

In Japan tabi had their origin in the custom of removing footwear when coming indoors. Tabi were worn outside with traditional thonged footwear such are the *zōri* and geta, but were also elegant enough to be worn formally indoors. They were worn by both men and women, and in the Edo period (1603–1868) they were worn primarily by the ruling samurai class. Sumptuary laws during the Edo period regulated clothing expenditures, and different social classes were restricted from certain materials, colors, and other forms of display. Since the Meiji period (1868–1912), when the feudal social classes were abolished, one of the major cultural shifts was the adoption of samurai culture by the entire population. While tabi are not mentioned specifically in the sumptuary edicts, their whiteness would have made them impractical for the working classes except for special occasions such as weddings. While white tabi were the most common color, especially in formal situations, there were also black and blue varieties for traveling. Samurai were required by law to spend alternate years in the city of Edo, and so traveling culture became very important.

In the twentieth century, tabi underwent a significant transformation in Japan, in parallel with, or perhaps even predated by, similar transformations in the United States. Working classes, particular those whose work required a heavy use of their feet also wore a variety of tabi called *jika-tabi*, or tabi that made contact with the ground. Construction workers, farmers, and rickshaw pullers favored these styles. Some of these had tough materials like rough fabric sewn in many layers on the sole; however, the big innovation came with invention and the widespread availability of rubber. In Japan, Ishibashi Tokuji-rō, brother of Ishibashi Shōjirō, founder of the Bridgestone tire company, is credited with their invention in 1923. Their popularity in Japan stems from the way they give the wearer tactile contact with the ground so that the wearer can be sure of what is underfoot. This

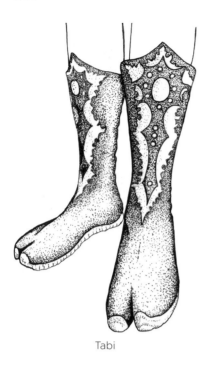

Tabi

was especially helpful for construction workers traversing scaffolding, and the separated toe also allowed objects to be held in place like an extra set of hands. Knee-high rubber varieties were also developed for work in rice fields and for fishermen.

Tabi in the United States

The first generation of Japanese immigrants to Hawai'i wore tabi with soft soles like the ones they had worn in Japan; however, they were not suitable for work on the sugarcane and pineapple plantations and lasted less than a month. Sharp rocks cut through the soft soles too easily, and Japanese women experimented to make them stronger. They used *ahina*, the Hawai'ian term for blue denim, sewn onto the base. Initially they used second-grade material with four or five layers, but they later found that the more expensive, top-quality *ahina* was more cost effective, as it lasted longer. As Japanese immigrants could not afford shop tabi, most tabi were sewn at home. After World War I there was sufficiently cheap surplus rubber from conveyor belts and tires for experimentation with rubber-soled tabi. Later these were imported from Japan.

In the United States, traditional white tabi were also part of a typical wedding trousseau brought to America by Japanese women in arranged marriages. Tabi were worn by the first Japanese winner of the Boston Marathon, Shigeki Tanaka, in 1951, but being only six years after World War II, there was no subsequent craze for tabi as running footwear. Sixty years later, however, divided-toe running shoes did experience a boom. Tabi also enjoy popularity in the United States as martial arts shoes and are sometimes referred to as ninja shoes. Although the covert mercenary of feudal Japan did wear special footwear to walk quietly, they had faded into popular myth by the time of the invention of rubber.

Influence and Impact

Like many aspects of clothing in modernity, tradition was being invented to provide a narrative of the past, to bind nations together, and to help make sense of the rapidly changing future. Japanese immigrants to the United States brought ceremonial tabi with them as a token of the world they were leaving behind, but it was only recently that it would have become common among their social class in Japan. Likewise, the tabi's use in martial arts and as an expression of some traditional knowledge in running shoes are also recent inventions.

See also HAORI; HAPPI; JAPANESE STREET FASHION; KIMONO; OBI
Compare to BIRKENSTOCKS; CLOGS; MOCCASINS; UGG FOOTWEAR

Further Reading

Dalby, Liza. *Kimono: Fashioning Culture*. London: Random House, 1993.
Kawakami, Barbara F. *Japanese Immigrant Clothing in Hawaii, 1885–1941*. Honolulu: University of Hawaii Press, 1993.
Minnich, Helen Benton. *Japanese Costume and the Makers of Its Elegant Tradition*. Tokyo: Tuttle, 1963.
Slade, Toby. *Japanese Fashion: A Cultural History*. Oxford: Berg, 2009.

■ TOBY SLADE

TALLIT

A tallit is a cloak to be worn around the shoulders of an observant Jewish male during morning prayer throughout the week and on Shabbat (the Sabbath) and other holy days. The word "tallit" is a combination of two Hebrew words, *tal* meaning "tent" and *ith* meaning "little." Tallitot (the plural of "tallit") are generally made of silk or wool, and they are white with navy or black stripes along the shorter ends so that threads of blue are present in each tassel found at the four corners. The tallit should be long enough to cover the entire body, but not so long that it drags on the floor. The tallit is folded precisely and draped over the shoulders like a shawl, but not worn around the neck like a scarf. Prescribed blessings are recited before putting on the tallit. Many times the blessing is embroidered on the ornamental collar (*atarah*) that lies against the wearer's neck. Most importantly, the purpose of the tallit is to hold the tzitzit (hanging tassels), which are attached on each of the four corners of the tallit. The tzitzit are meant to remind the wearer of God's commandments.

History

The tallit itself was not originally associated with prayer and has no religious significance. However, during the Middle Ages when the tzitzit was in danger of becoming obsolete, Jews began wearing the four-corned tallit with attached tzitzit to remind themselves of the commandments in the Torah. Nighttime wear of the tallit is prohibited to preserve the significance of the tzitzit.

The larger cloak version of the tallit is known as the *tallit gadol* (large tallit). However, a smaller poncho-shaped version of the garment exists for the more observant male who wishes to wear the tzitzit all the time. This is called the *tallit katan* (small tallit). It is about three feet long with a foot-long opening for the head. Ultra-Orthodox men begin wearing the *tallit katan* from childhood as an undergarment.

The tallit was originally daily wear that served the utilitarian purpose of protecting the wearer from climatic elements until it became a religious garment for prayer. It is actually a derivative of the Roman pallium (a church vestment) or the Greek himation (a garment worn by ancient philosophers). In fact, in Talmudic times, only wealthy, learned men and rabbis wore the tallit before the common man wore it. For almost two thousand years, only men could wear the tallit. In most Orthodox communities, men begin to wear the tallit only after marriage to signify their new status. The Ultra-Orthodox men wear the tallit over their head as they pray, where the act of wrapping the body and head with the tallit implies isolation of the person and protection during prayer. It can also be interpreted as wrapping oneself in God's laws.

The Tallit in the United States

The tallit, like many other Jewish garments, made its way into American culture through the Jewish Diaspora, the mass migration of Jews from Europe and Russia into the United States to avoid persecution in their homelands.

Today, everyone in the Reform, Conservative, and Reconstructionist synagogues may wear the tallit. Boys receive their first tallit on their Bar Mitzvah at the age of twelve or thirteen. Girls can now receive the tallit for their Bat Mitzvah. However, Orthodox synagogues still prohibit women from wearing the tallit because it is considered men's garb. The tallit is often present at other Jewish rites of passage. It is frequently used as a chuppah (the wedding canopy) during weddings and as a burial shroud for men.

Influence and Impact

Although it may be hard to imagine, this seemingly plain religious garment has been appropriated by the fashion industry on several occasions. In 2008, Korean-born designer Gunhyo Kim's *Hasidic Chic* line paraded male models down the catwalk sporting the new "hot Hasidic" look, complete with a *spodek* and *tallit katan*, taking the sacred garment and turning it into a high-fashion item. More recently, in 2012, Polish fashion magazine *Viva! Moda* featured a spread called "The Orthodox," showing a male model in skinny jeans and a leather bomber jacket, topped off with a tallit katan and yarmulke.

See also FEDORA; SHTREIMEL; SNOOD; TZITZIT; YARMULKE (KIPPAH)
Compare to BURNOUS; CHADOR; HIJAB; JILBAB; SHAWL

Further Reading

Emmett, Ayala. "A Ritual Garment, the Synagogue, and Gender Questions." *Material Religion* 5, no.1 (2007): 76–87.
Temple of San Jose. "The Tallit." http://www.templesanjose.org (accessed September 9, 2012).

■ JESSICA STRÜBEL

TAM-O'-SHANTER

A tam-o'-shanter is a cap, or male bonnet, of Scottish origin. It is named after the protagonist Tam O'Shanter in the poem of the same name, written by the Scottish poet Robert Burns and published in 1791. Often referred to as a tam, it is worn tight on the forehead facilitated by a band approximately one inch in width, with no brim, and a flat, round crown. The cap is traditionally constructed in a cylindrical fashion, with six equal "pie segments" that compose the top circle, often featuring a pom-pom in the center. Historically, the tam-o'-shanter was made of woven wool fabric, often of Scottish tartan. Tams are also knitted by hand and now are commercially manufactured. The tam is closely associated with traditional Scottish dress and military uniform.

History

During World War I, Scottish soldiers wore the tam as part of their official military uniform. This wartime tam was designed in khaki and resembled a Balmoral bonnet, a tam with ribbons attached at the center back of the head, which originally served to secure the hat to the head as a chin strap but often remained untied, the ribbons dangling down the back. Today, the uniform of the Royal Regiment of Scotland features a tam as its official headdress. The military-issued tam is distinguished between regiments by hackles, or small feathered plumes attached to the tam as decoration or trim. Some regiments in the British Commonwealth, including Canada and Australia, wear the tam.

In the 1920s, the hand-knitted tam became widely popular and featured traditional knitting designs from Fair Isle, an island in northern Scotland. Fair Isle knitting is characterized by colorful, two-stranded hand knitting that forms small, repeated, geometric motifs through the fabric. Fair Isle knitted tams were constructed in the same method as woven fabric tams, with typically six equal "pie segments" resembling a triangular design. Through the 1920s, Fair Isle knitting was endorsed by the British royalty and immortalized by Edward, Prince of Wales, who played golf in Fair Isle sweaters, which were also featured in his portraiture. British trends were brought into the United States in part as a result of the official visits of Prince Edward, who successfully shifted American attitudes toward British royalty through a democratic demeanor.

The Tam-o'-shanter in the United States

As an ambassador to the United States, Edward assumed an iconic status venerated both for his royal status and his modernity. As one of the first popular-culture celebrities, he became an international trendsetter, bringing many British clothing styles to American shores.

Influence and Impact

The tam is utilized in certain universities as part of academic ceremonial dress for doctoral candidates, in contrast to the mortarboard headdress associated with undergraduate education. The academic tam derived from the Tudor bonnet, a round fabric cap with a ribbon and tassel trim, the precursor to the modern-day graduation tassel.

See also KILT; SCOTTISH SWEATER
Compare to BERET; SLOUCH HAT (AUSTRALIAN)

Further Reading

Banks, Jeffrey, and Doria de La Chapelle. *Tartan: Romancing the Plaid*. New York: Rizzoli Publishing, 2007.
Burns, Robert. *Tam O'Shanter*. Edinburgh, Scotland: Birlinn Publishers, 2011.
Hannan, Martin. *Harvey Wallbangers and Tam O'Shanters: A Book of Eponyms*. London: John Blake Publishing, 2012.
Reid, Stuart. *Scottish National Dress and Tartan*. Oxford: Shire Publishing, 2013.

■ JENNIFER DALEY

TAQIYA

The taqiya is a small, soft skullcap worn throughout North Africa, East Africa, and the Middle East for reasons of climate or religious faith. Usually of white cotton, stitched and/or embroidered, the taqiya may also be crocheted, and either style may be colored. It is worn alone or as the base for further headdress. Its name varies by region (*'araqiyeh*, *taqiyeh*, *taqiyah*, *taqiyya*, *kap takiya*, etc.) and derives from the Arabic word meaning "to sweat"; such caps serve to absorb the wearer's perspiration so that it does not damage the outer head wear.

History

In addition to its practical function, the taqiya serves as the basic head covering for Muslims. It originated as part of early Islamic dress, based on verses in the Qur'an pertaining to covering the body as a moral imperative. Both men and women were expected to cover their heads and hair, as well as their indoor clothing, when in public.

In Africa, in the Republic of Djibouti, men of the Issa, a Somali clan, and the Afar, who also inhabit Ethiopia, wear the taqiya. Both groups are followers of Islam and wear urban Muslim dress including long white shirts over pants, or secondhand clothing originally manufactured for the West. In nearby Eritrea, the Bilen ethnic group and other Muslim men wear similar dress, adding a white vest or tailored jacket to the ensemble, which is topped off by a taqiya.

Turkish Ottomans arrived in Egypt in 1517 and influenced the dress of the Egyptians they employed, as well as others emulating the new elite. Men's headdress included a taqiya worn under a fez and, often, turban. Although the taqiya usually refers to a man's cap, a woman's cotton skullcap was described as a taqiya in this region in the early nineteenth century.

Examples of women's taqiya are also found in the Kyrgyz Republic (more commonly, Kyrgyzstan) in Central Asia. Married women wear plaited hairstyles and white turbans over a plain bonnet known in the north as *kap takiya* or simply *takiya*. In Lebanon, an elaborate headdress for a woman from Tripoli begins with a taqiya made of silk or cotton embroidered with colored or metallic threads, covered by a long veil, then a tarbush or fez. This is topped by several more layers, including metallic discs, and a shawl or veil that hangs to the ground.

The women of Ma'an, in southern Jordan, don festive dress that reflects the richness and variety of their city's place as a trading hub between Damascus and Mecca and Medina for over two thousand years. Their headgear starts with a taqiya, here meaning a small, embroidered cap held with a headband decorated with coins and glass beads. This is covered by the right sleeve of their dress, folded back and draped over the head, which in turn is covered by a coat made of patterned silk or silk and cotton.

The Taqiya in the United States

Despite these colorful examples, the taqiya most often refers to the aforementioned skullcap worn by Muslim men throughout the Eastern Mediterranean from medieval times to the present. These include urban dwellers as well as villagers and nomads in Syria; the Gulf states of Bahrain, Kuwait, and Qatar; and the United Arab Emirates. A typical Arabian man's headdress in the late twentieth and early twenty-first centuries starts with a taqiya, over which is worn a head cloth, held by a circlet called an *'aqal*. The taqiya comes to the United States via what is termed *al-zayy al-Islami*, or "global Islamic dress."

For men, *al-zayy al-Islami* comprises the taqiya, a loose white shirt over pants, and, often, a beard. Those wishing to visibly proclaim their observance of Islam and their adherence to Muslim organizations wear this style. The taqiya is traditionally a symbol of religious faith rather than a fashion statement. It meets the requirements of its Islamic wearers to cover their heads in public at all times, and to touch their foreheads to the ground in prayer without the need to remove the brimless taqiya. A Western convert to Islam might choose to wear the taqiya with the traditional clothing of his ethnic group or culture, provided such clothing is modest.

Influence and Impact

The taqiya is most often worn in order to signal the wearer's allegiance to Islam, and/or to display pride of ancestry. Western celebrities including athlete Mike Tyson and rap artist Snoop Dogg proclaim their Muslim faith by occasionally wearing the cap in public, although not as frequently as a more traditional adherent might. There are non-Muslim members of the entertainment and music industry who add a baseball cap–style brim to a colorful skull-cap base and thus fashionably adapt the taqiya. Such wearers may be honoring their ethnic heritage or simply proclaiming allegiance to a contemporary subculture or style tribe.

See also FEZ; KUFI; SIRWAL; THAWB
Compare to BLANGKON; SHTREIMEL; TOQUE; TURBAN; YARMULKE (KIPPAH)

Further Reading

Anawalt, Patricia Rieff. *The Worldwide History of Dress*. New York: Thames & Hudson, 2007.
Harvey, Janet. *Traditional Textiles of Central Asia*. London: Thames & Hudson, 1997.
Rajab, Jehan S. *Costumes from the Arab World*. Kuwait: Tareq Rajab Museum, 2002.
Topham, John M., Anthony L. Landreau, and William E. Mulligan. *Traditional Crafts of Saudi Arabia*. London: Stacey International, 1981.
Weir, Shelagh. *Palestinian Costume*. London: British Museum Publications, 1989.

■ TRACY JENKINS

TAQIYAH
See TAQIYA

TAQIYEH
See TAQIYA

TAQIYYA
See TAQIYA

THAWB

The thawb, also *thobe* or *thob*, is an ankle-length gown or tunic usually with long sleeves that is commonly worn in Arabic countries. "Thawb" is the Arabic word for clothing and

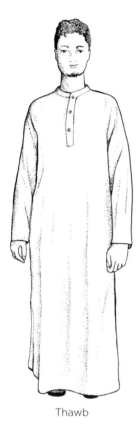

Thawb

is the word used specifically to describe the main garment worn by men in Arab states of the Persian Gulf. The thawb resembles a long-sleeved, ankle-length dress shirt with center front opening. The thawb has a pointed shirt collar with stand or a straight stand-up collar with a center front-button placket. The thawb generally has cuffed sleeves, but not in all cases or every version of the garment. It is most often made of a cotton or cotton/polyester-blended lightweight fabric. A sirwal—long, loose-fitting cotton trousers—is commonly worn underneath. In Iraq, Kuwait, and Oman, the same garment is known as the *dishasha*, and in the Emirates it is known as the *kandoura*. Regionally, small differences in styling exist. For example, in Qatar the sleeves are cuffed and secured by dress buttons or cuff links made of gold, precious stones, or diamonds.

The thawb worn in the Arab Gulf has three pockets: one square chest pocket on the left-hand side and two deep side-slit pockets on each hip. In the Emirates, the *kandoura* uses small cotton thread-ball buttons to fasten the center front and neck opening. The thawb is most often bright white or off-white but is sometimes soft gray or blue. Light colors are worn during summer months, with dark colors such as brown, gray, or deep green worn during winter months. The winter thawb is made from lightweight wool or wool-blended fabric. In Kuwait, the thawb is commonly made of silk fabric. Clothing worn in the Arabian Peninsula historically has been shaped by its harsh climate, characterized by extreme heat, little surface water, and great deserts. Arabian dress is adapted to the rigors of the desert. Temperatures during summer months can go as high as 122 degrees Fahrenheit (50 degrees Celsius) but are much cooler at night. The thawb, a loose layered garment, provides natural insulation and circulation for cooling. Geographically, the Arabian Peninsula has remained relatively isolated, and no foreign power has ever controlled the harsh inlands. The countries in this region seem to have been less influenced by the outside. It should be noted that the term "thawb" is also used to refer to similar garments worn by women in some Middle Eastern countries. The traditional Palestinian woman's gown, as well as long tunics worn by women in Syria, Jordan, and Oman, is also referred to as a thawb. The long tunic may have straight or triangular sleeves and is usually decorated with embroidery around the neck, chest, and sides. Often in black, red, and other solid colors, a variety of styling is found, reflecting individual cultures in the regions where worn.

History

Islam, one of the major monotheistic religions of the world, was founded in the early seventh century CE in the region that now comprises Saudi Arabia. The Islamic religion brought with it concepts of what was and was not acceptable in all aspects of life, including dress. During the pre-Islamic period, easygoing attitudes toward nudity existed; however, the arrival of Islam ushered in a new modesty code. Early Muslim traditions recommended modesty and austerity in dress and avoidance of extravagance. Islam holds a moralistic view on the purpose of clothing and dress in general, and dress has played an important role in the history of the Islamic world. During the medieval period, Islamic dress consisted of garments worn in three or more layers composed of under-, middle, and outer garments that covered and concealed the shape of the wearer's body. The number of layers and garments varied depending on a person's wealth. Garments worn outdoors by women were meant to further conceal the body, and men's clothing was to be modest and not ostentatious. Over time, with the expansion of Islam throughout Southwest Asia and northern Africa, three styles of dress prevailed, creating what is known today as the Islamic vestimentary system or Islamic style of dress. The three styles included (1) loose, flowing, and untailored garments, suitable for living in hot dry climates and conditions; (2) Greco-Roman tunics and wraps of various kinds that included cut and sewn garments; and (3) cut and shaped Irano-Turkic garments with tailored forms emphasizing the shape of the human body. It is important to note that many variations in Islamic style of dress have existed over time and continue to exist today.

The Thawb in the United States

Pan-Islamic dress is a global fashion that became popular at the end of the twentieth and beginning of the twenty-first centuries with the rise of nationalist and Islamist movements in Islamist countries. For men, this style of dress was comprised of a loose white shirt (*qamis*), baggy pants (sirwal), a skullcap (taqiya), sandals, and a beard. For women, emphasis is on hijab, or covering, always with some type of head veil and loose-fitting, floor-length outer garment such as a jilbab or *abayeh*.

In the United States the thawb is not commonly worn in an everyday working context but is worn by Islamic men when attending Friday prayers, on religious holidays, or when relaxing at home. Many Muslim men in the West choose not to wear pan-Islamic fashion daily due to its being perceived as foreign, outdated, and unfashionable as well as an indicator of religious fanaticism or political extremism.

Influence and Impact

In the early 2000s several British and American designers have emerged offering modest, contemporary styles of dress reflecting modern styles of today and traditional Islamic beliefs and values for women. Very recently, a Western interpretation of Islamic dress for men can be seen emerging. A British website offers customers worldwide designer thawbs made from a wide range of fabrics, styled with contrasting yokes, zippers, and trim. Styling integrates elements of what is perceived as Islamic and Western, creating thawbs suitable to be worn in the office, at home, or for formal functions.

See also SIRWAL; TAQIYA
Compare to BOUBOU; BURNOUS; CAFTAN; DASHIKI; DJELLABA; JILBAB

Further Reading

Coyler, Heather Ross. *The Art of Arabian Costume: A Saudi Arabian Profile*. Clarens, Switzerland: Arabesque Commercial, 1994.

Moors, Annelies, and Emma Tarlo. "Introduction." Special double issue of *Fashion Theory* 11, nos. 2–3 (2007): 133–42. doi:10.2752/136270407X202718.

Stillman, Yedida. *Arab Dress: A Short History from the Dawn of Islam to Modern Time.* Leiden: Brill, 2000.
Tarlo, Emma. "Islamic Fashion Scape." *Berg Fashion Library* 5 (September 2010). doi:http://dx.doi
    .org/10.2752/9781847888624/VISIBYLMUSLIM0009.

■ VIRGINIA M. NOON

THOB
See THAWB

THOBE
See THAWB

TIE-DYED APPAREL
Tie-dyeing is applied to apparel by folding the fabric into different patterns and binding it
with strings or rubber bands. Dyes are then applied to various parts of the fabric, resulting
in colorful designs. Most tie-dyers use reactive dyes because these dyes are effective on
cellulosic fibers like cotton, which happens to be the fiber most often used for tie-dye.

History
Bright colors have charmed humanity since prehistoric times. China has been producing
a method of tie-dye since the sixth century. In China, tie-dye cloth depicted status, worn
only by priests and the wealthy. Traders have traded tie-dye garments and merchandise in
Asia, India, and the Far East. Traders packed tie-dye cloths as part of their merchandise.
In Japan, tie-dyeing was applied on kimonos by using colored thread; Japanese tie-dye
has been named *shibori*. Other parts of the world that have enjoyed the art of tie-dye on
garments are Peru, Nigeria, and other parts of the west coast of Africa.

Tie-Dyed Cloth in the United States
Tie-dyeing was introduced in the United States around the turn of the 1900s, but it was
popularized in the 1960s. During the height of the hippie movement, modern psychedelic tie-dye became a popular fad in the United States and was also influenced by rock
stars such as Janis Joplin and John Sebastian.

   Tie-dye became popular in the 1960s as an inexpensive way to customize cheap T-shirts,
costumes, jeans, and other surplus garments into psychedelic creations. Tie-dye garments were
particularly prevalent among American youth who opposed the Vietnam War (1954–1975).

   Tie-dye garments lost popularity in the 1980s; however, they reappeared in mainstream fashion in the 1990s. But, unlike in the 1960s, the tie-dyed clothes were mass
produced and sold in large malls and retail outlets.

Influence and Impact
Tie-dye served as a form of artistic expression for the hippies, who were a psychedelic
generation and were free spirited. These uninhibited peace lovers of the 1960s embellished
T-shirts, draperies, embroideries, jeans, and whatever else would pronounce their uniqueness.

Tie-dye has remained the utmost symbol of the sixties. Tie-dye made people happy then, as it does today. Today, making a tie-dye T-shirt is a popular project idea for families, schools, and summer camps. Many department stores and online stores sell tie-dye T-shirts.

See also BATIK CLOTH APPAREL

Compare to CALICO AND CHINTZ; CHAMBRAY; KENTE CLOTH; PAJ NTAUB (HMONG FLOWER CLOTH)

Further Reading

Edwards, Eiluned. "Cloth and Community: The Local Trade in Resist-Dyed and Block-Printed Textiles in Kachchh District, Gujarat." *Textile History* 38, no. 2 (2007): 179–97.

Hedlund, Ann Lane. "Contemporary Tie and Dye Textiles of Indonesia." *American Anthropologist* 100, no. 3 (1998): 766–67. doi:10.1525/aa.1998.100.3.766.

Kusimba, Chapurukha. "Printed and Dyed Textiles from Africa (Book)." *Visual Anthropology* 17, no. 2 (April 2004): 197–98.

Pellew, Charles E. "Tied and Dyed Work: An Oriental Process with American Variations." *Craftsman* 16 (1909): 695–701.

"The Psychedelic Tie-Dye Look." *Time*, January 26, 1970.

■ PRISCILLA N. GITIMU

TOQUE (TUQUE)

A toque, or tuque, is a small, usually brimless knitted cap worn at the top toward the back of the head. The toque was originally made of red wool and was worn by French Canadians in Quebec and the Maritime provinces as well as by woodsmen in northern New England. The watch cap was a knitted navy blue hat worn by U.S. Navy seaman until the 1970s. Other U.S. servicemen wore similar head covers of various colors. Growing up in New England, children called this knitted hat a stocking cap. Usually this hat was much longer, and in the 1960s it could be as long as to the waist of the wearer. Sometimes a toque would be double-knitted, with one end turned into the other to form a very warm hat. Pom-poms, of the same or contrasting yarn, could be affixed to the very top or end of the cap. A white chef's hat is also called a toque.

History

Perhaps the toque began with the Persians or with the Assyrians, both costume styles including a cap-like head covering, but more conical in shape than the toque of today. The Phrygian cap worn by Trojans and often depicted on Greek vases resembles the toque worn in the eighteenth and twentieth centuries. A close relative of today's toque is the red cap worn by French revolutionists of the late eighteenth and early nineteenth centuries. It was worn to show camaraderie with the new government and symbolized liberty.

The Toque in the United States

The toque functioning symbolically as the "Cap of Liberty" is visible in many official examples in the United States. The state seals of Iowa, West Virginia, and North Carolina;

Toque

the seal of the U.S. Senate; some U.S. coins; and the U.S. Department of the Army seal all feature a red toque.

Influence and Impact

The toque was quite noticeable at the 2010 Vancouver Olympic Winter Games, especially with the athletes and on Mukmuk, one of the Olympic mascots. Many toques came to the United States as souvenirs of those games. French Canadian immigrants working in the northern woods of New England and New York are credited with first wearing the toque in the United States. Many northern New England ski teams and youth groups wore the toque as part of their team uniforms.

Today, the toque is a cap that is worn by many in the colder climates of the United States. It is mass produced in acrylic and cotton as well as wool. Manufactured by international and U.S. companies, they are available in various colors and patterns, brimmed or not, with or without pom-poms, earflaps or not. This modest head covering can be elaborately knitted and decorated.

Once worn by Canadian immigrants for cold-weather protection or group identity, one can now see toques on college campuses in the suburbs, as well as in cities, in warmer weather as well as cold. The toque, tuque, or beanie is worn by many.

See also CH'ULLU; RASTA HAT
Compare to BERET; SNOOD; TAM-O'-SHANTER; TAQIYA

Further Reading

Little, Gordie. *Toque, Tuque, Bruque: What's the Difference?* Plattsburgh, NY: Press Republican. http://pressrepublican.com/0205_columns/x1491887695/Toque-tuque-bruque-Whats-the-difference.

■ IRENE M. FOSTER

TRENCH COAT

The trench coat is a long belted raincoat, made from a waterproof fabric such as heavy-duty cotton, drill, or poplin. Typically the trench is a ten-button, double-breasted long coat in a tan, khaki, beige, or black color. The coat has cuff straps on the sleeves and epaulettes (a shoulder piece worn on military uniforms), which were originally used to hold gloves and folding service caps in the trench coat's former life as a military uniform. The belt design may sometimes have two small brass D-rings, further testament to its military origins, as these would have been used to hold swords, grenades, binoculars, or gas masks. In cases it may have a detachable lining.

History

The trench coat has journeyed from its origins as an item of military clothing to become an iconic fashion item popularized across the globe. It was created in England supposedly by the clothing manufacturer Thomas Burberry, the founder of the Burberry brand, and dates back to 1895. However, the British outerwear company Aquascutum, founded earlier in 1851 by Mayfair (London) tailor John Emary, also lays claim to creating the trench coat. The name Aquascutum is derived from Latin *aqua*, meaning "water," and *scutum*, meaning "shield." Emary patented a shower-proof technology in 1853 that was subsequently used to outfit British soldiers in waterproof coats during the Crimean War (1853–1856). However, it is through Burberry that the trench coat has its most documented history.

It began life as a waterproof smock-like garment worn by shepherds, farmers, and country gentlemen with a functional quality for protection from the rain and wind. In 1888 Burberry patented a revolutionary new waterproof fabric called gabardine out of which the trench coat would come to be made. This material was lightweight, breathable, and durable and thus perfect for its intended function as a military garment. This new innovative fabric led to the creation of weatherproof coats that were used during both World War I and World War II and that also became the practical attire of polar explorers including Ernest Shackleton on his trek to Antarctica in 1915.

In 1895 Burberry created the "Tielocken," the predecessor to the iconic Burberry trench coat. The Tielocken was worn during the Boer War in South Africa (1899–1902) and was adopted by many British generals such as Lord Kitchener and Lord Baden-Powell. In 1906 the British War Office gave its official seal of approval to this waterproof and durable coat. The year 1914 saw the start of "trench warfare" in Europe, and epaulettes and D-ring belt fastenings were added to the coats. This new version was named the "trench coat" by the soldiers who fought in the trenches, and the name remains today, although associations and functions have changed dramatically.

The trench coat was to become the standard uniform for many armies across the world. Between the wars, the trench coat became an item of everyday wear, and in 1924 Burberry added the now famous camel, black, red, and white pattern to the linings of their trench coat. This was formally known as the "Haymarket Check" after the street in London where Burberry had opened his shop in 1891. During World War II, the trench coat once again assumed its role as uniform and was worn by personnel in the U.S. Army, U.S. Army Air Corps, and U.S. Marine Corps. A more sinister version of the trench coat, made in black leather, was adopted by the Nazi SS and became the uniform of the Gestapo officer.

The Trench Coat in the United States

The trench coat arrived in the United States both through its function as an item of military clothing and its association with Hollywood movies. *Women's Wear Daily* reported that it was Greta Garbo who set the trend for the trench coat among stylish women, having worn a trench on the set for *A Woman of Affairs* (1928). In 1929 Gloria Swanson wore a double-breasted khaki-colored trench coat in *Queen Kelly*, and in the 1930s Bette Davis famously wore a black version. Burberry started advertising its female version of the trench coat in the 1930s; however, it was during the 1940s that the coat was to change its role and meaning and begin its passage into the sphere of fashion.

It was Hollywood's use and portrayal of the coat that was to really instigate this change, with Humphrey Bogart famously wearing a Burberry trench in the movie *Casablanca*

(1942) and Audrey Hepburn wearing one in *Breakfast at Tiffany's* (1961). Later the trench coat was to become the defining feature of Inspector Clouseau in *The Pink Panther* films. Through Hollywood, the trench coat became immersed in American popular culture and fashion. Intellectuals, writers, artists, and U.S. presidents have also favored the style.

Influence and Impact

Through advertising campaigns and continued marketing by the Burberry brand, the trench coat has maintained a key position in the fashion industry. The trench coat makes regular features on street style blogs such as *The Sartorialist*, indicative of its continued popularity in the United States as an iconic fashion article. Today the coat is a staple of the fashion wardrobe, having been featured in many other designer collections, including those by Yves Saint Laurent, Giorgio Armani, Gucci, Louis Vuitton, and Dolce & Gabbana. In 2009 Burberry launched a website titled "The Art of the Trench" whose purpose is to share photographs of people wearing their trench coats past and present. "The Art of the Trench" shows how the trench coat is a culturally significant item of clothing through which its wearers can express themselves. Through its long history the trench coat has embodied the hardships of war, British style and heritage, the glamour of Hollywood, and now luxury fashion and the globalization of style.

See also DUSTER; SHEARLING
Compare to INVERNESS COAT

Further Reading

Foulkes, Nick. *The Trench Book*. London: Assouline, 2007.
King, Peter. *The Burberry Book*. London: Bloomsbury Publishing, 2000.
Tynan, Jane. "Military Dress and Men's Outdoor Leisurewear: Burberry's Trench Coat in First World War Britain." *Journal of Design History* 24, no. 2 (2011): 139–56.

■ NAOMI BRAITHWAITE

TUQUE
See TOQUE

TUQYAH
See TAQIYA

TURBAN
A headpiece created by wrapping and securing a length of fabric around the head or around a cap on the head; also an engineered, stitched headpiece meant to resemble this wrapped style. The word "turban" in English is derived from the Persian word *dulband*, literally "scarf wound around the head."

History

The turban has played an integral role in the sartorial traditions of numerous cultures throughout the world, notably in the Middle East, Southern Asia, and Africa, where it is imbued with historical, cultural, and religious significance. Though its exact origins are unclear, one of the earliest examples of a turban-like headpiece appears on a royal sculpture from Mesopotamia (present-day Iraq) dated to 2350 BCE, although evidence exists that it could have been worn as early as 2600 BCE by the Sumerian and Babylonian people of this early civilization. The depiction of the turban on numerous deity sculptures of both cultures indicates its early religious connotations. It later finds mention in the Old Testament (1200–100 BCE) and the sacred Vedic texts of India (1500–1000 BCE), and it has played a prominent role in the sartorial histories of both Islam and Sikhism, where it became an intimate marker of one's religious identity.

In addition to its religious affiliations, the turban has historically served a practical role as well as existing as a social and cultural symbol. For the Tuareg people of North Africa, for example, the turban has simultaneously served as protection from the sandy, windy climate, as well as an indicator of their Islamic faith. For the Hmong people of Southeast Asia, the removal of a black and white striped cloth from a woman's turban on her wedding day symbolizes her newly married status, while in India—as in many countries—it is intimately related to a man's honor. The width and length of the fabric, as well as the color and material used in a turban, is as varied as the cultures in which it is found and can reflect many things about the wearer, including age, social status, religion, profession, and tribal affiliation. Traditionally the turban can be comprised of a long, narrow length of fabric or a square cut of cloth. Cotton is a common material as it is readily available and inexpensive in many regions, while silk is often reserved for royalty and affluent members of society.

The Turban in the United States

The multiple routes by which the turban arrived in America are a reflection of the garment's complex and diverse cultural history. West African women brought to America as slaves in the early seventeenth century are recorded to have worn turban-like head coverings. The wrapped headdresses were a reflection of the women's cultural heritage and would remain a staple of African-American women's dress in a variety of styles and forms for the next two centuries.

Turban

Waves of immigration throughout the nineteenth century would similarly bring the sartorial traditions of many different cultures to America. Many assimilated to American standards of dress while maintaining elements of their native heritage. Photographs from the latter part of the nineteenth century attest to the wearing of the turban by Indian immigrants, as well as Muslim immigrants who continued to wear the wrapped headdress as a symbol of their Islamic faith.

The turban had been part of fashionable European attire since the fifteenth century and made subsequent appearances in dress over the succeeding centuries. Its revival in the middle of the eighteenth century was a result of increased European trade with the vast Turkish-Ottoman Empire, but it also reflected Europe's continued fascination with the art and culture of Turkey, also known as *turquerie*. Wealthy members of American society mirrored their European counterparts and commissioned portraits that incorporated foreign clothing elements as an assertion of their worldliness, knowledge, and prestige. The turban's translation into American portraiture is evident in numerous eighteenth-century portraits by artists such as John Singleton Copley, in which both men and women are depicted in interpretations of the style.

The turban similarly made its way into the fashionable American woman's dress by influence of modes in Paris and England—the leading authorities in fashion at the turn of the eighteenth century. Dolly Madison, wife of U.S. president James Madison, was a tastemaker of the period and an early champion of the *à la turquerie* style in America. The turban would continue to make repeated revivals in American fashion throughout the nineteenth and twentieth centuries. Fashions of the 1910s saw a brief introduction of the turban when a wave of Orientalism hit fashion, while the close-fitting headdress was a fashionable alternative to the cloche in the 1920s. The austere years of World War II witnessed an emphasis on head wear that embraced the diverse qualities of the turban as well.

Influence and Impact

The turban has since experienced repeated revivals throughout the twentieth century, and today it continues to be worn both as the result of a fashionable trend and as a religious and cultural marker.

See also AFRICAN HEAD WRAP; BLANGKON; HAWLI; KUFI; TAQIYA
Compare to FEDORA; SHTREIMEL; SNOOD; TALLIT; YARMULKE (KIPPAH)

Further Reading

Bhandari, Vandana. *Costume, Textile and Jewelry of India: Traditions in Rajasthan*. New Delhi: Prakash Books India, 2005.
MacKenzie, John M. *Orientalism: History, Theory, and the Arts*. New York: Manchester University Press, 1995.
Starke, Barbara M., Lillian O. Holloman, and Barbara K. Nordquist, eds. *African American Dress and Adornment: A Cultural Perspective*. Dubuque, IA: Kendall/Hunt, 1990.

■ CASSIDY ZACHARY

TZITZIT

Tzitzit are the fringe tassels that hang from the four corners of the tallit, the prayer shawl worn by observant Jewish men. The sole purpose of the tallit is to hold the tzitzit, which serve as physical reminders of God's commandments. The fringe tassels and the knots tied in the fringe must include at least one thread of blue wool called *techelet* in Hebrew. The other threads are left white. The blue dye used in the *techelet* is very expensive and must be extracted exclusively from the murex shellfish, so most Jews today wear tzitzit of white. The blue color of the *techelet* has been interpreted in several ways, each with symbolic meanings attached. Some suggest that it symbolizes the Torah or the body and the soul of the wearer. Others say it represents something more mystical and transcendental, such as God's presence.

The tzitzit is created by inserting four strands of thread through a hole in each corner of the tallit, whereby the longer strand (the *shammash*) is wrapped around the three shorter strands. A properly wrapped tzitzit will have seven, eight, eleven, and thirteen winds between double knots. One interpretation is that the sets of windings represent the letters of God's name. The tzitzit should be worn and constructed in a very specific manner; otherwise it is considered invalid. Tzitzit must always be visible to the naked eye and worn at all times when a person is dressed during daylight. Tzitzit are not worn at night because there is not enough light to see them. This is why the tzitzit of the *tallit katan* are seen hanging from beneath a man's shirt.

History

Jews have been wearing the fringes since ancient times. The commandment of the tzitzit first appears in the Pentateuch (the first five books of the Torah) where God directs the children of Israel to put a tzitzit on each corner of the tallit to remind everyone of his commandments and that he is God. According to the Talmud (Jewish law), the tzitzit were later a method to identify Jews from Christians. They would hang the fringes from the four-cornered shawls, which were a part of the daily wardrobe.

The Tzitzit in the United States

The tzitzit were worn on the tallits of the various Jewish groups that migrated to the United States. It was a part of their daily inspiration to remember who they were, where they came from, and a constant reminder of their faith.

Today, Jewish men and boys wear tzitzit in one of two ways for prayer. They either wear a small poncho-type garment called a *tallit katan* (small tallit) that fits under their shirt, or they wrap themselves in the *tallit gadol* (large tallit), which is worn during the morning prayers. Modern women of non-Orthodox Jewish sects can also choose to fulfill the commandment of wearing the tzitzit.

Influence and Impact

Because of their length, the tzitzit can be cumbersome to the active man. A fun alternative to the *tallit katan* advertised on a Judaica website is a sleeveless T-shirt designed following the laws of *kashrut* (Jewish dietary and hygienic laws). The T-shirt is olive green, with the official seal of the Israeli Defense Forces on the front and kosher tzitzit on all four corners. Likewise, Tamir Goodman, an Orthodox Israeli-American basketball player, has designed a line of sports shirts with attached tzitzit for the active, athletic male. Goodman is most widely recognized for declining an offer to play basketball for the University of Maryland because games would be played on Friday nights and Saturdays (the Jewish Sabbath).

See also FEDORA; SHTREIMEL; SNOOD; TALLIT; YARMULKE (KIPPAH)
Compare to BURNOUS; CHADOR; HIJAB; JILBAB; SHAWL

Further Reading

Ginsburgh, Harav Yitzchak. "The Tzitzit." Galeinai Publication Society. http://www.inner.org (accessed November 2, 2012).

Green, Yosef, and Pinchas Kahn. "The Mystery, Meaning and Disappearance of the Tekhlet." *Jewish Bible Quarterly* 39, no. 2 (2011) 108–14.

"Techelet-Tzitzit and Women in the Talmud." Mayyim Hayim Ministries. http://mayimhayim.org (accessed September 26, 2012).

"What Is the Tzitzit and Tallit?" Chabad. http://www.chabad.org (accessed September 24, 2012).

■ JESSICA STRÜBEL

U

UDHENG

See BLANGKON

UGG FOOTWEAR

Uggs or ugg boots are simply designed boots, usually higher than ankle length and made of sheepskin, with a flat, relatively thin rubber sole. The skin, though cleaned and dyed for certain styles, remains relatively untreated so that the classic uggs are a basic tan color. The retained wool lines the inside, while the outer layer remains raw and porous. They originated in Australia and New Zealand in the early twentieth century when these countries were the world's largest producers of wool and sheep-related products.

History

While the period of origin is unclear, it is agreed that sheepskin boots were commonly worn in rural areas. In the early twentieth century these would have been made locally, according to a simple design. In 1933 they were being manufactured by Blue Mountains Ugg Boots in New South Wales. There were several manufacturers in the 1950s, and to-day there are over seventy manufacturers in and beyond Australia and New Zealand that incorporate the name or identify with the style.

Ugg boots and their related offshoots—slippers, slip-ons, shoes, and the like—were introduced in the United States as an official brand in 1978 by Brian Smith in Southern California. The year is significant, since it was the twilight of the protest and hippie era, and the name itself is not only humorous but nostalgic of a nameless primordial age when people ran free and did not worry about style.

The name of the brand itself is the primary indicator of this: Ug, the onomatopoeic name that arises from a grunt, is in popular mythology the generic name of a cave man. Indeed the austerity and the vernacular character of ugg design endow the footwear with a sense of always having been, hence the very name itself which connotes the Paleolithic origins of humankind. Other names for the boots include "ugh" and "fug," the former word relating to their "daggy," or plebeian, reputation.

Uggs

Uggs in the United States

Hence the austerity and simplicity of the ugg design template is important, as it shows an indifference to elegance and places a premium on function and effect, namely to keep one's feet warm. As the popularity of uggs grew in the 1970s, they became increasingly associated with clean and simple living, particularly due to their raw tactile character and their austere design that gives the impression of immediacy over artifice. Uggs are persistently associated with the surf and beach culture of the American West Coast, Florida, and Australia. By the mid-1970s, numerous surf shops in Santa Cruz and the San Fernando Valley were selling ugg boots, which they had obtained from Australian manufacturers. In 1973 in Cornwall, England, the shoemakers Hide and Feet started their own line of ugg boots, and in 1990, "UGG" was a registered trademark in the United Kingdom.

Influence and Impact

By the 1990s, uggs had become a standard wear by American surfers. Their association with sport and active living was cemented when the U.S. Olympic Team wore them during the 1994 Winter Olympics. After that, uggs were also marketed together with the mountain culture of the North American Rocky Mountains. They are also a popular item in Europe in winter and a fashion in après-ski wear.

More formal versions of the ugg have been appropriated by high-end shoe manufacturers such as Bally in collections of 2012, evident in the sheepskin lining and the porous, suede exterior. In such versions, the leather is usually colored and treated to give it more shape and resilience. The characteristic seam down the middle is usually dispensed with. In previous collections, Bally has produced derivatives such as fur-lined moccasins.

The UGG brand is itself a producer of quality and coveted products that extend well beyond the "essential" boot. It makes anything from hiking boots to lady's slippers. Its signature material is sheepskin, with the interior lined with raw wool. Other products branch out to use other fur products, dispensing altogether with the quasi-primitive simplicity. However, the original ugg style serves to maintain the mythology of the brand, namely that it is environmentally sound and linked to a natural, untainted past.

In recent years uggs have come up for criticism in relation to the movement against the use of animal skins. That they were singled out against the common leather shoe is probably attributable to the way in which the skin and fur are a centerpiece of the style's design and popularity.

See also SHEARLING; SLOUCH HAT (AUSTRALIAN)
Compare to BLUNDSTONE BOOTS; BRITISH RIDING BOOTS

Further Reading

Cronin, E. "The Story of UGG." *Telegraph*, January 30, 2011, http://fashion.telegraph.co.uk/article/TMG8283572/The-story-of-Ugg.html.

■ ADAM GECZY

V

VAQUERO

See BOLERO JACKET

VEST

See WAISTCOAT

WAISTCOAT

A waistcoat is a sleeveless, front-buttoned, upper-body garment often referred to as a vest. Waistcoats were traditionally worn with a tie over a dress shirt and under a formal suit coat, contributing to the development of the classic three-piece suit style.

History

The inner-jacket garment that eventually developed into the waistcoat was introduced in the mid-1600s by the court of King Charles II of England. During this early time period, men's outercoats and inner waistcoats were the same length. In the first part of the 1700s, men typically had a silk suit in which the coat, waistcoat, and breeches all were made of the same fabric. Toward the middle of the century, waistcoats were longer in length and traditionally covered a good portion of the breeches. By the late 1770s the waistcoats were much shorter, ending around the hip area. Fabrication for waistcoats fluctuated, with formal-wear waistcoats typically matching the outercoat and pants, and more casual styles featuring a contrasting waistcoat. The shorter-style waistcoat for men began emerging in the latter part of the 1700s and dominated garments in the nineteenth century. The shorter waistcoat style was traditionally worn under the coat and began the look of what developed into the male three-piece suit. The waistcoats transformed into what we consider vests in the United States and are still worn in the twenty-first century.

The Waistcoat in the United States

The United States was under British rule until the Revolution. This fact, coupled with the strong influence of British descendants on colonial culture, resulted in the incorporation of the British waistcoat into early American formal dress styles for men. By the time of the Revolutionary War, wool ivory waistcoats and matching breeches became part of the military uniform for officers. The coat was a dark blue or royal blue with ivory accents. In the South, waistcoats were made of lighter fabrics to help with the heat of summer. In contrast, the waistcoats were also made with sleeves to give an extra layer of warmth for the colder climates. Waistcoats in both Britain and the United States began to transform to include collars and double-breasted closures. In the 1800s, waistcoats were very colorful and often had elaborate decorations, remaining that way through the 1830s. By the late 1800s, decorative fabric became fashionable, including brocades, velvets, and paisley prints. Around the time period of the Revolutionary War, tailors in the American colonies began to use less expensive fabrics for the back of the waistcoat and more expensive fabric on the front. This allowed the purchaser to save money since a coat was consistently worn over the waistcoat.

Around the 1870s the necklines of waistcoats increased and peered above the collar of the suit coat. Many of the waistcoats were now black, although white was used for formal occasions. By the late 1890s the term "waistcoat" was replaced by "vest," which consisted of a collarless, high-buttoned garment. They were now normally made of the same fabric as the rest of the suit, with some contrasts coming from checks or plaids.

Influence and Impact

The traditional three-piece suit including the waistcoat, later referred to as the vest, remained popular from the sixteenth through the twenty-first century. In the twentieth and twenty-first centuries, vests began to be worn by men without the entire suit and as part of more casual ensembles, with khaki pants or jeans. Women began to cross over and wear the vest in large numbers in the 1970s, with the wearing of menswear styles first in the workplace. Following the lead of menswear, women also began to wear the vest as a casual accent in the last decades of the twentieth and the beginning of the twenty-first centuries.

See also HARRIS TWEED; OXFORD SHIRT
Compare to ZOOT SUIT

Further Reading

Baumgarten, Linda. *Eighteenth-Century Clothing at Williamsburg.* Williamsburg, VA: Wallace Gallery Decorative Arts, 2002.

■ LUANNE MAYORGA

WESTERN WEAR

Western wear is the original style of dress more widely associated with horses and which takes its inspiration from the nineteenth-century American "horse-and-wagon," "pioneer," and "Wild West" movement.

Whether reproduced to be historically representative or stylized with a contemporary twist, collectively it is "cowboy" clothing. The classic western-wear style consists of indigo jeans, denim (jean) jacket, high hat (Stetson style), leather boots, belt with buckle, shirt, waistcoat, bolo tie, chaps, and spurs. The poncho, pleated pant (*bombachas*), sombrero, and fringed jacket acknowledge the gaucho and vaquero cowboy. Associated styles are also "mountain men" who wore fur "trapper" hats/skins, "Civil War" wear, and cavalry shirts.

History

Inherently infused with the spirit of the wanderer, the cowboy relates to the nomadic horsemen and cattle herders who migrated to the United States around the late 1700s. The "vaquero" (Spanish for "cowboy") links to the Mexican cowboy skills and clothing that originated in Spain and Portugal and developed further in Mexico and the south-western United States where it was influenced by Pueblo Indian dress. The "gaucho" cowboy is predominantly associated with South America, especially the Argentinian/Uruguayan pampas area, and is a mixture of European and Native American horsemen and their relative traditional wear.

Contemporary western wear is associated with North America and the notion of "work" clothes. Layfolk and travelers ventured west in search of better quality of life, wearing mostly self-made and serviceable attire so as to protect them from the harsh environment and work conditions of the plains in the 1800s. Cowboy clothing consistently remains durable in order to serve its original purpose as work wear. The cowboy boot emerged in the 1870s after the Civil War from Europeans bringing boot making to the frontier and creating a "four-piece-construction" boot that was hardy, better fitting, and perfect for those establishing themselves as cowboys/cattle herders.

Jeans—denim, or *de-Nimes*—emerged out of France from the region of Nimes. The indigo-dyed thick cotton twill was introduced to the United States in the 1870s by Levi Strauss, whose enduringly iconic product brand, Levi's jeans, is now a global phenomenon. It maintains its role as a key component of western wear, though in 1974, Wrangler became the official rodeo brand for cowboys.

Western Wear in the United States

Western-wear style overall is North American, and though mostly associated with casual clothing, it maintains its often overstated/"showy" look in accordance with its showmanship origins. After the American Civil War (1861–65), the romance of the Wild West and pioneer movements was utilized as performance and pageant by entrepreneurial showman Buffalo Bill, whose subjective and oftentimes inaccurate representations of Native Americans as barbarians were depicted accordingly in reenacted battles. Nevertheless the success of the show, and key characters and their clothing, impacted radically on the American cultural psyche, especially in terms of the "art of the costume" (which in various guises remains popular at parties, festivals, celebrations, holidays, and especially Halloween). Buffalo Bill's "uniform" Stetson hat of 1865 remains the "contemporary" cowboy choice of head wear, mostly made from felt. "Annie Oakley," a sharpshooting, gun-toting *girl*, with her fringe-lined embroidered jackets and skirts combined with bolo necktie, cowhide waistcoat, costume "sheriff's" badge, Stetson, and long leather boots under "chaps" (more usually worn only by men), conveyed a capable and positive female image to great effect, and her influence endures beyond the aesthetic. The gaucho poncho entered the United States in the 1850s via the military and became popular as a fashion item in the 1960s. Originally in thick wool, the versatile vaquero utilized it as a human/horse blanket and item of protective clothing (a knife was often hidden underneath). Incorporating modern man-made materials, it is used as lightweight rainwear.

The media allowed the love of the "western" to flourish and in the 1940s and 1950s created popular TV heroes Gene Autry, Roy Rogers, the Lone Ranger (famous for his leather eye mask and influenced by the Mexican vaquero), and Hopalong Cassidy. Their adoption of bold and theatrical western shirts with checkered patterning, embroidery, and fringe—often worn with a fabric necktie "bandana" (with a nod to the vaquero) and/or a "bolo," a cord or leather necktie with metal decoration from the Southwest Native

American tradition of the 1950s—created a fashion for men that remains popular and is thus associated with those "strong and heroic" characters. Significantly, the nostalgic cowboy personified by John Wayne in the film *Rio Bravo* of 1959, in which he wore "distressed" cowboy clothing, is an iconic image.

Rodeos retain their importance today, with western wear offering opportunities for the celebration of commanding-looking performance clothing. Designer Nudie is synonymous with rhinestones and rodeo, and with dressing celebrity. His tailored, unique, and distinctive creations "dazzled" by utilizing concentrated jeweled embellishment on clothing, boots, saddles, and hats. Perfect for performers, in a career spanning fifty years he created costumes for Elvis, Gram Parsons, Bootsy Collins, Cher, Lou Rawls, and Judy Lynn, notably in the 1970s designing Robert Redford's outfit in the cowboy film *Electric Horseman*.

Larry Hagman of the 1980s TV hit series *Dallas* became infamously associated with his western-style Stetson. Modern iconic musicians including Willie Nelson, Johnny Cash, Tammy Wynette, Dolly Parton, Madonna, and Lady Gaga have incorporated their own style into "cowboy/girl" clothing, utilizing its now unisex look in a romantic, provocative, or ironic context pertinent to performance. The cowboy boot could be said to possess the most expressive artistic canvas. With its wooden Cuban heel, pointed toe, and metal adornments, and whether leather, snakeskin, or fish skin, stitched, colored, or carved, it, along with western wear as a whole, tells a tale.

Influence and Impact

In its contemporary context, with several constituent pieces and accessories, western wear is persistently evolving. When stripped "back to basics," it can be understood as the triumvirate—boots, jeans, and hat. Spawning lifestyle trends from interior design to art, film, festivals, TV, theater, line dancing, cheerleader outfits, and wedding dresses, there are few parts of American culture that have not been impacted. Brands such as Ralph Lauren's collections and advertorials, which reference riding and the freedom associated with the horse, evoke a romantic and nostalgic past as seen in his vintage *Americana* collections. Significantly his "prairie dress," with full-circle ruffled skirts, became assimilated into everyday fashion wear. Creatives continue to embrace a hybridized "western" of gold and glitz, a bold and wild look, symbolic of decadence and defiance, faded elegance, or a lost historical spirit. But its appeal endures and mutates in myriad new forms of fashion, art, and technology, utilizing global media such as the blog and Twitter to create a conversation on costume previously impossible.

See also BANDANA; BOLO TIE; BUCKSKIN; COONSKIN CAP; DUSTER; PONCHO; SERAPE
Compare to MARIACHI SUIT; PORCUPINE ROACH; POWWOW ACCESSORIES; SLOUCH HAT (AUSTRALIAN)

Further Reading

Cabrall, Mary Lynn, and Jamie Lee Nudie. *The Rodeo Tailor*. Layton, UT: Gibbs Smith, 2004.
June, Jennifer. *Cowboy Boots: The Art & Sole*. New York: Universe Publishing, 2006.
Whitaker, Julie, and Ian Whitelaw. *The Horse*. East Sussex: Ivy Press, 2008.

■ WENDY ROSIE SCOTT

WINDBREAKER
See ANORAK/PARKA

WINDSOR CAP
See FLAT CAP

WINGTIPS (BROGUE SHOE)

Wingtips evolved out of the more general brogue shoe, which has its roots in Ireland and Scotland during the late 1500s. The early brogue shoe was developed as a shoe for the field-worker and featured holes allowing water to drop out of the shoe during inclement weather, thereby keeping the worker's feet dry. The wingtip is a pointy toe-cap style with perforated wing lines that run along both sides of the shoe in an extended W wing shape.

History

Irish and Scottish field-workers had to work despite the climate conditions. Feet were often soaked by the end of the day, and that is how the brogue shoe was invented. The type of outdoor conditions was very harsh in both Ireland and Scotland, where many workers were farmers or tended fields. The shoes were created to help protect the feet from getting wet when it rained and allowed the water to drain through the holes perforated in the leather.

The original brogues, precursors to the wingtip, were made from layers of untanned leather that had perforations on top to allow the water to drain from the shoe and keep the feet more comfortable. Eventually the shoe caught on and became popular in many other sectors as an outdoor working or walking shoe. The shoe remained quite plain and simple in the early years. Ultimately the style transformed as this workingman's shoe moved from the closet of a field or blue-collar worker to that of a business professional, and in this transition it became known as a wingtip.

The Wingtip Shoe in the United States

Wingtips came into the American fashion scene with soldiers arriving home from World War I with easy-to-wear, low-sided lace oxfords from England. Leaving behind the prewar high-laced and narrow footwear, these young soldiers were attracted to the comfortable British wingtip, which they associated with the trend toward shoes evoking class distinctions and leisure.

Influence and Impact

In the 1930s, wingtip shoes came into popularity as a result of advancements in leather processing. The wingtip became an Anglo icon shoe for men in the United States with an article as recently as 2010 in the *New York Times* speaking to the popularity of the style due to its link to British class and culture, and its flexible, casual-yet-formal styling. In the twenty-first century, wingtips have become a classic women's boot and shoe style as well.

See also FLAT CAP; HARRIS TWEED; OXFORD SHIRT; SCOTTISH SWEATER
Compare to BIRKENSTOCKS; BLUNDSTONE BOOTS; ESPADRILLES; HUARACHES

Further Reading

Coleman, D. "Wingtips: Beloved, Classic Now Trendy." *New York Times*, October 27, 2010, http://www
    .nytimes.com/2010/10/28/fashion/28TRADE.html?_r=0.
Payne, Blanche, Geitel Winakor, and Jane Farrell-Beck. *The History of Costume*. 2nd ed. New York: Ad-
    dison Wesley Longman, 1992.

■ LUANNE MAYORGA

WORK SHIRT
See BUSSERULL (NORWEGIAN WORK SHIRT)

Y

YARMULKE (KIPPAH)

"Kippah" is the Hebrew word for a small, round head covering worn by Jewish men. The kippah is more commonly known as a yarmulke in Yiddish, and it is the most recognizable symbol of Jewish identity. The yarmulke is worn by Orthodox Jewish men at all times and by more nonobservant men only during prayer, when in the synagogue, or during religious observations, such as high holiday dinners. There are actually many differing opinions about whether a man is obligated to wear the head covering or whether it is a matter of aligning with a Jewish identity.

The term "kippah," in some interpretations, suggests a dome-shaped, cupola-type structure or half-sphere covering modeled after a structure that covers graves. In other forms of interpretation, the word "kippah" is used as the word for a prison or a bureau of taxation. The kippah is a head covering worn on the apex of the head, and it may come in the form of a small skullcap, while others will almost cover the entire head. Kippot (the plural of "kippah") come in many different colors, styles, and fabrication. They can be knit or crocheted, made of suede or satin, and embellished with embroidery. They are usually attached to the hair with bobby pins.

History

There is Talmudic literature (Jewish law) that serves as the basis for Jewish men covering their head. For example, in Kiddushin it says that a man should never walk four cubits (approximately eight feet) with his head uncovered, but it is not a Torah-based command-ment that a man should cover his head. In Europe during the Middle Ages, the Jewish hat, a horned skullcap, was worn by Jewish men during Torah prayer and to distinguish Jews from non-Jews. By the seventeenth century, people associated wearing a yarmulke with "Jewishness."

The Yarmulke in the United States

In the mid-1800s, the first mass movement of Jews to the United States began. Another wave of global migration occurred in the twentieth century with more than five million Jews immigrating to the United States as a result of the Diaspora. Each time, Jews brought their sartorial practices, including the practice of covering the head with the kippah.

Influence and Impact

Men traditionally wear the yarmulke; however, more women are choosing to wear the skullcap as an expression of their faith and a reminder that God is constantly above them. If a woman decides to wear a yarmulke it is wholly her choice because there is no direct commandment requiring women to do so. It is believed that women do not need to be reminded to stay focused on God because they are already spiritually closer to God than men. The Orthodox tradition requires Jewish women to cover their hair out of modesty, so the yarmulke can help to serve this purpose as well for more progressive women. The female version of the yarmulke can be found in a variety of fashionable colors and textures, and it is often gifted to a young girl at her Bat Mitzvah (the Jewish coming-of-age ritual).

In Hebrew schools and liberal yeshivas across the United States, young men are making fashion statements with kitschy yarmulkes emblazoned with pop-culture symbols and logos. Anything goes when it comes to personal statements about their favorite sports teams, political views, or cartoons, even if it is using counterfeit logos, such as Nike. The latest fad is to collect yarmulkes that reflect personality as well as religious identity. It has caused controversy not only with manufacturers who do not want their logos misused, but also with rabbis who feel that with commercialization the kippah loses its true meaning.

See also FEDORA; SHTREIMEL; SNOOD; TALLIT; TZITZIT
Compare to BLANGKON; FEZ; KUFI; TAQIYA; TURBAN

Further Reading

Kershaw, Sarah. "The Skullcap as Fashion Statement." In *The Meaning of Dress*, edited by Mary Lynn Damhorst, Kimberly A. Miller-Spillman, and Susan O. Michelman, 461–63. New York: Fairchild, 2006.
Landman, L. "The Hall of Reckoning Outside of Jerusalem." *Jewish Quarterly Review* 61, no. 3 (1971): 199–211.
Rabinowitz, B. "Yarmulke: A Historic Cover-Up?" *Hakirah* 4 (2007): 221–38.

■ JESSICA STRÜBEL

Z

ZOOT SUIT

The zoot suit is an exaggerated suit style worn primarily by African-American and Latino-American men and youth in the 1940s. It had trousers with a high waist and baggy legs that suddenly narrow into tight cuffs at the bottom of the trousers. The suit coat has unnaturally wide padded shoulders that narrow tight at the hips and end in a long coat hem. The coat features extremely wide lapels and was accessorized with a long watch chain looping from the waist to nearly the ankle and back. The coat and trousers were sometimes made of the same widely spaced pinstripes or wide plaids, or of contrasting colors—a brightly colored coat over a more subdued trouser color.

History

The origins of the zoot suit are clouded. Even at the height of their notoriety in the early 1940s, newspapers disagreed on their beginnings. These papers variously attributed the invention of the special characteristics of these suits to the jazz musician Cab Calloway, the actor Clark Gable, the Duke of Windsor, or a young African-American busboy in Georgia named Clyde Duncan. In addition, a number of tailors in Harlem, New York, claimed to be the inventor of the suit. The origins may be more ordinary. In the mid-1930s, mainstream suits exhibited similar, if less extreme, characteristics of the zoot suit: double-breasted coat with wider shoulders narrowing into a slim waist and a hem reaching mid-length, coupled with pleated trousers. With so many supposed origins, the zoot suit perhaps came from different sources, with each successive zoot suiter adding their own style and new exaggeration to their suit cut. In France during World War II, men who dressed in similar baggy clothing and engaged in black-market profiteering were called *zazous*.

The Zoot Suit in the United States

The zoot suit is an American style that became popular with African-American male youth in Harlem, Chicago, and other urban areas. Mexican immigrants in the Los Angeles area that were part of the pachuco, or gang, culture were also early adopters. The style did not have much time to infiltrate mainstream culture with the approach of World War II. Its extra fabric made them unpopular with ration regulators.

By the early 1940s, mainstream U.S. society associated the suits with Hispanic and African-American youth. Wearers were deemed unpatriotic as rationing took effect, and yet "zooters" looked for tailors who would illegally create the look. Coupled with the media associating the zoot suit with criminal activity and laziness, the suit took on a rebellious connotation. The Mexican gangs also used the suit to set themselves apart from the rest of the population.

In the spring of 1943, active-duty sailors and servicemen on furlough in Los Angeles clashed with Mexican immigrants in the barrios in a series of minor altercations. Many of these conflicts ended with sailors pulling the pants off zoot suiters, demonstrating their disdain for the excessive clothing and their negative feelings about Mexicans in their neighborhoods. These escalated into larger confrontations as each group retaliated against the other throughout May of 1943. The conflicts culminated in what was termed the Zoot Suit Riot that began June 3, 1943, and continued for five days. Mexican immigrants caught in the suits had their clothing nearly ripped off their bodies and were beaten heavily by naval men. The military command finally put an end to the riots by banning servicemen from shore leave.

Zoot Suit

Influence and Impact

Mexican and African-American wearers of the zoot suit enjoyed the sense of individualistic expression the clothing gave them. Even though it became associated with criminal activity, entertainers such as jazzman Cab Calloway and Mexican actor German Valdes, known as Tin-Tan, made the suit part of their personality that carried them into the early 1950s. The late 1990s saw a revival of the zoot suit with the interest in swing dance and bands. The Zoot Suit Riots were the subject of a song by the same name in 1997 by the Cherry Poppin' Daddies.

See also Beret; Cholo Style; Dashiki; Do-Rag; Fedora; Hip-Hop Fashion
Compare to Japanese Street Fashion; Mao Suit; Mariachi Suit; Nehru Jacket

Further Reading

Acuña, Rodolfo. "The Sleepy Lagoon Case and the Zoot Suit Riots." In *The Mexicans*, edited by C. J. Shane, 102–13. Farmington Hills, MI: Greenhaven Press, 2005.

Peiss, Kathy. *Zoot Suit: The Enigmatic Career of an Extreme Style*. Philadelphia: University of Pennsylvania Press, 2011.

White, Shane, and Graham White. *Stylin': African American Expressive Culture from Its Beginnings to the Zoot Suit*. Ithaca, NY: Cornell University Press, 1998.

■ JENNIFER VAN HAAFTEN

ZOUAVE

See Bolero Jacket

INDEX

ABOUT THE EDITORS AND CONTRIBUTORS

Annette Lynch, PhD, is a professor in the Textile and Apparel Program at the University of Northern Iowa. Her research focuses on the role of dress and appearance in negotiating gender-role transformation and cultural change.

Mitchell D. Strauss, EdD, is a professor of textiles and apparel at the University of Northern Iowa. Formerly he served as the dean at the Institute of Textile Technology. He has written about fashion theory in Berg's *Changing Fashion*.

CONTRIBUTORS

Linda Arthur Bradley, PhD, is professor of apparel, merchandising, design, and textiles at Washington State University, and author of *Aloha Attire: Hawaiian Dress in the Twentieth Century; the Art of the Aloha Shirt* and *The Hawaiian Quilt: A Unique American Art Form*.

Naomi Braithwaite, PhD, is a British research fellow in product lifetimes at Nottingham Trent University, England. Her interests include fashion, footwear, and material culture.

Steeve O. Buckridge, PhD, is director of area studies and associate professor of African and Caribbean history at Grand Valley State University.

Laura L. Camerlengo is an exhibition assistant with the Costume and Textiles Department of the Philadelphia Museum of Art. She has a master of arts degree in the history of decorative arts and design from Parsons, the New School for Design/Cooper-Hewitt, National Design Museum, Smithsonian Institution. She is the author of *The Miser's Purse* (2013).

Carol Ann Colburn, PhD, is a textile historian and craftsperson from Duluth, Minnesota. She is professor emerita of theatre costume at the University of Northern Iowa and currently teaches garment-making workshops at North House Folk School and Vesterheim Norwegian-American Museum.

Vishna Collins holds a bachelor of education (visual arts) and a master of museum studies and is a Sidney-based independent curator, designer, and arts writer specializing in fashion curation and sartorial display, and the social history of textiles.

Jennifer Craik is a research professor in the School of Fashion and Textiles at RMIT University, Melbourne, Australia. Her publications include *The Face of Fashion* (1993), *Uniforms Exposed* (2005), and *Fashion: The Key Concepts* (2009).

Jamie R. Cupit, MS, is an instructor at Stephen F. Austin State University in Nacogdoches, Texas, where she teaches undergraduate fashion merchandising courses. Her area of professional emphasis is in merchandising, particularly consumer behavior.

Jennifer Daley, PhD, researches uniforms, including the development of military clothing, the relationship between war and the textile industry, and the political, economic, and design influence of military fashion on civilian clothing.

Tameka N. Ellington, PhD, is an assistant professor of fashion at Kent State University. Her area of expertise is African American dress and self-esteem. She also has an interest in people with disabilities and how their worlds are connected with fashion.

Sandra Lee Evenson, PhD, is professor of apparel, textiles, and design at the University of Idaho. Her interests include cross-cultural aspects of dress and the global textile trade.

Marie-Claire Eylott is a graduate from the Master of Museum Studies Program at the University of Toronto. She specializes in textile collections as well as exhibition writing and French translation.

Dr. Irene M. Foster is a professor of fashion design and retailing at Framingham State University in Massachusetts. She is coauthor of *Research Methods for the Fashion Industry* for Fairchild Books.

Arianna E. Funk is an independent clothing historian interested in the material cultural aspects of American dress history. She is based in Stockholm, Sweden.

Blaire O. Gagnon, PhD, is an anthropologist and assistant professor in the Textiles, Fashion Merchandising and Design Department at the University of Rhode Island. She conducts historic and ethnographic research on the relationship between people and objects, intercultural markets, and the construction of value, particularly in relation to ideas of authenticity and power.

Dr. Adam Geczy is an artist and writer and senior lecturer at Sydney College of the Arts, the University of Sydney. Author of numerous books on art and fashion, his *Fashion and Orientalism* was published in 2013.

Karen J. Gilmer, MFA, is an assistant professor of theatre-costume design and costume history at Susquehanna University.

Priscilla N. Gitimu, PhD, is an associate professor and program coordinator of the Merchandising: Fashion and Interiors Program in the Department of Human Ecology at Youngstown State University, Ohio.

Rebecca W. Greer is professor of fashion merchandising at Stephen F. Austin State University.

Gowri Betrabet Gulwadi, PhD in architecture, environment-behavior studies, teaches interior design in the School of Applied Human Sciences at the University of Northern Iowa in Cedar Falls.

Silke Hagen-Jurkowitsch, PhD, is a cultural advisor, textile ambassador, and researcher from Lustenau, Austria. She is known for her research on African textiles including various decoration possibilities, particularly African lace in West Africa.

Laura McLaws Helms is a fashion historian, writer, and curator based in New York and London. Her book on fashion designer Thea Porter will be published in 2015.

Ellen Hlozan is an MMSt (master of museum studies) candidate in Toronto, Canada, with a focus on textiles and fashion. Her professional interests include curating, collections management, and coordinating exhibitions.

Rebecca Nelson Jacobs is a PhD candidate in cultural anthropology with a graduate certificate in human rights at the University of Connecticut. Her research focuses on ethical consumption, textile production, and volunteer tourism in Central America.

Tracy Jenkins is an independent fashion historian and curator. She works as a research assistant in the Costume Institute at the Metropolitan Museum of Art and as an adjunct professor at New York University.

Michelle M. Jones, MEd, is instructor at Stephen F. Austin State University in Nacogdoches, Texas. She teaches undergraduate courses in the Fashion Merchandising Program and serves as advisor to the student organization. Her emphasis area is visual merchandising, consumer behaviors, and historic costume.

Helen Koo, PhD, is an assistant professor of apparel design in the Department of Consumer and Design Sciences at Auburn University in Alabama.

Abby Lillethun specializes in dress history of the Bronze Age Aegean and early twentieth-century America. She coedited *The Fashion Reader* (2011) and is associate professor of art and design at Montclair State University, New Jersey.

Luanne Mayorga is an analyst with Northern Illinois University and has numerous years of teaching experience in both the business and fashion disciplines.

Ellen C. McKinney, PhD, is an assistant professor in the Apparel, Merchandising, and Design Program at Iowa State University. Her subject matter expertise area is in the interface between the body and the garment as revealed by garment size, fit, and consumer fit perception.

Marcella Milio is adjunct professor of the history of costume and textiles at Philadelphia University. Her expertise is in the late nineteenth-century and twentieth-century history of dress and culture.

Aprina Murwanti is a lecturer in the Department of Visual Art Education at the Universitas Negeri Jakarta, Indonesia. She recently finished her PhD in creative art at the University of Wollongong, Australia.

Susan Neill, MA, is a Chicago-based scholar and museum consultant with significant experience curating collections of historic fashion, textiles, and ethnographic dress.

Virginia M. Noon, employed in the textile and apparel industry for more than twenty-five years, is an assistant professor in the Department of Fashion Design and Retailing at Framingham State University and a doctoral student at the University of Massachusetts, Lowell, in work environment policy.

Anupama Pasricha, PhD, is associate professor and chair of the Apparel, Merchandising, and Design Department at St. Catherine University, St. Paul, Minnesota.

Victoria Pass is an assistant professor of art history at Salisbury University in Maryland. Her research examines the intersections between fashion and art in the twentieth century, with a particular focus on issues of gender, race, and identity.

Dr. Juliette Peers is senior lecturer in the School of Architecture and Design, RMIT University. She is widely published as an art theorist, freelance curator, and historian of women's art, nineteenth-century Australian art and design, and nineteenth- and early twentieth-century Australian fashion.

Lauren Downing Peters is a PhD candidate in the Centre for Fashion Studies at Stockholm University. She holds an MA in fashion studies from Parsons, the New School for Design.

Irina Zhoukova Petrova is coordinator of the Traditional Russian Costume Project. She has studied traditional Russian clothing and embroidery for twenty-three years, she publishes articles on the subject, and she makes replicas of traditional Russian outfits and embroidery.

Harini Ramaswamy is a master's student majoring in apparel studies (product development track), minoring in product design, at the University of Minnesota–Twin Cities. Her research interests include functional clothing design and quality testing of textiles.

Helen Ritchie is a freelance decorative arts researcher. She is currently a consultant at Christie's, London, and is cataloging the Hull Grundy gift of jewelry at the Mercer Art Gallery, Harrogate.

Jennifer Rothrock, MA, fashion curation, has researched, managed, and curated historical dress collections and exhibitions, specializing in the Victorian era, mourning dress, and customs. Jennifer is also a skilled seamstress, creating replica and reproduction garments for museums using historical sewing techniques.

Mary Ruppert-Stroescu, PhD, is an assistant professor of apparel design and textile science at Oklahoma State University. She teaches, practices, and researches creativity in areas related to apparel design for fashion and function.

Jessica Schwartz, MS, is an independent researcher specializing in contemporary fashion and curatorial practices within fashion collections.

Erica Suzanne Scott, MA, is an independent fashion and culture researcher, archivist, costume designer, stylist, and blogger based in New York City.

Wendy Rosie Scott is a London-based freelance journalist, stylist, and fashion anthropologist. Focusing on festivals, lifestyle, the City, vintage, and sustainable and native arts within the realm of culture and design, she contributes toward trend prediction, writes for BBC broadcasts, and teaches at the Paris American Academy.

Sabrina Skerston is an undergraduate student at Iowa State University studying apparel, merchandising, and design and marketing.

Toby Slade, PhD, is an associate professor at the University of Tokyo where he lectures in fashion theory and Japanese popular culture. His book *Japanese Fashion: A Cultural History* covers Japanese fashion from the earliest times to today.

Celia Stall-Meadows, EdD, is an international researcher and author whose numerous publications include the books *Why Would Anyone Wear That? Fascinating Fashion Facts* (2013) and *Fashion Now: A Global Perspective* (2011). She serves as a director of curriculum and instruction.

Susan M. Strawn, PhD, is a professor of apparel design and merchandising at Dominican University (River Forest, Illinois). Her research interests emphasize historical and cross-cultural influences on twentieth-century American dress and fashion.

Jessica Strübel, PhD, teaches merchandising at the University of North Texas in Denton, Texas, and is an editor for the journal *Fashion, Style and Popular Culture*.

Caitlin Tracey-Miller works as a program and exhibit specialist at the Museum of Natural History and Science in Cincinnati, Ohio. She recently completed a master's in museum studies from the University of Toronto.

Jennifer Van Haaften is curator of interpretation at Old World Wisconsin, a living history site in Eagle, Wisconsin, that explores the lives of immigrants. She has an extensive research background in historic clothing and clothing reproduction, and her master's of philosophy in history thesis at the University of Manchester explored influences on consumer behavior in women's clothing in England from 1835 to 1865.

Laura Van Waardhuizen has a bachelor of arts in textiles and apparel from the University of Northern Iowa and a bachelor of science in education from Grand View University. She is a family and consumer sciences teacher at Waukee High School and teaches adjunct courses for the Fashion Merchandising Program at the Des Moines Area Community College.

Rebecca Vang is a graduate from Oklahoma State University with a major in apparel, design, and production. She is a CAD designer at Fruhauf Uniforms in Wichita, Kansas.

Joan Webster-Vore is a mixed media artist and instructor of textiles, fiber arts, and design. She has a master's degree in textiles and a master of fine arts from the University of Iowa.

Linda Welters, PhD, is professor of textiles, fashion merchandising and design at the University of Rhode Island. She has written widely on European folk dress.

Juanjuan Wu, PhD, is an assistant professor of retail merchandising in the College of Design at the University of Minnesota. Her research interests include fashion studies, retail, and design.

Cassidy Zachary is a fashion historian, writer, and film and television costumer living in Albuquerque, New Mexico. She holds a master's degree in fashion and textile studies from the Fashion Institute of Technology.